WILLIAM LANGLAND'S PIERS PLOWMAN

MEDIEVAL CASEBOOKS

Christopher Kleinhenz and Marcia Colish, *Series Editors*

WILLIAM LANGLAND'S PIERS PLOWMAN
A BOOK OF ESSAYS

EDITED BY
KATHLEEN M. HEWETT-SMITH

ROUTLEDGE
NEW YORK AND LONDON

Published in 2001 by
Routledge
29 West 35th Street
New York NY 10011

Published in Great Britain by
Routledge
11 New Fetter Lane
London EC4P 4EE

Routledge is an imprint of the Taylor and Francis Group.

Library of Congress Cataloging-in-Publication Data

William Langland's Piers Plowman: a book of essays / edited by Kathleen M.
Hewett-Smith.
    p. cm. (Medieval casebooks; v. 30)
    Includes bibliographical references and index. *22535608*
    ISBN 0-8153-2804-4 (hb)
    1. Langland, William, 1330?–1400? Piers the Plowman. 2. Literature and
history—England—History—To 1500. 3. Christian poetry, English
(Middle)—History and criticism. I. Title: Piers Plowman. II. Hewett-Smith,
Kathleen M. III. Title. IV. Medieval casebooks; vol. 30.

PR2015.W5   2001
821'.1—dc21   2001016593

Printed on acid-free, 250-year-life paper
Manufactured in the United States of America

10 9 8 7 6 5 4 3 2 1

For Stan and Alexandra

Contents

WILLIAM LANGLAND'S PIERS PLOWMAN

Introduction

Interest in *Piers Plowman* has grown enormously in the past decade. Because it has much to contribute toward the lively contemporary debates over such issues as gender, dissent, representation, and popular religion and culture, the poem has enjoyed renewed critical attention. Likewise, because *Piers* is available in a number of new editions and translations, those scholars interested in teaching a more "integrated" version of four-teenth-century English literature and culture have turned to Langland's poem with great enthusiasm.

The present volume takes up some of the central (and in many cases long-standing) questions within *Piers Plowman* studies—How is the poem implicated in fourteenth-century literary and cultural history? How have nineteenth- and twentieth-century constructions of the author, even the text, of *Piers Plowman* affected our understanding of poet and poem? What is the nature of Langland's art? Of his allegorical poetics? How use-ful is literary theory to the study of early texts, especially *Piers Plowman*? These essays, ranging as they do from source study to critical historicism to queer theory, demonstrate the variety of critical tools presently brought to bear upon medieval texts. Nevertheless, in the midst of such diversity of method and approach, they all share an overwhelming interest in social context and meaning; three contend with Chaucer; four are concerned with gender; six with aspects of subjectivity; eight with rhetoric and rhetor-ical constructions—and *everyone* is worried, to varying degrees and for different reasons, about what C. David Benson calls the "myths" of poet and poem. Indeed, what all of these essays insist upon most energetically is the need for a fundamental reconfiguring of even our most basic and constitutive understandings of *Piers Plowman*—of its author and audience, the order of its texts, the power of its poetry, its understanding of women, of the poor, of allegory, of history, and its relation to fourteenth-century culture and ideology.

The volume's essays are arranged under a series of thematic rubrics which represent, in my opinion, the most important and productive areas of current thinking and writing on Langland's poem. "*Piers Plowman* in Context," by far the longest of the volume's sections, is also the most methodologically diverse. In "Making History Legal: *Piers Plowman* and the Rebels of Fourteenth-Century England," Andrew Galloway offers a striking example of the power of critical historicism to negotiate past texts. In this piece Galloway argues that Langland's vision of history can be more deeply understood when considered within a legal and social context "where history, law, and social relations were being placed under mutual pressure, driven by conflicts between newly politically self-conscious lower orders and their powerful landlords, a context of legal dissent in which tradition itself...became increasingly clearly a legal construction." Joan Baker and Susan Signe Morrison demonstrate the force and depth of Langland's social concern by exploring medieval attitudes toward marriage in "The Luxury of Gender: *Piers Plowman* B.9 and *The Merchant's Tale.*" Their essay argues, provocatively, that while Langland, like Chaucer, demonstrates an interest in gender issues, *Piers Plowman* ultimately "privileges the exigencies of human necessity over a concern for the burdens of gender." The final two essays in this section suggest that even the most fundamental contexts of *Piers Plowman* have yet to be explored fully. Stephen Shepherd's "Langland's Romances," a study of the possible connections between *Piers* and medieval English vernacular romance, reveals, for example, that the literary milieu in and through which Langland works is only incompletely understood; and C. David Benson's "The Langland Myth" observes that the persistence of assumptions about both the "author" and "text" of *Piers Plowman* have influenced scholarship on the poem.

In "The Poetry of *Piers Plowman,*" this volume's second section, Stephen A. Barney and Sister Mary Clemente Davlin remind us of the power of Langland's verse. Both critics illuminate Langland's prosody by comparing it with Chaucer's—a necessary strategy in a field still dominated by study of the poet who has defined the age—and argue that in the case of Langland, difference is a virtue. In "Langland's Mighty Line," Barney demonstrates persuasively that Langland's poetic lines have a broader range of both sound and sense than do Chaucer's. Sister Clemente, too, in "Chaucer and Langland as Religious Writers," observes that "whereas Chaucer, with Shakespeare, is the greatest poet we have of human character, Langland is the *only* poet we have (with the possible exception of Milton) who dares to probe at any length the nature of God, contemplating the central beliefs of Christianity."

In the fourth section, "Through the Lens of Theory," articles by James Simpson and Elizabeth Robertson demonstrate some of the ways in which literary theory has begun to inform the discourse and doctrine of the study of *Piers Plowman*. Simpson's "The Power of Impropriety: Authorial Naming in *Piers Plowman*" considers the question of the author—indeed the constitution of authorship itself—in Langland's poem through a focus upon the ways in which the developing logic of the personification of will/will "creates a communal authorial position." Elizabeth Robertson, looking through the lens of feminist criticism, argues that, in its association with measure and excess, "gender, or more precisely the 'feminine,' as it was understood in late fourteenth-century England...opens up possibility and possibilities" within *Piers Plowman*.

Essays in the volume's final section, "Allegory Reconsidered," address, and perhaps even begin to remedy, what James J. Paxson identifies as the "general exhaustion with and from allegory" in *Pier Plowman* studies. In his "Inventing the Subject and the Personification of Will in *Piers Plowman*: Rhetorical, Erotic, and Ideological Origins and Limits in Langland's Allegorical Poetics," Paxson asks us to reconfigure the relationship of *Piers Plowman* to theories of representation by showing how "sexualized rhetorical figures undergird the [poem's] allegorical poetics." The essay argues furthermore that "such a turn...enables a new way of theorizing the ideological and political implications of maleness, monarchical rule and social identity" in fourteenth-century England. In "'Nede ne hath no lawe:' Poverty and the De-stabilization of Allegory in the Final Visions of *Piers Plowman*," Hewett-Smith re-examines the relationship of allegory to history by demonstrating the ways in which the subject of poverty in the final passus of *Piers Plowman*, particularly as figured in the personification of Nede, involves the poem in an intense confrontation with its own modes of referentiality. Such essays remind us of the continuing relevance and vitality of *Piers Plowman* within the ever-changing landscape of critical discourse.[1]

---

[1] I would like to thank Christopher Kleinhenz, editor of the Medieval Casebook series, for giving me the opportunity to realize this project. Special thanks must go, however, to the contributors to the volume whose intelligence and hard work are evident in every page of these essays, and without whose patience and support I could not have brought this collection to fruition.

Piers Plowman in Context

Making History Legal: *Piers Plowman* and the Rebels of Fourteenth-Century England[1]

Andrew Galloway

> Forþi lakke þow neuere logik, lawe ne hise custumes,
> Ne countreplede clerkes, I counseille þee for euere.
> For as a man may no3t see þat mysseþ hise ei3en,
> Na moore kan no Clerk but if he cau3te it first þoru3 bokes.
> Alþou3 men made bokes {god was þe maister}
> And seint Spirit þe Samplarie, & seide what men sholde write.
>
> (B.12.97–102)[2]

Thus Imaginative, the stern if elusively definable allegorical teacher, to Will, the narrator of *Piers Plowman* who constantly "countrepledeþ" his authoritative interloculators of religious and secular "law" within the poem and often indirectly criticizes—sometimes directly confronts—his powerful legal audience outside it: "Ye legistres and lawieres" (B.7.60); "ye wise men þat wiþ þe world deleþ; / That riche ben and reson knoweþ"

[1] Previous versions of this essay were presented before marvelously challenging and encouraging audiences at the University Seminar at Columbia University, November 11, 1997; and as a Visiting Faculty Lecturer at the University of Illinois at Urbana-Champaign, March 8, 1998. I thank Professors Christopher Baswell at Columbia and Lori Newcomb, Charles Wright, and Lisa Lampert at Urbana-Champaign for these opportunities and for their warm hospitality.

[2] George Kane and E. Talbot Donaldson, eds., *Piers Plowman: The B Version*, rev. ed. (London: Athlone; Berkeley and Los Angeles: University of California Press, 1988). I cite *Piers* using the Athlone editions throughout: Kane, ed., *Piers Plowman: The A Version*, rev. ed. (London: Athlone; Berkeley and Los Angeles: University of California Press, 1988); George Russell and George Kane, eds., *Piers Plowman: The C Version* (London: Athlone; Berkeley and Los Angeles: University of California Press, 1997). Subsequent citations will appear parenthetically. All emendations of the Athlone editions that I consider based on slender empirical evidence, but which I retain, I leave bracketed, but I do not print their brackets for their other emendations of their copy texts. In the rare instances when I wish to print the archetypal textual reading instead of the Athlone emendation, I indicate this by curved brackets. While these may seem peculiar solutions to the textual complexities of *Piers Plowman* and to the Athlone editions, I take the position (as do the Athlone editors) that readers should be provoked to consider the matter of the text for themselves by

(B.17.262–63). But in the same breath as he stifles Will's aggressive 'coun-terpleading' of law, Imaginative's historical presentation of the originary moment of the New Law also implicitly attacks vengeful law and its cor-rupt practitioners, however officially sanctioned. For Imaginative is here elaborating the gospel account of Jesus's judgment on the woman taken in adultery, where Jesus's writing of "caractes" in the dirt is taken—as often by medieval exegetes—as indicting the sins of the woman's accusers, the Jews. Hence Jesus's writing becomes the "Samplarie," the original exem-plar, of all the books and learning ("Clergy") that encompass logic, law and its customs; a law that ideally, therefore, should provide merciful par-don for those accused who repent, and damnation for those, particularly corrupt judges, who do not:

> For þoruȝ caractes þat crist wroot þe Iewes knewe hemselue
> Giltier as afore god, and gretter in synne,
> Than þe womman þat þere was, and wenten awey for shame.
> [Thus Clergie þere] conforted þe womman.
> Holy kirke knoweþ þis þat cristes writyng saued;
> So clergie is confort to creatures þat repenten,
> And to mansede men meschief at hire ende.
> (B.12.78–84)

Thanks to valuable work on the legal terminology used in the poem, on its themes of justice and mercy, and on its relationship to judicial procedures like the chivalric duel and to social legislation like the Statute of Laborers of 1351 and 1388, modern readers of *Piers Plowman* will likely not need reminding, as Will does here, that law and "hise custumes" are crucial to this dream-vision poem's ways of "seeing."[3] But legal history in the four-teenth century—that is, law in the context of political struggle and social outlook, as an imaginative construction emerging, like literature, from tra-ditions remade in particular social contexts—can claim a still greater role for understanding the poem's participation with its world. In particular, the

---

means of the Athlone critical apparatus and introductions. On some of the advantages and peculiarities of the Athlone editions, with references to previous discussions, see my essay, "Uncharacterizable Entities: The Poetics of Middle English Scribal Culture and the Definitive *Piers Plowman*," *Studies in Bibliography* 52 (1999), forthcoming.

[3] See William J. Birnes, "Christ as Advocate: The Legal Metaphor of *Piers Plowman*," *Annuale Mediaevale* 16 (1975): 71–93; Myra Stokes, *Justice and Mercy in Piers Plowman: A Reading of the B Text Visio* (London: Croon Helm, 1984); Anna Baldwin, "The Double Duel in *Piers Plowman* B XVIII and C XXI," *Medium Ævum* 50 (1981): 64–78; John A. Alford, *Piers Plowman: A Glossary of Legal Diction* (Woodbridge, Suffolk: D. S. Brewer, 1988) and "The Idea of Reason in *Piers Plowman*," in Edward Donald Kennedy, Ronald Waldron, and Joseph S. Wittig, eds., *Medieval English Studies Presented to George Kane* (Suffolk: D. S. Brewer, 1988), 199–215; Lawrence M. Clopper, "Need Men and Women Labor? Langland's Wanderer and the Labor Ordinances," in Barbara Hanawalt, ed., *Chaucer's England: Literature in Historical Context* (Minneapolis, MN: University of Minnesota Press, 1992), 110–29; and Anne Middleton, "Acts of Vagrancy: The C Version 'Autobiography' and the Statute of 1388," in Steven Justice and Kathryn Kerby-Fulton, eds., *Written Work: Langland, Labor, and Authorship* (Philadelphia, PA: University of Pennsylvania Press, 1997), 208–317.

poem's constant projection of legal ideals into the ancient past may be more fully appreciated than heretofore if considered in relation to a pervasive element of many of the legal conflicts of fourteenth-century England, particularly those instigated by communities of the lower orders that become only fully—if then luridly and distortedly—visible in the accounts of the Rising of 1381: namely, the effort to use antiquity to transform or maintain legal status and capability. The most majestic dimension of Langland's work, its vision of history, can be better appreciated as part of this legal and social context where history, law, and social relations were being placed under mutual pressure, driven by conflicts between newly politically self-conscious lower orders and their powerful landlords, a context of legal dissent in which tradition itself—paradoxically, given Langland's and others' intense engagement with history—became increasingly clearly a legal construction.

The implied or overt use of history to justify, define, or challenge legal claims is common before the fourteenth century; indeed, it is central to the densely document-oriented style of post-Conquest medieval history writing.[4] Property claims, especially by the great institutions responsible for recording history, typically depended on some construction of the past, sometimes but not always a flagrantly imaginary construction.[5] In broader social applications beyond institutional or individual property disputes—that is, in issues of defining the legal status or freedoms of whole communities, or the law of the land as such—the topic of historically oriented legal endeavor deserves further exploration. Scholars have most thoroughly studied the strategies of claiming or assuming antiquity for English constitutional law in the seventeenth century, a context from which "antiquarianism" and medieval studies itself can be said to emerge.[6] The theoretical relation between law and history, considered in the most abstract terms by writers from Aquinas through seventeenth-century constitutionalists, can appear in either deductive or inductive forms; that is, this relation can be defined in such writings as either the view that the divine or collective "reason" contained in law adapted itself by custom and further devel-

---

[4] See Andrew Galloway, "Writing History in England," in David Wallace, ed., *Cambridge History of Medieval English Literature* (Cambridge: Cambridge University Press, 1999), 255–83.

[5] See Eleanor Searle, "Battle Abbey and Exemption: The Forged Charters," *English Historical Review* 83 (1968): 449–80, for just one example of institutional manipulations of history; I touch on others in my "Writing History in England," op. cit. See also Paul Brand, "'Time Out of Mind': The Knowledge and Use of the Eleventh- and Twelfth-Century Past in Thirteenth-Century Litigation," in Marjorie Chibnall, ed., *Anglo-Norman Studies* 16 (1993): 37–54 (Woodbridge: Boydell Press, 1994), for some individuals' uses of history in litigation.

[6] See J. G. A. Pocock, *The Ancient Constitution and the Feudal Law: A Study of English Historical Thought in the Seventeenth Century* (Cambridge: Cambridge University Press, 1987), and "The Origins of Study of the Past: A Comparative Approach," *Comparative Studies in Society and History* 4 (1962): 209–246; and Glenn Burgess' important critique of Pocock, *The Politics of the Ancient Constitution: An Introduction to English Political Thought, 1603–1642* (University Park, PA: The Pennsylvania State University Press, 1993).

opment into the forms necessary for particular times and places, or the view that the special "reason" of the law can be manifested only from cumulative custom and tradition.[7] But elaborations of the diverse uses of history for communities'—not monastic, individual, or national—legal ends are something distinctive to the fourteenth century, and generate special features that help lay the groundwork for post-medieval debates about the legal antiquity of the whole community of the realm.

My word "elaborations" is too tame by half to describe the striking density throughout the conflicts between rural and borough communities and their ecclesiastic landlords in the fourteenth century, a century as noted for its gradually centralizing legal systems as for its severe dangers to legal practitioners. Especially in the last decades of the century, attacks on lawyers and judges at all levels reached an unprecedented severity: the murder of a chief justice of the king's bench and numerous other lawyers by the mob in 1381; the execution by the Lords Appellant of another former chief justice of the king's bench in 1388 as one of the king's favorites; the Lords' Appellant sentences of death (commuted to exile in Ireland) imposed on all but one of the judges of the common bench in 1388 for supporting the king with affirmative answers to his infamous "questions to the judges" of 1387, where Richard II asked the judges to declare treasonous the earlier efforts by the Commons to constrain his closest advisors. Although the same sentiments against lawyers and judges have reappeared at various times, actual carnage, execution, or exile like this is unparalleled before or since.

Such attacks suggest with particular crudeness how politicized law became during the fourteenth century. Many legal issues that passed through the highest courts also riveted national attention, indeed constituted a form of national consciousness (if not administrative reality) that we may justly call "political" on a national scale both because of the social depth of the laws' purview and because of the politicizing consequences of their enactment and the resistance to them. In recent years, legal and social historians have argued that a solidarity between the artisan and laboring classes was hardened by the legal endeavors of the higher nobility to keep such lower classes in their place, such as the Ordinance (1349) and Statute of Laborers (1351 and 1388), resisting the massive demographic and hence wage and vagrancy changes wrought by the Black Death, and followed by a series of legal innovations and legal instruments by which the actions and products of artisans and laborers could be regulated.[8] At the same time, the

---

[7] For example, Aquinas, *Summa Theologica* I–II qq. 90–97 (henceforth *ST*). I use the convenient selection and translation in Dino Bigongiari, ed. and trans., *The Political Ideas of St. Thomas Aquinas: Representative Selections* (New York: Hafner Press, 1953, 1981). See Burgess, *The Politics of the Ancient Constitution*, for a lucid analysis of seventeenth-century understandings of the relation between law and custom.

[8] See Alan Harding, "The Revolt Against the Justices," in R. H. Hilton and T. H. Aston, eds., *The English Rising of 1381* (Cambridge and New York: Cambridge University Press, 1984), 165–93, and Robert C. Palmer,

continuous complaints by communities throughout the century against legal oppression by local magnates and landlords, who were granted special legal powers and seized legal influence with the collapse of the general eyres in the early fourteenth century, along with sporadic legal battles between communities of tenants and their great monastic landlords with their vast estates, burdensome and inconsistent labor and rent demands, and enormous legal resources and influence—all this created a further impetus for socially polarizing legal struggle between, on the one hand, the laboring and artisan classes and, on the other, the great institutions and lords of fourteenth-century England. This culminated in the Rising of 1381, an event notable for the rebels' hatred and murder of lawyers and justices and widespread destruction of legal records, as well as their own general political cohesiveness. This last element is clearest from the rebels' efforts in various parts of the Rising to establish new political rights based on claims to ancient legal rights, including both the general manumission of serfs and particular liberties from their powerful, institutional landlords.[9]

It should be emphasized that the immediate social effect of all such conflicts was to bring a new range of offenses into the jurisdiction of the king's courts, even if into the hands of corrupt local officials of the king.[10] But this general movement toward centralized law did not obliterate or even soften differences in legal and historical perspective between the ancient institutions and the newly political communities comprised of their tenants. On the contrary, the king's courts functioned in the fourteenth century as a main theater for conflicts between rebellious communities and overbearing landlords found throughout the country and throughout the century, of which the Rising of mid-June, 1381, was only the final act.

While *Piers Plowman* is often situated in response to the Rising itself, the poem's relation to the protracted series of legal struggles that found their way to the king's courts for decades *before* the Rising has never been explored. Yet it is logical to consider an array of these in relationship to a poem so manifestly in touch with, perhaps written not far from, the king' courts at Westminster. We may thus assess more fully the social implications and poetic depth of the poem's "counterpleading" of law from its earliest versions on, rather than simply its final, post-1381 version, including its persistent depictions of ancient models of true justice, where—in a

---

English Law in the Age of the Black Death, 1348–1381: A Transformation of Governance and Law (Chapel Hill, NC: University of North Carolina Press, 1993).

[9] See N. M. Trenholme, *The English Monastic Boroughs*, University of Missouri Studies 2:3 (1927); Harding, "Revolt"; and Rosamund Faith, "The 'Great Rumour' of 1377 and Peasant Ideology," in Hilton and Aston, *English Rising*, 71–74. Faith's essay treats this topic directly, focusing on the uses of Domesday Book in the late 1370s by rural tenants seeking to establish historical bases for their rights, and she points to the remarkable case of this by the tenants at St. Albans in 1381, a case I also take up below.

[10] So Edward Powell, "Arbitration and the Law in England in the Late Middle Ages," *Transactions of the Royal Historical Society*, 5th Series, 33 (1983): 49–67.

paradox found throughout the century—the fullest claims for freedom from the legal oppressions of tradition are expressed.[11] Thus in this essay I first discuss some aspects of the poem's ideals of justice from the ancient past in terms of conflict with as well as renewed assertion of tradition and history; next, I present some possible instances of the poem's more topical engagement with legal conflicts between tenants and their powerful, monastic landlords that led up to the Rising of 1381, where the poem's conflict between ideals of justice and traditional social identity reappears. Finally, I turn to the account of the Rising of 1381 by the chronicler at St. Albans monastery, Thomas Walsingham, to examine another text where claims to history infuse the legal debate, a context of historical debate that, as I shall suggest throughout this essay, complicated or even hollowed out belief in the very traditions on which the legal and social order of English culture was being established.

I thus place *Piers Plowman*, and, more cursorily, Walsingham's narrative, amidst a moment of cultural and legal history defined by historical visions emerging from sharply different perspectives. Yet in doing so I am already begging the question of my view of what "debate" of this kind meant in this period. How much mutual comprehension, much less agreement, between the historical and legal views of such profoundly divided social and linguistic realms was—could ever be—actually possible? In what sense does Langland's poem and Walsingham's chronicle "include" these diverse perspectives? It does not necessarily prove anything that Langland's poem was quoted or at least obliquely named by the rebels of 1381—"lat peres þe plowman my broþer duelle at home and dyȝt vs corne," states one rebel letter, quoted by the Leicester Priory chronicler Henry Knighton;[12] "Johon schep...biddeþ Peres plouȝman to his werke and chastise wel hobbe þe robbere...and do wel and bettre and fleth synne and sekeþ pees and hold ȝou þer inne," states another, supposedly found in the pocket of a man about to be hanged for rioting and quoted by Thomas Walsingham.[13] The Dieulacres Abbey chronicler goes further even than the rebel letters, stating that "Per Plowman" was himself one of the rebels in 1381 who were "striving to destroy the laws and customs of the realm" (*nitentes iura et consue-*

---

[11] On the plausibility of locating the poet and his original audience in the law courts and great houses of London, see Ralph Hanna, *William Langland* (Aldershot, G.B.: Variorum, 1993), 23–24, and Kathryn Kerby-Fulton and Steven Justice, "Langlandian Reading Circles and the Civil Service in London and Dublin, 1380–1427," *New Medieval Literatures* 1 (1997): 59–83, and *ibid.*, "Reformist Intellectual Culture in the English and Irish Civil Service: The *Modus tenendi parliamentum* and its Literary Relations," *Traditio* 53 (1998): 149–203. This context is increasingly plausibly established, although the evidence remains circumstantial.

[12] *Knighton's Chronicle, 1337–1396*, ed. and trans. G. H. Martin (Oxford: Clarendon Press, 1995), 222–23.

[13] Thomas Walsingham, *Chronicon Angliae, 1328–1388*, ed. E. M. Thompson, Rolls Series (London: Longman, Green, 1874), 322.

tudines regni destruere)—an accusation as absolute as Imaginative's warning to Will, which it closely parallels.[14]

No scholar, almost, would claim that the poet deliberately helped foment, or even that he foretold, the Rising, which occurred only after the B-Text was written and, as is often suggested, constituted part of the basis for the C-Text's revisions.[15] Langland typically comes off as surprised as well as horrified by the uses of his work, rushing to revise and clarify his socially orthodox intentions or at least his relentless indecisiveness about social action. But how *do* we assess the poem's remarkable accuracy in social prophecy—foretelling, for example, destruction of legal documents, one of the main actions of the Rising, in a conflict between a self-righteous plowman and a smugly legalistic clerk, as when from the A-Text on, the clerk reads the Pardon sent by Truth to *Piers Plowman* and punctilliously declares, "I can no pardoun fynde / But do wel & haue wel, & god shal haue þi soule, / And do euele & haue euele, & hope þow non oþer / þat aftir þi deþ day to helle shalt þou wende," leading Piers to rip the Pardon apart (A.8.97–100)? Or the prophecy of future disendowment of the monasteries, when friars will open "Constantyns cofres" and "þe Abbot of Abyngdoun and al his issue for euere / Haue a knok of a kyng, and incurable þe wounde" (B.10.329, 31–32)? The sixteenth-century answer was to consider Langland a "pronosticator" of the Reformation.[16] The usual modern scholarly answer is to point to the proposals to disendow the monasteries that had already occurred, and to place Langland within this "new anticlericalism."[17] We cannot seem to acknowledge or explain how Langland was at times capable of insightful social prediction, or grant that his elaboration of the dangers implied in departures from traditional identity and institutional loyalty—even when demanded by his ideals of jus-

---

[14] See M. V. Clarke and V. H. Galbraith, "The Deposition of Richard II," *Bulletin of the John Rylands Library* 14 (1930): 125–81, 164.

[15] David Fowler suggests that the A-Text was written to foment the rebellion, and B by another writer to suppress and denounce these implications ("*Piers the Plowman* after Forty-Five Years," *Æstel* 2 [1994]: 63–76). This claim for A's purposes is rare if not unique, although Anne Hudson, tracing and affirming the rebels' use of A, has similarly conjectured that B might be a response to 1381 ("*Piers Plowman* and the Peasants' Revolt: A Problem Revisited," *The Yearbook of Langland Studies* 8 [1994]: 85–106, especially 100–102). B's dating is indeed speculative; but its latest topical reference is apparently to the papal Schism (1378), and scholars have usually perceived C's rather than B's changes to reflect some response to the Rising, which thus falls between B and C (e.g., Hanna, *William Langland*, 12–17; Steven Justice's views on this are discussed below). Hudson's stimulating views about B are further incentives for the present essay; her brief comparison of its claims with those of the rebels are provocative and astute, although I explore such connections here as points of shared concerns *before* 1381. The question and its various implications deserve continued debate.

[16] See Anne Hudson, "Epilogue: The Legacy of *Piers Plowman*," in John A. Alford, ed., *A Companion to Piers Plowman* (Berkeley and Los Angeles, CA: University of California Press, 1988), 251–66, especially 260–62.

[17] See Wendy Scase, *Piers Plowman and the New Anti-Clericalism* (Cambridge: Cambridge University Press, 1989), especially chapter 4.

tice—might lead him to project where ideals of justice of this kind might lead. So too with Langland's presentation of an irate plowman tearing a document in half after a smug clerk tells him that it is no pardon: we do not read here a prediction of the destruction of legal documents in the Rising of 1381, but rather an accidentally inflammatory gesture that Langland, when a shocking series of real examples of it had come to pass, sought to cover up by excision from the C-Text.

Steven Justice, the most recent and provocative examiner of the 1381 rebels' uses of *Piers Plowman*, argues that they used the poem not just because it employs "the concrete vocabulary of labor as a vocabulary of reform," but also because it displays competing professional definitions of 'doing well,' which work to weaken those authories' absolute claims; and because it showed English capable of socially conceptual possibilities. Yet such elements "meant something to the rebels that [they] could not have meant even to Langland: that when a particular oppression was shared by a class, the oppressed could protest it as a class, and, once resistance began, could use these generalizing vocabularies to organize their action and critique."[18]

These are shrewd claims about the rebels' wresting of a social lexicon from the purposes of the poet. Yet I disagree with Justice's claim that Langland, like all of what Justice calls "official England," was "blind-sided" by and intent on suppressing from real consideration the Rising and the new kinds of class politics it represented, and I disagree, too, with Justice's general argument that "official England," particularly composed of the chroniclers who described the Rising, was unable to fathom the cogency of the rebels' ideology and concerns, reducing these by incomprehension and anxiety into mere parody and "noise." Nonetheless, Justice's terms for treating *Piers Plowman*, like much of his provocative book, are the starting point for many of my counterclaims; and the frequency with which I return to his study in this essay is testimony to its power and suggestiveness. Not just the Rising, but also law itself in the fourteenth century presented a mode of social conceptualizing that can be called political in a newly wide and deep way—both on the part of the communities designating themselves as the "poor" or the "middling people" in petitions to parliament demanding legal reform throughout the century,[19] and by the higher nobility responsible for the century's novel legal efforts to keep such lower classes in their place.[20] I propose that both Langland and Walsingham understood this political import of law and its uses of history in terms of the community struggles that were developing throughout the century, and that—an even more controversial claim—their narratives

---

[18] Steven Justice, *Writing and Rebellion: England in 1381* (Berkeley, Los Angeles, and London: University of California Press, 1994), 137–38.

[19] Harding, "Revolt," 169.

[20] See Palmer, *English Law*, passim.

assess the issues behind these struggles, and even the Rising, as cogent and coherent. In Langland's poem, however, the echo of the "counterpleading" by such communities shifts between expressing ideals of justice and appearing as mere subversion. In Walsingham's more sociologically analytical narrative, the cogency of the rebels' legal and historical claims is clearly visible by his legal and historical arguments against them. I consider both of their engagements with these matters something more than responses to mere noise.

I. *Piers Plowman* and the Justice of Antiquity

What I have just called Langland's poem's "subversive" criticisms of law and institutions, Imaginative sums up in the standard legal term "counterpleading," a posture or voice that, in *Piers Plowman*, invariably has an institution, broadly defined, explicit or implied, as its target. When figured most clearly as socially dangerous and parasitic, such a voice may cynically toy with historical questions that have a bearing on general ecclesiastic authority—such as when Dame Study contemptuously describes to Will how "heiȝe men etynge at þe table" (B.10.104) idly offer theological posers, such as why God would allow the serpent into Eden, or, since clerks tell us *"Filius non portabit iniquitatem patris, / Why sholde we þat now ben for þe werkes of Adam / Roten and torende? Reson wolde it neuere!"* (B.10.114–116). The invocation of "reson" here uses the key medieval synonym for "law": "law is reason," as all medieval legal theorists from Isidore on claim.[21] But it places reason in the role of a swift and simple corrector of custom.

Here, the challenge is to all divine law, as embedded in and expressed through sacred history rather than an individual's ready logic—rather as how Thomas Hobbes later challenged the dictum that law is reason in his *Dialogue Between a Philosopher and a Student of the Common Laws of England* on the grounds that anyone's reason might therefore be claimed as law, and that custom alone could never be law.[22] These challenges, by Dame Study's speaker or Thomas Hobbes', might be refuted with Aquinas' insistence that law, albeit based entirely on reason, cannot be created by the reason of any one person but requires the whole people or the viceregent of the whole people, since the law is for the common good; moreover, it reveals its authority through long duration (*ST* I–II q. 90 art. 3, q. 97 art. 3). Nonetheless, the challenge in Dame Study's scornful quotation of a wiseacre goes unanswered in the poem. Indeed, its criticism of the law on the grounds of readily available "reson" appears to foster rather than crush

---

21 See Alford, "Reason."
22 Thomas Hobbes, *A Dialogue Between a Philosopher and a Student of the Common Laws of England*, ed. Joseph Cropsey (Chicago: University of Chicago Press, 1997), 53–57, 94–97.

such counterpleading. Once given expression, the voice of 'reasonable' dissent against a law based merely on tradition and history opens up to encompass the next passus and a half, with a wide range of issues that finally touch on those proposed by the rebels of 1381.

This long, crucial, and notoriously tangled section of the poem (B.10.377–11.404) comprises Will's complaint against law in its broadest terms. Here Will counterpleads all bookish, Christian and legal knowledge, and finally, in a vision within the dream vision proper that surveys the innate moral actions of animals, counterpleads Reason himself, querying why "Reson rewarded and ruled alle beestes / Saue man and his make" (B.11.370–71)—thus interrogating the fundamental ideological principle of religious, human, and (with regard to the nesting and mating habits of animals) natural law. This series of attacks against law by the "reson" not of Reason, but of Will, swings between tones of social justice and obvious self-indictment, as when Will "counterpleads" Reason himself, 'aresoning' Reason, as Imaginative, with a fitting pun, describes it (B.12.218). The diatribe is initially driven by Will's questions about ancient and salvation history: How can knowledge and ethical living save one's soul, since these did not save the pagan philosophers? How can the thief next to Jesus on the cross, and Mary Magdalene, and David, killer of Uriah, all be saved and made "souereynes in heuene" (A.11.291; B.10.432), since they did not lead virtuous lives? In the B revision of the poem from the late 1370s, the complaint adds Scripture's curt remarks on how few are chosen, and this turns the narrator, seemingly by intention, away from counterpleading Scripture toward instead "disputing" with himself on "Wheiþer I were chosen or noȝt chosen" (B.11.117) for salvation, a topic Will pursues legalistically and with a legal analogy—but a surprising one:

> For þouȝ a cristen man coueited his cristendom to reneye,
> Riȝtfully to reneye no reson it wolde.
> For may no cherl chartre make ne his chatel selle
> Wiþouten leue of his lord; no lawe wol it graunte.
> Ac he may renne in arerage and rome fro home,
> As a reneyed caytif recchelesly rennen aboute.
> Ac reson shal rekene wiþ hym and rebuken hym at þe laste,
> And conscience acounte wiþ hym and casten hym in arerage,
> And putten hym after in prison in purgatorie to brenne;
> For hise are+rages rewarden hym þere riȝt to þe day of dome,
> But if Contricion wol come and crye by his lyue
> Mercy for his mysdedes wiþ mouþe or wiþ herte.
> (B.11.125–36)

Folded into an allegory of Christianity as historically imprisoning, this is a stunning miniature tale of the career of a serf seeking the freedom to contract land purchases and sell property, complete with echoes of a standard formula of sentencing ("riȝt to þe day of dome"), and of an appeal for pardon by a desperate wife, a role that Contricion here seems to mimic. Its unliberating, imprisoning, and judicial view of Christianity in particular presents history in general as serfdom, as legal bondage; the prisonhouse of history is here an inflexible law of institutional containments. More simply, the vehicle of the simile reminds us that Langland's contemporary Christendom contains serfdom, whose unreasonable and unjust constraints are emphasized by the slightness of the 'crimes' committed by the "cherl" in the simile: making a charter and selling his possessions. Such activities are abundantly documented among the unfree peasantry from the early fourteenth century onward and helped generate the most politically disruptive legal conflicts between the lower social orders and their powerful landlords. Langland could hardly have chosen a more provocative simile, calculated to invoke the passions and tensions surrounding literate and historically self-conscious but legally servile individuals in the fourteenth century.

Yet, almost immediately following this figuring of Christianity as an overbearing manorial legal system, bursts in the direct voice of the emperor Trajan, whose statements pick up the same image but transform its point to liberations, in a stunning shift of social references and ethical valences. For if the narrator sees himself in prison as subject to a law he cannot evade, Trajan has broken *out* of such prisons of history *into* Christianity:

> "Ye? baw for bokes!" quod oon was broken out of helle.
> [I] Troianus, a trewe kny3t, [take] witnesse at a pope
> How [I] was ded and dampned to dwellen in pyne
> For an vncristene creature; clerkes wite þe soþe
> That al þe clergie vnder crist ne my3te me cracche fro helle,
> But oonliche loue and leautee and my laweful domes.
> (B.11.140–45)

Trajan, who is the poem's only speaking human figure from the ancient past apart from Jesus, in one way epitomizes the poem's counterpleading of law that Imaginative asserts Will should suppress. Yet I imagine that most readers are likely to cheer, at least silently, at this point. Trajan is crucial for the poem's ideal of justice, as an equity not requiring any social or personal prerequisites, even of religion. Trajan, whose story as a just pagan posthumously saved by Gregory the Great's prayer was well known, appears from the depths of history paradoxically in order to define freedom *from* history as the principle of justice. Trajan states with imperious authority that he was saved by "his pure truþe" (B.11.156) rather than any "syngynge of masses" or "konnyng of lawes" (151, 166)—and here Langland aggressively rebuts the otherwise universal tradition of Gregory the Great's prayer as the cause for Trajan's salvation. Instead, it is Trajan's adherence to "truþe" defined in opposition to law or institutional ritual that saves him: "'Lawe wiþouten loue,' quod Troianus, 'ley þer a bene!'" (B.11.171)—a view presumably based on the incident in the *Golden Legend*'s Life of

Gregory the Great, where Trajan stops on the way to war to "see that justice is done" for a widow whose innocent son was executed.[23]

This presentation defines Trajan as embodying self-defined justice, justice that breaks out of the constraints of tradition or official proceedings,
just as he breaks out of the legalistic order of debate between Scripture and
Will in Langland's poem: he was not *pulled* by Gregory into heaven but by
his own efforts "was broken out of helle." Trajan's counterpleading makes
him a crucial figure in the poem both *from* history and *about* history, for
his presence and words imply that for one free or bound to servitude, heathen or Christian, salvation resides in self-definition and rupture from institutions and traditions. Right when the serf of the soul is imprisoned most
deeply in history and its institutional traditions, Trajan bursts out.

At the center of the poem, he thus constitutes the same liberating
movement that Jesus constitutes near the end of the poem, when Jesus
majesterially frees humankind from Lucifer's legal claim to own the souls
in hell as his serfs by right of ancient judgment against mankind's fall, but
even more simply by long duration of possession:

> "For by right and by reson þe renkes þat ben here
> Body and soule beþ myne, boþe goode and ille.
> For hymself seide, þat Sire is of heuene,
> If Adam ete þe Appul alle sholde deye
> And dwelle wiþ vs deueles; þis þretynge [driȝten] made.
> And [siþen] he þat Sooþnesse is seide þise wordes,
> And siþen I was seised seuene þousand wynter
> I leeue þat lawe nyl noȝt lete hym þe leeste."
> (B.18.278–85)

Jesus uses "reason" to free humanity from such corrupt law and the iner-
tia of legal custom, arguing that mortality, not damnation, was the sentence
for the Fall (330–31), and that the "old law" allows "lif for lif" (343), so
that by giving his life, Jesus can "by right and by reson raunsone here my
liges" (349).

As at once a prototype and an antetype of Jesus (prototype since his
righteous life was prior to, but antetype since his salvation was after Jesus),
Trajan—or Will: the division of these two here loses any certainty—even
goes on to invert the narrator's simile of Christian serfdom by suggesting
that with Christianity, there ought to be no basis in history for serfdom:

> For alle are we cristes creatures and of his cofres riche,
> And breþeren as of oo blood, as wel beggeres as Erles.
> For [at] Caluarie of cristes blood cristendom gan sprynge,
> And blody breþeren we bicome þere of o body ywonne,
> As *quasi modo geniti* gentil men echone,

---

[23] Jacobus de Voragine, *The Golden Legend: Readings on the Saints*, trans. William Granger Ryan, 2 vols.
(Princeton: Princeton University Press, 1993), 1:178; see also Frank Grady, "*Piers Plowman, St. Erkenwald,
and the Rule of Exceptional Salvation*," *Yearbook of Langland Studies* 6 (1992): 63–88.

> No beggere ne boye amonges vs but if it synne made:
> *Qui facit peccatum seruus est peccati.*
>   (B.11.199–204)

The claim, evidently made by Langland no later than 1378 when the last datable reference in the B-Text can be found, parallels accounts of the assertions of the rural and artisan rebels of 1381; Froissart declares that "these bad people" stated that "when the world began there had been no serfs and could not be, unless they had rebelled against their lord, as Lucifer did against God" ("No beggere ne boye amonges vs but if it synne made," as Trajan has it). Froissart adds that the leader of the Rising, John Ball, had for some time been preaching similar themes (211–13);[24] and Thomas Walsingham states that the proverbial couplet, "Whan Adam dalf and Eve span / Wo was thenne the gentilman?" was recited during the Rising.[25]

II. *Piers Plowman* and the Conflicts Before 1381

In the fourteenth century, no one claimed for himself a *sui generis*, ahistorical authority to change the law; it was always an image cast onto the Other. There it usually held a positive valence for heroic instances in the ancient past, and a nightmarish valence for instances in the present, a volatile possibility that displays how fragile the legal claims to history were, and how palpable the anxiety that they were all mere constructions of the present. In recounting the purposes of the Rising, the chronicler Adam of Usk—a civil lawyer and thus one of the targets of the rebels at their most bloodthirsty—stated that the rebels "boasted that they would kill all those in the kingdom who were nobler-born than them, and elect a king and lords from amongst themselves, and that they would make new laws; in brief, that they would transform—which meant, in fact, destroy— this whole island and its existing society."[26] But Wat Tyler, as leader of the London rebels, met the king at Smithfield in 1381 with a huge band of peasants, artisans, and lower clergy in order to demand that (as the *Anonimalle Chronicle* reports) there should be "no law but the law of Winchester and that henceforward there should be no outlawry in any process of law, and that no lord should have lordship in future, but that it should be divided among all men, except for the king's own lordship."[27] The "law of Winchester" apparently referred to the 1285 statute that allowed what Alan Harding has defined as "an ideal of communal self-

---

24 Geoffrey Brereton, trans. and ed., *Froissart: Chronicles* (London: Penguin Books, 1978), 211–13.

25 Thomas Walsingham, *Historia Anglicana 1272–1422*, ed. Henry Thomas Riley, 2 vols., Rolls Series (London: Longman, Green, 1863–4), 2:32.

26 *The Chronicle of Adam Usk, 1377–1421*, ed. and trans. C. Given-Wilson (Oxford: Clarendon Press, 1997), 5.

27 *The Anonimalle Chronicle*, ed. V. H. Galbraith (Manchester: Manchester University Press, 1927), 147.

policing,"[28] since the Statute of Winchester, like our Second Amendment, allowed a provision for "every man [to] have in house arms for keeping the peace," a legal atavism that registers the widespread hatred of corrupt royal officers and indeed the class oppression that characterized the laws passed by the central government in the later fourteenth century, which even Adam of Usk summarizes as "wanton evils, extortions, and other intolerable injustices upon the realm" that those around King Richard enacted.[29] Langland's darkest view of the law enacted and exercised by the higher nobility at the coming of Antichrist vividly depicts such class oppression, when he shows Simony as a powerful and rich lord barging through every court of law, secular and ecclesiastic, at Westminster:

> And cam to þe kynges counseille as a kene baroun
> And [knokked] Conscience in Court afore hem alle;
> And garte good feiþ flee and fals to abide,
> And boldeliche bar adoun wiþ many a bright Noble
> Muche of þe wit and wisdom of westmynstre halle.
> He Iogged to a Iustice and Iusted in his eere
> And ouertilte al his truþe wiþ "tak þis vp amendement."
> And to þe Arches in haste he yede anoon after
> And tornede Cyuyle into Symonye, and siþþe he took þe Official.
> For a Meneuer Mantel he made lele matrymoyne
> Departen er deeþ cam and deuors shapte.
>   (B.20.129–39)

This passage remains intact in the later, post-1381 C version. Yet it is hard to deny that the C-Text's changes are broadly clarifying of the need to avoid violence concerning just the issues that the rebels were concerned with: the violent act of Piers tearing the Pardon before the priest is effaced, the sharpest words of complaint against the wealthy are tempered. However, there is another place to put the emphasis in the common account of the poet revising his work to repress the many ways in which it bespoke the concerns of the rebels: that Langland's poem was remarkably in touch with the concerns which came to a head in 1381 but which preceded the Rising by decades, especially in conflicts at many of the monasteries; and that Langland's position as an arbiter of such issues preceded that of the rebels by several years at least. Even if he wished (who wouldn't?) to clarify his irenic social purposes—just because I praise poverty, do not go and kill the rich, he has even Recklessness himself declare—that does not imply that he was "blindsided" by the rebels' use of his poem. On the contrary, there are points where the poem seems to touch directly the issues of contention that spread across England from the early years of Edward III's reign on.

---

[28] Harding, "Revolt," 166. Harding quotes and trenchantly discusses the Statute.
[29] *Chronicle of Adam Usk*, 2–3.

I take two passages in *Piers Plowman* that may show some, or perhaps considerable, knowledge of these historically oriented legal conflicts between communities and religious landlords before 1381, as the communities began to consolidate, confect, or emphasize self-defined, ancient identities. A first possible echo to the legal struggles of the various tenant communities of the fourteenth century is cast not in a vision of the past but of the present and future. This appears in the poem's strongest assertion of disendowment of the monasteries, in Clergy's first speech, where, defining Dowel, he turns to castigate the clergy for not living up to Clergy's own ideals. Traditionally secluded in the holy settings of peaceful cloisters and schools, the clergy are now, Clergy states, worldly and arrogant landlords and cruel masters of their tenants:

> Ac now is Religion a rydere, a [rennere] by stretes,
> A ledere of louedayes and a lond buggere,
> A prikere on a palfrey fro place to Manere,
> An heep of houndes at his ers as he a lord were,
> And but if his knaue knele þat shal his coppe brynge
> He loureþ on hym and [lakkeþ] hym: who [lered] hym curteisie?
> (B.10.311–16)

Clergy moves on to an aggressive legal challenge of the monastic landlords. First he condemns mortmain, the granting of property by laymen to a church, which thus disinherits the layman's heirs—this was legislated against by Edward I but usually simply to yield a tax from the fee that abbeys could pay to be licensed to accept such property. Clergy implicitly addresses not the abbeys but those who might consider giving to them:

> Litel hadde lordes to doon to ȝyue lond from hire heires
> To Religiouse þat han no rouþe þouȝ it reyne on hir Auters.
> (B.10.317–18)

Then he addresses the personal indulgence their legal claims to benefice and lands allow them, in close parallel to the legal struggles between abbeys and their tenants that, as I shall show in more detail in a moment, were unfolding all over England by the 1360s and 1370s:

> In many places þer þei persons ben, be þei purely at ese,
> Of þe pouere haue þei no pite, and þat is hir pure [chartre] / {charite};
> Ac þei leten hem as lordes, hir lond liþ so brode.
> (B.10.319–21)

A manuscript variant leads us into questions about the precise legal subtlety of Clergy's wit here. On the principle (evidently) of preferring the more "difficult" reading, Kane-Donaldson conjecture here for the B-Text the reading "chartre," found in a handful of C manuscripts for the same passage, rather than the B archetypal "charite." But the textual principle of *difficilior lectio potior* is hard to weigh here, since what is 'difficult' is the

specific legal parody that *both* "pure chartre" *and* "pure charite" offer.
"Pure chartre," while not attested elsewhere, is justified by the sense
"absolute charter," that is, full possession, by analogy with the phrase
"pure alms," that is, a religious order's tenure of land in exchange simply
for spiritual services (*frankalmoign*). But by the same argument, "pure
charite," the alternate reading, might easily be taken as an ironically literal translation of, or troping on, "pure alms" or *frankalmoign*. In either
case, the other statements Clergy presents, "be þei purely at ese" and "Of
þe pouere haue þei no pite" end up as the contractual terms of the monks'
tenure of land that "liþ so brode." Quasi-allegorical unethical postures
rather than any historical claims define the monks' terms of ownership; the
everpresent historical claims to land tenure by the monastic houses are
swiftly satirized here by emptying ownership of any historical bases at all.

Following this much of the satire allows us to see the logic of the next,
more directly polemical and topical statements. The outcome of such materialism, arrogance—to their tenants, servants, and vicars—and ignorance,
Clergy declares, is that the friars shall find a way to take all the church's
endowed wealth, "shul fynden a keye / Of Costantyns cofres," as he puts
it, referring to the Constantine Donation, the charter by which the church
claimed all of its temporal possessions by grant from Constantine to Pope
Sylvester. Or perhaps Clergy means that the friars will lead to the undoing
of the church's wealth, even if the friars do not themselves acquire it. In
either case, the church will be economically and legally stripped and pun-
ished even beyond this, as metonymized by one monastery in particular:

> Ac þer shal come a kyng and confesse yow Religiouses,
> And bete yow, as þe bible telleþ, for brekynge of youre rule,
> And amende Monyals, Monkes and Chanons,
> And puten hem to hir penaunce, *Ad pristinum statum ire*;
> And Barons wiþ Erles beten hem þoruȝ *Beatus vir*res techyng;
> Bynymen that hir barnes claymen, and blame yow foule:
> *Hij in curribus & hij in equis ipsi obligati sunt &c.*
> And þanne Freres in hir fraytour shul fynden a keye
> Of Costantyns cofres þer þe catel is Inne
> That Gregories godchildren vngodly despended.
> And þanne shal þe Abbot of Abyngdoun and al his issue for euere
> Haue a knok of a kyng, and incurable þe wounde.
> That þis worþ sooþ, seke ye þat ofte ouerse þe bible:
>> *Quomodo cessauit exactor, quieuit tributum? contriuit dominus
>> baculum impiorum, et virgam dominancium cedencium plaga
>> insanabili.*
>
> (B.10.322–33)

For post-Reformation readers, the reference to the abbey of Abingdon has
both more and less meaning than it had for Langland and his first readers:
the abbey was indeed wealthy, and it was indeed utterly dismantled at the
Reformation, as all post-medieval commentators on the passage note. But

the *abbot* had a different fate in the fourteenth century. In 1368, he was "impeached" by his townsmen tenants for infringing on their ancient liberties, and thus made to appear before the king's council and embroiled in a difficult and expensive lawsuit for four years. The case displays an early instance of special procedures already attaching to the word impeachment (*impetitus*) before the use of this notion by the Commons to attack the king's favorites in the Good Parliament of 1376. The word had already been used at Cirencester in 1342 by the tenants of the monastery there in a very similar case against their abbot, where he too had been forced to journey to Chancery before the king's council.[30] The strategy by both groups of tenants seems to have been to evade the ordinary law courts, and to elide the king's interests with their own by claiming to be his tenants rather than the abbots'. As Gabrielle Lambrick argues, here and in other later cases including the Good Parliament, *impetitus* (whose translation as 'impeachment' had not appeared) thus seems to have taken on the sense of a legal action that concerned the joint interests of the king and a community of some kind, thus circumventing the need for an individual plaintiff as in common law cases.[31] It thus first appears as a legal instrument for making a law case into a means of collective social change and collective solidarity, a tool for politicizing law, for once in the tenants' and commons' interests.

I propose that Langland was aware of the case at Abingdon and that his "Haue a knok of a kyng," which is not directly stated in the Latin quotation from Isaiah, is his translation of *impetitus*, which he is taking, accurately, as the past participle of *impetito*, itself the frequentative of *impeto*, "attack," "assail." If this is true, here Langland was taking his language from the communities that generated the members and the strategies of the Rising, rather than the later rebels simply taking Langland's language from him. Clergy's projection of this "impeachment" into the open-ended future in the B-Text strengthens the connection. The Abingdon tenants ultimately failed to win their case, but they did not lose it; in 1372 the monastery was given its rents back and the tenants were instructed to seek individual remedy in the common law courts.

That they had at least managed a protracted battle bespeaks both their shrewdness and the nature of legal proof to antiquity required by the court they chose. The abbot had no charter to prove the abbey's ancient holding of the town and marketplace, although he orally claimed its foundation by Cedwalla in the seventh century: probably, Lambrick suggests, because the abbey's (as usual spurious) early charters were destroyed by tenants in the riots at the abbey in 1327. But a proceeding before the king's Council to

---

[30] See C. D. Ross, ed., *The Cartulary of Cirencester Abbey, Gloucestershire*, Vol. 1 (London: Oxford University Press, 1964), 110-13.

[31] Gabrielle Lambrick, "The Impeachment of the Abbot of Abingdon in 1368," *English Historical Review* 82 (1967): 250–76.

which the tenants forced the abbot would require some written record. So, to secure some authoritative claim about details of the abbey's original possession of the town, the abbot reverted to Domesday book in order to refute the tenants' simple assertion that the town had been free to the inhabitants and foreign merchants from time immemorial; yet Domesday book, it happens, makes no mention of Abingdon.[32] Therefore, the abbey's lawyers were forced to argue acrobatically that Abingdon was indeed present in Domesday book but as an unnamed part of another manor stated to be in the abbey desmene, Barton, which had ten market stalls outside the abbey door, two mills, fisheries, and twenty-four servants, features that, they claimed, identified Abingdon. The only shred of plausibility in this otherwise extremely dubious identification was the reference to the market stalls outside the abbey doors; but these had been a matter of open historical contestation within living memory of the later fourteenth-century abbot of Abingdon and his tenants. According to a chronicler at Abingdon abbey, the 1327 riots started when the townsmen "by their own authority" had moved the market stalls "which the abbot and convent are clearly seen to have possessed from the time before which there is no memory," and located and used the stalls "at their own pleasure," leading to the abbot's "defense" against such violation of history and tradition, and in turn to the townsmen's destruction of documents, moveables, and part of a building.[33] Clearly the center of both groups' historical claims was the market stalls, which may have defined the townsmen's most immediate community interest that led to the process of their seeking impeachment, while terms for market stalls probably featured like keywords in the abbey's lawyers' search through Domesday and other written records for a possible nearby manor.

Clergy's comments are a caustic assessment of the vacuity of the fourteenth-century church's claims to its wealthy holdings of land and service, in terms that precisely and informedly engage the legal issues that the church's tenants were similarly pursuing, issues that would be familiar to someone close to Westminster, where much evidence puts Langland for at least some of his life. These issues, moreover, are predictive of further collective, community-based legal assaults against the monastery and indeed all ecclesiastical landlords: if not sooner then later, if not Abingdon then another monastery—or *all* monasteries, as the C-Text finally asserts, when

---

[32] Still succinctly authoritative on the evidence for the abbey's pre-Conquest history and the development of its foundation narrative ("a pious, but incoherent, invention of the twelfth century") is F. M. Stenton, *The Early History of the Abbey of Abingdon* (Reading, G.B.: University College, 1913), quotation at 7. The reedification of the monastery in the tenth-century "Benedictine Revival" is fully documented with charters (albeit some clearly forged) from King Eadred; but that act never claimed foundational status, leaving the abbey's twelfth-century chronicler to develop the foundation narrative "upon the authority of the ancients" (*Historia Monasterii de Abingdon*, quoted by Stenton, 9).

[33] H. E. Salter, "A Chronicle Role of the Abbots of Abingdon," *English Historical Review* 26 (1911): 727–38, 731.

this passage becomes part of Reason's sermon to the "commune," and the phrase changes to "þe abbot of engelonde and the abbesse his nese / Shal haue a knok vppon here crounes" (C.5.176–77). Indeed, the actual soundness of the prediction is based on the logic of political, collective or institutional manipulation of legal history. The hollowing out of history by the institutions themselves would indeed lead to disendowment, as belief in the historical authority on which they depend gradually withered away. "Puyre chartre" or "pure charite" is a form of tenure that, like the phrases themselves, has no tradition at all.

My second example has a small point of entry but a large horizon of meaning for the poet's view of his own relation to legalistic history, both before and after 1381. Its entry is the reference to Sloth's knowledge of "rymes of Robyn hood and Randolf Erl of Chestre"—rather than of his Paternoster:

> I kan noȝt parfitly my Paternoster as þe preest it syngeþ,
> But I kan rymes of Robyn hood and Randolf Erl of Chestre.
>   (B.5.394–5)

The passage has always been an enticement to folklorists: it supplies the earliest references in English literature both to Robin Hood and Ranulph of Chester as heroes of the "rymes" of saga or ballad. Without any corroborating material for the "lost literature" on the second figure, scholars have had to guess which Ranulph of Chester is meant. Although Ranulph III is often assumed, since, as one of the most powerful knights in the thirteenth century, he was a heroic figure, James Alexander has plausibly argued for Ranulph II because he lived an outlaw's life and died defeated by King Stephen; and an outlaw, as Robin Hood is, not a hero would better suit Sloth's reprobate tastes.[34] In the "rymes of Robyn hood" that Sloth mentions, as Maurice Keen remarks, "it is the churchmen of rank whom the outlaws persecute, the bishops and archbishops, the abbots and the officers of the great monasteries." Thus, Keen adds, "it is probably no accident that our first certain reference to Robin Hood"—that is, here in *Piers*—"comes from the years just previous to the Peasants' Revolt,"[35] just as later riots and revolts invoked other instances of what Stephen Knight calls "symbolic liberators."[36]

The combination of the names and the disreputable context of their appearance is evidently significant. I suggest a more topical sense of such "symbolism." At Coventry, a struggle between the priory and the townsmen developed from the twelfth century on the basis of conflicting histor-

---

34 James W. Alexander, "Ranulph III of Chester: An Outlaw of Legend?" *Neuphilologische Mitteilungen* 83 (1982): 152–57.
35 Maurice Keen, *Outlaws of Medieval Legend*, rev. ed. (Toronto: University of Toronto Press, 1977), 152, 173.
36 Stephen Knight, *Robin Hood: A Complete Study of the English Outlaw* (Oxford: Blackwell, 1994), 51.

ical claims and came to a riot in 1321: the townsmen had the documentary evidence that earl Ranulph II of Chester had granted the town, or perhaps half the town, to the townsmen; the monastery, apparently slightly later, forged a charter by which it was claimed that Leofric in the eleventh century had given half the town to the monastery. Each side fiercely sought by this and other means to appropriate the liberties of the other; at one point the townsmen accused the prior before the pope of sortilege, which perhaps led to the prior accusing the townsmen of witchcraft in scheming to kill the king—the first case of prosecution of witchcraft in post-Conquest England. The struggle came to a head in the 1330s and 1340s when the queen mother Isabella took the townsmen's side and, by acquiring for the townsmen a royal confirmation of Ranulph II's charter to the townsmen (as well as by exchanges of property with other major landowners in the area), managed both to acquire lordship of manor in Coventry and to establish the historical basis for the townsmen to define the boundaries of a free borough as they claimed they had held it at least "in ancient times of the lordship of Ranulph III."[37] Such a "recovery" of the ancient boundaries gained the queen mother £1000 from the townsmen in exchange for enfranchising them with the various liberties she had thereby acquired. Coventry showed, perhaps with dangerous attractiveness to monastic tenants, how high the stakes of historical reconstruction or revision could be in the context of the community politics in the fourteenth century.

Many communities of monastic tenants sought similar endeavors claiming ancient or more recent liberties in 1326, 1327, and into the 1330s—Bury St. Edmunds, St. Albans, Abingdon, and Dunstable are the best documented, but others appeared at Darnhall, Cheshire (the tenants of Vale Royal), and at Great and Little Ogbourne (the English tenants of Bec). Perhaps the first great year for such claims of ancient liberties was 1327, not simply because of the "great disruption" of the forced abdication and imprisonment of Edward II and the succession of the young Edward III; it may also be that the sudden possibility of petitions from the Commons to parliament that appeared in this year made it a moment to seize, for tenants who wished to present directly to the highest secular court their historical claims of being free burghers, a means more direct than the notoriously corrupt trailbaston courts, much less the manorial courts of the abbeys and priories themselves where their suits would have been unimaginable. It is worth pausing to note the courage of making such historical claims at all, in the face of the massive historiographical and social authority of the religious houses that the tenants combatted; "Appeals...to a not necessarily mythical or remote past are to be found in...cases in which proof of past conditions was necessary, not involving a plea of ancient demense," Rodney Hilton remarks, adding that such efforts were inherent-

---

[37] Arthur and Eileen Gooder, "Coventry Before 1355: Unity or Division? The Importance of the Earl's Half," *Midland History* 6 (1981): 1–38, 20.

ly unlikely to succeed even at royal courts, thus often forcing the peasants and tenants to direct action: "Royal courts would protect the rights of men who were uncontrovertibly free...But it would be foolish to imagine that projects for the general emancipation of the unfree could be entertained by government officials or royal judges, whose social and political outlook was that of their class."[38] As Steven Justice asserts, the letters of the rebels in 1381 placed the rebels "in what had been defined immemoriably as a clerkly space, a space of writing and documentary record marked by specialized forms and formulae, by specialized languages and hands, by all the parchment that flowed into the royal chancery and back out again. The [rebel] letters announced that they were taking over this space, and taking over the forms that went with it."[39] But this "announcement" had in fact been made for many decades, as the religious houses at many of the places where the Rising flared up most acutely well knew, and indeed they defined their own cartulary and historiographical responses around it. It is hardly surprising that the historical arguments and documentary strategies of the rebels in 1381 did not spring fully born from the head of John Ball but needed at least half a century of tempering as a political and historical conviction. The Coventry townsmen's success in 1355, of course, would, if known, have contributed greatly—and dangerously—to the confidence of all such efforts. The synchronicity or near-succession of risings in the late 1320s and again in the 1350s shows that even before 1381, tenants across England seem to have some knowledge of other such efforts: a prelude to the massively coordinated revolt of 1381. But none of the later efforts would have a member of the royal family on their side, and in this sense the misleading model of Coventry was the exception that proved the rule.

Thus, to return to the small moment in *Piers Plowman*, perhaps Ranulph of Chester was, after the events at Coventry in mid-century, a "symbolic liberator" in a more specific way than, for example, Trajan, one that would make him an appropriate candidate as a subject of Sloth's ballads. I can prove this suggestion no more than that, but it is possible to explore supporting implications of Langland's legal and historial vision implied in Sloth that do not depend on such an allusion. If present, the allusion to triumphant townsmen over an abbey would show in direct terms how Sloth's portrait brings to focus a range of social tones more topically rebellious than scholars usually perceive. Sloth, in this case, is not simply too slothful to obey religious law; he is also subversive of clerical authority, slothful in his resentful obedience to such authorities, although not in his pursuit of things more to his liking. He is in fact energetic in pursuit of a life that is rebellious against the orthodox communities of church and

---

[38] Rodney Hilton, "Peasant Movements in England Before 1381," in *Class Conflict and the Crisis of Feudalism: Essays in Medieval Social History*, 2nd ed. (London and New York: Verso, 1990), 49–65, 225–28; here, 58.

[39] Justice, *Writing and Rebellion*, 66.

local life. Even without the allusion's support, but guided by its possibilities, we can see that Sloth's balance of anti-institutional energies and slothful obedience to clerical authority is more complex still, for he evidently
functions as a partial shadow of the narrator, as John Bowers has most
thoroughly shown, who displays similar symptoms (falling asleep in church
to have a dream-vision, or wandering as a vagrant) and even uses the same
Latin quotation to define himself: *"Heu michi quia sterilem vitam duxi
Iuuenilem"* (440a).[40] And Sloth is, like the narrator at times, the epitome
of a half-stifled, muttering counterpleader.

The energetic rebelliousness and institutional lassitude in Sloth's portrait can be perceived further in the C-Text's elaboration of the narrator,
produced after the Rising. Now, Will is officially interrogated for sloth in
a legal sense, that is, vagrancy, legislated against by the Statute of Laborers
as reissued in 1388, and here enforced by Reason and Conscience, who in
the C-Text have become the king's chancellor and king's chief justice. Will's
counterpleading rises here—*after* the Rising—to its highest, if also its most
unstable pitch, in social and ethical terms. He first counterpleads that he is
a clerk and should therefore do no physical labor. Yet as Conscience replies,
Will has no official church position to justify his lack of other occupation:
"y can nat se this lyeth; / Ac it semeth no sad parfitnesse in Citees to begge
/ But he be obediencer to prior or to mynistre" (C.5.89–91). Will admits he
has "ytynt tyme and tyme myspened" but hopes for a final repayment that
will justify a lifetime of socially uncategorizable endeavor and seemingly
fruitless investment:

> "...as he þat ofte hath ychaffared
> And ay loste and loste and at þe laste hym happed
> A boute suche a bargayn he was þe bet euere
> And sette his los at a leef at the laste ende
> ...
> So hope y to haue of hym þat is almyghty
> A gobet of his grace and bigynne a tyme
> That alle tymes of my tyme to profit shal turne."
>   (C.5.94–101)

Will then yet more clearly displays that, however vigorously he gives assur-
ances to Conscience and Reason of hastening to lead a "lyf þat is
louable"—including bustling to church as Conscience orders—and however desperately energetic he seems in his quest to gain final recuperation of
all the time he has lost, he nonetheless remains decisively, even aggressively slothful in precisely the orthodox, institutional forms that Reason and
Conscience demand of him:

---

[40] John Bowers, *The Crisis of Will in Piers Plowman* (Washington, D. C.: The Catholic University of
America Press, 1986), chapters 5–7.

> And to þe kyrke y gan go god to honoure;
> Byfore þe cross on my knees knokked y my brest,
> Syhing for my synnes, seggyng my paternoster,
> Wepyng and waylyng til y was aslepe.
>   (C.5.105–8)

Rather than a retreat after the Rising from the B-Text's complex political posture of counterpleading the law and the institutions it upholds, in tones shifting between slothful subversion and demands for justice, the poet of C fashioned a further development of precisely this issue, now raised to a more daring if more general claim that slothfulness in commitment to traditional institutions may be *necessary* for energetic definition of new social endeavors and non-traditional identities. Sloth's subversive counterpleading is shifted into the narrator's claims for an ethics of justice that *he* must teach to Conscience and Reason: a posture of justice beyond institutional loyalty and constraints, the justice of Trajan and Jesus.

Yet even as a paeon to this emerges, the narrator simultaneously attacks the implications of his own posture. Will's final counterpleading to Reason and Conscience includes a diatribe against the present decay of traditional social identity, an anticipatory defense against Reason's and Conscience's claim that there might in the modern world be any "lyf þat is louable" available for Will—and what is routinely considered an instance of the poet's extreme social conservatism, of a species even harder and more anti-rebel than ever before:

> Ac sythe bondemen barnes haen be mad bisshopes
> And bar[o]nes bastardus haen be Erchedekenes
> And sopares and here sones for suluer han be knyhtes,
> And lordes sones here laboreres and leyde here rentes to wedde
> For the ryhte of this reume ryden aȝeyn oure enemyes
> In confort of the comune and the kynges worschipe,
> And monkes and moniales þat mendenantes sholde fynde
> Imade here kyn knyhtes and knyhtes fees ypurchased,
> Popes and patrones pore gentel blood refused
> And taken Symondus sones seyntwarie to kepe,
> Lyfholynesse and loue hath be longe hennes
> And wol til hit be wered out or oþerwyse ychaunged.
>   (C.5.70–81)

Steven Justice remarks that this is "possibly the most uncompromising assertion of class privilege in the whole poem" and a comment on the damage to the social hierarchy that (Justice proposes) Langland thought the Rising of 1381 had already accomplished. But the passage has a remarkable similarity to how the late fourteenth-century chronicler Henry Knighton also explained the anti-vagrancy legislation of 1388:

> For the lesser people were so puffed up in those days in their dress and
> their belongings, and they flourished and prospered so in various ways,

that one might scarcely distinguish one from another for the splendor
of their dress and adornments: not a humble man from a great man,
not a needy from a rich man, not a servant from his master, not a priest
from another man, but each imitating the other...Wherefore the magnates insisted upon a remedy, to remove the abuses and impose a better order....[41]

A poet in touch with the legislation at Westminster could well have known
this rationale for the reissuance of the Statute of Laborers—a complaint
that indeed is rather typical throughout the fourteenth century legislation
against the "lower" or "middling" estates.[42] Yet I think it somewhat misses the point to define Langland's similar passage simply in terms of an
injured sense of lost social privilege.[43] Instead, Langland's passage, while
echoing these complaints of the gentry, introduces his broadest assertion
that social appearances are now unreconcilable with tradition, that history
itself, in the everyday way that medieval trappings of social identity presents it, is thoroughly hollowed out both by demands for a justice that
boldly pays no heed to tradition as such, and by self- or institution-serving
presentist manipulations of tradition that accomplish the same ends. What
Langland has shown Trajan and Jesus doing as an expression of justice—
achieving liberation from servitude to tradition, into a just freedom—he
here shows as a principle of social destruction: "bondemen barnes haen be
mad bisshopes." The legal petitions by the magnates and by the chronicler
Henry Knighton apply this criticism of self-made, traditionless legal identity entirely to the Other; Langland presents his passage in terms that directly reflect on his protagonist. In this sense, Langland's new passage is not
simply collusion with the magnates disturbed by an evaporation of traditional identity and a confection of new social identities by those like Will
himself whose traditional estate is so unclear. Rather, it is also a statement
of the consequence of his own ideals of justice as freedom from custom and
traditional identity, hence a statement of the modernity in which the narrator finally locates his own legal identity. The argument Will's petulant
and defensive remarks here serve is not, after all, to reimpose the Statute of
Laborers, but instead to claim the freedom to lead a non-traditional and

---

[41] *Knighton's Chronicle*, 509. Justice's views on Langland's passage are at *Writing and Rebellion*, 245.

[42] Knighton's passage resembles the rationale for the Commons' petition for a sumptuary ordinance in
1363; see *Rotuli Parliamentorum, ut et petitiones et placita in parliamento*, 6 vols. (London: Record
Commission, 1767–1832), 2.278 (section 25). That resemblance leads me to think it likely that Knighton
was here recording official parliamentary rhetoric, which would increase the possibility that Langland had
also heard such rhetoric in the context of the 1388 legislation. The enrolled copy of the statute from the
Cambridge Parliament of 1388 has been lost (see J. A. Tuck, "The Cambridge Parliament, 1388," *English
Historical Review* 84 [1969]: 225–43); thus it is even conceivable that both Knighton's rhetoric echoes, and
Langland's obliquely mimes, the preamble of the parliamentary form of the statute.

[43] See also Middleton, "Acts of Vagrancy," 256–60, for another view against this consensus, and passim
for the fullest discussion of the 1388 legislation in relation to the claims of the narrator at C.5.1–104.
Middleton does not note the parallel passage in Knighton's presentation of the 1388 legislation.

impoverished life: he is not seeking a hypocritical justification of the social privilege of being a bishop, archdeacon, or knight, but rather the right to proceed in *and to define the legal identity of* his vagrant dreaming, now displayed as the self-conscious embrace of modernity.

III. Thomas Walsingham and the Dialogue of Legal History at St. Albans

Thomas Walsingham's magisterial continuation of the *Deeds of the Abbots* at St. Albans abbey allows us both a contrast with and a parallel to Langland's engagement with the communities' uses of history to claim novel legal authority.[44] For Walsingham's house history concludes with a vivid, sustained drama of the legal demands and illegal actions of the rebels at St. Albans, to which Walsingham gave the large rubric in his autograph manuscript, "*Processus tenentium Monasterii Sancti Albani*," which may be translated either as "The Narrative of the Tenants of St. Albans Monastery" or, more likely, and displaying Walsingham's typically elusive combination of belittling irony and quasi-sympathy with all enemies to the monastery, "The Lawsuit of the Tenants of the Monastery of St. Albans," as if his presentation of the events constituted the best case they might be able to make for the new (or, in their view, ancient) liberties they sought.

Of all the claims by the rebels of 1381, the endeavor by the St. Albans tenants to gain an ancient charter of liberties from King Offa which they believed the monastery was hiding from them is the most complex, both in its vision of history and in the evidence Walsingham presents of his own view of that claim. Walsingham presents this near the end of his narrative of the Rebellion—indeed, seemingly as an afterthought, since much of his narrative has recounted how the rebels structured the rising at St. Albans around their demands for another ancient charter describing their liberties. This other charter guaranteed freedom from the abbey's seignorial control of milling, and borough status of the town, both flash points for conflicts at St. Albans and many other monastic villages and boroughs since the early fourteenth century. And the rebels could at best merely openly force the abbot to forge a new one, which of course had no legal authority whatsoever. But as Walsingham reveals near the end of his narrative, the rebels' demands were ultimately based on their persistent, false belief in a grant from the ninth-century founder of the abbey, King Offa, who, they thought, had given the liberty of the vill to the craftsmen who had built the monastery; they further believed that the monastery had hidden this charter to deny them this right. This belief, passed down, Walsingham states, by

---

44 Thomas Walsingham, *Gesta abbatum Monasterii Sancti Albani*, ed. Henry Thomas Riley, Rolls Series, 3 vols. (London: Longman, Green, 1867–69). Henceforth this work will be abbreviated *GA*.

a narrow lineage of retellers, most sparked the villeins' resentment against the monastery and for decades kept it alive—an explanation that Walsingham reserves for a final, dramatic *recapitulatio*:

> *Recapitulation of the many wrongdoings of the villeins of St. Albans attempted against the abbot and convent, as is aforesaid*
>
> The villeins were especially incited to rebellion and to seeking liberties by the lies of certain elders of the said vill, who led the younger ones to this by false fables, so that they believed that they formerly held liberties and privileges from King Offa which had later been violently removed and injustly annulled by the abbots and monks. Of these old scoundrels the first purveyor was Richard Bude, Henry de Porta, and a certain Benedict Spichfat, and others, followed in their lie by William atte Halle and others, who, continuing the lies into our times, incited the community of the vill and consequently drove it to misery, as the narration above has sufficiently taught. For they asserted that the most illustrious King Offa, when he had gathered artificers, craftsmen, carpenters, masons, and stone-cutters for constructing the monastery, with his officers, gave this vill to the stone-cutters and other laborers to dwell in, and honored it with liberties and privileges provided by his regal munificence.[45]

These details, so carefully located near the end of the narrative, start to reveal the import they held for the rebels, and for Walsingham too, when we place them in the context of a century and a half of the monastery's and the tenants' historically based legal efforts.

For although St. Albans monastery itself was purportedly founded on a grant from King Offa in 793 (*GA* 1.147–52), the abbey's ancient territorial claims were given full, official historical context only in the mid-thirteenth century, when Matthew Paris also wrote a Latin life of Offa and his fourth-century namesake, describing Offa's dream vision of St. Alban, his invention of the body, and his founding of the monastery.[46] Only at this point did the abbey being to claim a long list of legal rights over its tenants and lands that "of old" belonged to it. In Edward I's nation-wide *Quo warranto* proceedings of 1280–81, the abbey paraded an imposing list of its liberties, all resting on its claims from the charter of Offa, who is said to have granted them the hundred of Cashio with all possessions, which turn out now, through a series of royal confirmations, to be return of writs, gallows, view of frankpledge, free warren, fines for all transgressions of their tenants, and all liberties and free customs that royal power might confer on

---

[45] *GA* 3.365.

[46] See *The Victoria History of the County of Hertfordshire*, Vol. 2, ed. William Page (London: Institute of Historical Research, 1908), 477–83, 149–50, 319–22; Wilhelm Levison, "St. Alban and St. Albans," *Antiquity* 15 (1941): 337–59; and *GA* 3.70–74. Matthew's *Vitae duorum Offarum* is printed in William Wats' edition of the *Historia Majorca* (London: A. Mearne, T. Dring, B. Tooke, T. Sawbridge, and G. Wells, 1684), 961–88.

a monastery, none of which is present even in the mid-thirteenth-century forged charter.[47]

Rosamond Faith has shown how, as early as 1246, small groups of tenants of the monastery withdrew labor services, and she traces some of the continuities of those groups of later tenants who protested or resisted the monastery's demands.[48] Faith's succinct comments can be elaborated and her consideration of the materials extended. In 1253 the townsmen of St. Albans resisted what were probably the monastery's new impositions on its tenants:[49] the townsmen managed to elicit from Henry III a charter granting them exemption from charges of attaint—that is, freedom from the abbot's overturning of their jury decisions on the grounds of false judgment or perjury.[50] In 1308 the townsmen forced the abbot to accept Edward I's writ confirming their ancient liberties, by confirming a perambulation they made of the boundaries of what they claimed as their free territories.[51] As Matthew Paris's drawing of the monks and King Offa perambulating the boundaries in his Life of Offa shows, this gesture intersects the monastery's own rituals and narratives of privilege.[52] In 1316 the townsmen managed to have Edward II confirm the 1253 charter from Henry III granting them freedom from attaint.[53] The abbey suppressed the town's latest ancient claims only in 1327 under the next abbot, who, after a series of counter-lawsuits and fines that exhausted the townsmen's funds and energies in their "illegal" efforts to defend their rights, confiscated the royal charters the townspeople possessed, including that confirming the 1253 charter. A brief note in the *Gesta* asserts that these negotiations were carried out in such secret that "even to this day" the villagers believe the said charters to be still in the Chancellor's keeping—perhaps a surmise of their belief rejected as unlikely, perhaps an early fourteenth-century monk's reflection on their legitimate reasons for festering anger against the monastery; a later fourteenth-century hand has cancelled this note, in turn perhaps because

---

[47] William Illingworth, ed., *Placita de Quo Warranto temporibus Edw. I, II, & III* (London: Record Commission, 1818), 288.

[48] Rosamond Faith, "The Class Struggle in Fourteenth-Century England," in *People's History and Socialist Theory*, ed. Raphael Samuel (London, Boston and Henley: Routledge and Kegan Paul, 1981), 50–60. Faith adds shrewd remarks about the "radical conservatism" suggested by their appeals in 1381 to ancient tradition in the form of Offa's charter. See also her essay, "The 'Great Rumour' of 1377," op. cit.

[49] For the general downgrading of semi-free and unfree tenants' status in this period, see M. A. Barg, "The Villeins of the 'Ancient Demesne,'" *Studi in Memoria de Federigo Melis*, 2 vols. (Naples: Giannini, 1978), 1.213–37.

[50] *Calendar of Patent Rolls, 1247–58* (London: Her Majesty's Stationary Office, 1908); *GA* 2.255.

[51] *GA* 2.161–70.

[52] For a reproduction of this drawing see Eileen Roberts, "St. Albans' Borough Boundary and its Significance in the Peasants' Revolt," in *The Peasants' Revolt in Hertfordshire: The Rising and its Background: A Symposium* (Stevenage Old Town, Hertfordshire: Hertfordshire Publications, 1981), 128–85, 132; for its identification as Matthew's, see Suzanne Lewis, *The Art of Matthew Paris in the Chronica Majora* (Berkeley, CA: University of California Press, 1987), 441.

[53] *Calendar of Patent Rolls, 1313–17* (London: Her Majesty's Stationary Office, 1898), 454.

the belief recorded was so similar to the villagers' belief that the monastery had hidden their charter from Offa.[54] The late thirteenth century might well have been when the townsmen's account of Offa's grant to their artisan ancestors—the "lie" Walsingham records at the end of his account of the Rising—was first elaborated. Walsingham's list of the lineage of tellers of this grant stretches back to the period when the abbey first began insisting on its ancient privileges over the town: Henry de Porta, one of the story's earliest tellers, featured in the struggle of 1290; Benedict Spichfat, a later teller, appeared in the conflicts of 1313 and 1327.[55] In the early fourteenth century, some illustrator added to the monastery's copy of the *Lives of the Two Offas* a careful scene of the workmen who built the monastery (Fig. 1). Perhaps the debate about this history was already underway.

Figure 1. Building St. Albans Abbey. Matthew Paris,
Vitae duorum Offarum, early 14th century.
British Library, Cotton MS Nero D.I., fol. 23v,
reproduced by permission of the British Library, London.

Intriguingly, Langland presents a parallel—or rather negated parallel—to the story of the workers rewarded, when, during his long counterpleading to Scripture, Will declares that the workers who built the Ark were not saved:

Ac I wene it worþ of manye as was in Noes tyme
Tho he shoop þat ship of shides and bordes:
Was neuere wrighte saued þat wroȝte þeron, ne ooþer werkman ellis,
But briddes and beestes and þe blissed Noe

---

[54] *GA* 2.254–5.

[55] *GA* 2.151, 167. The townsmen's version might date from earlier, since as noted above, already in the mid-thirteenth century the St. Albans chronicle attributed to John of Wallingford mentions many uncertain stories of Offa; for this suggestion, see Faith, "The 'Great Rumour' of 1377," 64–65.

And his wif wiþ hise sones and also hire wyues;
Of wrightes þat it wroȝte was noon of hem ysaued.
(B.10.405–10)

Langland uses the story allegorically, to threaten the clergy who are, he notes, the first carpenters of Holy Church: why should they think they will be saved any more than were the Ark's workmen? Thus he aggressively unsettles the clergy's historical claim to privileges of salvation. Presumably, then, in spite of his own plaintive repetitions about these original "werkmen" who were not saved, Langland is presenting the story against the very sort of historical claims to monastic virtue and sanctity that Walsingham is presenting throughout his account of the wretchedly erring rebels.

But even Walsingham's treatment of the townsmen's fable grants it a special authority, even plausibility; he presents it in a form that tacitly registers at least its coherence of counterpleading against his own historical-legal argument. Walsingham closes his account of the Rising, and indeed concludes his entire, massive *Deeds of the Abbots*, by disputing the townsmen's story, treating it as the legal epitomy of the rebels' cause. He answers it on what might seem to us rather narrow, even irrelevant points in assessing it as a forgery: first, its use of the name "St. Albans" for the town, instead of the name used until the tenth century, "Warluamchestur"—and it is a sign of Walsingham's verbatim consideration of the claim that he cites the early English form of ancient Verulamium, as if assuming that if a real charter *had* existed for villeins, it would have been in ninth-century English.[56] Thus, in spite of its oral lineage, Walsingham treats the townsmen's account as if it were a charter presented in a court of law.[57] But Walsingham refutes the charter for a second, and less transparent reason, on the basis of the inconsistency of the present town boundaries with the ones of ancient Verulamium, which he reconstructs in detail—even though there is no statement of a boundary in his recitation of the rural charter. Then, curiously, Walsingham turns to a geographical history of the whole local area, showing its difference from present boundaries although that has not appeared as an issue in his summary of the townsmen's claims to Offa's charter.

The strategy is identical to that used by the lawyers of the abbot of Abingdon in 1368 when they were forced to speculate with historical geography to argue that the town of Abingdon, although not mentioned in Domesday book at all, is referred to in the description in Domesday book of another manor that is stated to be in the abbey desmene. The difference is that the Abingdon abbey lawyers were forced to this tenuous argument because they had no explicit charters laying claim to the town; in Walsingham's case, the townsmen are the ones lacking a charter, and as

---

[56] *GA* 3.365–66.
[57] *GA* 3.366.

Walsingham has recited their putative charter there is no need to answer a question of boundaries. Why then does Walsingham refute an unrecorded claim?

In taking this extra step of offering a fuller defense than the alleged charter, as he has recorded it, demands, Walsingham reveals a sensitivity to the villeins' historiographical consistency and textual appropriation that reaches deep into his account. This sense may explain, for example, Walsingham's remark that the townsmen did not wait for the abbot's seal of his new charter granting their ancient liberties but instead made a perambulation, pouring out beer at the point of each boundary mark, "as a more effective memorial and evidence to their neighbors and children of the seisin they had gained over the liberty," hence obviously rejecting the authority of the latest monastic charter and, implicitly, since they immediately return from the perambulation to demand again the grant from Offa, implying that they rest their real authority on that ancient grant.[58] (In his study of literacy and the Rising, Steven Justice comments perceptively on this scene, but he denies that Walsingham noticed the meaning of the rebels' rejection of the present abbot's seal or the sequence of the demands.)[59] But the proof that Walsingham saw the tenants' belief in the townsmen's Offa story as the basis of their perambulations is in his sudden leap to discuss the ancient boundaries when refuting the townsmen's story. That he *there* defined with the greatest precision he could muster the boundaries of Verulamium shows that, even though the townsmen's charter, as he briefly but climactically summarized it, does not mention boundaries, *Walsingham assumed that its narrative was the justifying basis for the townsmen's rebellious perambulations of 1327 and 1381,* described at length in the earlier sections of the *Gesta abbatum.* His rebuttal of the boundary claims *later,* when he refutes their claims to a charter from Offa, reveals that he believed they were reinscribing in both 1327 and 1381 the precise area of their liberties that they thought Offa had granted them in their charter. That later rebuttal displays his view that their previously described perambulations respond precisely to details of the townsmen's Offa charter beyond what he summarizes. In his "Lawsuit of the tenants," he responds to their evidence with full appreciation of its interlocking historical coherence.

Walsingham's sense of the coherent claims of the townsmen's Offa story may even explain a seemingly unrelated incident to which Walsingham gives much attention. While the abbot in one part of the monastery tried to assuage the townsmen by promising to draft a new version of the ancient deed they sought (an inadequate substitute, as both sides would know after the 1327 conflict, when new charters were as easily annulled as granted), another band of "ribalds" broke into the abbey's

---

[58] *GA* 3.320.

[59] Justice, *Writing and Rebellion,* 169–72.

"parlor" (*locutorium*) where they retrieved the millstones that the abbey had confiscated in the 1327 conflict over the villagers' rights to private mills. Walsingham now reveals that these had been used at some point to pave the parlor floor. Tearing them out, the ribalds broke them into small pieces to distribute to the others of the commons, "giving some to each, just as it is customarily done in parish churches on Sunday to break and distribute the blessed bread, so that, when they saw these pieces, they would see for themselves that they had been victorious in their case against the monastery."[60]

Steven Justice, who has made this scene the center of an intriguing argument in which Walsingham was the unwitting medium for the rebels' ideologies—a form of 'Orientalizing' (in Edward Said's sense) in which the monk does not see the implications of the materials he transmits—regards this episode as a characteristic glimpse of another world through the "fissures" of Walsingham's narrative, a clue Walsingham inadvertently left of how the rebels successfully wrested away historical meaning from the monastery and its writers. "Those who jimmied them up from the floor made the stones mean more than the monastery had," Justice comments, "even as they seized the meanings for themselves. The documents (the stones) belonged to them, and so did the sacrament. The millstone eucharist emphasized the agricultural work without which the mass was impossible...a eucharist...which located Christ not in the miracle of transubstantiation but in the task of subsistence."[61] Any counterpleading on the rebels' behalf, it seems from Justice's approach, must be done outside Walsingham's range of awareness. Yet it is Walsingham's simile that asserts that the stones functioned "as a document and memorial of an old dispute between the villeins and the monastery," and it is Walsingham, not the rebels, who provides the still more suggestive eucharistic simile that allows Justice to contemplate the townsmen's collectivity and agrarian theology.[62] As the fight over the merchant stalls at Abingdon shows, in this period objects subjected to conflicted historical interpretation begin to resemble charters: they reveal their multiple possibilities for historical narrative as those narratives are carefully constructed and just as carefully disputed.

I propose that when Walsingham emphasized the rebels' destruction of the monastery's floor in conjunction with the pursuit of the ancient charter he both plausibly perceived and adroitly inscribed in the episode several worlds of meaning. On the rebels' side, as he clearly surmises, it precipitously avenged the confiscation of 1327 but also reopened the issues of that conflict, which pivoted on a struggle over ancient liberties; Walsingham implies the rebels' awareness of the struggle for historical legitimacy when he adds the striking detail that they sought to commemorate the present

---

[60] *GA* 3.309.

[61] Justice, *Writing and Rebellion*, 169.

[62] *GA* 3.309.

event by handing out fragments of the stones, like the Eucharist. The simile captures a holy zeal for a new sense of collectivity based on a belief in
ancient liberties, but also a false belief; Walsingham's simile shows he
noticed what we notice, and theorized before we theorize, that the rebels
were involved in the creation of a new sense of community drawing on the
resources of claims to antiquity. But of course Walsingham, his contemporaries, and modern historians all differ on the value of such a novel construction of class-consciousness based on shared claims to ancient rights.
Walsingham perceived their unlicensed appropriation of the millstones,
what he calls the monastery's "documentation" of the earlier settlement,
just as he would or perhaps did perceive the close relation of the unlicensed
townsmen's Offa story to the monastery's stories of Offa's endowments: as
a consistent and self-defining but false belief. Moreover, Walsingham, who
alone emphasizes that the millstones had been embedded in the monastery's
parlor *as* the pavement—the charter to the king describing the event merely says that the stones have been brought to the parlor, and that the rebels
broke the stones *and* tore up the pavement—may be making an even deeper reference to the townsmen's story of the rebels' ancestors having built the
monastery.[63] According to the terms of their own version of Offa's grant,
they are breaking the covenant: they are *de*constructing the monastery that
their ancestors had constructed. Thus his narrative argues both that the
townsmen's story was inaccurate, and that, if it *were* accurate, the modern
rebels (at least the impetuous *ribaldi* he mentions here) violated its terms.

   I am thus led to posit that, however supportive of political repression,
Walsingham's vision of the Rising included both parodic dismissal of the
rebels' historical consciousness and legal claims, and simultaneously a keen
sense of the tenants' legal sophistication, political self-consciousness, and
ideological consistency in fashioning a collective, historical identity from
the late thirteenth-century onward. His work is evidence of how the fourteenth century was shaped by novel efforts of communities to seize legal
authority by means of historical claims—efforts and debates that writers
participated in deeply even when they did not openly acknowledge such
debates. I also propose that, of all fourteenth-century writers, Langland
most completely and overtly included within his work the kinds of legal
"counterpleading" of history that the rebellious communities at St. Albans
and elsewhere, and for decades before the Rising, generated. For most of
the centuries after its making, *Piers Plowman* in all its versions has been
seen to play an active and calculated role in the history of dissent, which
only recent commentators have sought to deny. In terms of the prior history of the Rising of 1381 if not the Rising itself, *Piers Plowman* should be
restored to this position, a hypothesis of the poem's social engagement that
is founded in the first instance on the poet's legal ideals and his probable
access to information about the community-based legal struggles staged

---

[63] *GA* 3.293.

before the king's court at Westminster. But Walsingham too, in his aware-ness of the tenant communities' manipulations and appropriations of tex-tual authority, should be granted more insight than he has usually been credited: he had perhaps an even keener sense than Langland of such rebel-lious, legal counterpleading of history, a hypothesis sustainable not just by his greater proximity to the communities' long struggles to claim title to history, but by the even better reason that his own institution had a long history of doing the same thing. However fraught with paradoxes and anx-ieties, the signs of both works' participation in the period's long-building conflicts of historical vision and law affirm a view of culture, especially its visions of law and history and its struggles over authority in both, as a con-tinual if subtle dialogue, and of literary and historical narrative as a vital, penetrating, and majestic part of those real and symbolic confrontations.

The Luxury of Gender: *Piers Plowman* B.9 and *The Merchant's Tale*[1]

Joan Baker and Susan Signe Morrison

This essay is based on the premise that Chaucer knew the B version of Langland's poem[2] and argues that *The Merchant's Tale* represents a sustained response to Passus 9, to the extent that the tale might be considered an exemplum of the passus. Yet the argument does not depend on such direct dependence. The dominant theme of both *The Merchant's Tale* and Passus 9 is marriage, the blessedness and bliss of those made in heaven versus the purgatory of "unkynde" earthly unions, which, in their "wreched engendrynge," have exacerbated the consequences of the Fall. Thus, this particular pairing of texts—Chaucer's disquisition on marriage and Langland's "marriage homily"—provides a common vehicle for exploring and exposing each poet's attitude toward gender as it is couched in his treatment of the institution and of its worthy and, especially, unworthy practitioners. We are indebted to M. Teresa Tavormina's study, *Kindly Similitude: Marriage and Family in Piers Plowman*, for focusing attention on an issue in *Piers Plowman* that Chaucerians have for decades taken for granted as a central theme in the *Canterbury Tales*.[3] Although we draw

---

[1] This essay has been developed from our discussion of this passus and tale during a seminar at the NEH Chaucer and Langland Institute, University of Colorado, Boulder, July 1995. We are indebted to the directors of the Institute, C. David Benson, Elizabeth Robertson, and James Simpson, for providing the impetus to read Chaucer and Langland together. We thank Professor Simpson and fellow participant Kathleen Hewett-Smith for their input at various stages in this project. The essay first appeared in and is reprinted with permission from the *Yearbook of Langland Studies* 12 (1998): 31-64.

[2] See J. A. W. Bennett, "Chaucer's Contemporary," in S. S. Hussey, ed., *Piers Plowman: Critical Approaches* (London, Methuen, 1969), 310–24; George Kane, *Chaucer and Langland: Historical and Textual Approaches* (London: Athlone, 1989), 56–58, 134–49; Helen Cooper, "Langland's and Chaucer's Prologues," *Yearbook of Langland Studies* 1 (1987): 71–81; and Frank Grady, "Chaucer Reading Langland: *The House of Fame*," *Studies in the Age of Chaucer* 18 (1996): 3–23. Cooper argues that the version Chaucer knew was the A text ("Prologues," 71).

[3] M. Teresa Tavormina, *Kindly Similitude: Marriage and Family in Piers Plowman* (Cambridge: D. S. Brewer, 1995).

upon a number of Tavormina's findings, we will argue that in this specific tale and passus, it is an *unkyndely similitude*—that is, a mode of self-reflective, self-gratifying fashioning of others and manipulation of the world— that most concerns the poets and serves as an unvirtuous, anti-social, and life-denying model antagonistic to the "trewe wedded libbynge" (B.9.108) that is Dowel.[4]

As our discussion will illustrate, *The Merchant's Tale* sustains and revalues the currency of a striking number of themes in Passus 9, and both poetic texts register a concern for women—especially how they must live "as the world asketh." But reading their works in tandem, we find that Chaucer and Langland diverge in their literary treatment of the victims of social injustice. Chaucer's January points to the difference in the closing lines of *The Merchant's Tale*: "And on hire wombe he stroketh hire ful softe/And to his palays hoom he hath hire lad" (4.2414–15).[5] May's feigned craving ("covetise") for the pear is in contrast to the very real hunger that deprives helpless women and men of their Inwit in B.9.70–71. Appetite thus assumes the urgency of hunger—the necessity of human survival, of *being*. Both Langland's passus and Chaucer's tale condemn excessive sexual appetite, "*luxuria*," as transgressive. Langland, however, distinguishes agents of "covetise" who fail to control their desires—whether gluttony for food or sex—from those desperate "victims" of involuntary deprivation whose appetites arise from a need to be filled, as opposed to a desire for more than one's fill. Throughout this essay, we employ the term "luxury" both to encompass and distinguish deprivation or want from excess.

The notion of luxury not only conveys the contrasting states of the haves and have-nots, but also suggests a principle for our reading of gender in *Piers Plowman*. Because Langland situates his discourse on marriage in a communal sphere that frequently expands to encompass the sweep of salvation history, his poem speaks to the whole rather than to any one segment of humankind—or any one element of human appetite. At the same time, his recurring references to the plight of the world's wretched engage the reader at the affective level so as to arouse empathy for the victims of social injustice and outrage toward its perpetrators. In terms of thematic focus, gender is a luxury in Passus 9 and elsewhere in *Piers Plowman* because of the scope and involuntary nature of the human misery the poem depicts: Langland privileges the exigencies of human necessity over a con-

---

[4] All references to the B-Text are from A. V. C. Schmidt, ed., *The Vision of Piers Plowman*, Everyman paperback, 2nd ed., (London: J. M. Dent, 1995). A-Text references are from George Kane and E. Talbot Donaldson, eds., *Piers Plowman: The A Version* (Berkeley and Los Angeles: University of California Press, 1997). Subsequent citations shall appear parenthetically.

[5] All citations from Chaucer are from Larry D. Benson et al., eds., *The Riverside Chaucer* (Boston: Houghton Mifflin, 1987). Subsequent citations shall appear parenthetically.

cern for the burdens of gender.[6] Chaucer, on the other hand, assumes an unthreatened physical existence that allows him to play with and counter gender constructions and expectations. He brings the themes of Passus 9 (including salvation history) to bear on the exemplary "unkynde" marriage of January and May to arouse our antipathy towards those who, not unlike ourselves, are the victims of their own volition—who misdeem because they misconceive.

Marriage is a topic that conventionally invites discussion of power relationships and female agency. Thus we would expect two works sharing the theme of marriage to reflect a common concern for gender-sensitive issues. Contrary to these expectations, we find that although issues of gender often assume priority for Chaucer, for Langland they appear, at most, secondary to the demands both of the "wombe" and soul—they are superseded by social and salvific pressures. We will argue that Langland's revisions of Passus 9 strongly suggest his awareness of and responsiveness to gender, including the possibility of a female audience of the A version. Hence, his subordination of gender becomes all the more significant as evidence of a calculated strategy. We hope that our discussion will encourage further intertextual study of these two poets and will serve as a caveat against reading gender *into* Langland—to resist making gender more central to Langland's poetic enterprise or burdening his text or texts with more claims for gender than they can reasonably support.

Our discussion is organized into four sections that we take up in the following order: (1) the chivalric allegory of Castle Caro, with discussion focused on the gender implications of the Inwit passage; (2) an examination of the notion we term "unkyndely similitude," as figured by Lady Mede and the "unkynde" marriages of Passus 9 and *The Merchant's Tale*; (3) a reading of *The Merchant's Tale* as an exemplum of the "unkyndely similitude" of Passus 9 with an emphasis on January's misapplication of the *imago Dei*; and (4) an analysis of Langland's revisions of Passus 9 and the implications for a female audience.

I

The crux of our argument for the luxury of gender in Passus 9 is found in the context of Langland's rather surprising use of romance imagery in the chivalric allegory of Castle Caro in the opening of A.10 and B.9 (also

---

[6] See Carol Clover, "Regardless of Sex: Men, Women and Power in Early Northern Europe," *Speculum* 68 (1993): 363–87, who further argues that "what finally excites fear and loathing in the Norse mind is not femaleness, per se, but the condition of powerlessness, the lack or loss of volition, with which femaleness is typically, but neither inevitably nor exclusively associated" (379–80). Clover's discussion of the "social binary," which distinguishes "dependents" from "breadwinners," and her assertion that this is "*the* binary, the one that cuts most deeply and the one that matters: between strong and weak, powerful and powerless" applies to our reading of Passus 9.

C.10). Although the wooing of the soul by Christ is not a new image, it is uncharacteristic of Langland, who later uses chivalric imagery in the strictly martial depiction of Christ as a jousting knight (B.18). Here, the female Anima is the object of masculine desire and discourse, as she is transformed within the allegory from beleaguered lady, to a place "in the herte [which] is hir hoom and hir moost reste" (B.9.56), to "trewe wedded libbynge" (B.9.108). Kynde, or God, who traditionally assumes the role of the lover wooing the soul, appears instead to have abandoned his beloved Anima to aggressive and manipulative courtship by the "proud prikere of Fraunce, *Princeps huius mundi*" who would "wynne hire awey with wiles and he myghte"(B.9.8–9). Presumably unable to defend herself, Lady Anima is entrusted as a royal ward to Sir Dowel, who sends for his five sons to aid in her rescue. The constable Inwit oversees her mortal defense while Dobest, acting as bishop, attends to her spiritual security.[7] Clearly, Lady Anima is the object, not the subject, of the chivalric allegory—unlike the masculine Anima of Passus 15, who, as controller of both desire and discourse, is the subject of the entire passus.

Although it is Lady Anima who must endure the allegorical assault, the architectural allegory of Castle Caro appears constructed solely in terms of masculine salvation. As we will see, only the husband's salvation is of any concern to Langland's Wit and Chaucer's Parson, not to mention January. And only the husband's point of view is accommodated. May's rebuke to January in the garden, albeit delivered just prior to her signaling Damian, is not, then, altogether ironic: "'I have,' quod she, 'a soul for to kepe / As wel as ye, and also myn honour'" (4.2188–89).

The Castle Caro passage illustrates two points that bear on our argument. First, although marriage and women are conventionally depicted as threats to *men's* salvation, we find in this passage that marriage and men appear to be necessary to *women's* social and spiritual welfare. Second, although man has been endowed with carnal desires (appetite) and the means of controlling this physical passion (reason), he does so, we argue, by subordinating the object of his desire (woman) rather than the desire itself. It should not be surprising, then, that we are somewhat confused as to who is attacking or under attack in the siege on Castle Caro. Desirable as well as desiring, the interiorized, feminized soul appears to invite her own ruin, while masculine desire, figured as the "proud prikere of France," exerts external force but little in the way of the rational self-control that is Inwit. It is Inwit in the head, we are told, who leads Anima dwelling in the

---

[7] James Simpson offers a helpful summary of the faculty psychology employed in the third vision noting that the psychological aspects of this vision correspond more closely to the philosophical psychology of Aristotle than subsequent visions based more on Augustine's religious conception of the soul (*Piers Plowman: An Introduction to the B-Text* [London: Longman, 1990], 97–99). The Inwit passage, in particular, reflects the influence of the twelfth-century pseudo-Augustinian tract *De Spiritu et Anima* in which the upper reason (which Simpson reads as Inwit) is synonymous with wisdom; the lower, with prudence (102).

heart; but he first seeks a nod from Anima with respect to what is pleasing or displeasing: "Ac Inwit is in the heed, and to the herte he loketh / What Anima is leef or looth—he lat hire at his wille"(B.9. 57–58).[8] In this sense, Anima could be said at most to govern by consent but to lack sovereignty or power—a situation analogous to a woman's role in society.

The significance of the allegory with regard to gender becomes somewhat clearer as we move outside the architectural allegory of the castle to the community. Langland groups widows and maidens, whose very survival outside the institution of marriage is threatened, with other victims of circumstance:

> Fooles that fauten Inwit, I fynde that Holy Chirche
> Sholde fynden hem that hem fauteth, and faderlese children
> And widewes that han noght wherwith to wynnen hem hir foode,
> Madde men and maydenes that helplese were—
> Alle thise lakken Inwit, and loore bihoveth.
>
> (B.9.67–71)

This passage could be read simply as a springboard for the familiar Langlandian plea that "Sholde no Cristene creature cryen at the yate / Ne faille payn ne potage, and prelates dide as thei sholden" (B.9.80–81). But the fact that he views unmarried women, although pure and chaste, as spiritually endangered because need has rendered them the intellectual and moral equivalent of the young child or the town fool—powerless to exercise rational control—is disturbing to modern readers. The distance between the innocent souls of the indigent and the "wight that mysruleth his Inwit, / And that ben glotons glubberes—hir God is hire wombe" (B.9.60–61) is distressingly narrow. Langland deromanticizes the salvific currency of a Christian poverty that rewards patience by drawing our attention instead to its equal potential to corrupt or seriously imperil the soul. Here Langland concedes that the affective, experiential mode of "kynde knowing" that he elsewhere privileges in matters of faith is by its very nature vulnerable to external forces. Indeed, without the protection of Sir Dowel, social necessity would appear to threaten Anima and the soul of Everywoman as much as the *Princeps huius mundi* himself. Significantly, the B version expands the protective safety-net to include all those "pore and cateles" whose circumstances have reduced them to a state of helplessness, among them poor widows and maidens.[9]

The issue of social necessity raised in the Castle Caro passage also illustrates our argument that gender is a luxury in *Piers Plowman*. The very fact that women are subsumed into categories of the socially helpless along with dependent men and children suggests that in this instance gender des-

---

8 In Canto XVI of the *Purgatorio*, Dante refers to the childlike innocence and behavior of the feminized soul that "will turn to anything it likes" (l. 90), "she will run after it / if guide or curb do not divert her love" (ll. 92–93); *Purgatory*, trans. Mark Musa (New York: Penguin Books, 1985), 173.

9 See Tavormina, *Kindly Similitude*, 68–69.

ignates a non-essential category of human being. Although the victims in *Piers Plowman*, especially those of Passus 9, suffer physical and spiritual distress, they appear all but helpless either to control or change their circumstances. Bereft of Inwit, the desperately needy are as disabled as the physically and mentally impaired, unable to repair their wounds of necessity; others, the practitioners of the seven deadly sins of Passus 5, seem corrupted beyond repair—beyond feeling their wounded souls. Langland impresses human necessity upon the reader in much the same affective mode that Will (as the human will, *voluntas*) must assume if he is to achieve "kynde knowing," the knowledge that is acquired only to the extent that it is tasted (savored), touched, and translated into experience.[10] This is why the Inwit passage is at once troubling and paradoxical, for it is the will alone that can achieve "kynde knowing"—the "savour after the sire" (B.9.152) that seeks and savors "direct and experiential knowledge of God."[11] Dire necessity and the concommitant loss of Inwit, then, would weaken the human will, thereby condemning those about whom Langland professes most concern for their lot in this life, while at the same time leaving them spiritually ill-equipped to fare much better in the next. In contrast, even Chaucer's most deliberately affective tales of Custance and Griselda depict women who endure and morally transcend the dramatic changes in their circumstances through sheer force of will, notably a willed submission to God, not man. At the other end of the spectrum, in the *fabliaux*, adversity appears to enable rather than disable Chaucer's female figures: their collective inward wits are pressed into the service of outwitting their adversaries. Our poets' treatments of gender thus appear related to the role each assigns to the rational and desiring faculties, especially when under duress.

II

What becomes increasingly clear as Passus 9 and *The Merchant's Tale* are considered in light of one another is that for all the attention each gives to marriage and procreation, the prevailing mood and dominant theme is that of physical and spiritual barrenness. Humans beings, it seems, have succeeded only in defeating the natural, social, and spiritual aims of the institution because of their predilection from biblical times for pursuing "unkynde" marriages. This does not bode well for women for whom marriage is often the only safety net available. Indeed, as these two works

---

[10] See James Simpson, "From Reason to Affective Knowledge: Modes of Thought and Poetic Form in *Piers Plowman*," *Medium Ævum* 55 (1986): 1–23; here, 6–7; and Anne Savage, "*Piers Plowman*: The Translation of Scripture and Food for the Soul," *English Studies* 74 (1993): 209–221; here, 209, 215–16, 221.

[11] See Simpson, "From Reason," 7, who notes that Anima enclosed in Castle Caro in Passus 9 reappears in Passus 15 to counsel Will that he cannot know charity "thorugh wordes ne werkes, but thorugh wil oone" (B.15.210).

demonstrate, the outcome of marriage may be even less benign. Rather than rescuing women, an "unkynde" marriage can place them in double jeopardy—subject to "unkyndely similitude" as well as subordination. Such a union is unilateral and all but erases female subjectivity: the wife is valued neither for herself nor even as Other, but only as she reflects and fulfills her husband's self-centered desire. This malignant similitude is at once the source and consequence of problems arising from the marriages depicted in Passus 9 and *The Merchant's Tale*. In this section we examine the implications of "unkyndely similitude" for women, taking up first the dimension of luxury characterized by insatiable "covetise" that begets nothing but more desire as figured in *Piers Plowman* by Mede, and second, the sexual manifestation of luxury as it pertains to the marital sin of *luxuria*. Each poet illuminates the other's treatment of these issues and, once again, differs significantly in the degree of agency ultimately granted to female figures.

It is apparent from Langland's rendering of Lady Mede that the implications of the mercantile ethos for gender are not lost on him; to explore these implications, we step outside Passus 9 briefly to consider his extended treatment of the business of marriage. Effectively playing off of the notion of the "goods" of marriage, he deploys Wit's injunctions against marrying for "goods" (discussed below), to evoke Augustine's counter-definition of the "goods" of Christian marriage: offspring, mutual fidelity, and the sacramental bond.[12] In his anti-Manichean writings, Augustine adopts a pro-reproductive schema which elevates the "first good" that he further promotes by linking *matrimonium* etymologically with *mater*.[13] Particularly significant for our purpose is his argument that not only the offspring of sexual relations tainted by original sin, but even those of adulterous unions, are regarded as good works blessed by God.[14] This view is not, however, borne out in Passus 9 where bastardy—allegorical and literal— comes under increasing attack in the three versions.[15] The progeny or "goods" of "unkynde" unions are not among the blessed. Desired only for

---

12 For a very helpful conspectus of both the content and context of Augustine's commentary see Elizabeth Clark, "'Adam's Only Companion': Augustine and the Early Christian Debate on Marriage," in Robert R. Edwards and Stephen Spector, eds., *The Olde Daunce: Love, Friendship, Sex and Marriage in the Medieval World* (Albany: State University of New York Press, 1991), 15–31, 240–54; especially 25. Clark cites Book I of *De nuptis* (*Corpus Scriptorum Ecclisiasticorum Latinorum* [hereafter *CSEL*] 42. 224–25, 231, 236). She argues that Augustine, forced to respond to the demands of controversy with extreme ascetics (Manichean, Pelagian, and Julian), was drawn away from the volitional to physical aspects of marriage (31).

13 Clark, "Adam's," 21, 246 n64. Clark cites *Contra Faustum* 19.26 (*CSEL* 25 (1), 529).

14 Clark, "Adam's," 21, 246 n75. James Brundage notes that procreative intent could excuse *luxuria* in marriage in his *Law, Sex and Christian Society in Medieval Europe* (Chicago: University of Chicago Press, 1987), 280–81.

15 Tavormina, *Kindly Similitude*, 220–21. The pattern of revision on the subject of marriage from the A to B (and C) versions depicts an increasingly spiritual and idealistic view of marriage while increasingly attacking "unkynde" marriage and bastardy.

her "goodes," Lady Mede is consumed and all but used up—and by Passus
4, so little desired and of so little value that she, like the cursed progeny of
Passus 9, is reduced to a social outcast. As the product of an "unkynde"
marriage if not an incestuous relationship,[16] she shares an affinity not only
with the misfits of Passus 9, but also with Chaucer's May, whose commercial courtship precludes satisfactory consummation of her marriage.

Where Mede is concerned, we are dealing with a pattern based on
exchange not reproduction, in which the goods succeed only in reproducing or replicating themselves: "In marchaundise is no mede, I may it wel
avowe: / It is a permutacion apertly—a penyworth for another"
(B.3.257–58). Langland seduces us with the figure of Mede so that we forget that she represents a *medium*, a process, and impute to her attributes
and power she does not possess. Instead, our material girl becomes
"inescapably associated with how men exchange her, with masculine
desires for woman and wealth," as a "vehicle of relations between men"
that "ensures reproduction of social institutions."[17] Clare Lees argues that
Mede has "no subjectivity, no agency, of her own"; rather, her status is that
of the "produced object," a female textual figure produced "by the
processes of use and exchange."[18] Because of the ambiguity of her figure
both as beautiful victim, corrupted by those around her, and as "magnetic
courtesan" corrupting all who enter her circle—potentially wife or whore;
reward or bribe—Mede cannot be fixed but must circulate in a continuous
cycle of desire and reward.[19] And because her arbitrary exchange value is
determined in relation to an external standard, Mede (like all women on
the market) is dispossessed of any intrinsic or natural value: she is reduced

---

[16] See Tavormina, *Kindly Similitude*, 5–11, 7, and 7 n20, for an explication of Mede's tainted lineage.

[17] Clare Lees, "Gender and Exchange in *Piers Plowman*," in Britton J. Harwood and Gillian R. Overing,
eds., *Class and Gender in Early English Literature: Intersections* (Bloomington, IN: Indiana University
Press, 1994), 117, 129 n27 (quoting Luce Irigaray, *This Sex Which is Not One*, trans., Catherine Porter
[Ithaca: Cornell University Press, 1985]), 123.

[18] Lees, "Gender and Exchange," 125 and 117. Lees extends Yunck's study of venality satire—his construct of women and money—to apply the Marxist notion of use value to women in which women are
essentially "material depositiories of exchange value"—a social form of money—which achieves reality
only by consumption (128 n19). See J. A. Yunck, *The Lineage of Lady Meed: The Development of
Mediaeval Venality Satire* (Notre Dame: University of Notre Dame Press, 1963), 285–306.

[19] Lees (116, 128 n16, & 121) expands upon Malcolm Godden's description of Mede: "The fundamental question about the place of wealth in the good society is brilliantly captured in the ambivalence of
Mede's own personality: beautiful innocent led astray by those around her, or magnetic courtesan cynically corrupting all she can reach?" (Godden, *The Making of Piers Plowman* [London: Longman: 1990], 36;
quoted in Lees, 116). See also David Herlihy, *Medieval Households* (Cambridge: Harvard University Press,
1985), who notes that the church's preoccupation with incest had forced a wider circulation of women
across social boundaries (61). Carolyn Dinshaw's reading of the *Man of Law's Tale* (*Chaucer's Sexual
Poetics* [Madison, WI: University of Wisconsin Press], 88–112) is particularly relevant to a discussion of
Lady Mede and May in Langland and Chaucer. Dinshaw articulates the nature of the exchange of women
drawing upon of Gayle Rubin's notable study, "The Traffic in Women: Notes on the 'Political Economy' of
Sex," in R. R. Reiter, ed., *Toward an Anthropology of Women* (New York: Monthly Review Press, 1975),
157–210.

to an indifferent abstraction.[20] As a "conduit of a relationship rather than a partner to it,"[21] "Mede is ymaried moore for hire goodes / Than for any vertue or fairnesse or any free kynde" (B.2.76–77). In figuring Mede as female, the object and vehicle of both wealth and desire, Langland critiques the civil and ecclesiastical institutions where she circulates but where she lacks real power of her own.[22] Mede is not the point of her own allegory. Rather, she brilliantly implicates the intended targets of Langland's social critique.

Passus 9 specifically addresses the human consequences of marriages based on Mede as evidenced by Wit's repeated injunctions against marrying for goods: "For coveitise of catel unkyndely ben wedded" (157); "For goode sholde wedde goode, though thei no good hadde" (160); "Or wedden any wodewe for welthe of hir goodes" (164); "For coveitise of catel ne of kynrede riche" (174); "For no londes, bot for love, loke ye be wedded" (177). To so marry is to enter into an "unkynde" marriage, a union based on self-serving and exploitive intent in which a spouse is sought not because of any inherent qualities, but indifferently, solely for exchange value. Although the increasing practice and legalized encouragement of consensual marriage presumably militates against such indifference, these injunctions do not redress the asymmetrical nature of the relationship: "The wif was maad the w[y]e for to helpe werche" (B.9.113). Consent, "as thei two myghte acorde" (B.9.116), is implied in Langland's handling of similitude in marriage. Wit counsels: "Ac maidenes and maydenes macche yow togideres; / Wideweres and wodewes, wercheth the same" (B.9.175–76), as he inveighs against the "unkynde" match, the "yong wenche" married to "an[y] olde feble" (B.9.163). Similitude, then, extends to class, age, sexual experience, and marital status, as counseled in Mirk's *Festial:* "by Goddys ordynaunce, a man schal takon a wyf lyke of age, lyk

---

20 Irigaray, *This Sex,* esp. ch. 8, "Women on the Market": "The exchange value of two signs, two commodities, two women, is a representation of the needs/desires of consumer-exchanger subjects: in no way is it the 'property' of the signs/articles/women themselves. At the most, the commodities—or rather the relationships among them—are the material alibi for the desire for relations among men...On this basis, one may affirm that the value of the commodity takes on *indifferently* any given form of use value. The price of the articles, in fact, no longer comes from *their* natural form, from *their* bodies, *their* language, but from the fact that they mirror the need/desire for exchanges among men" (180–81). Lester K. Little notes that money facilitates transactions in an urban society in which parties in an exchange are total or partial strangers (*Religious Poverty and the Profit Economy* [Ithaca, NY: Cornell University Press, 1978]). He quotes Max Weber's apt definition: "Money is the most abstract and impersonal element that exists in personal life" (33).

21 See Rubin, "Traffic," 174; also Irigaray, *This Sex,* 181, who here seems to describe Lady Mede: "A preeminent mirror, transcending the world of merchandise, it guarantees the possibility of universal exchange among commodities."

22 Elizabeth Fowler discusses the role of Mede as "a kind of surplus value, a conceptual tool that allows Langland to analyze the exchange of services for money" (250) in "Misogyny and Economic Person in Skelton, Langland, and Chaucer," *Spenser Studies* X: 245–73, ed., Patrick Cullen and Thomas P. Roche, Jr. (New York: AMS Press, 1992); see also 250–54, 263–67.

of condicions, and lyk of burth; for þereos þese ben acordyng, it is lyk to fare wel, and ellys not."[23] In "kynde" marriages based on similitude, the bodily members are also more likely to be in accordance with the will so as to avoid sinful performance of the "derne dede."[24] Had January sought a "kynde" match, he might have had to rely less on such performance-enhancing resources as textbook authorities, aphrodisiacs, and erotic art (Priapus).

Performance anxiety notwithstanding, January's major problem is that he convinces himself that he can do no sin with his wife. *Contra!* First and foremost, he deviates from Wit's exhortation drawn from I Cor. 7:1–2 to marry in order to avoid fornication:

> Whiles thow art yong, and thi wepene kene,
> Wreke thee with wyvyng, if thow wolt ben excused:
> *Dum sis vir fortis, ne des tua robora scortis.*
> *Scribitur in portis, meretrix est ianua mortis.*
> [While young and strong, give not your strength to whores:
> "Harlot is Death's Gate" is written on (her) doors].
> (B.9.182–183a)

This passage would undoubtedly hit a bit too close to home for January who, having spent himself with unvirtuous women for his sixty years and is now literally at death's door, belatedly and misguidedly seeks to amend his situation. We must turn to the Parson to set the record straight regarding the issue of sin in marriage: "And for that many man weneth that he may nat synne for no likerousnesse that he dooth with his wyf, certes, that opinion is fals. God woot, a man may sleen hymself with his owene knyf, and make hymselve dronken of his owene tonne" (*The Parson's Tale*, 10.858). How? According to *The Book of Vices and Virtues*, which also avers that a man may "slen hymself wiþ his owne swerd, and also a man may do dedly synne wiþ his owne wife"(45), the deed of wedlock may be lawfully done in three ways: in hope of offspring, as just return to one's mate or conjugal debt, and as a venial sin to prevent lechery and adultery.[25] In *The Parson's Tale*, marriage is discussed under the heading "*Luxuria*" or "Lechery"; here, "man" is cautioned not to love his wife excessively (too ardent relations are considered adulterous) but instead with "discrecioun, paciently and atemprely, and thanne is she as though it were his suster" (10.860). The seven-branched Tree of Lechery in *The Book of Vices and Virtues* depicts the third branch as married people, with the sixth branch representing *luxuria*: that in which man "wiþ his owne wif doþ þing forboden and defended, aȝens kynde and aȝens the ordre of wedloke" (i.e., to *slen hymself*). The seventh branch of Lechery is incestuous relations: "and

---

[23] Tavormina, 94 n83 cites Mirk's *Festial*, 290.

[24] Clark, "Adam's," 21.

[25] W. Nelson Frances, ed., *The Book of Vices and Virtues*, Early English Text Society, Old Series, 217 (London: Longman, Green, 1942), 246–47. See also *The Parson's Tale*, 10.938–42.

euere it [lechery] clymbeþ vpper and vpper and alwey wors and wors."[26] The image evoked parallels that of May clambering ever higher, the danger to her mortal soul escalating with each step borne on the back of her bent-over husband.

However, were January to adhere to the conditions under which sex in marriage is *not* sinful—theologically "safe sex," so to speak—he would, in the words of Jacques de Vitry, find "marriage more morally demanding than the monastic life."[27] In Passus 9, Wit unequivocally places the blame for the cataclysmic consequences of Cain's legacy on another of the First Couple's violations:

> Whan ye han wyved, beth war, and wercheth in tyme—
> Noght as Adam and Eve whan Caym was engendred.
> For in untyme, trewely, bitwene man and womman
> Ne sholde no [bedbourde] be: but if thei bothe were clene
> Of lif and of soule, and in [leel] charite.
> (B.9.184–88)

According to *The Book of Vices and Virtues* and Robert Mannyng's *Handlyng Synne*, there is no sin in the "werke of wedloke" unless it is done for pleasure only, or done at the wrong time or in the wrong place. The wrong time includes during menstruation, during holy times such as "high festes that ben solempne in holy chirche" (248), during fasting time, and lying-in time. Nor can one have sex in the church or church yard.[28] In both quantitative and qualitative terms, then, *luxuria* entails the notion of excess and transgression within the bonds of marriage. Wit warns that the wedded man must guard himself against such *luxuria*: "For lecherie in likynge is lymeyerd of helle" (B.9.181). As noted by A.V.C. Schmidt, the lymeyard, with a pun on *yerde*, was "a twig smeared with thick glue to trap birds,"[29] so that a man could indeed slay himself with his own knife, whether knife is read as the wife[30] or as his "wepene kene."

---

[26] *Vices and Virtues*, 44–45. See also Anthony Annunziata, "Tree Paradigms in *The Merchant's Tale*," *ACTA: The Fourteenth Century*, (CMERS: Binghamton, NY, 1978) 125–33; esp. 131–32.

[27] Brundage, *Law*, 450. John Bromyard (d. ca. 1390) "pictured marriage as a 'life-long curbing of desire,' punctuated occasionally by serious and solemn attempts to conceive a child" (quoted in Brundage, 503). See Brundage, 503–09, regarding sexual behavior in marriage.

[28] *Vices and Virtues*, 247–49. See also *Handlyng Synne*, 30–34 (noted by E. Talbot Donaldson in his *Speaking of Chaucer* [New York: Norton, 1970], 170–71, who cites the prohibitions). John T. McNeill and Helena M. Gamer cite *The Penitential of Columba* (ca. 600) in their *Medieval Handbooks of Penance* (New York: Columbia University Press, 1938; rpt. 1990), 254; note also the extensive treatment of "Irregularities in Marriage," 195–98; and "Matters Relating to Marriage," 208–11, in *The Penitential of Theodore*, Archbishop of Canterbury (668–690); The Corrector and Physician of Burchard of Worms (ca. 1008–12), 329, offers his remedies for marital sin.

[29] Schmidt, *Vision*, 442 n181, notes that "yard" could mean 'penis' *Oxford English Dictionary* (Oxford: Clarendon Press, 1933), s.v.11.

[30] See Donaldson, *Speaking*, 171, n1.

What we wish to stress is that when preaching on *luxuria*, Langland's Wit and Chaucer's Parson and January echo—or at least parallel—one another, inasmuch as they view the wife "as an inanimate object in marriage," little more than a generic object of desire.[31] They think of marriage literally in terms of husbandry; the wife herself merits concern only to the extent that she threatens the husband's salvation. January, a most unlikely cleric, nonetheless co-opts clerical arguments, ignoring the technicalities and twisting them to his purpose: *luxuria* in the guise of virility—the promise of the "goods" of marriage, is celebrated as a virtue. We see that even in the domestic economy, woman is consistently objectified and treated with the same indifference as Lady Mede who, as the object of political desire in Passus 2 through 4, is animated only by those who use her. We could say then, that in the passages under consideration, Langland and Chaucer would likely agree that, insofar as she is a product and not a producer, Everywife, like Mede, is denied any substantive power.[32] A closer look at *The Merchant's Tale* takes our discussion of "unkyndely similitude" to a new level and helps to illustrate the manner in which Chaucer's response to the social impotence of women departs from Langland's.

III

January functions as a caricature of Wit, and the *The Merchant's Tale* itself burlesques Langland's critique of the commercial and "unkynde" marriages condemned in Passus 9. January is a caricature not only of the mismatched spouse, but also of the frustrated husband bound by regulations from rendering his conjugal debt without damning his soul. With his "likynge of lecherie as by lokynge of his eighe" (B.13.344), his "coveitise and unkynde desiryng" (B.13.356), and the fact that for him "Swiche werkes...were nevere out of seson" (B.13.351), he is also the perfect candidate for Hawkyn's besmotered coat. January can never get his intent, his words, and his actions satisfactorily aligned, so that ultimately he fulfills Innocent III's prediction that "they become the instruments of his punishments that had been the pleasures of his sins."[33] The tale demonstrates how January brings this punishment on himself through a series of misconceptions based on "unkyndely similitude"—that is, based on his propensity to construe both words and the world so as to support his assumptions and promote his self-interest.

January co-opts a clerical argument—for the sheer purpose of misinterpreting it—that he could have lifted directly from Passus 9:

---

[31] Donaldson, *Speaking*, 170.

[32] See Lees, "Gender and Exchange," 125.

[33] Robert Lewis, ed., *De Miseria Condicionis Humane*, Innocent III [Lotario dei Segni], (Athens, GA: University of Georgia Press, 1978), 1.14. 23.

> The wif was maad the w[y]e for to helpe werche,
> And thus was wedlok ywrought weith a mene persone—
> First by the fadres wille and the frendes conseille,
> And sithenes by assent of hemself, as thei two myghte acorde;
> And thus was wedlok ywroght, and God hymself it made;
> In erthe the heven is—hymself was the witnesse.
>
> (B.9.113–18)

January first misconstrues the account of creation in Genesis and then seeks to serve his own, rather than God's will, in pursuit of self-authentication—counsel that accords with his rather than his friends' ideas of marriage.[34] In his handling of the Creation story, January is led by sexual appetite to privilege those elements in the two versions that satisfy his desire. Unlike Wit, who explains to Will that God created all things "And made man [moost lik] to hymself one / And Eve of his ryb bon withouten any mene" (B.9.33–34), January argues,

> That womman is for mannes helpe ywroght.
> The hye God, whan he hadde Adam maked,
> And saugh him al allone, bely-naked,
> God of his grete goodnesse seyde than,
> "Lat us now make an helpe unto this man
> Lyk to hymself"; and thanne he made him Eve.
>
> (4.1324–29)

January eschews the first account in Genesis 1:27, which suggests that Creation as conceived in the mind of God contains both masculine and feminine attributes and, thus, that male and female were created in the image of God, at one and the same time: "And God created man to his own image: to the image of God he created him: male and female he created them."[35] Like most Christian commentators, he opts, instead, for the second version, Genesis 2:20–24, a sequential creation in which woman is derived from man:

> ...but for Adam there was not found a helper like himself.
> Then the Lord God cast a deep sleep upon Adam: and when he was fast
> asleep, he took one of his ribs, and filled up flesh for it.
> And the Lord God built the rib which he took from Adam into a
> woman: and brought her to Adam. And Adam said, This now is bone
> of my bones, and flesh of my flesh: she shall be called woman, because

---

[34] For a full discussion of Chaucer's treatment of biblical passages in *The Merchant's Tale*, see L. L. Besserman, "Chaucer and the Bible: The Case of *The Merchant's Tale*," *Hebrew University Studies in Literature* 6 (1978): 10–31; 16–17, 28. Holy Writ, January argues, cannot be false; but it can be, and is, misconstrued in the tale. Helen Cooper, *The Canterbury Tales*, 2nd ed., (Oxford: Oxford University Press, 1996), reminds us that there is neither debate nor advice, that January "none argumentes make" (206–207).

[35] John Fyler offers a helpful etymological summary and analysis of the text in Genesis in his "Man, Men, and Women in Chaucer's Poetry" in Edwards and Spector, eds., *The Olde Daunce*, 154–176. The Hebrew allows for the wordplay on *ish/isha* that fosters an effect of similitude between man and woman lost in the Vulgate *vir/mulier*; hence Jerome employs *virago* to restore the similitude of the Hebrew text.

she was taken out of man. Wherefore a man shall leave father and mother, and shall cleave to his wife: and they shall be two in one flesh.[36]

But we see that January takes liberties with the text, emphasizing that Eve is made like unto Adam—in *man's* image. Here again, he is in accord with authorities who argue that without the mediating figure of the male, woman is not created in God's image.[37] In both Passus 9 and *The Merchant's Tale*, woman seems more or less a divine afterthought, "made *from*, *after*, and *for* Adam."[38] John Fyler reminds us that in the prelapsarian state, "God's injunction 'Increase and multiply'(Genesis 1:22) has a wholly benign effect, for the Creation mirroring the original act of its Creator, divides and subdivides but with the bond of virtuous similitude holding together its disparate multiple parts."[39] January exploits the tension between Creation accounts by trying to achieve an artificial equivalence, an awkward attempt, perhaps undertaken to compensate for his "unkynde" marriage: he anticipates molding his young wife in his image "Right as men may warm wex with handes plye" (4.1430). His attempt is doomed to failure because it functions like a self-indulgent, incestuous union—an unvirtuous, "unkyndely similitude." Elaine Tuttle Hansen notes that the Merchant's version of the second account of Creation, generally taken to differentiate Adam and Eve, "actually implies their similiarity, the failure from the beginning of a reassuring difference between male and female."[40] This similitude problematizes the notion of innate female infe-

---

[36] Biblical quotations are from the Douay-Rheims version (1914).

[37] Clark , "Adam's," 28, 250 n133. Clark cites Augustine's *De Trinitate* 12.7.10 (*Corpus Christianorum, Series Latina*, 50.364). See Kari Børresen, *Subordination and Equivalence: The Nature and Role of Women in Augustine and Thomas Aquinas*, trans. Charles H. Talbot (Washington: University Press of America, 1981); "*Imago Dei* as Inculturated Doctrine," in her *Image of God and Gender Models in Judaeo-Christian Tradition* (Oslo: Solum Forlag, 1991), 7–10; and "God's Image, Man's Image?: Patristic Interpretation of Gen. 1:27 and 1.Cor.11:7," in *Image of God and Gender Models*, 188–207. Børresen's studies approach scriptural accounts of Creation as an interaction of anthropology and theology: "Patristic interpretation of human God-likeness, *imago Dei*, presupposes andromorphic or metasexual God-imagery....It follows that women cannot be God-like *qua* females, with corresponding lack of fully human status, i.e. full religious capacity, *qua* women. Traditional Christian anthropology starts with two contrasting tenets: (1) Androcentric gender hierarchy or female subordination is established by God's creative order. (2) Human equivalence in the sense of women's parity with men is realised through Christ in redemption. The ensuing asymmetry between women's creational inferiority and their salvational equality is affronted by 'feminist' church Fathers, in order to include women in human God-likeness *already* from creation, *in spite* of their God-alien femaleness." As elaborated by Augustine, this stratagem "defines *imago Dei* as an incorporeal and consequently sexless quality, linked to human capacity of virtue and intellect. This genderfree privilege in man-like disguise permits *back*dating women's redemptive Christ-likeness to the creational level, without affecting their God-given subservience *qua* females, a split which has been upheld in theological anthropology until this century" (188).

[38] Børresen, "God's Image," 190.

[39] Fyler, "Man," 159.

[40] Elaine Tuttle Hansen, *Chaucer and the Fictions of Gender* (Berkeley: University of California Press, 1992), 247.

riority and makes the business of January's "unkynde" marriage a self-reflexive, self-reflecting trap.[41]

The Merchant's Tale is perhaps reworking the problems of gender similitude and difference implied in those passages of *Piers Plowman* B.9 describing God's paradoxical prohibition of marriage between Seth's sons and Cain's daughters and God's endorsement of the union of Seth's kin with its own (Genesis 6:1–4). In Langland's view, man and woman have different natures, but she reflects the male and has the same Father, or, in B.9.125–26, the same grandfather, Adam. In *Piers Plowman*, this union of Seth's kin with its own is not an example of incest, but suggests the union of citizens of the City of God. The union of Seth's sons with Cain's daughters, however, carries the actual stigma of incest, where the two lines are both too similar—with the same grandfather—but also too different, suggesting the union of the citizens of the Heavenly City with those of the earthly city.[42] In Augustine's (and Langland's) view, these miscegenations engendered a race so wretched that God destroyed what he had created in his image.

Langland employs the passages on the Cainites and Sethites in order to critique "unkynde" marriages that ignore natural and divine law. To reclaim virtuous similitude, *Piers Plowman* projects ideals of mutuality in "kynde" marriage and spiritual parity despite social asymmetry—ideals that are sabotaged at every step by the seminal notion of subordination in human relationships. In contrast, Chaucer gives us in January a narcissistic figure who abuses and perverts *kindly* similitude, twisting the divinely instituted union of marriage solely to his own ends. As John Fyler notes, "January gets what he deserves as his similitude when he marries May."[43]

January's second misconception arises from the first, from his playing God with May. In his pursuit of self-gratification, he suffers the consequences of misplaced love and misdirected will, a theme articulated throughout *Piers Plowman*. For example, at B.3.311 Conscience wishes "Preestes and persons with *Placebo* to hunte" (the reference is to Psalm 114.9, "*I will please* [the Lord]"). In seeking to please not the Lord but only himself, to follow his "owne conseil," January not surprisingly succumbs to May's false medicine, the "strugle with a man upon a tree" intended "to heele with youre eyen" (4.2374, 2372). Nowhere, however, is the narcissistic basis of his spiritual blindness more apparent than in his

---

[41] Hansen, *Fictions of Gender*, 248. Made of the same stuff—as Eve was of Adam—May will come to resemble the men who desire and devise her (251, 255). Hansen extends the blurring of gender differences to include Damyan and January, and Damyan and May: Damyan is like January in that he too is ravished by May (255), whereas May and Damyan are alike in knowing "entente" and their ability to communicate (257).

[42] See Augustine, *The City of God*, trans. Henry Betteson (Hammondsworth, Middlesex: Penguin, 1984). 15.22–23. See also Schmidt's note to lines 124–26: Langland got the idea of God's prohibition to Seth from Peter Comestor's *Historia* dealing with Genesis 31 (Schmidt, 441–42).

[43] Fyler, "Man," 159.

subtle reversal of the letter and spirit of St. Paul's admonition to husbands: "Love your wives, as Christ also loved his church and delivered himself up for it: That he might sanctify it...He that loveth his wife, loveth himself" (Eph. 5:25, 28), which the narrator of *The Merchant's Tale* translates, "Love wel thy wyf, as Crist loved his chirche. / If thou lovest thyself, thou lovest thy wyf" (4.1384–85). The excessive self-love that leads to his self-destructive *luxuria*—his excessive lust for May—entangles him in two other sins usually depicted with *luxuria* in medieval iconography: Idolatry and Avarice and, by association, with what Langland calls False.[44] Here the text of Innocent III is fulfilled: "For as the idolater serves the image, so the avaricious man serves his treasure" (2.15.2). In particular, January embodies Origen's comment, that he who creates an idol "makes what is not. A form which the eye does not see, but which the mind imagines for itself."[45] The only May that exists for January, the only woman he sees, is the one shaped in his mind. January's attempts to mimic God are thwarted in large part because, unlike God who creates *ex nihilo*, he must create out of that which is already completed, already created.[46] In the hierarchy of creativity posited by Hugh of St.Victor, January ranks as a mere artificer of nature, one who works in artifice, an adulterer (*moechus*) of the truth, "one who pollutes the marriage bed of another." In the "adulterate realm of the copy...representation appropriates or steals that which it should not."[47]

As Barbara Raw observes, idolators repeat the sin of Adam and Eve who fail to remember "that man is the image of God because he resembles him, not because he is equal to him. He is not a perfect image, but an inferior copy, imprinted on an alien nature as a king's image is imprinted on a coin."[48] Aelred of Rievaulx defines this sin as an act of theft, *per rapinam Dei usurpat similitudinem*. The only perfect human "image" of God, of course, would be Christ, who shares his nature.[49] January's anachronistic description of Adam as "al allone, bely-naked" is not a pretty sight, and certainly affirms man's alienation from the *imago Dei*. If January, like

---

[44] Michael Camille, *The Gothic Idol: Ideology and Image-Making in Medieval Art* (Cambridge: Cambridge University Press, 1989), 15, notes an illustration in Paris, Bibliothèque Nationale, MS.fr.146 (*Roman de Fauvel*) fol. 12v, in which Idolatry sits beside her sisters Luxuria and Avarice. Camille (50) also cites Isidore of Seville's derivation of the word "idol" from *dolus*, or fraud.

[45] Camille, *Gothic Idol*, 37, 359 n16, from Origen's *Homiles of Genesis and Exodus*.

[46] See Camille, *Gothic Idol*, 35.

[47] Camille, *Gothic Idol*, 35. Hugh of St. Victor (1096–1111) ranks works as (1) the work of God; (2) the work of nature; and (3) the work of the artificer who imitates nature.

[48] See Barbara Raw, "Piers and the Image of God in Man," in Hussey, 143–79; 150–51, 337n19. Raw notes, 156–59, that Langland in B.15.342–46 (B.15.348–53 in Schmidt) uses the medieval image of the coin, in this case the counterfeit coin, to express the concept of man as the imperfect image of God. The metaphor of the coin appears first in the writings of St. Augustine, followed by Bede, Anselm, and Aquinas. See also R. A. Shoaf, *Dante, Chaucer and the Currency of the Word* (Normon, OK: Pilgrim Books, 1983), 71.

[49] Raw, "Piers," 151.

Adam, is but a frail copy of his Creator, then what can we expect of May, the creation of a self-reflective idolatry? Fashioned out of the misogynist matter cluttering January's head, she becomes a self-fulfilling fantasy of his own worst fears: "whan a man is oold and hoor / Thanne is a wyf the fruyt of his tresor" (4.1269–70).[50]

In taking up the third of January's misconceptions and violations of an ideal of "similitude" between men and women, we see in Chaucer an extension of the notion of luxury to include the sense of 'luxuriant'—fertile, fruitful, and productive. In his role as courtly lover, January constructs a garden so inimical to Nature and Reason as to become the locus of deceit and "privitee"—secret signs and meetings, counterfeit keys, a false pregnancy, and parodic salvation. The garden is more the purgatory predicted by Justinus than his anticipated earthly paradise. Nor is this garden witness to a *felix culpa*. Like the pear, an inverted Christian motif and a noted symbol of *luxuria* in many of its senses,[51] the design, the trees, and the statuary of January's garden everywhere portend the unnatural consequences of *his own* appetite.[52] In flights of "heigh fantasye" he has envisioned himself a green knight who, albeit hoary, would "fare as dooth a tree / That blosmeth er that fruyt ywoxen bee; /...Myn herte and alle my lymes been as grene / As laurer" (4.1461–66). Nonetheless, he professes also to worry about keeping away from the tree of the seven deadly sins (4.1641). His vision of his wedding night reaches epic proportions as he imagines himself the lover: "That he that nyght in armes wolde hire streyne / Harder than evere Parys dide Eleyne" (4.1753–54). The sinfulness of too ardent relations has been noted above; here, the violent, unnatural nature of January's fantasies clearly aligns him with Pluto and the incestuous rape of Proserpine.[53] Significantly, January's truncated account of Genesis in the

---

[50] Shoaf, in his chapter "The Merchant and the Parody of Creation" (185–209), notes that when January converts May into a coin, she is money that is available also for Damyan to borrow, for "just like money, she will be ready to change hands. Coined by January's 'fantasye'...she will, in fact, be spent by another man, who seeks to deposit his 'interest' on this 'loan'" (190).

[51] Kenneth Bleeth, "The Image of Paradise in *The Merchant's Tale*," in Larry Benson and David Staines, eds., *The Learned and the Lewed: Studies in Chaucer and Medieval Literature* (Cambridge: Harvard University Press, 1974) 45–60; 53, 53n15. See also Hansen, *Fictions of Gender* (257, 257 n18), for an ambiguous symbol of pears as male and female genitals and, citing Karl P. Wentersdorf, 51–52, "Imagery, Structure and Theme in Chaucer's *Merchant's Tale*, in Leigh A. Arrathoon, ed., *Chaucer and the Craft of Fiction* (Rochester, MI: Solaris Press, 1986), 35–62, as a sign of effeminacy and infamy. On the scientific authority and popular practices and tradition imputing contraceptive properties to the pear, a virtual antidote to "kynde," see Carol Heffernan, "Contraception and the Pear Tree Episode of Chaucer's *Merchant's Tale*," *Journal of English and Germanic Philology* 94 (1995): 31–41.

[52] Bleeth , "Image of Paradise," cites Ovid's account of Priapus's attempt to rape the nymph Lotis, 51 n10.

[53] In addition to the medieval views on this presented above (section II), Bleeth, "Image of Paradise," 49–50, notes that too ardent relations were considered adulterous and the fantasy of violent unnatural lust would be equated with rape. See also Elizabeth Simmons-O'Neill, "Love in Hell: The Role of Pluto and Proserpine in Chaucer's *Merchant's Tale*," *Modern Language Quarterly* 51 (1990): 389–407, who emphasizes the incestuous nature of the rape: Proserpine is Pluto's niece (392–94).

encomium ignores the temptation and fall scenes. If Chaucer associates Nature with Reason, as he does in the *Parliament of Fowls*, then January's blind, instinctive passion is unnatural and most "unkynde," in Langlandian terms.[54] In this context, it is January's unwillingness to control his desire rationally and the self-indulgent nature of that desire that most violates Langland's ideal of virtuous human relationships governed and bound by *caritas*. Blessed by Nature, or Kynde, these relationships bear fruit physically and spiritually. But whereas the image of the garden "full of grene and of faire trees and of good fruyt" tended by the "grete gardener," a "model for the paradise of virtue within the heart," is a popular medieval topos,[55] January's virile fantasies construct a mock Eden that parodies the figure of the good man as garden. Likewise, the simile of the mirror in January's "heigh fantasye and curious bisynesse" (4.1577)—drawn from Nature's Confession to Genius in the *Roman de la Rose*—is symbolic of the generative process, and, with its capacity to reflect or distort the truth, of true or false (parodic) generation:[56]

> Many fair shap and many a fair visage
> Ther passeth thurgh his herte nyght by nyght,
> As whoso tooke a mirour, polisshed bryght,
> And sette it in a commune market-place,
> Thanne sholde he se ful many a figure pace
> By his mirour; and in the same wyse
> Gan Januarie inwith his thoght devyse
> Of maydens whiche that dwelten hym bisyde.
>   (4.1580–87)

This mirror is the false, distorting mirror that Jean de Meun identifies as "the perilous mirror of Narcissus—an imperfect and incomplete glass of love."[57] Elizabeth Simmons-O'Neill argues that the mirror image "emblematizes both January's reflected mercantile gaze, and the illusory, narcissistic nature of his sense of power," which likewise implicates him in his own deception.[58]

---

[54] See George Economou, "Januarie's Sin Against Nature: *The Merchant's Tale* and the *Roman de la Rose*," *Comparative Literature* 17 (1965): 251–57; 256.

[55] Bleeth, "Image of Paradise," 52, 52 n11, quoting from *The Book of Vices and Virtues*.

[56] See Economou, "Januarie's Sin," 252–53.

[57] Economou, "Januarie's Sin," 254, paraphrasing line 20423 from the *Roman de la Rose*.

[58] Simmons-O'Neill, "Love in Hell," 399. In a similar vein, George Economou has described Januarie's sin against nature as a "one-sided, self-centered love" that is "vain and futile," and destined by nature to be "fruitless and deceived" (256–57). In a passage evocative of May, Luce Irigaray elaborates on the effect of the mercantile gaze: "In other words, for the commodity, there is no mirror that copies it so that it may be at once itself and its 'own' reflection....For when we are dealing with commodities the self-same, mirrored, is not 'its' own likeness....The likeness here is only a measure expressing the *fabricated* character of the commodity, its trans-formation by man's (social, symbolic) 'labor.' The mirror that envelops and analyzes the commodity specularizes, speculates (on) man's 'labor.' *Commodities, women, are a mirror of value of and for man*....They yield to him their natural and social value as a locus of imprints, marks, and mirage of his activity" (*This Sex*, 176–77).

If he cannot discipline his own flesh, it is not surprising that he is powerless to discipline May: "The wif is oure wikked flessh, wol noght be chasted" (B.17.330). January labors at sex because he must, and in doing so he parodically usurps the female punishment of labor in childbirth as he feverishly sows his seed.[59] His works are as vain as his imagining, for the only heir he is likely to conceive from a quasi-incestuous union is the sort of morally monstrous progeny prophesied in B.9.193–94: *gedelynges, fals folk, fondlynges, faitours,* and *lieres—wastours* all. According to scripture, we are to bring forth fruit, fruit that remains (John 15:16), but as Langland predicts, this "unkynde" marriage will engender only "foule wordes; / Have thei no children but cheeste and chopp[es] hem bitwene" (B.9.168–69). And, thanks to Proserpine's timely intervention in *The Merchant's Tale,* it is similarly only the words that remain.

In *Piers Plowman* the five sons of Inwit are sent to save Lady Anima, among them Se-wel and Sey-well (B.9.19–20); these correspond most conveniently for our purpose to the garden gods Pluto and Proserpine. Pluto will grant January sight to see-well his wife's deception; Proserpine will enable May to say-well in order to extricate herself. As an equally ill-matched couple, Pluto and Proserpine are the perfect literary match for January and May, not only in terms of age disparity, but also in terms of the violent and callous manner in which Proserpine and May were "taken" as wives.[60] January, who worried that wedded bliss would jeopardize his salvation, unwittingly elicits the divine intervention that assures for May and all women that "For lak of answere noon of hem shal dyen" (4.2271). By giving May a voice, Chaucer has at the very least granted her a degree of agency, if only to help her help herself.[61] May certainly is no kin to the helpless females of Passus 9 (she is, after all, married—"unkyndely" or no), but rather a survivor, a kindred spirit to Lady Mede. Dupe though he be, January correctly deems that May can be bought off with his "towns" and "tours." But despite his belated generosity, his admissions and apologies, these are but dubious cures, placebos as it were, for the misery of those trapped in an "unkynde" marriage. The merchant—and, we presume, Chaucer's female readers and auditors—ask, "This Januarie, who is glad but he?" (4.2412). The question, then, is whether here and elsewhere in Chaucer, women, like Januarie, have been offered a placebo or the real thing.

---

[59] Wolfgang Rudat, "Chaucer's Spring of Comedy: *The Merchant's Tale* and Other 'Games' with Augustinian Theology," *Annuale Mediaevale* 21 (1981): 111–120; here, 113–14.

[60] See Barbara Gates, "'A Temple of False Goddis': Cupidity and Mercantile Values in Chaucer's Fruit-tree Episode," *Neuphilologische Mitteilungen* 77 (1976): 369–75; 370. Dante, for example, depicts Pluto as the god of Avarice; Proserpine, as the goddess of wealth, thus linking sexual love with avarice.

[61] May's quick response perpetuates the *fabliaux'* stereotypical depiction of female speech as cunning, designed to outwit and deceive. To the extent that Chaucer's victims are shaped by the conventions of the *fabliau,* January and May might more aptly be viewed as subjects of literary as opposed to social determinism.

IV

We do not wish to suggest from our reading of these texts that Langland is indifferent to the gender concerns Chaucer delightedly and delightfully explores. On the contrary, we regard Langland's relentless seach for Truth throughout his poem as evidence that he would be uneasy at the very least about offering a painless placebo, a quick fix, for the problems of gender. We conclude our study, therefore, with a close look at the revisions of *Piers Plowman* to assert that Langland was, indeed, not only aware of, but deeply concerned with such issues, particularly those concerning a gendered readership of his text. And this, we contend, makes his ultimate subordination of gender to other social and spiritual agendas a more deliberate and hence more compelling argument for the "luxury" of gender. For the purpose of this discussion, we will regard the A version as an integrally complete work.[62]

Recently there have been a number of articles suggesting that the A-Text is not, as it has traditionally been seen, the first version of the poem chronologically. One solution to the "problem" of the A version has been proposed by Jill Mann, who, arguing against the traditionally understood order of the three major versions of *Piers*, suggests that the A-Text could be an abridged version of the B- and C-Texts, revised with a different audience in mind, an audience consisting of "non-Latinate (or perhaps in the very elementary stages of education), as lay, and possibly young."[63] In fact, she argues that A was "designed" to fill the role as a "condensed version" of *Piers Plowman*.[64] In a parallel revisionist vein, Charlotte Brewer refers to George Kane's edition of the A version, as "the *putative* first version."[65] She goes on to propose that variations among A versions could be due, not to scribal error, but to Langland himself, who may "have touched up or altered individual readings, so that some manuscripts may consequently bear traces of alternative authorial, not just scribal, variants....Langland might have come back to his first version of A and improved some of its

---

62 According to Míceál Vaughan, ("The Ending(s) of *Piers Plowman* A," in Míceál Vaughan, ed., *Such Werkis to Werche: Essays on Piers Plowman in Honor of David C. Fowler* [East Lansing: Colleagues Press, 1993], 211–41), the general consensus that views the A version as an "abandoned early fragment of a work carried to conclusion by its author in the B and C versions" has impeded study of the A version "as a poem with its own integrity and appeal" (225). Based on his analysis of the various endings of the A-Text(s), Vaughan asserts that the pious closings confirm the possibility that the poem was complete, "that it achieved closure in its own terms; and we might do well to recover those terms rather than insist on our own." Nor, he argues, can we "assert uncritically that the shorter version is *in itself* incomplete since other readers have accepted it as complete" (240).

63 Jill Mann, "The Power of the Alphabet: A Reassessment of the Relation between the A and B Versions of *Piers Plowman*," *Yearbook of Langland Studies* 8 (1994): 21–50; 24. Mann notes Howard Meroney's claim that the A-Text was "an abridgement for a non-clerical audience by a redactor of the B version" (22).

64 Mann, "Power," 27.

65 Charlotte Brewer, "The Textual Principles of Kane's A Text," *Yearbook of Langland Studies* 3 (1989): 67–90; 67 (our emphasis).

readings."[66] John M. Bowers asks "whether the A-Text might not be the last, rather than the first, version of *Piers Plowman* written as an abridgement or abbreviation begun late in life by Langland himself."[67] Bowers cites several other writers who tended to reduce and simplify late in their careers, including Shakespeare. But this revisionist view of the order of the various versions of *Piers* is far from universally accepted, as Traugott Lawlor's refutations of both Mann and Bowers make clear.[68]

Regardless of chronology, an analysis of the various versions of *Piers Plowman* inevitably raises questions of audience, which Mann, among others, has tackled. Anne Middleton argues that *Piers Plowman* had a "heterogeneous" readership—the actual "audience" the text acquired.[69] Following Walter Ong, Middleton defines the poem's "public" as that constructed audience of the poem imagined by the poet. On the basis of the manuscripts and evidence of early ownership, she observes that "[t]he audience of *Piers Plowman* is best characterized neither by regional peculiarities nor by 'estate' as such, but by a common social location and range of activities and interests."[70] Robin Lister agrees that the poem addresses all orders of society, but asserts that it is the peasant class, unable to represent themselves in literature, who are directly addressed by Langland: "[t]here is every likelihood that vernacular texts would have been read aloud to audiences including members of the lower strata of society."[71]

Derek Pearsall is one of the few scholars to have emphasized that the audience of *Piers* was mixed in terms of gender.[72] For example, women owned manuscripts of *Piers*.[73] Felicity Riddy argues for a female readership of the Vernon manuscript, which includes the A version of *Piers Plowman*. The manuscript includes "a strikingly large number of works

---

[66] Brewer, "Textual Principles," 78, 84.

[67] John M. Bowers, "*Piers Plowman*'s William Langland: Editing the Text, Writing the Author's Life," *Yearbook of Langland Studies* 9 (1995): 65–90; 83.

[68] Traugott Lawlor, "A Reply to Jill Mann, Reaffirming the Traditional Relation Between the A and B Versions of *Piers Plowman*," *Yearbook of Langland Studies* 10 (1996): 145–80; and "Response to John M. Bowers," *Yearbook of Langland Studies* 9 (1995): 94–98.

[69] Anne Middleton, "The Audience and Public of *Piers Plowman*" in David Lawton, ed., *Middle English Poetry and Its Literary Background: Seven Essays* (Woodbridge, Suffolk: D. S. Brewer, 1982), 101–23, 147–54; here, 104.

[70] Middleton, "Audience," 104. She goes on to point out that the A version appears more often in manuscript collections than either the B or C versions, most often with didactic religious works and narrative histories. Additionally, Middleton discusses the use of the alliterative long line as suited to such a wide readership.

[71] Robin Lister, "The Peasants of *Piers Plowman* and Its Audience," in Kathleen Parkinson and Martin Priestmann, eds., *Peasants and Countrymen in Literature* (London: English Dept., Rochampton Institute of Higher Education , 1982), 71–90; 73.

[72] Derek Pearsall, "The Courtly World of Chaucer vs. the World of Langland," paper delivered to the NEH Summer Institute: Chaucer and Langland, Boulder, Colorado, July 12, 1995.

[73] William Palmere, rector of St. Alphage, Cripplegate, London, from 1397 until 1400, left his copy of "peres plowman" in his will to Agnes Eggesfeld (see Robert A. Wood, "A Fourteenth-Century London Owner of *Piers Plowman*," *Medium Ævum* 53 [1984]: 83–90).

written specifically for women readers."[74] Such texts include an abridged version of Aelred of Rievaulx's *De institutione inclusarum*, addressed to his sister, a nun. Also in the Vernon manuscript are several works by Richard Rolle written for women, including his *Form of Perfect Living* specifically directed to Margaret Kirkby, a nun at Hampole and later a recluse at Ainderby. A version of the *Ancrene Riwle* which was written for a group of female anchoresses is included, as well as *The Abbey of the Holy Ghost*, which as Riddy notes "instructs the lay reader how to build a nunnery in his or her heart and is translated from a French text originally destined for women."[75] Other works directed to women are also included. The A version present in the manuscript, as Riddy observes, "is not only the shortest of all the versions but the most accessible to those not literate in Latin."[76] Taking up these various suggestions, we pursue further Pearsall's and Riddy's points concerning a possible female audience for *Piers Plowman* in reading B.9 and its corresponding passus in the A version, Passus 10. Our evidence suggests that if the traditional order of the A, B, and C versions in fact holds true, then it is possible that Langland wrote for an increasingly masculine audience in B and C. If the A version is a later revision of the B-Text, as Mann and Bowers suggest, then one audience the redactor may have intended to address included women.

The first of a number of details that suggest a more gender-inclusive audience for the A version is to be found in the puzzling reference to Seth's sister—"Seth and his sister"—a phrase used three times in the A-Text (10.153,159,179) and not at all in the B- or C-Texts. Both B.9.124–31 and A.10.151–62 concern Seth and his disobedience of God's prohibition against coupling with Cain's kin. Seth appears in Genesis 4:25–5:8 as the son of Adam and Eve begotten after Cain's death. Tavormina points out that Langland adheres to one of the most common interpretations of the passages in Genesis, which follow Genesis 6:1–7, "according to which the descendants of Seth ('the sons of God') and of Cain ('the daughters of men') intermarried, against God's command to Seth; these miscegenations produced the lustful and violent race destroyed by the Flood."[77] Augustine in *The City of God* (15.17) argues that Cain's line of succession is that of the earthly city, while Seth is the father of the heavenly city, thus making him a signifier of the resurrection. The Vulgate's reference to Seth as Adam's "seed" may explain Langland's emphasis on Seth as a "seeder."[78]

---

[74] Felicity Riddy, "'Women Talking About the Things of God': A Late Medieval Sub-culture," in Carol M. Meale, ed., *Women and Literature in Britain 1150–1500* (Cambridge: Cambridge University Press, 1993), 104–127; here, 106.

[75] Riddy, "'Women Talking'," 106.

[76] Riddy, "'Women Talking'," 106–107.

[77] Tavormina, *Kindly Similitude*, 85.

[78] See Thomas Hill, "Seth the 'Seeder' in *Piers Plowman* C.10.249," *Yearbook of Langland Studies* 1 (1987): 105–108.

Augustine, however, provides a possible explanation for why Langland would include the phrase "his sister." Unlike Cain's line, which is destroyed in the Flood, the description of Seth's line mentions no women by name. Cain's descendants, by contrast, are continually described with the names of their wives:

> For in the resurrection there will be no generation, when regeneration has brought them to that state. In this connection it is not irrelevant, I think, to point out that among the generations derived from the man called Seth although the birth of sons and daughters is recorded, no woman is expressly mentioned by name in that line. In contrast, among those descended from Cain, at the very end of the whole list, the last woman to be born is named....This is a neat way of suggesting that the earthly city, right up to its end, will have carnal births, resulting from the union of male and female....In contrast with [Cain] is Seth, whose name means 'resurrection.' He is the father of generations which are separately listed.[79]

In linking Seth with the Resurrection and with the City of God, Augustine places Seth in his cosmic vision as a prefiguration of Christ himself. In adding Seth's sisters to Seth's name, then, Langland appears to offer a more gender-inclusive Resurrection and heavenly city.

Another aspect of the A-Text that might suggest a nod to a female audience is found in the argument concerning Inwit. The A version does not suggest, as does the B-Text (9.67–71), that women do not have Inwit. Furthermore, the A-Text focuses continually on marriage, something most lay women would be experienced in. We propose that the A-Text consistently constructs a more inclusive gender argument and, thus, audience. For example, all three texts remind the reader not to work "in vntyme," in other words, not to have sex at improper times as did Adam and Eve who thereby engendered Cain. But the A-Text reminds *spouses* while both B and C remind *husbands* only.[80] The A-Text also significantly omits the crude exhortation for the young man with "thi wepene kene" (B.9.182) to marry to avoid lechery.[81] This provides further evidence that the A-Text is concerned with a mixed-gender audience. Additionally, as Tavormina points out, A.10 focuses on "familiar duties to immediate kin and on the vocations of ordinary Christians who support the *comune* by working in any state of life....[W]e find [the concepts of works and words] exemplified in A mainly by the physical, worldly work of the ordinary good person, and by the teaching passed on in families and in schools."[82] This is in contrast

---

[79] Augustine, *The City of God*, 627.

[80] See Tavormina, *Kindly Similitude*, 100.

[81] See Mann, "Power," 35. Mann also points out the omission in Mede's confession (B.3. 52–62) that the friar treat lechery as a "cours of kynde" (B.3.52 cf. A.3.50–52)—"presumably because an unsophisticated audience might not see the irony here and might be led astray by Meed's arguments."

[82] Tavormina, *Kindly Similitude*, 105.

to the B and C versions that focus on prelates and the spiritual teachings of the Church. The A-Text thus emphasizes a world that would be familiar and meaningful to lay married women. Tavormina sees a development from A to B to C, one in which Langland universalizes his points concerning social responsibility, in that he shifts from the local and secular bonds of lay persons to kin to broader, more spiritual obligations, especially those of churchmen.[83] One could also read these shifts as shifts in audience. A lay female listener or reader of Langland's A-Text would be directly addressed, as opposed to the B- and C-Texts, wherein she could obviously draw spiritual conclusions, but would not specifically be included in the moral atmosphere.

More evidence for the differences between A.10 and B.9 concern tone. B contains more highly sustained literary images that carry out the idea of incest, such as B.9.147–152 on grafting fruit. The fruit image is repeated in B.9.168 concerning the bad fruit of ill words engendered in a bad marriage, whereas in A.10 the complex grafting passage does not prefigure the reference to the fruit of ill words, suggesting a simplified text for a less educated audience.[84] Another example of variance in the A and B versions is to be found at the end of each passus in the discussion of good and bad marriages. The A-Text has considerably fewer examples of mismatched marriages. When Wit argues that marriage is good between single people who love each other, that argument is underscored in the B-Text with a quotation in Latin (B.9.192). The A-Text lacks this quotation and gives a loose translation of it (A.10.206–8), suggesting an audience unversed in Latin.[85]

Tavormina has pointed out numerous differences among the various versions that could also be used to support our argument that Langland quite possibly directs the A-Text to women readers and listeners. For example, Tavormina argues that, in defining Do-wel and Do-best, Wit uses concrete examples in A.10 that refer to parental and schoolroom instruction.[86] Additionally, she argues that Do-best in the A version is shown to grow out of "honest, God-fearing, steadfast (i.e., place-keeping) work in one's proper station and long-suffering meekness, *lou3nesse* and *kyndenesse*."[87] The A-Text is more interested in "obedience and humility"[88] than the other versions, an aspect that coheres with contemporary texts prescribing female

---

83 Tavormina, *Kindly Similitude*, 106.

84 Mann, "Power," argues that the excision of Wrath with the extensive references to grafting "is that this tree-metaphor is applied to a clerical squabble, which is not a fitting subject for a lay audience" (40). And as Charlotte Brewer cautions, "How can we be sure that Langland would not have retouched his poem [here referring to the A-Text] at some points to achieve precisely these sorts of effects, with the aim of communicating more clearly to his audience?" (73).

85 Mann, "Power," discusses the omission of Latin quotations as one of the main principles in abridging B to create A (28, 35).

86 Tavormina, *Kindly Similitude*, 73.

87 Tavormina, *Kindly Similitude*, 75.

88 Tavormina, *Kindly Similitude*, 76.

conduct and behavior such as those outlined in Riddy's study. Tavormina also notes that while A offers a fairly comprehensive list of the estates, the B-Text focuses on more elite ranks and the C-Text emphasizes religious classes.[89] Finally, A.10.117–34 (including the image of the rose) suggests a kind of authority to wedded folk that would have appealed to lay married women: even Do-best is a possibility in virtuous married life.

Clearly, the A version is more appropriately addressed to women and lay people; the revisions—if revisions they are—reflect Langland's awareness of the importance of gender distinctions and his response to them. But the fact that he chooses, finally, even in this version to subordinate gender concerns to other social and salvific urgencies, particularly as they are reflected in the Inwit passage, underscores the "luxury"of gender as he sees it. Langland is consciously not addressing (or transforming, or revaluing, or redirecting) these questions in his poem as Chaucer is. He refuses to give gender the kind of priority Chaucer gives it, electing, instead, to make feminine self-interest—whether construed as political, social or gender-based—subordinate to larger or more abstract and, for him, more fundamental, theological issues.

In *The Merchant's Tale*, while drawing on the same general social and moral themes, Chaucer foregrounds gender. The feminine self becomes subject to masculine definition and desire in the context of such gender-sensitive issues as marriage, fertility, and rape, if only to accommodate the female point of view or momentarily to grant women a few well-directed, well-timed words. While implicitly acknowledging the contingencies of gender, Chaucer neither speaks for nor protects his protagonists, but risks granting them just enough literary free will to save or damn themselves—victims of their own as well as others' desires. But in the end, *The Merchant's Tale* is about men, their role in their own deception and fall and the life-threatening, life-denying consequences of their lust and violence. Solomon, January, and Pluto—lechers all—are rendered impotent by the very women they have subdued. The three serve as literary exempla of Elaine Hansen's theory that "when men bring Woman into being they both see themselves more truly and induce or reveal their own feminization."[90] If nothing else, there is in May's one-upmanship a temporary, compensatory shift of power that is momentarily liberating for women. We must conclude that the victory for May, as for her sympathetic auditors and readers, is short-lived and presumably as hollow as her womb that January paternally strokes. Were May to bear him an heir, he would have yet another possession to ply as wax, to mold in his image.

The Merchant's Tale exemplifies the self-reflexive, self-gratifying mode, what we have defined as "unkyndely similitude," that is at the root of the wretchedness engendered by the "unkynde" marriages explicated in Wit's

---

[89] Tavormina, *Kindly Similitude*, 80.
[90] Hansen, *Fictions*, 249.

homily. As Chaucer perhaps discerned in his reading of Passus 9, similitude is the problem not the solution: it is the lack of mutual recognition of the Other that renders such unions emotionally and spiritually barren. The "kyndely" similitude that constitutes a life-enhancing, spiritually regenerative marriage, which Langland projects as the literal and metaphorical ideal in *Piers Plowman*, entails a recognition of the significance, albeit not the equivalence, of the Other. "Kyndely" similitude in terms of age and class does not erase the difference imposed by gender; it cannot tolerate, for example, the indifference of the marital exchanges of Lady Mede. Langland could be said to lay out the paradoxical problem of "kyndely" versus "unkyndely" similitude that Chaucer picks up and explores with relish in *The Merchant's Tale*. It is January, we must remember, not his creator, who is indifferent to the complexities of gender and sexual relations.

Nor, as we have argued throughout, can Langland be regarded as indifferent to questions of gender. How, then, can we conclude that gender is a luxury in Passus 9? In bringing our discussion to a close, we turn, as does Langland, to focus upon the role of women and marriage in Christian salvation. Whereas Chaucer's *fabliau* can accommodate the divine only to the extent that it can be parodied (divine intervention evens the score between a man and a woman but not between man and his God), Langland becomes increasingly interested in man's potential for restoring the divine image in himself, in becoming god-like not by equality but, dare we say it, by similitude. He must imitate God, or the perfect image of God that is Christ.[91] Because Christ incarnate was a poor man, the poor acquire a status as chosen people, and humility is elevated as a virtue. In this "redemptional democracy," the female in the salvational couple, the nuptial Christ and Church, "serves as a simile for human dependency on divine omnipotence," and as submissive humanity.[92] In Christian salvation as in earthly marriage, it appears that women continue to be objects of desire; in the former, however, they have acquired a salvific use-value, so to speak, as the beneficiaries of piously motivated good works. In the grand scheme of salvation that Langland's Will is working out and working toward, human suffering—however graphically it is depicted and however keenly it may be felt by the reader—becomes sublimated as a means to an end. Read in an eschatological context, gender essentially becomes moot, as kinship bonds and gender and class boundaries dissolve.[93]

The poet who works through his intellectual and spiritual crises in his poem as if his and humanity's salvation depended upon it does not dismiss gender but absorbs it into greater, more cosmic concerns. The earthbound

---

[91] Raw, "Image," 167. "Whereas Piers represents the imprint of the divine image on humanity as a whole, Will stands for the particular, individual man" (168, 338 n48).

[92] Børresen, "God's Image," 189–90. In Passus 17.337a Langland quotes 2 Cor.12:9: "For power is made perfect in infirmity," directly after comparing a wife to the "wikked flessh" (B.17.330).

[93] See Galatians 3:28.

Langland, upon whom discord and distress impinge, chooses to subordinate gender in the face of what he perceives, in Passus 9 at least, to be the more pressing demands of social justice for humanity at large, as opposed to, for example, May's individual justice. Yet, as the A-Text reveals, the poet is all the while aware of gender differences in the reception of his poem. If for everything there is a season, then the season for addressing questions of gender in *Piers Plowman* is long overdue. It is our hope that by reading Passus 9 and *The Merchant's Tale* together, we have heightened our readers' appreciation of Langland's subtle but distinctive handling of gender and suggested his place among Chaucer's literary benefactors. We hope also that those examining gender in Langland's poem will, unlike January, heed our counsel—our caveat—and test such claims as are made for gender, particularly female agency, against the Castle Caro and Inwit passages of Passus 9.

Langland's Romances

Stephen H. A. Shepherd

To what extent does Langland make use of vernacular romance beyond his adaptation of accidental features of the genre—knights, the life and language of the court, jousts and sieges?[1] Is there nothing less narrowly allusive than his fleeting, if not perjorative, references to Randolph Earl of Chester[2] or Felice (12.46)? Finding a responsible answer to such questions cannot be easy, nor can there in all likelihood be a complete answer. As Anne Middleton says:

> [the poem's] readability depends on its tantalizing and continued resemblance to familiar instructive, factual, authoritative kinds of...discourse, the peculiar power of the literary fiction depends on the evasion or deferral of instrumental claims, on its own insistence that it but 'plays' the part of the useful....Langland makes equivocal what he received as univocal.[3]

---

[1] For the purposes of this essay vernacular "romance" is taken simply to correspond with those texts identified in J. Burke Severs, ed., *A Manual of the Writings in Middle English 1050–1500, I, Romances* (New Haven, CT: Connecticut Academy of Arts and Sciences, 1967). A less arbitrary definition of the genre is beyond the need of the present study but continues to be a valid matter of debate; important representations of the issue are Kathryn Hume, "The Formal Nature of Middle English Romance," *Philological Quarterly* 53 (1974): 158–80; John Finlayson, "Definitions of Middle English Romance," *Chaucer Review* 15 (1981–82): 44–62, 168–81; Susan Crane, *Insular Romance* (Berkeley and Los Angeles: University of California Press, 1986), 10–11; and Joerg O. Fichte, "Grappling with Arthur, or Is There An English Arthurian Verse Romance?," in Piero Boitani and Anna Torti, eds., *Poetics: Theory and Practice in Middle English Literature* (Cambridge: Cambridge University Press, 1990), 149–63.

[2] *Piers Plowman* B.5.396. All references to *Piers Plowman* are from the B version only, as edited by A. V. C. Schmidt, *The Vision of Piers Plowman*, Everyman paperback, 2nd ed. (London: J. M. Dent, 1995). Subsequent citations shall appear parenthetically.

[3] Anne Middleton, "The Audience and Public of *Piers Plowman*," in David Lawton, ed., *Middle English Alliterative Poetry and Its Literary Background* (Woodbridge, Suffolk: D. S. Brewer, 1982), 101–23; here, 121.

Many of Langland's sources are notoriously difficult to trace. His quotations, and especially his allusions, are often drawn, as John Alford has revealed so thoroughly, from such indirect sources as "florilegia, encyclopedias, commentaries, and alphabetical reference books."[4] Langland's intertextual manner is thus likely to conjure multiple referents from single references: sometimes the quotations bring with them an acquired meaning or context and act as what Alford calls "liveried servants";[5] sometimes they act "as *incipits* whose full meaning can be determined or completed only within a context outside the poem."[6] In the absence, then, of any overt identification of direct romance sources in *Piers Plowman*, such considerations as those voiced by Alford and Middleton must set the parameters for further inquiry: besides the romances themselves, we would do well to look for texts which have great allusive/analogous potential in relation to the romances as well as to *Piers Plowman*—it seems less likely to find a passage or set of details derived exclusively from one romance than to find a cluster of mutually-reminiscent passages from a number of different, though possibly related, sources and genres.

Studies that attempt to identify romance elements in *Piers Plowman* beyond incidental plot-independent details, or that do not resort to broad generalizations, are understandably few, yet they bear out the suggestion that such romance elements are most likely to share in a manifold-allusive, multi-generic context—they will be the liveried servants, so to speak, of Langland's associative equivocation. Nicole Clifton, for instance, finds that "Jesus' duel with Longeus [B.18] reflects a common motif from medieval romance: the battle between two disguised knights who end their strife by yielding to one another once their true identities are revealed."[7] She finds the parallel with the duel between Yvain and Gauvain in Chrétien's *Yvain* to be the most compelling—as in *Piers Plowman* the deadlock between combatants "paradoxically brings resolution" and "the joust between Longeus and Jesus, like that of Yvain and Gauvain also reconciles sisters: the Four Daughters of God."[8] In contrast to antecedent religious texts like the *Ancrene Wisse* that use amatory romance conventions (the allegory of the King and the Lady) that consequently restrict the allegory ("earthly love figures divine love, so that the allegory cannot work on both levels")[9]

---

4 John A. Alford, *"Piers Plowman": A Guide to the Quotations* (Binghamton, N. Y.: Medieval and Renaissance Texts and Studies, 1992), 16.

5 Alford, *Guide*, 16.

6 Alford, *Guide*, 8.

7 Nicole Clifton, "The Romance Convention of the Disguised Duel and the Climax of *Piers Plowman*," *Yearbook of Langland Studies* 7 (1993): 123–28; 123.

8 Clifton, "Romance Convention," 127. For a mid-fourteenth-century Middle English translation/adaptation of Chrétien's poem, see *Ywain and Gawain* in S. H. A. Shepherd, ed., *Middle English Romances* (New York and London: Norton, 1995), 75–173. For evidence of the widespread popularity of this story in medieval England, see James A. Rushing, Jr., *Images and Adventure: Ywain in the Visual Arts* (Philadelphia: University of Pennsylvania Press, 1995).

Langland's borrowing of a romance motif "shows Christ in this scene not as Other, as he is in allegories where he appears as Lover-Knight, but as brother, as almost-Self....The joust motif encourages the audience to identify with Jesus, to internalize an ideal of Christian perfection."[10]

Equally as important as these findings is Clifton's recognition that more than one example of this motif comes to mind: Balin and Balan (in Malory's Old French source), Reinbrun and Heraud's son in *Guy of Warwick*, Erec and Guivret in *Erec et Enide*, and Perceval with Sagremor and Kay in *Le Conte del Graal*. The consequence is that "even an audience unacquainted with all the parallels that *Yvain* contains would recognize and respond to the motif of the disguised joust and the complex questions of loyalty, honor, and identification that accompany it."[11] Langland's borrowing here—if one agrees that it is probable—is specific enough to invite his reader's recognition of a typical motif, yet broad enough in its application to invite an understanding of the motif not just as *typical*, possibly even centered on a particular identifiable source, but in effect as *typological*, enhancing his meaning by several associations. To Clifton's list might be added the final meeting between Roland and Oliver in the *Chanson de Roland*, a text popular in Britain since the early twelfth century.[12] The blinded Oliver strikes his friend Roland, the greatest warrior in the world, one whose mission on earth is sanctioned by God (through the bestowal, first to Charlemagne, then to Roland, of the sword Durendal, 11. 2316–37). Once Roland identifies himself (i.e., causes Oliver figuratively to "see," as Christ, once struck, causes Longeus to see), Oliver asks forgiveness—"I have struck you? Forgive me then, I beg" (2005)—as does *Piers'* Longeus—"For the dede that I have doon I do me in youre grace. / Have on me ruthe, rightful Jesu!"(18.90–91)—and both are pardoned. Both episodes are followed not long after by scenes of divine intervention leading to victory over the enemies of God. Perhaps for Langland's readers it would have been impossible to comprehend the apposite romances in the same way again; the episodes in question might inevitably invite a rereading of their host romances as types of what might be called a higher romance intertext dedicated to a salvific redefinition of knightly action.

Clifton's is the most convincing elucidation of a romance motif in Langland to date; and yet further such studies will continue to face similar difficulties in establishing Langland's sources. It seems, therefore, that any other approach that might afford even a slight advantage in tracing

---

9 Clifton, "Romance Convention," 127.

10 Clifton, "Romance Convention," 127.

11 Clifton, "Romance Convention," 128.

12 All references to the *Chanson de Roland* are to the translation by D. D. R. Owen, *The Song of Roland* (Woodbridge, Suffolk: D. S. Brewer, 1990). For an account of the popularity of the story of the *Chanson* in Britain see S. H. A. Shepherd, "The Middle English *Pseudo-Turpin Chronicle*," *Medium Ævum* 65 (1996): 19–34.

Langland's steps ought to be explored. To this end, the remainder of this essay will attempt to provide a strategy for using evidence of the reception of Langland's poem as a guide to discerning which romance texts and romance-oriented themes some of Langland's medieval readers saw fit to associate with *Piers Plowman*. It begins simply by considering manuscripts that contain both *Piers* and one or more Middle English romances, and then treats of Middle English romances showing some material link with *Piers Plowman*, insofar as they have been copied in a manuscript by a scribe who also rendered a copy of *Piers Plowman* in another manuscript, or contain clear verbal borrowings from the poem. Such study reveals reception profiles with some notable commonalities. Using such commonalities as a guide, we will then return to Langland with one suggestion of where to look for further clues to the components of Langland's "romance intertext."

Nine Middle English Romances are found with *Piers Plowman* in five manuscripts:[13]

Manuscript	PPl version	MS date	Romance
Lincoln's Inn 150	A	1400–1425	**Libeaus Desconus**, **Arthur** and **Merlin**, **Kyng Alisaunder**, **Seege** or **Batayle of Troy***
Vernon	A	c.1400	*Robert of Sicily*, **King of Tars**
Trinity C. Dublin D.4.12	A	1475–1500	*Wars of Alexander*[14]
Huntington 128	B	early C15	*Siege of Jerusalem*
Laud Misc. 656	C	c.1450	*Siege of Jerusalem*

*Titles in **boldface** represent texts possibly written prior to Langland's A version—i.e., c.1365–70.

It is surely significant that most of these romances (seven of nine) appear with an A version of *Piers*; and that in each of the manuscripts this is a "pure" A version, without B or C conflations. All but one of these

---

[13] Unless otherwise stated, the information in this chart is derived from Gisela Guddat-Figge, *Catalogue of Manuscripts Containing Middle English Romances* (Munich: W. Fink, 1976).

[14] The poem's recent editors, Hoyt N. Duggan and Thorlac Turville-Petre, find that a *terminus ad quem* of 1450 allows them to say only that "the poem could have been composed at any point within the [previous] century" [*The Wars of Alexander*, Early English Text Society, Supplementary Series, 10 (Oxford: Oxford University Press, 1989), xlii].

romances have a proposed date of composition conceivably before that of Langland's poem; and all have sources which antedate *Piers Plowman*. *Piers Plowman* A would then seem to stand as a relative newcomer to an established literary tradition. It may well be that these would be useful texts with which to begin a study both of the ways in which the A version might have been thought to correspond with its companion romances as well as of possible romance influences on at least the A readings of *Piers Plowman*. Space does not permit a full study of such correspondence here—the door is open for further research—but a brief survey will reveal a number of general affinities.

All of the romances found in maunuscripts with A versions of *Piers* feature *will*-ful lone male heroes involved repeatedly in life- (or soul-) threatening struggles. Four (the two *Alexander*-romances, *Merlin*, and *Libeaus*) take in the life-history of their hero and include a period of youthful precociousness. Four (the two *Alexander*-romances, *Troy*, and *Tars*) concern worthy non-Christian heroes (and it is worth noting that *Merlin* and *Robert* both feature precocious heroes who for a time occupy conditions of moral apostasy). All are non-courtly romances, given over less to the refinements of chivalry than to an emphasis on the historical or didactic (or a combination of both). These are, of course, broad strokes with which to paint a comparison with *Piers Plowman* A; and yet the similarities are substantial enough to warrant further inquiry. One of these correspondences, the interest in the worthy non-Christian (the "virtuous pagan" or the "righteous heathen") is especially inviting because it may be found not only in romances associated with A manuscripts of *Piers*, but also in romances associated either in manuscript or in content with B and C versions of the poem. It is upon this correspondence that the remainder of this essay will concentrate.

The only romance found in the same manuscript with B or C versions of *Piers Plowman* is the *Siege of Jerusalem* (SJ), composed probably in the 1370s or 1380s.[15] Now, *SJ* is a nasty piece of anti-Semitism any way one looks at it—and so most students of Middle English literature have not looked at it at all—but scholarly interest in this "chocolate-covered tarantula"[16] has recently begun to stir, most notably in the work of Ralph Hanna and David Lawton.[17] Of special interest to this study is the work of another recent student of the poem, Gregory O'Molesky, who observes that characters in *SJ* present a spectrum of proximity to Christian values.[18] At one end of the spectrum are the inevitable subjects of the poem's desire for vengeance, the Jews of Jerusalem; "somewhere in the middle stands

---

[15] Ralph Hanna III, "Contextualizing the *Seige of Jerusalem*," *Yearbook of Langland Studies* 6 (1992): 109–121; 113.

[16] Hanna, "Contextualizing," 109.

[17] Daivd Lawton and Ralph Hanna are preparing a new edition of the *Siege of Jerusalem*. See also Hanna, "Contextualizing."

[18] Gregory O'Molesky, *Re-contextualizing the "Siege of Jerusalem"* (M.A. Thesis, Southern Methodist Univeristy, Dallas, 1997).

Josephus, the book-making Romanized Jew, an *auctor* with great Christian potential"; and at the other end are the worthy Christians-to-be, Titus and Vespasian.[19] In other words, the poem projects relative conditions of non-Christian worth; and it is to this kind of relativity that Langland also subscribes.

Langland's position will need to be considered in more detail—it is set out mainly in his depiction of Trajan—but the "romance" component of this issue first needs the support of further evidence. Two more romances have obvious connections with *Piers Plowman*, and both, it can be argued, touch on the issue of the virtuous pagan: the *Awntyrs off Arthure* and the *Sowdone of Babylone*. The scribe of the Lambeth 491 text of the *Awntyrs off Arthure* (composed in the first quarter of the fifteenth century) also copied the conflated B and C version of *Piers Plowman* found in Huntington Library manuscript HM 114;[20] and the Charlemagne romance of the *Sowdone of Babylone* (*SB*; composed after 1400), though not connected in manuscript to *Piers Plowman*, presents the most direct link of all between Langland's poem and a vernacular romance. It would seem to derive its lines 963–68, quoted with additional context below, from the first line of Langland's Prologue and lines 365–68 of Passus 11, the latter coming from Kynde's nature idyll, which follows, interestingly enough, very soon after Trajan's discourse on non-Christian salvation.[21]

> In the semely seson of the yere,
> Of softenesse of the sonne,
> In the prymsauns of grene vere,
> Whan floures spryngyn and bygynne,
> And alle the floures in the frith
> Freshly shews here kynde,
> Than it is semely therwyth,
> That manhode be in mynde;
> For corage wole a man to kith,
> If he of menske haue mynde,
> And of loue to lystyn and lithe,
> And to seke honur for þat ende
> For he was neuere gode werryour,
> That cowde not loue a-ryght;
> For loue hath made many a conquerour
> And many a worthy knighte.
> This worthy Sowdan, though he heþen wer,
> He was a worthy conquerour....[22]

---

[19] O'Molesky, *Re-contextualizing*, 49.

[20] See Ralph Hanna, "The Scribe of Huntington HM 114," *Studies in Bibilography* 42 (1989): 120–33. This scribe is also responsible for the copy of *SJ* found in Lambeth 491—yet another correspondence between *SJ* and the later versions of *Piers Plowman*.

[21] *SB* also appears to borrow from Chaucer. For details, see H. M. Smyser, "Charlemagne Legends" in Severs, ed., *Manual*, 82–84.

[22] Emil Hausknecht, ed., *The Romance of the Sowdone of Babylone and of Ferumbras His Sone Who Conquerede Rome*, Early English Text Society, Extra Series no. 38 (London: Trübner, 1881), ll. 963–80.

This passage values the Sultan not only as a worthy warrior but also as someone capable of love; indeed, his capacity for love admits him to the category of all "gode werryoure[s]," Christian or non-Christian. Though there can be no guarantee that this borrowing was done with any thought beyond a taste for the superficial and modish, *Piers Plowman* seems a curiously arcane place from which to cull such material, unless there was something about *SB* which invited recourse to *Piers Plowman* in the first place. Perhaps the proximity of Trajan is the key to those subsequent lines which value the Sultan's condition beyond that of mere extinguishable infidel. Perhaps the author of *SB* had the same compulsion to connect *Piers Plowman* with his Saracen as that which appears to have governed the compilation of the (misnamed) *Liber Glastoniensis*. Also known as Cambridge University Library MS Dd 1.17, this is one of the most voluminous manuscripts to contain a copy of *Piers Plowman*. It includes with its Latin contents

> British histories and chronicles...and other histories of romance 'matters'—Turpin's [chronicle] of Charlemagne, Guido della Colonna's *Historia Troiana*—several works concerning eastern travels, crusades, and geographical and religious surveys...and...works on the Saracen faith and its foundations....The book surveys the very foundations of rule in the Western kingdoms, from Troy to Britain and Charlemagne, and it looks to the east neither for wonders nor wisdom *per se*, but for its faith, government, and the prophecies and prospects of its conversion.[23]

Perhaps little more can be made of the *Piers* borrowings in *SB* than to suggest they may represent a *Liber-Glastoniensian* response to Langland writ very small. For that matter, it is wise to note Anne Hudson's observation about *Piers Plowman*'s companion texts in manuscript: "The most that can be perceived by way of identifying mode amongst the other items [found in *Piers* manuscripts] is an interest in pseudo-historical romance—works such as *The Wars of Alexander*, the *Siege of Jerusalem*, *Kyng Alisaunder*, *The Sege or Batayle of Troy*....But this may tell us more about the relative popularity of these other works than about the medieval understanding of Langland's poem."[24]

"Relative popularity" is indeed a powerful counter-argument that threatens the ruin of the present study. Nevertheless, one or two more fragments may be shored against the ruin. In this capacity, the case of the *Awntyrs off Arthure*—copied in one of its four manuscripts by a *Piers Plowman* scribe—is especially interesting. Whoever produced the *Awntyrs* could well have been reading Langland. If that were the case, then the poem was influenced by that aspect of Langland's method that David

---

23 Middleton, "Audience and Public," 106.
24 Anne Hudson, "Epilogue: The Legacy of *Piers Plowman*," in John A. Alford, ed., *A Companion to "Piers Plowman"* (Berkeley and Los Angeles: University of California Press, 1988), 251–66; 253.

Lawton calls "a ceaseless questioning of received ideology."[25] For instance, within the first of the poem's two main episodes the ghost of Guenevere's mother begins to speak to Guenevere and Gawain with the implicit authority of a spirit that endures the pains of Purgatory or Hell; and yet, in spite of such apparent authority, she goes on to misidentify the Corporal Acts of Mercy as the "giftes of the Holy Goste."[26] The misidentification is common to all four manuscripts of the poem, suggesting that it is no mere scribal error; and it is compounded when the ghost continues speaking, only to report an incomplete list of the Acts. To recall Anne Middleton's characterization of *Piers Plowman*, the impression is less one of a failure of authority than of a "resemblance to familiar instructive, factual, authoritative kinds of...discourse" that "depends on the evasion or deferral of instrumental claims."[27] Indeed, it is not clear whether the ghost's request for the singing of trentals (11. 218–221)—a request modeled on the popular *Trental of St. Gregory*—is successful in relieving her from purgatory. All we are told is that Guenevere extra-dutifully orders "a mylion of masses" to be sung (1.706).

The correspondence here between the *Awntyrs* and *Piers Plowman* in their skeptical reception of respective streams of Gregorian legend is compelling.[28] In *Piers Plowman* Trajan claims, in a pointed rejection of the tradition that Gregory the Great redeemed him through prayer, that he was in fact saved "withouten syngynge of masses" (11.150). There are other such fault lines drawn throughout the *Awntyrs*,[29] all of which contribute to a mercurial allusiveness that Helen Phillips has characterized very well—and it is remarkable how much of her account, barring the names of certain sources, could be read as an account of *Piers Plowman*:

> [The poem's] complexity arises from its multiple affinities: [sources such as] the *St. Gregory's Trental* stories, *Summer Sunday*, *Three Dead Kings* and the alliterative *Morte Arthure* all provide contexts in which it can usefully be read. The structure does not offer us simply two discrete sections which can be labeled secular or spiritual according to their subject matter, but a curious network of repetitions, recurrent patterns and episodes which become frames for other episodes, through which the secular becomes a context for the spiritual and the spiritual for the secular, and in which the same motifs and patterns—

---

[25] David Lawton, "The Subject of *Piers Plowman*," *Yearbook of Langland Studies* 1 (1987): 1–30; 15.

[26] *The Awntyrs off Arthure at the Terne Wathelyne*, l. 254, in Shepherd, ed., *Middle English Romances*. All references to *Awntyrs* are to this edition.

[27] Middleton, "Audience," 121.

[28] A good introduction to the traditions that held Gregory capable of redeeming tormented souls is Gordon Whatley, "The Uses of Hagiography: The Legend of Pope Gregory and the Emperor Trajan in the Middle Ages," *Viator* 15 (1984): 25–63 (n.b. 27, n. 7 on early analogues to the *Trental of St. Gregory*). On distinctions between the "Trajan" and "Trental" streams of Gregorian legend, see James Root Hulbert, "The Sources of *St. Erkenwald* and *The Trental of Gregory*," *Modern Philology* 16 (1919): 149–157.

[29] See the commentary in Shepherd, *Middle English Romances*, 365–69.

for example, of lordship, of shrieks for help, of high and low—recur in both secular and spiritual form....[30]

To be sure, the ghost of the *Awntyrs* is not a "virtuous pagan," and yet, as a contrite yet infernal harbinger of wisdom—however jumbled—she does share in that unsettling displacement from the certainties of Christian lore also manifest in valued figures like Trajan, Josephus, or *SB*'s "worthy Sowdan."

Just how well the "virtuous pagan" model derived from the romances considered above accounts for Langland's reading of vernacular romance remains to be seen. The method for deriving the model, it must be remembered, is largely arbitrary, its definition rather broad, its evidence at best suggestive. Yet, however tenuous, it is a start. The challenge now will be to identify romances or their sources and analogues which either antedate or are contemporary with Langland and that present virtuous pagans—or otherwise worthy figures displaced from Christian orthodoxy—who are involved in circumstances reminiscent of any of those presented in Langland's poem. A re-reading of one passage in *Piers Plowman* suggests that the model might just possess some degree of viability. In Passus 12 Ymaginatif lectures Will on the salvific advantage of learning:

> ...he that knoweth clergie kan sonner arise
> Out of synne and be saaf, though he synne ofte,
> If hym liketh and lest, than any lewed, leelly.
> (12.171–73).

Ymaginatif presents the example of the thief who, though not steeped in Christ's teaching, yielded to Christ on Good Friday and was saved; but who, nevertheless, received a relatively low station in heaven: "Ac though that theef hadde hevene, he hadde noon heigh blisse, / As Seint Johan and othere seintes that asserved hadde bettre" (B12.195–96). Immediately following Ymaginatif's example are eight lines that extend it through graphic analogy:

> Right as som man yeve me mete and sette me amydde the floore:
> I have mete moore than ynough, ac noght so muche worshipe
> As tho that sitten at the syde table or with the sovereynes of the halle,
> But sete as a beggere bordlees by myself on the grounde.
> So it fareth by that felon that a Good Friday was saved:
> He sit neither with Seint Johan, ne Symond ne Jude,
> Ne with maydenes ne with martires ne [mid] confessoures ne wydewes,
> But by hymself as a soleyn, and served on the erthe.
> (B12.197–204)

---

[30] Helen Phillips, "The *Awntyrs off Arthur*: Structure and Meaning, A Reassessment," in James P. Carley and Felicity Riddy, eds., *Arthurian Literature* XII (Woodbridge, Suffolk: D. S. Brewer, 1993), 63–89; 87–88.

One editor notes that the scriptural basis for the well established doctrine that there are degrees of bliss in heaven is John 14:2 ("In my Father's house are many mansions"),[31] but he and other editors do not comment directly on Ymaginatif's choice of the potentially allusive "beggere bordlees." The analogy could well derive from an episode in the very popular *Pseudo-Turpin Chronicle*, composed in the mid-twelfth century. The *Pseudo-Turpin* (*Ps-T*) claims to chronicle Charlemagne's expeditions against the Saracens in Spain, culminating in the great ambush of his rearguard at Roncevaux and the deaths of Roland and Oliver. As well as detailing Charlemagne's military activities, it contains a number of *exempla* and other moralizing passages and also gives an account of Charlemagne's last days; nevertheless, martial interest predominates and the text easily crosses into the realm of romance. The early fourteenth-century Middle English romances of *Roland and Vernagu* and *Otuel and Roland* are essentially versified renderings of the *Ps-T*;[32] it also appears as the third book of Caxton's late prose romance *Charles the Grete*.[33] Interestingly—perhaps significantly—a Latin *Ps-T* is, as noted above, one of *Piers Plowman*'s companions in Cambridge MS Dd 1.17.

The particular *Ps-T* episode in question was evidently quite popular in fourteenth-century England and would easily have been accessible to Langland through a variety of indirect sources of the kind listed by Alford: it is retold in Higden's *Polychronicon*; it is cited by John Bromyard (d. c.1352) in his popular *Summa Predicantium*;[34] and it is used in two sermons by Thomas Brinton, one of which probably dates from July 17, 1377, the day after the coronation of Richard II.[35] (This was a year after Brinton's sermon on the occasion of the Good Parliament, in which he relates the anecdote of the Rat Parliament, which has in turn been used to date the allusion in the Prologue of Langland's B-Text). Here is the episode as translated by Trevisa:

---

[31] Derek Pearsall, ed., *Piers Plowman: An Edition of the C-Text* (Berkeley and Los Angeles: University of California Press, 1978), 241, note to 14.135. The parables of Luke 14:7–24 could provide another scriptural basis for the passage.

[32] See R. N. Walpole, "Charlemagne and Roland: A Study of the Source of Two Middle English Metrical Romances, *Roland and Vernagu* and *Otuel and Roland*," *University of California Publications in Modern Philology* 21 (1944): 385–452.

[33] William Caxton, *The Lyf of the Noble and Crysten Prynce, Charles the Grete*, ed. Sydney J. H. Herrtage, Early English Text Society, Extra Series nos. 36, 37 (London: Tr̩bner, 1880, 1881). The portion dervied from the *Ps-T* extends from 201, l.16 to 249, l.13.

[34] There is no modern edition of the *Summa Predicantium*. The edition consulted for the present essay was produced in Venice in 1586. In any edition, the *Ps-T* episode should be found under Bromyard's entry for *Eleemosyna*, at the paragraph beginning "*Quod etiam de hoc scandalizentur, patet ex gestis Karoli magni....*"

[35] See Sister Mary Aquinas Devlin, *The Sermons of Thomas Brinton, Bishop of Rochester (1373–1389)*, 2 vols. Camden Third Series, vols. 85, 86 (London: Offices of the Royal Historical Society, 1954) I, 196 (Sermon 44; probably July 17, 1377); II, 351 (Sermon 77).

De Libro Turpini. In a day whan trewes was i-graunted [in] eiþer side, Aigolandus, a strong prince of Spayne, com to Charles to be i-cristned, and sigh al þat were at þe bord realliche i-cloþed and likyngliche i-fedde, and sigh after þrittene pore men sitte on þe grounde and have foule mete and symple wiþ oute eny bord, and he axede what þey were. Me answerde hym and seide: 'þese þrittene beeþ Goddes messangers, and prayeþ for us, and bringeþ to us mynde of þe nombre of Cristes disciples.' 'As I see,' quod Aigolandus, 'ȝoure lawe is nouȝt riȝtful þat suffreþ Goddes messangers be þus evel bylad; he serveþ evel his lord þat so fongeþ his servauntes;' and so he was lewedliche offended, and despised cristenynge, and wente hoom aȝen; but Charles worschipped afterward pore men þe more.[36]

The concluding lesson of the episode as found in the *Ps-T* proper is a little stronger, finding that all true Christians must help the poor, that they must do the "proper works of baptism," and that faith without works is like a body without a soul. In using the story to recommend better treatment of the poor, Brinton and Higden are consistent with the *Ps-T*. Brinton adds that the story demonstrates how "daily even the Saracens are scandalized because those poor whom we call the servants of Christ we treat so unmercifully and dishonourably."[37] If we assume that this story in one of its manifestations is Langland's source then Langland has clearly changed it from a lesson on the proper treatment of the dispossessed that had been thrown into strong relief by the patently righteous vision of a heathen, into a lesson on the relative merit in salvation. But if it was still intended to act with Langland's characteristic manifold allusiveness, perhaps the force of the *original* lesson is also meant to be recollected. It is intriguing that Langland still has Trajan on his mind at this point. Ymaginatif says of the thief who was saved that he dwells as shallowly in heaven as Trajan dwelt in hell (12.209–211). A little later Ymaginatif suggests that Trajan himself now occupies a low position in heaven (the Latin is a quotation of 1 Peter 4:18):

> ..."*Salvabitur vix iustus in die iudicii*;
> *Ergo— salvabitur!*" quod he, and seide no moore Latyn.
> "Troianus was a trewe knyght and took nevere Cristendom,
> And he is saaf, so seith the book, and his soule in hevene."
> (B12. 278–281)

It does not pay to dwell on this evidence as the source cannot be proved; but it is not inconceivable that Langland would have wished with his lines about the "beggere bordlees" allusively to reinforce not just the view that there are ranks of salvation, but also that the (lower) ranks can admit those

---

36 *Polychronicon Ranulphi Higden Monachi Cestrensis*, ed. C. Babington and R. Lumby, Rolls Series 41, 9 vols. (London: Longman, Green, 1865–86), VI, 251–53. Higden's Latin text is printed on facing pages. Subsequent references to the *Polychronicon* are to this edition.
37 Translated from Devlin, *Sermons*, Sermon 44, 196.

worthies that this world's Christian tradition—but not God—would mistakenly exclude.[38]

The true viability of the model can only be confirmed through its application to further passages in *Piers Plowman* and through its drawing on further likely romance contexts. In the former case, inclusiveness is to be encouraged; passages already familiar from their adaptation of accidental romance elements warrant re-examination. For instance, a return to the Longeus episode of Passus 18 with the model in mind draws out not just the romance convention of the "disguised duel" but also the type of the worthy heathen warrior whose severe aggression against Christianity fails and who, in his failure, willfully converts to gain the true victory of salvation. Fierabras—the Sultan of Babylon's son—is a prominent example of the type. Notorious in Christendom for his conquest of Rome, he challenges Oliver (who has recently been wounded in the side) to single combat. Despite his wounds, Oliver prevails over Fierabras, compelling him to convert: "Hoo, Olyvere, I yelde me to the, / And here I become thy man /.... Baptised nowe wole I be" (*SB* 1353–59).[39] And if there is any definitive recommendation to be made from the foregoing study, it is to look more closely at the relation—be it a debt on Langland's part in sourcing or the mark of Langland's influence—between *Piers Plowman* and "Saracen" romances, most obviously the Charlemagne romances, but also texts incorporating sympathetic non-Christians such as *The King of Tars*, *Bevis of Hampton*, or the *Troy*- and *Alexander*- romances.

In the case of examining further likely romance contexts, it cannot be emphasized enough that such contexts will inevitably draw within their purview a spectrum of genres in related source/analogue material—and also in manuscript companion-texts. A case in point is *Piers Plowman*'s most common manuscript companion, *Mandeville's Travels* (composed mid-fourteenth century). One of the more remarkable features of this imaginative travelogue is its willingness "to assert the moral successes of the virtuous heathen while containing them within a larger Christian context."[40] Naturally, this correspondence moves the search away from romance *per*

---

[38] It is worth noting at this point that Trevisa offers his own interpretation of the *Ps-T* episode in his 1387 Translation of Higden. His interpretation, though comparatively superficial, does suggest that he may have had Langland's analogous passage in mind. Trevisa asserts:

> Aigolandus was a lewed goost, and lewedliche i-meved as þe devel hym tauȝte, and blende hym þat he kouþe nouȝt I-knowe þat men schulde be i-served as here astaat axeþ.
> (*Polychronicon*, VI, 251).

It is also worth noting that Trajan recommends love of the poor and the pursuit of poverty at length in his speech (11.179–99, 230–95).

[39] Three Fierabras verse romances—all translated from French originals—survive in Middle English; one is *The Sowdone of Babylone*, the other two are the "Fillingham" *Firumbras* (c. 1375–1400) and the "Ashmole" *Sir Ferumbras* (C. 1380). For details, see Severs, *Manual*, 82–87.

[40] Frank Grady, "*Machomete* and *Mandeville's Travels*," in John Victor Tolan, ed., *Medieval Christian Perceptions of Islam* (New York: Garland, 1996), 271–288; 278.

se, but of necessity it invokes just the kind of associative *tour detour* that Langland himself used and would approve in his readership. With this in mind we will do well to see the definition of "Langland's Romances" as dynamic and trans-contextual, opening up any number of the regions of literary excursion through which Langland requires us to pass in order to receive his poem in all its meaningful exigence.

The Langland Myth

C. David Benson

In a "Note on the Author" that begins his popular 1995 Everyman edition of *Piers Plowman*, A.V.C. Schmidt expresses an understanding about the poet's life and the composition of his poem that, in general terms, appears to be accepted by most (though certainly not all) Langlandians today: "William Langland lived from c.1330 to c.1386. He was born near Malvern, in Worcestershire, and educated for a career in the Church, but appears to have married and never proceeded beyond minor orders. Little is known about his life apart from what can be learnt from the work on which he spent the years from 1360 or earlier to the time of his death, earning his living as a psalter-clerk in London, mainly, and possibly returning to the West Country in his last years. His great alliterative poem *Piers Plowman* exists in three versions, A, B and C."[1]

There is nothing new about this account of poet and poem, for all its essential claims were made more than a century ago by the first modern editor of *Piers*, the great Walter W. Skeat.[2] Derek Pearsall has declared that

---

[1] All references from *Piers Plowman* are from A.V.C. Schmidt, ed., *The Vision of Piers Plowman*, 2nd ed. (London: Everyman, 1995), vii. Subsequent citations shall appear parenthetically, with an indication of version (i.e., B.5.10). Schmidt goes on to suggest the possibility of an earlier Z-version, first proposed by A. G. Rigg and Charlotte Brewer in their *Piers Plowman: The Z Version* (Toronto: Pontifical Institute of Medieval Studies, 1983) in his *Piers Plowman: A Parallel Text Edition* (London: Longman, 1995), vii.

[2] Skeat's views were most influentially stated in his two-volume parallel-text edition *The Vision of Piers the Plowman in Three Parallel Texts* (Oxford: Oxford University Press, 1886), 2: xxxii–vii. See also his article on the poem in the *Encyclopedia Britannica*, 9th ed. (New York: Scribners, 1882), 14: 285–6. The argument of this essay is that Skeat's biography of Langland has been generally accepted by scholars for more than a century, though some of its details (such as the poet's birth in Cleobury Mortimer, Shropshire) have dropped away. In writing about the history of the Langland myth, I am following the pioneering work of John Bowers ("*Piers Plowman*'s William Langland: Editing the Text, Writing the Author's Life," *Yearbook of Langland Studies* 9 [1995]: 65–90) and Charlotte Brewer (*Editing Piers Plowman* [Cambridge: Cambridge University Press, 1996]).

Skeat's work on *Piers Plowman* marks "the end of the 'myth' of the poem, and the beginning of a more accurate historical appraisal of it."[3] Skeat's monumental labors did sweep away many previous fancies about *Piers*, but in the process he established a new and more persistent myth, or, more accurately, two closely related and interdependent myths: the myth of the poet's life (including Malvern, marriage, a marginal clerical life in London, and final return to the West country), which explains and is explained by the myth of the poem (Langland obsessively rewriting his single work to get it right and producing at least three separate versions). By using the term *myth* for these ideas about poet and poem, I do not mean to dismiss what so many have for so long believed. Myths are often good things and can be very productive—they may even be true. The Langland myth has inspired sophisticated editing and powerful critical interpretations, yet its very success has tended to obscure the awkward fact that the myth is based on very little solid evidence. More importantly, it has blocked other potentially fruitful approaches to *Piers Plowman*.

Skeat's myth, created in the mid-nineteenth century, was a major achievement that satisfied a real need. Previous accounts of the author had offered not much more than a personal name and local habitation, about which there was much dispute. Editors and commentators on *Piers* could not even agree on what to call the author ("Robert" as well as "William" Langland were proposed, the former long the most popular, not to mention others such as "John Malvern"). In the century before Skeat, there was growing acknowledgement that the many manuscripts of *Piers* contained radically different versions of the work, but there was no consensus about their number or order.[4] Into this confusion about poet and poem, Skeat brought clarity, common sense, and a strong imagination, with results that continue to make him one of the most influential scholars of *Piers Plowman* today.

---

[3] Derek Pearsall, *An Annotated Critical Bibliography of Langland* (Ann Arbor: University of Michigan Press, 1990), 218.

[4] In the prefatory note to his first edition of *Piers*, *The Vision of Pierce Plowman, now firste imprynted* (London, 1550), Robert Crowley begins the tradition of publicly naming the poet as Robert Langland, information apparently from the circle of John Bale [see R. W. Chambers, "Robert or William Longland," *London Mediæval Studies* 1 (1939): 430–62]. The poem was also attributed to others, including John Lydgate, of all people [see Vincent DiMarco, "Eighteenth-Century Suspicions Regarding the Authorship of *Piers Plowman*," *Anglia* 100 (1982): 124–29]. A sixteenth-century tradition begun by John Stow and accepted by such as Anthony Wood identifies the author as John Malvern, a fellow of Oriel College [see DiMarco, esp. 9, 16 and A. S. G. Edwards, "*Piers Plowman* in the Seventeeth Century: Gerard Langbaine's Notes," *Yearbook of Langland Studies* 6 (1992): 141–44].

The first published statement that *Piers* had been revised is by Joseph Ritson in 1802 and Richard Price first publicly announced a third version in 1824, though as early as 1725 Thomas Hearne seems to have been the first to suspect a revision of the poem, thoughts he confined to his journal. Ritson himself had apparently earlier made a private note of the possibility of the third version. For all this, see DiMarco (above), and the relevant citations in his magisterial bibliography [*Piers Plowman: A Reference Guide* (Boston: G.K. Hall, 1982)].

Skeat was the first to offer anything like a systematic life of Langland, which he constructed not from outside historical sources (they were and remain virtually non-existent), but from stitching together the scattered comments about the dreamer/narrator found within the various versions of *Piers*, especially a unique passage in the C version about the dreamer's life on Cornhill.[5] Not that Skeat ignored documentary evidence when it was available. He was the first to recognize the importance of an early fifteenth-century memorandum in a Dublin manuscript of the C-Text: the only near-contemporary record that provides a name for the author of *Piers Plowman* (William Langland) and suggests a social identity by describing his father as holding land under the Despensers (though it says nothing more about the poet himself).[6] Given the paucity of such external information, Skeat's bold innovation was to construct a life of the poet by turning to the poem itself, which he described early in his editing project as "a true *autobiography* in the highest sense of the word."[7] With the self-confidence that marked all his work, Skeat insisted that "the internal evidence of his poem really reveals much more [than the external evidence], quite enough, in fact, to give us a clear conception of [Langland]."[8] The great appeal of this new biographical narrative caused many to overlook what will become customary with later versions of the Langland myth—the tendency to beg central questions. Here the question is whether the poet of *Piers Plowman* actually intends to portray himself through the figure of the dreamer. The two previous nineteenth-century editors of *Piers*, Thomas Whitaker and Thomas Wright, thought not, but Skeat, although he was the first to make such a case, regarded the self-portrait as so obvious that it did not require proof.[9]

In addition to the poet's life, Skeat also invented the related myth of the poem. He argued that *Piers* was written and rewritten over the course of the poet's life and first established the traditional sequence of these versions, which he labeled and put into chronological order as A, B, and C.[10]

---

[5] In the prefatory note to his 1550 edition, Crowley had only minimal biographical information about the poet: "The Autour was named Roberte langlande, a Shropshire man borne in Cleybirie, about viii myles from maluerne hilles."

[6] Langland is identified as the son of Stacy (or Eustace) de Rokayle. For transcription of this memorandum, see George Kane, *Piers Plowman: The Evidence for Authorship* (London: Athlone Press, 1965), 26, and Ralph Hanna III, *William Langland* (Aldershot: Variorum, 1993), 26. It was dismissed in Wright's edition of *Piers* earlier in the century: "I do not think this memorandum ought to be considered as overthrowing the old tradition relating to Roberte Longlande" (Thomas Wright, ed., *The Vision and Creed of Piers Ploughman*, 2nd ed., 2 vols., [1855; repr. London: Reeves and Turner, 1887]), ixn.

[7] Skeat, *Piers Plowman*, EETS OS 28 (London: Trübner, 1873), A-Text, xxxviii, his emphasis.

[8] Skeat, "Section VIII," in Thomas Warton, *History of English Poetry*, ed. W. Carew Hazlitt, 4 vols., (London: Reeves and Turner, 1871), 245.

[9] John Bowers, *The Crisis of Will in Piers Plowman* (Washington, D.C.: Catholic University of America Press, 1986), 166.

[10] The A, B, C order is already assumed without proof in Skeat's mind in his earliest publication on *Piers, Parallel Extracts from Forty-Five Manuscripts of Piers Plowman*, EETS OS 17 (London: Trübner, 1866), 1.

The two myths were clearly intertwined in Skeat's mind as they would be for later scholars, for he described the poet and his poem as growing and declining together like the Sphinx's three ages of man. The first shape of *Piers* is the youthful A version, "written with great rapidity and vigour;" the second is the mature B version, expanded by Langland's greater learning and experience of London and providing the best example of the poet's "peculiar powers;" and the last is the feebler C version in which "there is a tendency to diffuseness and to a love for theological subtleties."[11] Skeat's fullest justification for the order of composition he proposed is casual to the point of breeziness: "Now, when we proceed to place the *three* texts side by side, it is at once apparent that the B-Text is *intermediate* in form between the other two; so that the order of texts must either be A, B, C or C, B, A; but the A-Text so evidently comes *first*, that the C-Text can only come *last*; and this settles the question."[12] In the best British empirical (not to say imperial) tradition, the true shape of the poet's text, like the truth of his life, is not really difficult to discern because (from the right perspective at least) it is so apparent and evident. To achieve such a settled conclusion, however, important questions again have to be begged, including whether the different versions of *Piers* are indeed successive authorial drafts that express his views at different stages of his life.

Skeat's Langland myth was a brilliant and imaginative achievement, though it convinced more because of the coherence and sweep of its invention than because it is based on demonstable evidence. The shape that the myth assumed was not inevitable but was clearly influenced by the era during which it was first constructed. As a Victorian, Skeat echoes earlier Romantic conceptions of the poet of *Piers* as a rural Wordsworthian bard come to the city to tell home truths and combines it with a newer Tennysonian idea of public poetry that stresses Langland's political views.[13] By producing the first complete life of Langland, Skeat rescued the poet from the obscurity of an anonymous medieval bard so that he might take his place with Chaucer and other named canonical authors. With his own chapter in the Lives of the Poets, Langland was able to earn a substantial entry in that massive contemporary project, the *Dictionary of National Biography*. Other nineteenth-century forces may be detected in the Langland myth. The claim that the poem evolved from a short, simple A version through the more complex B and C versions seems clearly Darwinian.[14] Even the influence of Freud can be detected. Skeat's interest

---

[11] Skeat, "Section VIII" in Warton, 245-47.

[12] Skeat, *Piers Plowman*, *C-Text*, EETS OS 54 (London: Trübner, 1873), xiv (his emphasis).

[13] For Whittaker's earlier Wordsworthian conception of the poet see Bowers, "Editing," 70–72; Bowers also notes how Skeat's portrait of Langland's life corresponded to the editor's own standards for Victorian industriousness.

[14] Bowers, "Editing," 82–83.

in the poet's life was quickly developed in the first book-length study of the poem by J.J. Jusserand using new Continental ideas about human psychology (Jusserand was French after all): he diagnosed Langland's problem as a disease of the will that made him unable to act.[15]

Skeat's myth probably reveals its Victorian origin most clearly in its confidence and practicality. Although it was once believed that better editions of *Piers Plowman* would solve the authorship question, we have come to understand that the editing of *Piers Plowman* can only proceed *after* a determination has already been made about who wrote it (a myth of the poet) and of the number and order of its versions (a myth of the poem).[16] Like many another contemporary British explorer into strange territory, Skeat did what he had to do to get where he wanted to go, without worrying too much about the precedents he was setting or the consequences that would follow. His intertwined account of poet and poem are enabling myths that allowed him to get on with the job at hand. Absolute proof of these myths was as irrelevant as it was impossible. In a great English tradition, Skeat becomes a textual theorist on instinct.

The most intriguing thing about the Langland myth is that concepts that were so much of their time and so utilitarian should have proved so persistent. Skeat himself, though the inventor, always retained a certain skepticism.[17] Thus for a long time he was attracted to the possibility that the poet's surname might have been "Langley" (it appears as an alternative name on the title page of his student's text of the *visio* and was still there in a 1968 reprinting of the 10th edition), and he notes that in the manuscripts the poem existed in up to ten forms, rather than just three, though not all of them authorial.[18] It is those after Skeat who take his enabling myth as dogma.

Not of course that the myth has been central to all writing about *Piers Plowman*: it plays little part in the wonderful books by Mary Carruthers

---

[15] J.J. Jusserand, *Piers Plowman*, rev. ed. (London: Unwin, 1894).

[16] E. Talbot Donaldson admitted that he and Kane found themselves unable to proceed with their edition of the B-Text "until we had committed ourselves to a position of authorship" (*"Piers Plowman*: Textual Comparison and the Question of Authority," in Arno Esch, ed., *Chaucer un Seine Zeit* (Tübingen: Nuemeyer, 1968), 241–247; here, 241).

[17] Skeat himself often makes clear that his myths are speculative and provisional. An obituary notice by A. J. Wyatt noted that Skeat's "judgment did not appear to be founded upon great principles; he was apt to reverse a decision" [see Arthur Sherbo, "William Walter Skeat (1835–1912) in the *Cambridge Review*," *Yearbook of Langland Studies* 3 (1989): 109–130; 112]. In his first version of the Langland biography in his edition of the A-Text, Skeat uses such phrases as "the balance of evidence," and "the probability" (*A-Text*, xxxvi). The fuller formulation of 1871 is still cautious: "we may now piece together the following account of him, which is probably true, and, at any rate, rests chiefly upon his own statements" (Warton, *History*, 247). Although he believed that the poet's given name was William, he is careful not to claim too much even in his parallel-text edition: "The author's Christian, or at any rate his assumed Christian, name, was William" (2: xxvii).

For early objections to Skeat's biography see A. S. Jack, "The Autobiographical Elements in *Piers the Plowman*," *Journal of English and Germanic Philology* 3 (1901): 393–414.

[18] Skeat, parallel-text edition, 2: xxii–xxiii.

and Elizabeth Kirk (though Kirk does assume that B is a later revision of A), for example, and, to choose a prominent recent example, in the work of Wendy Scase.[19] Nevertheless, the myths of poem and poet have underlain most scholarly belief among Langlandians, all the more influential for so often being assumed rather than argued.

Until very recently there was virtually no dissent from the textual side of the myth: the belief that *Piers* exists in three and only three versions composed in the sequence A, B, C (the most prominent exception was Meroney, who was not very influential).[20] The related myth of the poet, however, was strongly challenged by John Manly at the beginning of this century, first in a short article and then in a long essay in the *Cambridge History of English Literature*.[21] His sensational claim that *Piers* was written by five different authors began a spirited debate, though neither he nor his followers ever supplied the definitive proof he always claimed to have ready at hand. In fact, although the debate sputtered on for decades, the most lasting effect of Manly's heresy was to inspire renewed devotion to the Langland myth. The first to defend it was Jusserand, who, in contrast to Skeat's more pragmatic approach, used the language of religious apologetics (which we shall see again) to urge his readers to be "skeptical about such skepticism."[22] He insisted that we are justified "in adhering to our former faith"[23] of a single poet whose narrator is autobiographical "so long as no positive text or fact contradicts the plain statements in the poem."[24] The myth is a question of belief and of innocent until proved guilty.

The most persistent and effective supporter of the myth of the poet during the debate with Manly and his supporters was the estimable R.W. Chambers, who is a link between Skeat and the later Athlone general editor, George Kane.[25] Chambers's most important contribution to the biographical myth, which was later developed by Kane, was to show that in medieval allegorical visions the narrator is usually meant to represent the poet in some way.[26] Conceding that everything we learn about the *Piers*

[19] Mary Carruthers, *The Search for St. Truth: A Study of Meaning in Piers Plowman* (Evanston: Northwestern University Press, 1973); Elizabeth Kirk, *The Dream Thought of Piers Plowman* (New Haven: Yale University Press, 1972); Wendy Scase, *Piers Plowman and the New Anticlericalism* (Cambridge: Cambridge University Press, 1989).

[20] Howard Meroney, "The Life and Death of Long Wille," *English Literary History* 17 (1950): 1–35.

[21] John M. Manly, "The Lost Leaf of *Piers the Plowman*," *Modern Philology* 3 (1906): 359–366; "*Piers the Plowman* and Its Sequence," in the *Cambridge History of English Literature*, ed. A. W. Ward and A. R. Waller, vol. 2 (Cambridge: Cambridge University Press, 1908), 1-42.

[22] J. J. Jusserand, "*Piers Plowman*: The Work of One or of Five," *Modern Philology* 6 (1909): 271–329; 327.

[23] Jusserand, "Work," 329.

[24] Jusserand, "Work," 328.

[25] Chambers was not only an able, though not uncritical, defender of Skeat's work, but he also received the older editor's blessing to revise the A-Text; see R. W. Chambers and J. H. G. Grattan, "The Text of *Piers Plowman*: Critical Methods," *Modern Language Review* 11 (1916): 257–75.

[26] See Chambers, "Robert," 439–51; "The Authorship of *Piers Plowman*," *Modern Language Review* 5 (1910): 1–32, here 30; and "The Three Texts of *Piers Plowman* and Their Grammatical Forms," *Modern Language Review* 11 (1916): 257–75, here 130–131.

narrator cannot be literal autobiography because so many details "are conventional and fictitious,"[27] Chambers is perhaps too confident that he can distinguish historical fact from literary invention.[28]

Chambers also added a powerful new narrative to the myth of poet and poem when he argued that the A version "breaks off sharply" because the dreamer/narrator Will raises challenging questions about salvation (especially of non-Christians) that Langland was himself unable to answer for many years.[29] Although Chambers's explanation for the shape of A has been widely accepted, its reasoning is hardly compelling. Are we really to believe that many contemporary readers (including the poet) would have been impressed (let alone reduced to silence) by Will's desperately pessimistic arguments at the end of A? An example of his feverish reasoning is that good deeds are irrelevant because sinners such as Mary Magdalene, King David, and Paul, who "wrou3te wykkidly in world whanne þei were" (A.11.292), now reign in heaven. Rather than serious challenges to the faith of the author of *Piers Plowman*, as Chambers claimed, these are familiar debating points with rather obvious answers, some of which are already implied in their very statement (the Magdalene, David, and Paul are, of course, not rewarded for their wickedness but for their repentance) and some of which Imaginatif provides without much difficulty in the longer B version. There is no reason to think that Langland himself ever suffered from the naive doubts expressed by the dreamer.

Chambers was so concerned to refute Manly's assertion of multiple authorship and to affirm the biographical truth of the narrator in the different versions of *Piers Plowman* that he even cautiously welcomed the most reckless attempt to discover the poet's life in the poem: Allan Bright's *New Light on Piers Plowman*.[30] Bright purported to identify real-life models even for Langland's allegorical characters: for example, Scripture is said to be based on the second wife of a neighbor with whom the poet was possibly carrying on a romance.[31] Bright also claimed to locate the very spring near Great Malvern where the poet first had his vision,[32] as well as the fair field full of folk.[33] As it turns out, almost all of the places named by Bright are on land that he himself owned near the Malvern Hills. Given the Disneyfication of our world, we might be tempted to imagine that Bright had some mad scheme to create a *Piers Plowman* theme park: Longlands! Bright is an extreme, if finally disarming because so enthusiastic, example of the results of believing that the poet describes himself in the poem,

---

27 Chambers, "Robert," 447.
28 Chambers, "Robert", 449.
29 Chambers, "Three," 133; and *Man's Unconquerable Mind* (London: Cape, 1939), 129–49.
30 Allan H. Bright, *New Light on Piers Plowman* (London: Oxford Univesity Press, 1928).
31 Bright, *New*, 61–63.
32 Bright, *New*, 50.
33 Bright, *New*, 51ff.

though he resembles more sober adherents of the Langland myth in a tendency to assert rather than prove his central claims.

The Langland myth has fueled the work of scholars far more brilliant than Bright. For example, the composition of three separate texts in a particular sequence by the same poet has been fundamental to the Athlone project, the most ambitious and influential edition of *Piers Plowman* since Skeat's. Not that everything in the myth was accepted by the Athlone editors or even that they have always agreed among themselves. George Kane, the general editor, passionately defended the single authorship of *Piers* even as he denied the possibility of a Langland biography—the sort of biography whose most popular modern formulation was by his co-editor Talbot Donaldson.[34] In his persuasive essay "The Autobiographical Fallacy in Chaucer and Langland Studies," Kane acknowledges the irrepressible desire of readers to discover the personalities of both poets in their poems, but argues that the results are "attained by inferences both logically dubious in themselves, and unauthorized by the literary history of the fourteenth century."[35] This "free biographical inference" has within itself "no element to control its accuracy, and therefore no means by which its logical necessity or even its probability can be checked."[36] The accounts of Langland's life thus produced may seem "wise, perceptive, full of insight," but they remain "unverifiable": "We can then, as things are, have no biography of Langland, only speculative 'lives,' without historical necessity."[37] Yet despite his dismissal of Skeat's traditional biography, Kane does not abolish the myth of the poet so much as refine and aestheticize it.[38] The poet, if not his biography, remains central to Kane's editing and criticism—as the creator of all three versions, as a developing literary character within these poems, and, most sublimely, as the poet of genius whose writing transcends the particularities of history and psychological struggle to achieve an artistic completeness far above the defacements of his scribes and readers.[39]

---

[34] E. Talbot Donaldson, *The C-Text and Its Poet*, (1949, repr. London: Frank Cass, 1966), 199–26.

[35] George Kane, "The Autobiographical Fallacy in Chaucer and Langland Studies," Chambers Memorial Lecture (London: H. K. Lewis, 1965), repr. Kane, *Chaucer and Langland* (Berkeley, CA: University of California Press, 1989), 1–14; 2.

[36] Kane, "Autobiographical," 5–6.

[37] Kane, "Autobiographical," 6 and 14.

[38] In the same year as his essay "Autobiographical Fallacy," Kane published his *Piers Plowman: The Evidence for Authorship* (London: Athlone, 1965), which marks the effective end of any widespread belief in multiple authorship. But despite Kane's initial promise to produce an "unambiguous answer" and a "single truth" (1), his conclusions are actually heavily nuanced and, as John Bowers has noted, remarkably modest: one poet named William Langland wrote all versions of the poem whose title was *Piers Plowman* (Bowers, "Editing," 75). Although most of Kane's effort goes toward establishing the name of the author, that name does not appear on the title pages of the Athlone edition.

[39] See Lee Patterson, "The Logic of Textual Criticism and the Way of Genius: The Kane-Donaldson *Piers Plowman* in Historical Perspective," in Jerome J. McGann, ed., *Textual Criticism and Literary Interpretation* (Chicago: University of Chicago Press, 1985), 55–91. Deliberately exaggerating Patterson,

The greatest influence of the Athlone edition (extending far beyond *Piers* or even Middle English literature) has been on textual theory and practice brought about by Kane and Donaldson's highly interventionist editing of the B-Text. And yet, for all their sophisticated discovery or creation of individual readings, Kane and Donaldson accepted the essence of Skeat's myth of the poem without change: *Piers* was issued in three separate versions written in a particular sequence over the course of the poet's life. Many of the textual emendations in the B-Text depend on it having been composed after A and before C.[40] Despite its importance to their editing, however, the ABC sequence is assumed rather than argued. Kane-Donaldson begin boldly (and I think correctly) by conceding that the supposed historical allusions in the different versions are "equivocal" and therefore cannot be used for dating.[41] That leaves the editors with only a subjective assertion and a theory to defend the traditional sequence: "Thus the order of composition of the three versions of *Piers Plowman*, however conceived, must both appear obvious, and be strictly hypothetical."[42]

For the obviousness, Kane-Donaldson cite Skeat's now one-hundred-year-old appeal to the self-evident quoted above, which seems quaintly dated amidst the modern textual apparatus of the Athlone edition. Nor is their theory of the ABC hypothesis much better supported. Consider the justification for believing that the A version of *Piers* was written first: "In the absence of other considerations, a natural presumption that a poem under revision will grow in content, scope and meaning, rather than diminish, must make this seem the earliest form of *Piers Plowman*."[43] Not only

---

Pearsall aptly calls this a "sublime notion" of a poem "whose words will always be discerned to be ineffably superior among the mass of scribal variants, and in a sublime notion of the editor as another unique someone who will always be able to discern them" (Derek Pearsall, "Authorial Revision in Some Late-medieval English Texts," in A. J. Minnis and Charlotte Brewer, eds., *Crux and Controversy in Middle English Textual Criticism* [Cambridge: D. S. Brewer, 1992], 43).

Kane is finally not very interested in Langland's public life, but rather in an aesthetic version of Skeat's "true" autobiography. For Skeat, that meant the poet's opinions and for Chambers, his inner moral struggles; but Kane's Langland is less personal and more literary: he can be glimpsed in the verbal icon he worked so long to edit and in the developing literary character within the text that bears his name. Both are largely free from history (see Bowers, "Editing," 75). In his "Autobiographical Fallacy" article, Kane argues that Langland's actual life has been refined into a fictional "construct," which is "both more and less than the poet" (12). Like the real author, the constructed narrator/poet has "an identity" (11) and "distinctive modes of being" (12), which grow organically over the three versions of *Piers* (11). This figure gradually acquires "temperament," "personality," and "character" as well as "the circumstances of life" (11), but he exists only in literary rather than material history like other "imaginary creations" (12).

40 Thus readings in both A and C are assumed to have originally also been in B, even if recorded in no manuscript. No consideration is given to the possibility that the poet might have changed his mind then changed it back again. "For if the texts of A and C, the earliest and latest versions of the poem, agree in reading, their agreement sets up a presumption that no revision occurred at that point" (George Kane and E. Talbot Donaldson, eds., *Piers Plowman: The B Version* [London: Athlone Press, 1975], 76).

41 Kane-Donaldson, *B Version*, 71 n3. Such topical allusions were very important for Skeat and have come to be used again by Hanna, though they are not necessarily now any more persuasive.

42 Kane-Donaldson, *B Version*, 71.

43 Kane-Donaldson, *B Version*, 71.

is a "natural presumption" not much on which to base a central hypothesis, but, as we have seen elsewhere, the central question is begged: is *Piers*, in fact, a work under revision? Kane-Donaldson conclude so without seriously examining alternatives. Moreover, what they first call a hypothesis is quickly allowed to become a certainty. They argue that because "in its major features B resembles A more than C does, and also resembles C more than A does...it occupies the medial position. This physical sequence is a fact."[44] Sequence, however, is precisely what is in doubt. The resemblances Kane-Donaldson cite would also exist if B had been the author's first version, with A and C both derived from it. If anything is a fact about the three versions of *Piers*, it is difference, not sequence. Skeat's myth has once again been taken largely on faith.[45]

We have no reason to feel superior to Kane and Donaldson, still less to Chambers or Skeat. These scholars, like more recent believers in the Langland myth, have much to tell us about *Piers Plowman*. If their work depends on unexamined assumptions, so does everything we do, including, of course, this essay. One cannot start from first principles with everything. What I am suggesting, however, is that we not allow ourselves to be restricted by the boundaries of the traditional Langland myth, but rather try to imagine new, and equally defensible, ways of approaching *Piers Plowman*: these may not necessarily tell us better things than has the myth, but they will tell us new and different things.

This is a good time to reconsider the Langland myth, for it has been coming under increasing pressure. Although supporters of the myth of the poet finally fought off the Manly challenge, Kane himself, as we have seen, doubted whether any Langland biography was really possible, even as he continued to affirm the single authorship of *Piers*. More recently and from very different perspectives, John Bowers and David Lawton have strongly questioned whether the narrator/dreamer of *Piers* is meant to represent the poet in any significant sense.[46] But it is the myth of the poem that has been particularly battered of late. A new authorial version of *Piers* to supplement the old ABC trio, the Z-Text, has been proposed by Rigg and Brewer and tentatively accepted by several prominent Langlandians. If this addition to ABC were not enough, the sequence itself has been challenged increasingly in recent years.[47]

---

[44] Kane-Donaldson, *B Version*, 72.

[45] Despite the magisterial tone of the Kane-Donaldson introduction, Donaldson in his own voice is often more playfully subversive and skeptical about such certainties. In his essay "Textual Comparison," Donaldson stresses less the ultimate truth of the editorial method of the Athlone B-Text than its bracing originality. He declares that the results of using A / C to edit B, "whatever their status in the realm of abstract historical truth, are good for intellectuation" (246). For Donaldson it is less important that others accept his edition than that it "make them think" (247).

[46] Bowers, *Crisis*; David Lawton, "The Subject of *Piers Plowman*," *Yearbook of Langland Studies* 1 (1987): 1–30.

[47] See Jill Mann, "The Power of the Alphabet: A Reassessment of the Relation between the A and B Versions of *Piers Plowman*," *Yearbook of Langland Studies* 8 (1994): 21–49; Bowers, "Editing"; and for an earlier suggestion, Anne Hudson, "The Variable Text," in Minnis and Brewer, eds., *Crux*, 49–60.

Yet despite these cracks in the facade, Skeat's myths of poem and poet are still alive and well. In whole or part they remain at least the starting point, the unexamined assumption, for most major Langland scholars, though in a formulation that may be subtle and nuanced. The new parallel-text edition of *Piers Plowman* by A.V.C. Schmidt in imitation of Skeat's pioneering work is now appearing (with the Z-Text somewhat cautiously added to A, B, and C), one of whose purposes is "to keep the evolution of the poem in the forefront of scholarly attention;"[48] and perhaps the best recent general reading of *Piers Plowman*, by James Simpson, reasserts that Langland spent at least two decades "constantly revising his single poem."[49] Despite the postmodernist privileging of texts over authors, scholars remain fascinated with what Donaldson called the poet's "curiously provocative and attractive personality"[50] and still search (so far in vain) for records about him. In a ruefully amusing section of an important article, Lawrence Clopper describes the frustration of searching for contemporary traces of the poet in a variety of likely medieval archives only to come up empty.[51]

Two studies by Ralph Hanna III and Anne Middleton demonstrate the persistence of the myths of poem and poet in very different, interesting modern works on *Piers Plowman*. Hanna's short manual is an exemplary work of bibliographical research that clearly and concisely presents what is known about the poet, his possible family, the manuscripts, and early printed editions.[52] Anne Middleton's "William Langland's 'Kynde Name,'" is a more theoretical study of the politics of self-representation in *Piers*, whose rich if sometimes elusive arguments proceed by implication, association, and pun.[53] Neither simply repeats Skeat's myth, for both have a more sophisticated sense of the theoretical issues involved, especially those pertaining to the myth of the poet. Middleton pays little attention to the actual events in the poet's life, though she does seem to assume, as Skeat had suggested, that the poet moved from the country to London as an adult.[54] Instead of a biography, Middleton concentrates on what she takes to be the poet's naming of himself at various places within the poem, his "signatures," especially in the famous line from the B-Text, which Skeat first drew attention to: "I have lyved in londe...my name is Longe Wille"

---

48 Schmidt, *Parallel*, viii.

49 James Simpson, *Piers Plowman: An Introduction to the B-Text* (London: Longman, 1990), 5.

50 Donaldson, *C-Text*, 199.

51 Lawrence Clopper, "Need Men and Women Labor: Langland's Wanderer and the Labor Ordinance," in Barbara Hanawalt, ed., *Literature in Historical Context: Chaucer's England* (Minneapolis: University of Minnesota Press, 1992), 111–114.

52 Hanna, *William Langland*.

53 Anne Middleton, "William Langland's 'Kynde Name': Authorial Signature and Social Identity in Late Fourteenth-Century England," in Lee Patterson, ed., *Literary Practice and Social Change in Britain: 1380–1530* (Berkeley: University of California Press, 1990), 15–82.

54 Middleton, "William," 55–59.

(B.15.152).[55] Hanna gives something more like the traditional biography of the poet drawn, as usual, mostly from *Piers* itself (including youth in Malvern and later married life in Cornhill as a marginalized cleric), though he is well aware of the autobiographical fallacy argued by Kane and very circumspect in his phrasing. He declares that most biographical information remains "inferential" and is accessed "only through the poet's representation of himself within his text," which results not in an actual life but in information that suggests "the parameters of a life."[56] Even though this material is subject to "scholarly contention," Hanna concludes that some of the most persistent details "may have their basis in fact."[57]

For all their differences in aim and approach from Skeat (and from one another), both Hanna and Middleton still echo the fundamental assumptions of the Langland myth: the poet's name was William Langland; he presents himself through the figure of the narrator/dreamer Will; the poem exists in three versions; and the order of composition was A, B, and C.[58] Many orthodoxies are questioned by Hanna and especially Middleton, but these are not.[59]

An example of how the myth can take on a life of its own regardless of evidence is Schmidt's suggestion, quoted at the beginning of this essay, of Langland's "possibly returning to the West Country in his last years," which Hanna echoes when he argues that the apparent origin of most C manuscripts in the Worcestershire area "support[s] the theory that Langland returned late in life to Malvern."[60] But theory is too grand a word for this echo of Shakespeare's retirement back to Stratford at the end of his life. As far as I know, the original idea and only argument for such a return by the author of *Piers* is Skeat's long discredited belief that the same poet also wrote *Richard the Redeless*, which locates itself at Bristol.[61]

Modern followers of the myth are rarely naive and sometimes frankly acknowledge the lack of solid evidence for their position. John Burrow has long accepted the biographical myth of *Piers Plowman*, but his recent *Langland's Fictions*, a study of a Christian poem by a critic who proclaims

---

[55] Skeat, *Parallel*, 2:xxxi, n2, notes the "remarkable line" and wonders, "Is this a mere chance?" As often, Skeat is more tentative than later scholars. Authorial signatures are discussed in Kane, *Evidence*, 52–70.

[56] Hanna, *William*, 6. This phrasing might almost suggest a (poor) *New Yorker* cartoon—two bored yuppies talking at a fern bar: "I don't have a life, just the parameters of a life."

[57] Hanna, *William*, 17.

[58] One way of explaining the differences between these two is that whereas Hanna works with archives and the realm of facts (though others might question the validity of some of these), Middleton wants to collapse distinctions between external and internal biographical evidence, and regards the "proof" of even a "far-fetched" claim to lie in "the quality of the readings of this poem that such a hypothesis enables" ("William," 44).

[59] For example, see Middleton: the poet of *Piers* "signs [his work] in all three of its surviving versions (the A-, B-, and C-Texts representing three successive states of composition), inscribing these signatures more fully, deeply, and indelibly in the fabric of the narrative with each version" ("William," 17).

[60] Hanna, *William*, 17.

[61] Skeat, *Parallel*, 2: lxxxiii–lxxxvi.

himself an atheist, makes it clear that the idea that Langland describes his own life in *Piers* is not something that can be objectively proved or disproved but is a matter of individual "belief" or "disbelief."[62] Burrow recognizes the subjectivity, at times verging on religious faith, that from the first has supported the biographical myth.[63]

Skeat's myth is also directly evoked at the very beginning of Steven Justice's introduction to *Written Work*, an ambitious and innovative 1997 collection of essays on *Piers Plowman*, edited by Justice and Kathryn Kerby-Fulton.[64] While admitting that the language of Skeat's assertions is no longer available to contemporary scholars and with careful qualification (or is his use of "seems" having his cake and eating it too?), Justice directly links the new work he is introducing to what Skeat first invented. First citing the great editor's declaration that *Piers Plowman* "is a true autobiography in the highest sense of the word," Justice notes that all the contributions to his volume "take as a point of departure or conclusion the single C passage [C.5.1–104] in which Langland seems explicitly to offer autobiographical detail."[65] Having identified the importance of the myth of the poet to contemporary scholars, Justice in his second paragraph invokes the myth of the poem. He insists that what Skeat "most famously said about *Piers Plowman* is that Langland wrote it three times," which he glosses as "Langland seems to have refused to create a poem separable from his continuing labor of authorship."[66] Like the aforementioned writings of Burrow, Hanna, and Middleton, the volume edited by Justice and Kerby-Fulton (which includes new essays by Hanna and Middleton) demonstrates that the Langland myth is still generating interesting work. But even as we celebrate these achievements, we ought to consider what has been excluded. The Langland myth has encouraged scholars to approach *Piers Plowman* by certain well-worn paths and thus to avoid others. I can only begin to suggest some of the roads not taken in *Piers* criticism, but I hope that these brief concluding remarks will encourage others to go much further.

Let me begin with the most widely accepted part of the Langland myth: the myth of the poem. For over a century, most Langland scholars have started from the premise that *Piers Plowman* exists in three discrete versions, although this is only uncertainly represented in the manuscript evi-

---

[62] John A. Burrow, *Langland's Fictions* (Oxford: Clarendon Press, 1993), 83–86.

[63] See also Donaldson, who cheerfully concludes that, like their opponent Manly, the Athlone editors worked under an assumption about the authorship and order of the texts that was "subjective in a high degree" ("Textual," 247).

[64] Steven Justice, "Introduction: Authorial Work and Literary Ideology," in Steven Justice and Kathryn Kerby-Fulton, eds., *Written Work: Langland, Labor and Authorship* (Philadelphia: University of Pennsylvania Press, 1997), 1–12.

[65] Justice, "Introduction," 1.

[66] Justice, "Introduction," 1. Justice himself qualifies the idea of there being only three versions of *Piers* later in his essay.

dence, as the poem's editors have always, in fact, acknowledged.[67] As already mentioned, Skeat suggested that the poem might have existed in as many as ten different shapes, not all of them authorial. Although the Athlone project is based on the integrity of the three versions, its editors actually describe a more chaotic reality. In his A-Text, Kane admits that he cannot tell how much of the so-called "John But ending" that appears in three manuscripts is authentic; the co-editor of the B-Text, Talbot Donaldson, once famously suggested that the versions we have might be no more than accidental "snapshots" of a more organic process; and the co-editor of the C-Text, George Russell, has long argued that its final shape was determined by literary executors and not the poet.[68] The surviving manuscripts contain a bewildering mixture of forms of *Piers*, including six A-Texts completed with C endings; two distinct B traditions and evidence of an alternate C tradition; three B-Texts with A and C openings; one B version that eventually turns into an A-Text; and, most complex of all, a Huntington Library manuscript (HM 114) that is a careful conflation of all three versions by a sophisticated editor: not all that different, I suspect, from the *Piers Plowman* that many of us carry around in our heads. These manuscripts show how few medieval readers would have been able to read a "pure" version of A, B, or C and that despite the preeminent importance of the author of *Piers*, he is not the sole creator of meaning. Paying greater attention to the production and reception of individual manuscripts would allow us to understand *Piers Plowman* less as a personal document and more as a social text. One result of such an approach would be to make us more careful about basing general interpretations on individual passages that may have been available only to certain readers.

Beyond the myth of the poem, another possibility for new work on *Piers Plowman*, is to reconsider the ABC sequence. Although it is essential to their work, neither Skeat nor Kane-Donaldson (nor anyone else) has provided real evidence for ABC beyond its obviousness. For a long time this seemed enough, but recently questions have been raised by Hudson and Bowers and, most fully, by Jill Mann, who suggests that the A-Text is not the poet's first version but a later adaptation for a non-clerical audience. Whether or not Mann's argument gains general acceptance, it stands (remarkably) as the first sustained attempt to explain (rather than just assert) the order of composition. Those who wish to defend the tradition-

---

[67] This is the assumption behind not only Skeat's and Schmidt's parallel-text editions as well as the Athlone edition, but also most interpretive criticism of *Piers*. Even Manly and his followers accepted Skeat's ABC order, though they did not believe they were composed by a single author. The Z-version proposed by Brewer and Rigg and included in Schmidt's new parallel-text edition extends the usual sequence but does not overthrow its basic assumptions.

[68] See Kane, *A-Version*, 51; Donaldson, "MSS R and F in the B-Tradition of *Piers Plowman*," *Transactions of the Connecticut Academy of Arts and Sciences* 39 (1955), 211, a position retracted in a footnote to Kane-Donaldson (64 n101), though it remains influential; and George Russell, "'As They Read It': Some Notes on Early Responses to the C-Version of *Piers Plowman*," *Leeds Studies in English*, n. s. 20 (1989): 173–189.

al sequence will not only have to refute her case but also make a positive one for their own hypothesis.[69]

Questioning the ABC order is another way of moving away from exclusive focus on the author. Instead of evidence of compulsive rewriting for personal reasons, the different forms of *Piers Plowman* could be seen as attempts (either by the poet himself or with others) to address individual audiences with particular interests, just as a literary talk might be successively adapted for a general audience, a graduate seminar, and a specialized academic conference. No doubt new ideas would occur to a writer as he made these different versions, but his primary attention would be outward, and on those he was addressing at each occasion, not inward. Thus the simplicity (but not simplemindedness) of A, as Mann suggests, may result from the particular audience for which it was designed. Freed from the prejudice that A is an early, perhaps failed, attempt, we can appreciate it for its own individual virtues, which include some fine original passages.[70] Similarly, the form of the C version might be explained by a desire to appeal to a less metropolitan audience, as indicated by so many surviving manuscripts having been in an area near the Malvern Hills. A version for such an audience would not be better or worse, only different. Thus instead of enigmatic puzzles such as the tearing of the pardon from Truth, the C version provides powerful passages about the life of the poor and marginal, including "lunatic lollers" (C.9.98–161), our needy neighbors (C.9.71–161), and even the failed narrator on Cornhill (C.5.1–104). To consider how the needs of readers might have influenced the versions of *Piers Plowman* does not eliminate the author, rather it attempts to reinsert him into the historical reality in which he wrote his poem.

There are also things to be learned outside the myth of the poet. Perhaps the most insidious effect of this biographical myth is that it allows critics to believe that they can discover Langland's own views and personal conclusions. When Skeat says that the "poem is a true *autobiography* in the highest sense of the word," he goes on to explain that this means that it "abounds with [Langland's] opinions, political and religious, from end to end, all expressed in the most decided language."[71] Although *Piers* is full of views and didactic moments, what the poet himself believes and means to teach is far harder to determine than Skeat thought. This has been recognized by some of the best modern readers of the poem, such as Carruthers or Kirk, the latter of whom notes that we "seek continually in the argument for a stability and satisfaction that it does not provide."[72]

---

[69] Traugott Lawlor has already made such an attempt; see his "A Reply to Jill Mann, Reaffirming the Traditional Relation between the A and B Versions of *Piers Plowman*," *Yearbook of Langland Studies* 10 (1996): 145–80.

[70] Manly and his followers thought the A-version (or rather the *visio* of A) was a superior form of *Piers*.

[71] Skeat, *A-version*, xxxviii.

[72] Kirk, *Dream*, 200. The evidence that when the poet produced C the only copy of the poem he had was a defective manuscript of B (a fundamental assumption of the Athlone edition) may suggest he was not as

Because *Piers* contains so many passionate statements, we may assume we know which are the poet's own. Surely we are on safe ground when we say he is sympathetic to the poor and suspicious of the rich or on the side of truth and against wrong. But if we try to go much beyond this (and just about all of us do), we fall into the careless habit of attributing a specific lesson (or apparent lesson) to the poet. We ignore context and, most importantly, we ignore the character who is actually speaking, which results in fatuities on the order of, "As Shakespeare teaches us, 'To thine own self be true.'" Even the most magisterial interpretations of single versions of the poem, such as those by Dunning, Frank, and Simpson, though they may recognize discursive complexity, are forced by the need to produce a coherent account of an unruly poem to make crooked places straight and rough places plain.[73] But it is the crooked and rough that gives *Piers Plowman* its special greatness.[74] For though it is a serious Christian poem, *Piers* offers anything but clear and consistent instruction. As Sternberg says about the Hebrew Bible, *Piers* "is ideological but not didactic."[75]

Those who are most certain about the poet's positions in the poem rarely agree on what they are. Langland has been called "the most Catholic of English poets,"[76] but his poem was originally published by Crowley to support the Protestant cause and, more recently, David Aers has argued that at the end it literally walks away from the Church.[77] Langland has long been judged a social conservative and defender of aristocratic privilege, but he has also been seen as a radical (not least apparently by the rebels in 1381), even a prophet of democracy or at least of the English parliament, by such as Jusserand.[78] *Piers Plowman* contains all of these competing positions (and more), but which (if any) represent the poet's own is unclear. For example, Donaldson suggests that the Rat Parliament in the prologue of B and C means that the poet "seems to have thought" that the

---

obsessed with his poem as the myth assumed. He could have been asked for a copy of *Piers* by some Western friends, found an inferior one somewhere (perhaps he had none of his own), and then corrected it as best he could while adapting it to the taste and interests of his new audience.

[73] T. P. Dunning, *Piers Plowman: An Interpretation of the A-Text* (1937, repr. Westport, CT: Greenwood, 1971); Robert Worth Frank, Jr., *Piers Plowman and the Scheme of Salvation: An Interpretation of Dowel, Dobet, and Dobest* (1957; repr. Hamden, CT: Archon Books), 1969; and Simpson, *Introduction*.

[74] A. C. Spearing argues that in contrast to most medieval allegories, which are self-interpreting and accessible, *Piers* is often obscure, not because the poet sought to veil the truth but because "the truth was to him obscure and uncertain" (*Medieval to Renaissance in English Poetry* (Cambridge: Cambridge University Press, 1985), 248–249.

[75] Quoted in Robert Alter, *The World of Biblical Literature*. (New York: Basic Books, 1992), 68.

[76] Christopher Dawson, "The Vision of Piers Plowman," 1934 as *Medieval Religion*; rpt. *Medieval Essays* (Garden City, NJ: Image, 1959), 212–40; here 213.

[77] David Aers, "Reflections on the Allegory of the Theologians: Ideology and *Piers Plowman*," in *Medieval Literature: Criticism, Ideology and History*, ed. David Aers, (New York: St. Martin's Press, 1986), 58–73.

[78] J. J. Jusserand, *Piers Plowman*.

people should endure oppressive rulers,[79] even though the same fable was used by Thomas Brinton in 1376 to draw the opposite conclusion.[80]

The debate on kingship in the B-Text, like so many other episodes in *Piers*, is indeed a debate, with speakers from different discursive traditions trying to lay claim to a disputed authority—in *Piers*, a lunatic is not necessarily outranked by an angel, let alone a goliard. To identify one position in this epistemological welter as that of Langland himself is reductive.[81] The sense of stability and clarity sometimes offered by the myth of the poet is an illusion. We need to consider more seriously that there is no single authoritative voice to be discovered in *Piers Plowman* and that it offers no clear didactic message. Once beyond the myth of the poet, it will be easier to approach *Piers* as an interactive work, open to being shaped by readers as well as by the original poet. The essential dramatic quality of *Piers Plowman*, its parliament of different voices, needs further analysis and appreciation.

I do not intend this essay to be understood as a call to do away with Skeat's myths of poet and poem, which have produced so much good work and continue to do so. I only want to question the overwhelming dominance that has made them the Microsoft™ operating system of *Piers* scholarship. There is other critical software out there (and yet to be invented) that is worth using in trying to understand this great and difficult poem. Rather than suppressing Skeat's brilliant construct, we need to be inspired by it to create two, three, many more Langland myths.

---

[79] Donaldson, *C-Text*, 94.

[80] Pearsall, *C-Text*, 38. Donaldson also quotes a subsequent statement by Piers himself to his son found only at C.8, which also insists upon sufferance to the orders of higher authorities, as "probably the fullest statement in *Piers Plowman* of the author's political beliefs, so far as they concern the lower classes" (C-Text, 102–103).

[81] Some hear Langland's voice everywhere, for they claim that the various characters in the story are the flimsiest masks for the poet himself. As we might expect, Skeat again leads the way, asserting that the allegorical figures in *Piers* are "all mouthpieces of the author himself, uttering for the most part his own sentiments," though Skeat does concede that they sometimes speak "in accordance with the characters which each is supposed to represent" (*Encyclopedia*, 286). In Dorothy Chadwick's 1922 study it simply does not matter to whom words are assigned: thus she writes, "*the poet complains* that steeds, hawks and hounds devoured money which should have clothed and fed the needy...," when it is actually Wit speaking; "The monk's business, *according to Langland*, is to obey his own Rule, and not to wander abroad on pilgrimages...," when it is Reason speaking; and that basic necessities should be common to all, "*according to Langland*," when the actual authority is Truth in his Pardon (*Social Life in the Days of Piers Plowman* (New York: Russell and Russell, 1922), 13–14, 29–49, my emphasis. We expect this confusion between creator and creations in older critics, who often say "Langland" or "the poet" when they simply mean "the poem," but the habit has persisted in *Piers* scholarship in a way that it has not in discussion of Chaucer's work. For example, Steven Justice recently echoes Skeat in referring to *Anima* as "one of [Langland's] mouthpieces" ("Introduction," 8).

The Poetry of *Piers Plowman*

Langland's Mighty Line

Stephen A. Barney

The Sweet Fruition of an Earthly Crown

Marlowe's mighty line took a long time agrowing, and developed from the tradition in which Chaucer worked. Langland's form of poetry died out for reasons too complex to fathom, but even though it had no mighty progeny, its death should not occlude our notice of its virtues—he too made mighty lines.[1] His craft should first be examined against the poetic form that he inherited, the alliterative long line. But because *Piers Plowman* stands (probably with *Winner and Waster* and *William of Palerne*) among the earliest surviving extended instances of that form, and because Langland differs from his fellow poets in the details of his prosody, close comparison with his fellow workers is hampered. Broader comparison with the line-making of the other, Chaucerian tradition is in any case more striking.[2]

---

[1] The tradition of poetry directly influenced by Langland is now handily gathered in Helen Barr, ed., *The Piers Plowman Tradition* (London: J. M. Dent, 1993).

[2] Langland worked line by line; study of his lines needs no apology. But little has been done aside from A. V. C. Schmidt's efforts in *The Clerkly Maker* (Cambridge: D. S. Brewer, 1987) and George Kane's essay "Music 'Neither Unpleasant nor Monotonous,'" 1981, repr. in his *Chaucer and Langland* (Berkeley and Los Angeles: University of California Press, 1989). Among the reasons for this neglect: 1) until recently, editions of *Piers Plowman* have been too poor to permit close study; 2) since the death of the New Criticism, stylistic analysis of poetic craft has been unfashionable; 3) readers tangled in Langland's tangles of thought are not invited to examine individual lines; 4) in sharp contrast with Chaucer, Langland's personae seem to neglect his own craftsmanship, his meddling with makings, and he has thereby misled his readers. For an introduction to Langland's "Alliterative Style," see the chapter by that name, with bibliography, by David A. Lawton in *A Companion to Piers Plowman*, ed. John A. Alford (Berkeley and Los Angeles: University of California Press, 1988), 223–249. A study comparing Langland's craft with that of his fellow poets in the alliterative tradition would be welcome.

Hence here I begin scrutiny of Langland's craft by comparison with Chaucer. Although I think Langland at his best makes better lines than Chaucer at his best, I should acknowledge that the comparison that follows is skewed in Langland's favor. In the preface to his *Iliad* Pope said, "Nothing is more absurd or endless than the common method of comparing eminent writers by an opposition of particular passages in them and forming a judgment from thence of their merit upon the whole." I began this study by collecting what seemed to me especially skillful lines of Langland, and then I ransacked Chaucer for lines that somehow shed light on what Langland does; had I worked in reverse order, Chaucer would win. Further, both poets produce feeble lines, and Langland produces them more often. I aim not to put the two poets in competition, but to illuminate Langland.

Sound cannot be entirely separated from sense. I have attended to our poets' sound effects, but much of this comparison will rest on parallels of general expression, primarily on content, even on mere diction. As a warmup, then, I begin with very close parallels of content in Langland and Chaucer, with an aside on couplets. Thereafter I turn to look at several categories of characteristic line-work in the two poets. Finally, I've given a set of lines in *Piers Plowman* that I think have no parallel in Chaucer, and that especially distinguish Langland's art.

A Ramble Through Closely Matched Pairs

Some pairs of lines have similar content but differ so as to begin to mark what is distinctive about each poet.[3] I offer first a group of lines in which Langland and Chaucer position themselves as poets, as professional users of language. Lewte asks why Will should fear **To reden it in retorik to arate dedly synne?** (**11.102**);[4] the Nun's Priest says *And if a rhetor koude faire endite* he might write how ever the latter end of joy is woe (*NPT 3207*). Rhetoric implies "fine writing" with the note of mild contempt that this phrase can imply—one of the "sotile craftes" (**15.48**). Langland's line works by opposition—use this clever art to flay vice!—where Chaucer's works by self-deprecation, as we remember that Priest and poet are perfectly comfortable with *Youre termes, youre colours, and youre figures* (*ClPro 16*). Lewte is angry, the Priest is sly; no work demands more than

---

3 Lines from *Piers Plowman* are cited in bold face by passus number and line number from the B version only, as edited by A. V. C. Schmidt, *The Vision of Piers Plowman*, Everyman paperback, 2nd ed. (London: J. M. Dent, 1995). Lines in italic from Chaucer are cited from *The Riverside Chaucer*, ed. Larry D. Benson et al. (Boston: Houghton Mifflin, 1987), with the usual abbreviations of titles of Chaucer's works (*Riverside*, 779). FrT is *The Friar's Tale*, FrankT is *The Franklin's Tale*.

4 **Reden**, complexly, "to read it out aloud, to give instruction or counsel, to exhort"; **arate**, "berate," a word common in Langland, rare (as is "raten") elsewhere—once in Chaucer. "Berate" is not Middle English. I rely on the *Middle English Dictionary* (*MED*), (Ann Arbor: University of Michigan Press, 1956—).

the rhetoric that Will neglects, while the Priest smoothly distances himself from an antique tradition that would elevate the cliché that joy and grief alternate.

Langland is seldom snobbish, but the modern decline in knowledge of French got his goat: Coveitise allows **And I kan no Frenssh, in feith, but of the fertheste ende of Northfolk** (5.235). Chaucer's line is less padded (in feith) and more precise—the Prioress's French is *After the scole of Stratford atte Bowe* (GP 125)—but rather arch. The light subsidiary *f*-rhyme in -**folk** may help justify the length of Langland's line, but it is hard to like his lines when they are too long. The wit of both lines lies in the question of distance: we almost expect ultima Thule, or at least Avignon, when we get to Northfolk; the Prioress's *scole*, a school manqué, is too close to home.[5]

On the matter of *auctoritee* our poets diverge radically. Dame Studie, in her virtuoso diatribe on misused learning, attacks theologasters: **Austyn to swiche argueres, he telleth hem this teme:/ *Non plus sapere quam oportet*** (10.118).[6] Langland takes *auctoritas* and its abuse in deadly earnest; Chaucer carries his learning lightly: impersonating his Monk, his narrator says *Lat Austyn have his swynk to hym reserved!* (GP 188).[7] Often Chaucer's satire operates by indirection, Langland's by derision. Some of the difficulty in reading Langland derives from his reluctance to speak untruths even indirectly through his fallacious speakers; the confessions of the deadly sins are a striking exception. Comparable, and requiring no comment, is the pair **With glosynges and gabbynges he giled the peple** (20.125) and *Glosynge is a glorious thyng, certeyn* (SumT 1793).

Again, expressing his sense of vocation, Langland offers plenty of plain instruction. Anima informs us that **'Hethen' is to mene after heeth and untiled erthe** (15.458).[8] Perhaps one needs long steeping in Langland to enjoy this line. *In propria persona* Chaucer could scarcely bear so pedantic a tone, but with propriety he has the Second Nun say *Or Cecilie is to seye "the wey to blynde"* (SNPro 92). Etymologies are the common coin of school discourse, Langland's world, and they accord nicely with the alliterative line because a word and its etymon usually begin with the same sound. Chaucer is truant from school, and he generally leaves such instruction to pedants like Pandarus or the friar in *The Summoner's Tale*, or to

---

5   Conversely, for both poets the use of French can signify affectation or (the French being the way they are) licentiousness: see *Piers* 14.122 and *SumT* 1838, discussed below. Langland also regrets declining latinity: **Grammer, the ground of al, bigileth now children** (15.371)—here **bigileth** means "perplexes."

6   **Teme**, "theme" as of a sermon. *Non plus*, "Not to know more than is fitting," from Romans 12:3. To inquire why Studie attributes the saying to Augustine would seek to know more than is fitting. The line's alliterative pattern is of a kind labelled by Schmidt as "T-type," characteristic of Langland, wherein an irregular aa/bb pattern is supplemented by an alliterating but unstressed word, here **he**, before the first lift of the second half-line: AA/aBB (Schmidt, *The Vision*, p. 507).

7   *Swynk*, "(manual) labor." Augustine wrote a treatise on the need for monks to perform manual labor.

8   **is to mene after**, "derives from the word"; the etymology is correct, and the definition of "heath" as "untilled earth" is exact.

professionals like the Parson, or to non-fictional prose like the "Treatise on the Astrolabe"—and even in the treatise he hedges his book-learning with a gesture of gentlemanly amateurism, *I n'am but a lewd compilator* (61). Melibee is the exception that proves the rule, as remote from Chaucer's usual way (but no parody) as is its paired effusion, Sir Thopas.

Among these instances of our poets' consciousness of their stance as writers is a famous pair on the subject of their names.[9] Will wants to know where he can find this generous friend Anima speaks of, this Charity, and as if by the way **"I have lyved in londe,"** quod I, **"my name is Longe Wille"** (15.152). As a particular human being, with human experience, he admits his distance from the greatest of virtues; inevitably his name personifies desire and longing here on this broad earth, will-lang-land. Chaucer's narrator never names himself, but the eagle in the *House of Fame* calls him 'Geffrey' (729), and in the same poem, his Apology for Poetry, the same narrator wishes *That no wight have my name in honde* (1877). Their lines perfectly express the two poets' persons: Will's tormented egotistic humility, and Geffrey's comic humble egotism.[10]

The poets work in a medium—dream vision. Will talks about his dreaming in a line in which the first half, with its series of long loosely-stopped vowels, echoes its sense with its sound: **And lay longe in a love-dreem; and at the laste me thoughte** (16.20).[11] We have to figure out why this is a love-dream. Alliteration, a collocative craft, draws things together. Here **love** links with **longe**, but as **Longe** with **Wille** above means at first merely "tall," in this instance it merely means "for a long time"; any hint of longing we bring in because we know about love-longing. Chaucer of course undercuts the visionary import of his medium—*ne do no fors of dremes* (NPT 2941)—and produces the line that, when I first read Chaucer, I remember as making me aware that he was funny. In the midst of a long curse on those who might misinterpret his dream he asseverates, *That (dreme he barefot, dreme he shod)* (HF 98). Chaucer's dreams are playfully circumscribed by scholarly knowledge of antique *Traumdeutung*; Langland's dreams render moral theology into human experience.

The next few examples bring out qualities of diction, tone, and technique that help describe each poet's art. The figure Liar, temporarily routed from the court, goes **Lurkynge thorugh lanes, tolugged of manye** (2.217). In fact Lady Meed's allies **Alle fledden for fere and flowen into hernes** (2.234). The Canon's Yeoman tells us that he and the Canon inhab-

---

[9] Anne Middleton has shown how crucial these signatures are in fourteenth-century imagination: "William Langland's 'Kynde Name': Authorial Signature and Social Identity in Late Fourteenth-Century England," in *Literary Practice and Social Change in Britain, 1380–1530*, ed. Lee Patterson (Berkeley and Los Angeles: University of California Press, 1990).

[10] Compare a wonderful pair of self-identifications: "**I am Wrathe,**" quod he, "**I was som tyme a frere**" (5.135) and "*I am a feend; my dwellyng is in helle*" (FrT 1448).

[11] I wish Langland had written **lone dreem**, as only one late copy reads, and he may have: "love" and "lone" are often indistinguishable in the manuscripts.

it the suburbs of a town where thieves dwell, *Lurkynge in hernes and in lanes blynde* (*CYPro* 658). Are there any earlier representations of blighted urban spaces in English poetry? These lines—they seem as dark to me as Blake's "I wander thro' each charter'd street"—point to a real coincidence in our two poets: they have found in the city the locus at once of social decay and of satire. Langland was a few years ahead of Chaucer here, and it is the presumably late Chaucer—of the *General Prologue*, the tales of the Nun's Priest, Pardoner, Canon's Yeoman, Friar, and the *fabliaux*—that is most like *Piers Plowman*. A century ago critics like ten Brink would call this the work of Chaucer's "English period." Chaucer may have been influenced by Langland when he wrote his Prologue,[12] and I suspect he had Langland's lines in mind when he wrote this one, which closely accords with alliterative style.

Where Chaucer finds health in laughter, comic release, Langland finds it suspect—**galle is in thi laughyng** (16.155)—a sign of the Pride of Life. Hence, **This Lecherie leide on with laughynge chiere** (20.114). We are surprised therefore by Chaucer's famous dark line about *The smylere with the knyf under the cloke* (*KnT* 1999). Not this knife, or a knife, but *the knyf*, the one we expect, just as Lechery comes as our familiar, **This Lecherie**.

Or our poets can express unrelieved grief. Pacience says **Allas, that richesse shal reve and robbe mannes soule** (14.132). The Wife says *Allas, allas! That evere love was synne!* (*WBPro* 614). Both statements are paradoxes generated by a shift of context: when we think of sin and of our souls, our goods turn bad.

These last lines exemplify, too, a matter of technique. Langland's line has five strong lexemes—richesse, reave/reive ('steal'), rob, man, soul—and Chaucer's two. Chaucer rarely compresses; his generally easy colloquial style needed beefing up before it developed into the mighty line of the sixteenth century. Langland is more writerly than Chaucer. Of course Langland's line is longer, but even his short ones cram in more lexical words and fewer function words. **Cristene kynde to kille to dethe** (10.424) may be the shortest line in *Piers Plowman*, and its effect comes partly from its economy, even with its semantic redundancy (kill to death).[13] But then Chaucer matches it with an equally compressed and chilling *The colde deeth, with mouth gapyng upright* (*KnT* 2008). A more typical pair: **For lat a dronken daffe in a dyk falle** (11.425) with four lexemes, and *Til he was in a marle-pit yfalle* (*MilT* 3460), with two. The alliterative line luxuriates in lexis.

Of course Chaucer also employs alliteration, as several of the lines quoted above display. Further, initial rhyme is only one of the resources of phonic play in our poets. For instance, a happily matched pair near the

---

[12] See Helen Cooper, "Langland's and Chaucer's Prologues," *Yearbook of Langland Studies* 1 (1987): 71–81. We can only guess that the works named here are late Chaucer.

[13] Another good short line: **Envye herfore hatede Conscience** (20.295).

beginnings of their big poems: **Pilgrymes and palmeres plighten hem togidere** (Pro 46); *Thanne longen folk to goon on pilgrimages* (GP 12). Langland exploits the interplay of *p* and *l* and *i*, where Chaucer plays on *l* and *g* and *o*. The interlocked consonants make the assertions seem inevitable, but the effects (perhaps aided by the decelerating weight of Chaucer's long vowels) are utterly different: Langland's crabbed and critical eye (Will worries much about **lakkynge**, chastizing) opposes Chaucer's fluent generosity.

When Chaucer more directly affects the technique of alliterative poetry he shows what he thinks it's good for: boffo battle poetry.[14] Both poets cast a cold eye on the excitement of combat. But the two main arenas, the stock in trade, of the Middle English alliterative tradition seem to have been (perhaps later) battle poetry and (perhaps earlier) satire.[15] Chaucer saw the potential in the form for mimetic sound, as the lines can clash and pound like men and weapons clashing and pounding. But the particular effects of the alliterative long line that make it apt for satire are less easy to assess.

Of two such effects, one is obvious and the other I think can be demonstrated but not explained. The first is the receptiveness of the alliterative long line to a kind of nervous fullness, a busy-ness, characteristic of satire from Juvenal to Pope. Fools rush. Examples in Langland range from brief couplings that first surprise then seem inevitable—**Marchaundise and mede mote nede go togideres** (3.226);[16] **For sith charite hath ben chapman and chief to shryve lordes** (Pro 64); **For the fend and thi flessh folwen togidere** (1.40)—to full-scale polysyndetic lists: **Ac Symonie and Cyvylle and sisours of courtes** (2.63), with hissing, or **Taillours and tynkers and tollers in markettes** (Pro 221),[17] which accord with Chaucer's Friar's *A theef, and eek a somnour, and a baude.* (FrT 1354).[18]

---

[14] Chaucer's three parodies of the alliterative long line are at *KnT* 2602–2616, *LGW* 635–648, and briefly (the war is serious) *TC* 4.39–42. Chaucer nowhere imitates the heteromorphism of the alliterative long line. See note 19 below.

[15] On the early link between the alliterative tradition and satire, see especially Ralph Hanna, "Defining Middle English Alliterative Poetry," 43–64, esp. 54–55, in *The Endless Knot: Essays on Old and Middle English in Honor of Marie Borroff*, ed. M. Teresa Tavormina and R. F. Yeager (Cambridge: D. S. Brewer, 1995).

[16] Another "T-type" (see note 6 above). As I read *Piers Plowman* looking for good lines I found that a surprising number of the lines I picked were of this type. Perhaps Langland shook off the sterner constraints of his form when he was onto something good. The shape of the line is uncommon in Chaucer, but compare *Freres and feendes been but lyte asonder* (SumPro 1674), where association is put negatively.

[17] **Tollers,** "toll gatherers." The grouping of workers into three types, with the third modified, parallels the sets of three proper names with a final epithet called "tricolon abundance" and characteristic of epic: "Heorogar and Hro®gar ond Halga til" (*Beowulf* 61). See Klaeber's note to the line in his edition of *Beowulf* (Boston: Heath, 1922, 1950).

[18] But lists may have wholly non-satiric effects, as in "The Complaint unto Pity," *With Bounte, Gentilesse, and Curtesye* (68) or *Assured Maner, Youthe, and Honeste* (40). Chaucer is a terrific list-maker; see my "Chaucer's Lists," 189–223, 297–307 in *The Wisdom of Poetry: Essays in Early English Literature in Honor of Morton W. Bloomfield*, ed. L. D. Benson and S. Wenzel (Kalamazoo, MI: Medieval Institute Publications, 1982).

The other effect follows from a recently noticed and definitive feature of the alliterative long line, its heteromorphism—that is, its requirement that each line conclude in the *b*-verse *avoiding* regular alternation of stressed and unstressed syllables.[19] Apparently most of the alliterative poets required, with extremely rare exceptions, two or more weakly stressed syllables before either, but not both, of the two lifts of the second half-line; they also welcomed immediately adjacent ("clashing") lifts. This practice diametrically opposes Chaucer's practice (and the practice of all his iambic successors), in which regular alternation of stressed and unstressed syllables is enforced the more rigorously the closer we come to the end of the line. The difference accounts for large differences in the poetics of the two poets. The rhythmic imbalance at the end of the alliterative line typically lets the sense too seem imbalanced, as if more were needed to bring stability; it releases energy, potentiates, drives forward. In contrast, the close of the iambic pentameter line typically makes things stand pat, with an effect of poise and remote control.

Here follow first some lines from *Piers* that contradict what I have just said and display something like a static balance:

> Ther the cat is a kitoun, the court is ful elenge (Pro 194)
> My wif was a webbe and wollen cloth made (5.211)
> Til I foryat youthe and yarn into elde (11.60)
> Ac whiche ben the braunches that bryngen a man to sleuthe? (13.410)

and so forth, often with proverb-like solidity of closure, often marked with a copulative verb, or such pithy, Chaucerian *sententia* as

> That I makede man, now it me forthynketh (9.130)[20]
> And maken hym murie with oother mennes goodes (20.289)
> Right so is the Sone the science of the Fader (17.172)
> Ac blood may noght se blood blede, but hym rewe (18.396)

Such lines, which exploit the fact that the alliterative long line tends to fall into two pairs of two strong lexemes, need no illustrative parallels from Chaucer's work—balance runneth oft in Chaucer's art. Comparable to this distinction between tumbling and poised lines are the distinctions between the Latin poets' dactylic hexameter and elegiac couplets, or between the blank verse and heroic couplets of the Augustan Age in England. The former types want to draw out the sense, as Milton puts it, into sequences of

---

[19] The heteromorphic property of the alliterative line, named by Angus McIntosh, is exploited as definitive of the corpus of alliterative poetry by Hanna ("Defining"). It rests on simultaneous discoveries by Hoyt Duggan and Thomas Cable about the prosody of the *b*-verse. For a review of studies of Langland's meter, see my "Langland's Prosody: The State of Study," 65–85, in Tavormina, ed., *Endless Knot*. Line 5.235, quoted above, is one of a number of lines in *Piers Plowman* that appear to break the rule.

[20] *it me forthynketh*, "I regret." This is one of a number of Langland's stunningly apt translations of Latin (*Penitet me fecisse hominem*), which a longer study might examine. Nice instances of the same: 1.186, 8.89, 9.61, 14.60.

lines, periodic verse paragraphs, that resist stasis; the latter types naturally fall into couplets, whose closure reduplicates the lines' closure.

Chaucer's meter comes to rest; Langland's meter presses on with an energy suited to satire. As if partly to compensate for the enclosing effect of his line, Chaucer often opens his couplets, so that the major breaks of sense come not before and after the couplets but at their middle. The making of couplets is Chaucer's business, not Langland's. It involves, in the eighteenth-century sense, pointing and wit. Langland is not bereft of wit, and he can make pairs of lines that, couplet-like, are positively, Chaucerianly, sly:

> **Thei konne na moore mynstralcie ne musik men to glade**
> **Than Munde the Millere of *Multa fecit Deus***
> (10.43–44)[21]

or with a clever enjambment,

> **And for a menever mantel he made lele matrymoyne**
> **Departen er deeth cam, and a devors shapte**
> (20.138–39).[22]

This latter can be paired with a similar enjambment-joke in Chaucer. In the procession following her husband's bier the Wife sees Jankyn from behind and thinks

> *me thoughte he hadde a paire*

of what? Buttocks? Ballocks?

> *Of legges and of feet so clene and faire.*
> (*WBPro* 597–98)

In another fine couplet Langland concludes with a line strikingly like iambic pentameter:

> **For lowliche he loketh and lovelich is his speche**
> **That mete or money of othere men moot asken.**
> (14.228–29)

This is wit but not humor, rather compassion for beggars.[23] On the whole, couplets and Langland are strangers.

But other lines will remind us of the characteristically kinetic urge of Langland's line. I choose a few from the wildly vigorous Passus 5 that have motion in both sense and sound, and observe in passing that Langland stuffs his lines with verbs of motion:

---

[21] konne, "have knowledge of"; the Latin need not be understood to make the point.

[22] menever mantel, an expensive fur coat; lele, here "true," almost "steadfast"; shapte, "made." Langland seems to accent prefixes readily (emphasizing imbalance?), here two de-'s in one line; on this see Hoyt N. Duggan, "Stress Assignment in Middle English Alliterative Poetry," *Journal of English and Germanic Philology* 89 (1990): 309–29.

[23] Compare the Man of Law: *If thou be povre, farwel thy reverence!* (*MLPro* 116).

> Ech a word that he warp was of a neddres tonge
> (5.86)[24]
> And kaireth hym to kirkeward his coupe to shewe
> (5.298)
> And thanne gan he to go like a glemannes bicche
> (5.347)
> The first word that he warp was—'Where is the bolle?'
> (5.363)[25]
> And blewe alle Thi blessed thennes into the blisse of Paradys
> (5.496)
> Sholde I never ferther a foot for no freres prechyng
> (5.633)

Such lines seem properly Langlandian; a comparable handful of distinctly Chaucerian lines would lack this strenuous energy.

Chidynges and Knavyssh Speche

Among the terrains satire works are direct expressions of savage indignation and pomp-deflating vulgarity. A few examples of each kind, played off Chaucer, will show Langland at his second-best.

Chaucer, and even his Parson, are relatively coolly indignant; the Pardoner, who of course assumes the pose of an outraged preacher, is the exception: *O wombe! O bely! O stynkyng cod* (*PardT* 534). Langland is hot. Compare the blunt attack on bad clerisy, **Thus thei dryvele at hir deys the deitee to knowe** (10.56), with the indirection of *As clerkes ben ful subtile and ful queynte* (*MilT* 3275). Langland attacks not just *ad hominem*, but *ad corpus*. Both poets exploit France's reputation for luxury, but Langland's **And Dives in deyntees lyvede and in** *douce vie* (14.122) is angrier than Friar John's mincing chirking, "*Now, dame," quod he, "now* je vous *dy sanz doute*" (*SumT* 1838), which characterizes rather than buffets.

Hopping about is undignified. Langland praises the work of the martyr Thomas and warns other bishops **And naught to huppe aboute in Engelond to halwe mennes auteres** (15.528); Chaucer has his alter ego Pandarus deprecate himself, "*By God," quod he, "I hoppe alwey byhynde!*" (*TC* 2.1107). Compare, too, the styles of vehement dissent: **'Ye? Baw!' quod a brewere, "I wol noght be ruled"** (19.400) and "*Nay, nay," quod he, "thanne have I Cristes curs!*" (*PardT* 946). Harry Bailey is forceful, but the

---

[24] **warp**, "hurled"; **a neddres**, "an adder's." Here and in line 363, quoted below, Langland plays off the alliterative tag in which the narrator "warps forth his word"; compare Chaucer's more elegant rhymes on writing and enditing. We might expect the Pardoner, who shares Will's homiletic passion, if not his integrity, to produce an equally energetic line, *Thus spitte I out venym under hewe / Of hoolynesse* (*PardPro* 421–22).

[25] **Bolle**, "bowl." Compare Chaucer's equally happy but quieter line, *This Nicholas answerde, "Fecche me drynke"* (*MilT* 3492).

brewer, perhaps because of the energizing stress thrown on **be**, the refusal to admit the passive, is more forceful. Finally, I hear barely suppressed anger in **And maken hym murie with oother mennes goodes** (20.289), taking its energy from the cliché, "make merry," as opposed to another line from *The Pardoner's Tale*, *"Now lat us sitte and drynke, and make us merie"* (*PardT* 883), whose irony is cool and allusive[26] and not completed until the closure of the couplet, *"And afterward we wol his body berie."*

An angry satirist shakes material reality in the victim's face. Langland's and Chaucer's tempers differ nowhere more clearly than in their uses of vulgarity, the baser matters of excretion and sex, and this difference appears at the level of the line. Whereas for Langland churls' terms have values of anger, earthiness, sometimes even regret, for Chaucer, with rare exceptions like the Canon's Yeoman's *Poudres diverse, asshes, donge, pisse, and cley* (*CYT* 807), where *pisse* connotes mere sweaty materialism, there is usually a value of impropriety and rudeness. Larry Benson perhaps overstates the case for English unconsciousness of the indecency of four-letter words before Chaucer, but he surely is right to observe that Chaucer in a way invented prudery, was first to exploit a distinction between decent and indecent language as signs of gentle and churlish speech. The Wife of Bath's playful mastery of euphemism marks the origin of this distinction.[27]

Not because he preceded Chaucer, but because he bore a clerkly indifference to the marks of upper-class discourse, Langland has no prudery, and therefore cannot be obscene. His attitudes toward swearing and toward the common language of bodily functions are closer to those of a medical writer, or to the Parson and the Pardoner, than to the Prioress or Knight or Troilus. They are attitudes formed by Christianity rather than by the essentially comic work of social discrimination. Compare the New Revised Standard Version's translation of 2 Kings 18:27, "to eat their own dung and to drink their own urine," with the late-fourteenth century translation, "eat her toordis and drynke her pisse."[28] The latter formulation was not intended, we may think, to arouse embarrassed laughter; turds and

---

[26] The allusion is to Isaiah 22:13, 1 Corinthians 15:32.

[27] Some of Benson's printed essays touch on Chaucer's uses of vulgar language, but his main arguments about Chaucer's invention of prudery, presented in essays especially on farting in Chaucer, have so far only been presented in talks before learned assemblies. See Benson's "The Beginnings of Chaucer's English Style" and "Courtly Love and Chivalry in the Later Middle Ages," and on euphemism "The 'Queynte' Punnings of Chaucer's Critics," 243–65, 294–313, and 217–242 in *Contradictions: From "Beowulf" to Chaucer*, ed. Theodore M. Andersson and Stephen A. Barney (Aldershot, G.B.: Scolar Press, 1995).

Of the little list of four-letter words, neither Chaucer nor Langland uses "cunt" or "fuck"; both use "piss" and (as a verb) "shit," as well as "fart" and "arse." Langland does not use "turd" or "dighten" in the sexual sense or "swyve," all in Chaucer. It is not their diction, but the way the poets speak of the referents of these rude terms that distinguishes Langland from Chaucer.

[28] *MED* s.v. pisse. So Moses said, in the Wycliffite Bible, "& ᵀᴹe part of ᵀᴹe body by ᵀᴹe whiche tordys been shetyn out" (Deut. 28:27, cited in *MED* s.v. shiten), from the Vulgate *"et partum corporis per quam stercora egerunt,"* cleansed to "by which the dung is cast out" in the Douai version, and altogether lost in the New Revised Standard Version. Note that much of Langland's earthiness is in fact biblical.

piss in that world of discourse simply had no value as improper, and Chaucer shows us both the old unconscious world, especially in his *fabliaux*, alongside the emergent world of "gentle" delicacy of diction.

The specific contrary to knavish speech is courtly speech. Where we can imagine Langland emerging from the literary context of Raoul de Houdenc, Robert Grosseteste, Rutebeuf, the *South English Legendary*, and *Winner and Waster*, we know that Chaucer emerged from Guillaume de Lorris, Froissart, Machaut, Boccaccio. More often than has commonly been recognized, Langland will imitate a kind of courtliness, that of those English romances which Chaucer parodies in Sir Thopas as well as of the alliterative romances contemporary with him, for his own kind of satiric parody.

Lady Mede is **Purfiled with pelure, the pureste on erthe** (2.9)[29] like many a lady in the junk romances. Chaucer, with a broader range in this area, does this too: he says of the Prioress *Ful fetys was hir cloke, as I was war* (*GP* 157), and more distinctly parodies bourgeois aspirations toward courtliness with

> *His robe was of syklatoun*
> *That coste many a jane.* (*Thop* 734–35)

It seems in fact that to describe noble ladies as wearing fine clothes was out of style; Emelye of *The Knight's Tale* is clothed in nature (*KnT* 1035–55), like Alysoun! (*MilT* 3233–70), and Criseyde is *Simple of atir and debonaire of chere* (*TC* 1.181), an observation out of Langland's ken.

Now follow three further examples of Langland's parody of a courtly diction itself not up to Chaucerian, presumably Ricardian, standards. The **raton of renoun** says he has seen men in the city of London **Beren beighes ful brighte abouten hire nekkes** (Pro 161), and this gives him the idea of belling the cat. *Beagas* were fine things in Old English poetry, but the *MED* shows that word itself, along with the idea of jewelry as the sign of courtliness (here bourgeois aspiration), are alien to Chaucer; these objects are found in the English romances and alliterative gestes, and not in Chaucer's continental lexis. By way of contrast, addressing the noblest lady of them all in a way that Langland could not, Chaucer (following Guillaume de Deguileville) has *Help, lady bright, er that my ship tobreste* (*ABC* 16).

Again, mocking the "courtly," really courtly-manqué, diction of minstrels' delight in their superiors' heraldry, Langland has Will ask the herald-of-arms, Feith, **"What berth that buyrn,"** quod I tho, "so blisse thee **bitide?"** (16.180).[30] "Bern"—'man, warrior'—is an old word [OE *beorn*] that the *MED* shows is almost exclusively preserved in the alliterative tradition; it is not used by Chaucer. Further, **so blisse thee bitide** is an old-fashioned asseveration, a phrase of the kind preserved in the English romancers

---

[29] See *Piers* 4.116, 5.26, and 20.176 for rougher versions of this parody.
[30] The **buyrn** is Christ.

and used by Chaucer mainly in parody, as in *Sir Thopas: Bityde what bityde* (874) and *Bitid a sory care* (759).[31] In its proper context within the normative alliterative tradition we find, in *Pearl* 397, "Blysse, burne, mot þe bytyde."

And again, Will observes that Haukyn thinks himself wittiest, or wisest, **Or strengest on stede, or styvest under girdel** (13.294). This is *Thopas*-speak again: *And slepe under my goore* (789) or *So worly under wede* (917). In its own romance context the phrasing is common and appropriate; *Sir Gawain and the Green Knight* has "Stifest vnder stel-gere on stedes to ryde" (260), that is, "Strongest in armor to ride on steeds." But Langland's line is comic, especially if we imagine what might be stiff under Haukyn's girdle.

Chaucer, then, wields a truly courtly diction, mainly French, against which he can play both the comic pseudo-courtly diction of the old rum-ram-ruffing style, as in *Sir Thopas*, and the distinctly churlish diction of the *fabliaux*. His churl-craft is never simple: when the Manciple, for instance, finally gets down to cases, he manages for two lines to advance his plot, *His wyf anon hath for hir lemman sent*, and forthwith interrupts himself, *Hir lemman? Certes, this is a knavyssh speche!* (*MancT* 204–5). He then digresses again on the topic of plain speech regardless of dignity of estate. But to Chaucer's gentils surely 'lemman' is the mildest of knaveries, not much stronger than "boyfriend." The Manciple, for his own purposes, adopts the ethos of the Parson; he objects not to the word but to the thing—adultery. The Manciple, *somdeel squaymous*, Chaucer might have said, or of a somewhat *spiced conscience* (*MilT* 3337, *GP* 526), makes a show of resisting low speech, unlike the Miller who *nolde his wordes for no man forbere* (*MilPro* 3168). In contrast, Langland's **Lyf lepte aside and laughte hym a lemman** (20.152). The **lemman** is Fortune, and there is no hint of social impropriety, but rather moral contempt, expressed with fierce energy.

Langland's talk about sexual intercourse is direct, and rings with the righteous indignation of the satirist rather than the leer or guffaw of the comedian of manners. Adopting the lingo of misogynist satire, Conscience says of Lady Mede **For she is frele of hire feith and fikel of hire speche** (3.122), and more harshly *ad feminam*, **For she is tikel of hire tail, talewis of tonge** (3.131).[32] In contrast, the merchant's wife in *The Shipman's Tale* wins out, like a clever clerk in a *fabliau*, with a coy, tale-wise pun, *I am youre wyf; score it upon my taille* (416). With regard to the results of promiscuity, in his wonderful speech Wrathe says Dame Pernele, a priest's mistress, won't make it to the rank of prioress **For she hadde child in chirie-tyme, al oure Chapitre it wiste!** (5.159). We see here a whole world of cler-

---

[31] But Chaucer uses *bityde what bityde* non-parodically in *TC* 5.570.

[32] Sharper is **Trewe of youre tonge and of youre tail bothe** (15.105)—does Chaucer have any zeugmas of this kind?

ical vice and the spiteful gossip of an enclosed community. This outcome of the progress of wooing is not merry enough for Chaucer, who only hints of pregnancy a few times in his comic mode (*GP* 212–13, *RvT* 3943, *MerT* 2414). When Chaucer approaches Langland's directness in this arena, in fact, he denies pregnancy in a triple attack on friars for their multiplicity, their sexual rage, and their impotence:

> *In every bussh or under every tree*
> *Ther is noon oother incubus but he,*
> *And he ne wol doon hem but dishonour.* (*WBT* 879–81)[33]

So such lines as Wit's advice to marry **Whiles thow art yong, and thi wepene kene** (9.182) to avoid sin fall outside the courtly mode of Chaucer, but also—because they are serious—out of his *fabliau* mode. We find no counterpart in Chaucer to Will's regret that old age has incapacitated him, **For the lyme that she loved me fore, and leef was to feele** (20.195) can no longer work his wife's will. Chaucer cannot handle these matters with such directness, the stuff of the confessional. More Chaucerian is Will's observation that Haukyn's coat is soiled by his lechery, as with each maid he met he **Aboute the mouth or bynethe bigynneth to grope** (13.347), combining the activities of hende Nicholas (*MilT* 3276) and friar John (*SumT* 2148), but again with more moral disgust than condescending appreciation— Haukyn would do this on **fastyng dayes and Fridaies and forboden nyghtes** (13.349), imperilling his soul.

Although the Parson and the Wife of Bath each speak of piss more often (twice) than any others of Chaucer's characters, pure *Miller's Tale* (3798) is Gloton: **He pissed a potel in a** *Paternoster*-**while** (5.342). Gloton makes us laugh. Not so the wastrel Bretoner who challenges Piers **And bad hym go pissen with his plowgh, forpynede sherewe** (6.155). This is mere anger directed at the thematic heart of the poem—might Langland have heard some jangling rival say these words? Equally angry is the description of those who respond to a pardoner's preaching and **Comen up knelynge to kissen hise bulles** (Pro 73). Perhaps I am improperly influenced by Harry Bailly's angry response to that other bull-laden Pardoner, Chaucer's (*kisse the relikes...kisse thyn olde breech...I wolde I hadde thy coillons in myn hond—PardT* 342, 944–952), but *I* hear "balls" in this pardoner's pseudo-papal bulls.[34]

Let the word "arse," a common thing in Chaucer's Miller's and Summoner's tales (not found elsewhere in Chaucer) and no very vile term, conclude this effort to distinguish our poets' exploitation of the values of vulgarity. Langland writes of Wrath being whipped on the bare arse (5.173) and of Dame Study wishing of self-congratulating theological masters that

---

[33] Pees knows of a more potent friar confessor: **He salved so oure wommen til some were with childe** (20.348).

[34] "Bal" can mean "testicle" in Middle English (see *MED* "bal," 8); more common is "ballok."

their eyes were in their arse and their fingers after (10.125). But the great line speaks of a roaming religious, who rides about with **An heep of houndes at his ers as he a lord were** (10.308). This sword has two edges: the regular clergy look like fools with their genteel pretensions, and lords themselves, gone ahunting, look none too dignified with their hounds nipping at their butts. This is pure satire, of broader range and sharper bite than Chaucer would manage.

High Seriousness

In *The Study of Poetry,* Matthew Arnold granted that Chaucer's poetry was large, free, shrewd, and benign, but he would not grant him the virtue of "high seriousness" as displayed in Dante's line, "*In la sua voluntade è nostra pace.*" He would only admit that Chaucer has charm, a "truth of substance," and "an exquisite virtue of style and manner." He offers in evidence a line from *The Prioress's Tale, O martir, sowded to virginitee* (579). Perusal of Arnold's touchstone lines shows that by "high seriousness" he means especially the heroic and the experientially religious, especially the eschatological: the serious gazes at mortality.

Whether, like the young Byron, Arnold preferred *Piers Plowman* to the work of Chaucer I do not know. Both our poets produce, indeed, lines that I think Arnold would say have "truth of substance": with Langland's **Forthi I rede yow riche, haveth ruthe on the povere** (1.175) we have Chaucer's *O riche marchauntz, ful of wele been yee* (MLPro 122), and for **For to loven thi Lord levere than thiselve** (1.143) we have *God loved he best with al his hoole herte* (GP 533). Moreover, I think the poet who wrote, near the end of *Troilus, Dispitously hym slough the fierse Achille* and *And to that sothfast Crist, that starf on rode* (5.1806, 1860) was not bereft of Arnoldian high seriousness. Still, as part of my argument that Langland's lines in fact have a broader range both of sound and of sense than Chaucer, I offer in conclusion a dozen lines that I think are not matched by our archpoet, and that partake in fact of the sublime.[35] They are not heroic lines; that first kind of Arnoldian seriousness had to wait in English (after *Beowulf,* where the poet can make his heroes simply sit down with epic dignity) until Marlowe wrote. I have tried to choose lines that do not get their force from the weight of later tradition, as phrases like "remembrance of things past" and "great expectations" in Shakespeare's sonnets affect our sensibilities after the fact.

Let us pass by, then, fine lacerating invective (**And gnawen God with the gorge whanne hir guttes fullen,** 10.57) and Chaucer-like delight in the

---

[35] That is, Chaucer has no lines with a scope like **And bicam man of a mayde, and** *metropolitanus* (15.515), "archbishop," or with rage like **In paltokes and pyked shoes and pisseris longe knyves** (20.219). He also has few lines of the open-eyed, holy simplicity that I am calling sublime.

natural world (**I seigh floures in the fryth and hir faire colours**, 11.364) and profoundly simple theology (**Here is breed yblessed, and Goddes body therunder**, 19.389) and political savvy (**Forthi I kan and kan naught of court speke moore**, Pro 111; **For she copeth the commissarie and coteth hise clerkes**, 3.143) and the high pathos of lines like one that Skeat admired (**Pitousliche and pale as a prison that deieth**, 18.58) and even grand prophecy (**Ac ther shal come a kyng and confesse yow religiouses**, 10.316), but rather let us locate Langland's sublime in humble lines of religious intensity.

Here are my dozen; I think they need no comment, and I provide only their context for legibility.

Holicherche speaks of love taking on flesh and blood, **Was nevere leef upon lynde lighter therafter** (1.156). Holicherche again: **Forthi chastite withouten charite worth cheyned in helle** (1.188, repeated nearly verbatim six lines later). Repentaunce preaches, **And gart Wille to wepe water with hise eighen** (5.61).[36] Will argues against Scripture that ignorant people can **Percen with a *Paternoster* the paleys of hevene** (10.462).

Ymaginatif has moved Will to meditate on his end, **And how fele fern-yeres are faren, and so fewe to come** (12.5). In a single line Will summa-rizes what will happen in Passus 18: Jesus **Deide, and deeth fordide, and day of nyght made** (16.166). At his death God shuts out the light: **The lord of lif and of light tho leide hise eighen togideres** (18.59). Jesus berates Lucifer: **For I that am lord of lif, love is my drynke** (18.366).

The repentant Will speaks of the power of the cross: **May no grisly goost glide there it shadweth!** (18.433). Conscience reviews the *vita Christi*: **He made lame to lepe and yaf light to blynde** (19.125). In the reign of Antecrist **Deeth cam dryvynge after and al to duste passhed** (20.100). In answer to Will's last question in the poem: **"Lerne to love," quod Kynde, "and leef alle othere"** (20.208).

---

[36] Gart, "made," If *[For] pitee renneth soone in gentil herte* is Chaucer's favorite line, on the evidence of repetition (*KnT* 1761, *MerT* 1986, *SqT* 479, *LGW* F 503), then to weep water with one's eyes is Langland's favorite phrase (here and 5.473, 14.324, 16.116; cf. 19.381–2). My thanks to Traugott Lawlor for his help with this essay.

Chaucer and Langland as Religious Writers

Mary Clemente Davlin, O.P.

Much of what has been written about Chaucer and Langland[1] would suggest that they are too different from one another to compare. "They do not belong together, in the established history of English poetry, as representatives of a single period, like Pope and Swift, or Tennyson and Browning"; "it would seem impossible for a work of art to have less in common with Chaucer [than *Piers Plowman*]."[2] Chaucer is the master of rhyme and meter, Langland of the alliterative line; *Piers Plowman*, "different from what literature has come to mean in the twentieth century,"[3] but Chaucer, the source of what poetry and perhaps narrative have come to mean. Chaucer is a supreme storyteller in many genres, whereas Langland seems to practice "the frustration of narrative."[4] Chaucer seems to many readers to be continental, whereas Langland seems English.[5] Chaucer is influenced by French, Italian, and Latin texts, Langland mostly by Latin; Chaucer is comfortable with the traditions of chivalry and courtliness that Langland rarely uses. Chaucer is easier to read, more immediately accessible; in comparison, Langland seems difficult and confusing. Chaucer is one of the supreme erotic poets, and Langland avoids the erotic almost completely.

---

[1] In writing about "Langland" I do not wish to assume that the question of single or multiple authorship of the *Piers Plowman* manuscripts is settled with certainty. I use "Langland" throughout for convenience, to signify the author or authors of the various *Piers Plowman* versions.

[2] John Burrow, *Ricardian Poetry* (New Haven: Yale University Press, 1971), 1; Elizabeth D. Kirk, "Chaucer and His English Contemporaries," in George Economu, ed., *Geoffrey Chaucer* (New York: McGraw Hill, 1975), 111–127, here 117.

[3] C. David Benson, "The Aesthetic of Chaucer's Religious Tales in Rhyme Royal," in Piero Boitani and Anna Torti, eds., *Religion in the Poetry and Drama of the Late Middle Ages* (Woodbridge, Suffolk: Boydell and Brewer, 1990) 101–117, here 114.

[4] C. David Benson, "The Frustration of Narrative and Reader in *Piers Plowman*," in Robert R. Edwards, ed., *Art and Context in Late Medieval English Narrative* (Cambridge: D. S. Brewer, 1994), 1–15, here, 1.

[5] Conrad Pepler, O. P., *The English Religious Heritage* (St. Louis, MO: Herder, 1958), 41.

Yet, "Topographically and biographically speaking, no two English poets for two centuries so closely overlap. They must have passed each other on the street."[6] They have, according to Bennett, a "cluster of common sympathies...sane and sanative qualities."[7] He lists three: Englishness with knowledge of the wider world, earthiness fused with sublimity in contrasts of style; similar structures, especially the pilgrimage; and similar characters (like the plowman and the worldly religious). Both are lay, and learned, though they prefer rather different books; both are interested in dream lore; both are severe moralists and therefore satirists; both (unlike Dante) are interested in this world more than in the next.

Even among those who do compare or contrast Chaucer and Langland, very few scholars compare their religious work; perhaps this is because although Langland is obviously a religious poet, Chaucer has not usually been considered to be so until the last few years when some scholars have argued that "Chaucer is as much a religious artist as a comic artist."[8] And among those who discuss Chaucer's "religious," "ethical," "serious," or "clerical" writings or poetry of "faith,"[9] there still is no general agreement on what should be included in these categories, or how they should be defined. For the purpose of this paper, I shall use Aquinas's definition of the virtue of religion as "a relationship to God" (IIa IIae 81:1) and define religious literature as literature that communicates an experience of relationship with God, reflecting or creating a world within which bonds between people and God are real and central. Clearly, in this sense *Piers Plowman* is religious, and so are many of Chaucer's works: some, like the ABC, "Truth," *Troilus and Criseyde*, *The General Prologue* to *The Canterbury Tales*, *The Man of Law's Tale*, *The Second Nun's Tale*, *The Parson's Tale*, and the miracle story in *The Prioress's Tale*, because they focus on relationships with God, and others because they satirize the misuse of Christian vocation or sacrament, the perversion of charity, and the ignoring, abandonment or betrayal of relationship with God. In this latter group, whose humor and satire depend upon an understanding of religious belief and practice, I would include the *Friar's*, *Summoner's*, *Merchant's*, *Pardoner's*, *Shipman's*, and *Miller's Tales*, and *The Prioress's Tale* as a whole. The *Summoner's*, *Shipman's* and *Pardoner's Tales* depend upon an

---

[6] J. A. W. Bennett, "Chaucer's Contemporary," in S. S. Hussey, ed., *Piers Plowman: Critical Approaches* (London: Methuen, 1969), 310–24; 322.

[7] Bennett, "Chaucer's," 324.

[8] Benson, "Aesthetic," 102.

[9] David Benson and Elizabeth Robertson have a collection on *Chaucer's Religious Tales* (Cambridge: D. S. Brewer, 1990); Gregory Kratzmann and James Simpson write on *Medieval English Religious and Ethical Literature* (Cambridge: D. S. Brewer, 1986); Ralph Elliott writes of "Chaucer's Clerical Voices" (in Boitano and Torti) op. cit.; and Paul Ruggiers of the "Serious Chaucer," (in Edward Vasta and Z. P. Thundy, eds., *Chaucerian Problems and Perspectives* [Notre Dame, IN: University of Notre Dame Press, 1979]), and Przemyslaw Mroczkowski writes of "faith" in his "Faith and the Critical Spirit in Chaucer and His Time" (in Boitani and Torti, eds., op. cit.), 83–100.

understanding of a friar's, a monk's, and a pardoner's proper vocation for their comic irony. The *Merchant's* and *Miller's Tales* are "spiced" with sufficient religious flavor to sharpen their irony, such as Absalon's "sensynge" (*MilT* 3341) and Alysoun's trip to church, "Cristes owene werkes for to wirche" (*MilT* 3308), and January's religious scruples lest he "shal have myn hevene in erthe heere" (*MerT* 1647).[10] The irony of *The Friar's Tale* lies in the contrast between the summoner's lack of faith and the devil's certainty about the reality of hell. The bitter irony of *The Prioress's Tale* depends upon awareness of the psychological gap between piety and vengefulness and the logical gap between antisemitism and the veneration of a Jewish mother and her Son. All of these tales can be called "religious," then, because relationship with God is an essential element of each narrative, but in this essay, I shall concentrate on Chaucer's non-satiric religious tales.

Chaucer and Langland are quite different as religious writers. As a number of scholars have pointed out, Chaucer uses pathos in his religious tales, and he tends to identify Christian sanctity as the prerogative of women or of men who have learned from women.[11] Although his range of religious emotion is wide, including humor[12] associated with poetic justice as in *The Friar's Tale*, and the wonder, triumph, and exaltation of miracle as in *The Second Nun's Tale* and *The Prioress's Tale*, his religious verse is especially marked by the pathos of little children and their mothers, helpless and alone, invoking Mary and her son. Here, "abstract virtue takes on flesh, [and] suffers."[13] Chaucer tends to choose these mothers and other women as icons of Christian virtue in the religious tales, the supreme example being Mary, as in the ABC, the prologues to *The Prioress's Tale* and *The Second Nun's Tale*, and the odd last line of *Troilus and Criseyde*: "To Chaucer, women and Christian spirituality occupy the same marginal space."[14] These qualities are not totally foreign to Langland, of course. He, too, uses pathos, as, for example, in the scene where Glutton's family bring him home from the tavern:

> With al the wo of this world, his wif and his wenche
> Baren hym to his bed and broughte hym therinne.
>   (B.5.358–59)[15]

---

10 All citations from Chaucer are from *The Riverside Chaucer*, Larry Benson, ed., (Boston: Houghton-Mifflin, 1987). Subsequent citations shall appear parenthetically.

11 Cf. Benson, "Aesthetic," 115–117.

12 Daniel F. Pigg, notes "the overriding sense of comedy" in the religious tales ("The Semiotics of Comedy in Chaucer's Religious Tales," in Jean Jost, ed., *Chaucer's Humor* [NewYork: Garland, 1994], 321–348.

13 Robert Worth Frank, Jr., "*The Canterbury Tales* III: Pathos," in Piero Boitani and Jill Mann, eds., *The Cambridge Chaucer Companion* (Cambridge: Cambridge University Press, 1986), 143–58; 150.

14 Elizabeth Robertson, "Medieval Medical Views of Woman and Female Spirituality in the *Ancrene Wisse* and Julian of Norwich's *Showings*," in Linda Lomperis and Sarah Stanbury, eds., *Feminist Approaches to the Body in Medieval Literature* (Philadelphia: University of Pennsylvania Press, 1993), 143–167; 146.

15 All citations of *Piers Plowman* are from *The Vision of Piers Plowman: A Critical Edition of the B-Text*, 2nd ed., edited by A. V. C. Schmidt (London: J. M. Dent, 1995). Subsequent citations shall appear parenthetically.

But pathos is rather rare in *Piers Plowman*. So are mentions of Mary. Langland's saints are both men and women, whom he seems to treat simply as persons, not particularly different because of gender.[16] The dominant characteristics of *Piers Plowman* as religious poetry are perhaps its biblical, liturgical character and its focus upon the central Christian mysteries with their implications for human life. Morton Bloomfield's wonderful statement that Langland "speaks Bible",[17] is true, especially Bible filtered through liturgy.[18] John Alford, by identifying the biblical quotations in *Piers Plowman*, has shown the breadth of Langland's knowledge of the Bible, however he gained this knowledge. *Piers Plowman* is especially steeped in the Psalms, the wisdom books, including the gospel and first letter of John, and the prophets, whereas Chaucer uses the Song of Songs over and over and retells *stories* from throughout the Hebrew Scriptures. Langland uses the Bible as monks used it in *lectio divina*, with deep attention to words and a mental concordance relating each use to other uses in other contexts.[19] His sense of God, too, is biblical, for example in his privileging of the name "Truthe" for God, *emet* in Hebrew, "the faithful one, the one who can be counted on."[20] His spirituality is liturgical[21] and therefore public while at the same time deeply personal; the seasons of the church year are revelatory for him, so that of course the revelation of Christ finally comes to Will during the Paschal weekend (Passus 18),[22] and he sees the Holy Spirit come during the feast of Pentecost (Passus 19).

And whereas Chaucer, with Shakespeare, is the greatest poet we have of human character, Langland is the *only* poet we have (with the possible exception of Milton) who dares to probe at any length the nature of God, contemplating the central beliefs of Christianity: the Trinity, the incarnation, the church, the indwelling of God in people, the causes of salvation. In doing this, he always balances one aspect of a mystery against another

---

[16] Yet, as Elizabeth Robertson has noted, some of Langland's stylistic characteristics are those attributed especially to women writers, such as emphasis on the concrete and sensual and upon bodily fluids ("Medieval," 146), and structure which is repetitious, "experiential and relational...fluid, nonteleological" (*Early English Devotional Prose and the Female Audience* [Knoxville: University of Tennessee Press, 1990], 197). She attributes the fact that Langland has these qualities, noted in Julian and Margery Kempe, to the fact that he, like the women, has a lay audience.

[17] Morton Bloomfield, *Piers Plowman as a Fourteenth-Century Apocalypse* (New Brunswick, NJ: Rutgers University Press, 1961), 37.

[18] J. A. W. Bennett, *Middle English Literature*, ed. Douglas Gray (Oxford: Clarendon Press, 1986), 449.

[19] John Alford, "The Role of the Quotations in *Piers Plowman*," *Speculum* 52 (1977): 80–99; 81–83.

[20] Jacques Guillet, *Themes of the Bible,* trans. Albert J. La Mothe, Jr. (Notre Dame, IN: University of Notre Dame Press, 1960), 34–35.

[21] Pepler, *English*, 52–54.

[22] On Langland and liturgy see, for example, Conrad Pepler, O. P., "The Spirituality of William Langland," *Blackfriars* 20 (1939): 846–854, and *English*; Greta Hort, *Piers Plowman and Contemporary Religious Thought* (New York: Macmillan, 1936); and the works of St. Jacques. J. A. W. Bennett says that "Langland was impregnated, divinely intoxicated with the offices of Holy Week" (*Poetry of the Passion* [Oxford: Clarendon Press, 1986], 91).

that seems contradictory to it, creating paradox; thus Christ is always seen as both God and man; God is "Oo God withouten gynnyng" (2.30) and yet "thre lovely persones" (17.44); salvation depends upon both works and grace as in 12.280–294. Langland seems to abhor dichotomies in religion, since they tend to be oversimplifications, and to think in terms of "both/and" rather than "either/or," as the great formulations of Christian faith have traditionally done. Thus in religion as in other matters, Langland is a poet who "concentrates on essentials."[23] Chaucer, on the contrary, seems to be more interested in such religious elements as miracles, pilgrimages, Mary and the saints, in everything about how people (including religious people) act, and in the contrast between their suffering and triumph.

Like Chaucer, Langland is a poet of religious experience, not theology (though Chaucer did love the theology of predestination). Anne Middleton says that Langland invented "experience as a literary category,"[24] and Bloomfield calls him the first poet of the existential.[25] The experience his poem recreates is that of a believer struggling to find a *kynde knowyng* of God, at the same time that God is seeking him.[26] Langland communicates this experience not by direct appeal to emotion, but through such devices as wordplay and paradox, first engaging the mind and then the heart.

Two passages may exemplify these qualities of the two poets as religious writers. The first is from *The Man of Law's Tale*, when Custance is falsely accused of the murder of Hermengyld:

> Allas! Custance, thou hast no champioun,
> Ne fighte kanstow noght, so weylaway!
> (*MLT* 631–632)

The narrator's voice is filled with pathos in this addition to Trivet's story.[27] He bewails the situation, speaking both to the heroine, "Allas! Custance...weylaway!" and also to an audience of queens and other aristocrats:

> O queenes, lyvynge in prosperitee,
> Duchesses, and ye ladyes everichone,
> Haveth som routhe on hire adversitee!
> An Emperoures doghter stant allone; (652–5)

---

23 Bennett, *Middle*, 452.

24 Anne Middleton, "Narration and the Invention of Experience: Episodic Form in *Piers Plowman*," in L. D. Benson and Siegfried Wenzel, eds., *The Wisdom of Poetry* (Kalamazoo, MI: Medieval Institute Press, 1982), 91–122; 110.

25 Morton Bloomfield, "Allegories of Dobest," *Medium Ævum* 50 (1981): 30–39; 37.

26 See John Lawlor's "The Imaginative Unity of *Piers Plowman*," *Review of English Studies* 8 (1957): 113–126; repr. in Robert J. Blanch, ed., *Style and Symbolism in Piers Plowman* (Knoxville, TN: University of Tennessee Press, 1969), 101–116.

27 Ann Astell, "Apostrophe, Prayer, and the Structure of Satire in the *Man of Law's Tale*," *Studies in the Age of Chaucer* 13 (1991): 81–97; 82.

He emphasizes Custance's aloneness and helplessness, her submissive posture ("She sette hire doun on knees...") (638), her pale face. Custance herself introduces elements of pathos by speaking about mother, daughter, and child in her prayer:

> ...and thou, merciful mayde,
> Marie I meene, doghter to Seint Anne,
> Bifore whos child angeles synge Osanne...(640–642)

In the next stanza, "one of his starkest, most moving passages,"[28] Chaucer uses a favorite technique, a close-up of a particular detail in a vast panorama, as if with a telephoto lens:

> Have ye nat seyn sometyme a pale face,
> Among a prees, of hym that hath be lad
> Toward his deeth, wher as hym gat no grace,
> And swich a colour in his face hath had
> Men myghte knowe his face that was bistad
> Amonges alle the faces in that route?
> So stant Custance, and looketh hire aboute. (645–651)

This rhetorical question is rather convoluted yet absolutely clear, the language extremely simple and piercing, without narratorial comment. The episode has a victorious ending for Custance, and the audience moves from feelings of pathos to triumph:

> A voys was herd in general audience,
> And seyde, "Thou hast desclaundred, giltelees,
> The doghter of hooly chirche in heigh presence;
> Thus hastou doon, and yet holde I my pees!"
> Of this mervaille agast was al the prees;
> As mazed folk they stoden everichone,
> For drede of wreche, save Custance allone. (673–679)

The word "allone," which previously (655) evoked pathos, here distinguishes Custance as perfectly unafraid (679), no longer an abandoned victim but "The doghter of hooly chirche" (675), vindicated miraculously. Instructed by the fact that "Of this mervaille agast was al the prees," the audience, too, is "mazed" at the wonderful divine rescue from an almost hopeless situation.

A description of Christ's crucifixion from *Piers Plowman* is equally moving, but significantly different from Chaucer's passage because of its biblical character and the manner in which its focus on mystery balances pathos.

> 'Consummatum est', quod Crist, and comsede for to swoune,
> Pitousliche and pale as a prison that deieth;

---

28 Frank, *The Canterbury Tales*, 152.

> The lord of lif and of light tho leide hise eighen togideres.
> The day for drede withdrough and derk bicam the sonne.
> The wal waggede and cleef, and al the world quaved.
> (B.18.57–61)

Here, typically, Langland expresses "the most elevated of religious feelings in the simplest terms,"[29] weaving the Vulgate ("*Consummatum est*") into the English line and adding very little to the biblical account except details of human experience like the swoon and closing of the eyes;[30] there is no narratorial lament. As David Aers points out about *Piers Plowman* in general, there is "no attention to the standard [late medieval] focus on the physical tortures and sufferings of Jesus."[31] Yet the scene does include elements of pathos: "...comsede for to swoune, / Pitousliche and pale as a prison that deieth...tho leide hise eighen togideres": human weakness, the tiny detail of the young man closing his eyes in death, the gentle alliterating sounds of *s*, *p*, and *l*, paleness like that of Custance, even the word "Pitousliche" and the same association with a prisoner to be executed that Chaucer makes in the *Man of Law* passage (645–650)—if these were all, we would have a beautiful poem of pathos. But the poet complements these pathetic elements with something that causes us to see the crucifixion not simply as a moment of pathos, but also as the revelation of an awesome mystery. The young man, "Crist," (the name that implies his divinity) is "The lord of lif and of light." The paradox of the lord of life dying, the lord of light closing his eyes, the pun in the next line, familiar from liturgical hymns associating the Son of God with the glorious sun of light ("and derk bicam the sonne"), and the terrifying reactions of nature to the crucifixion, retold from the gospel account[32] with onomatopoetic power: "The wal waggede and cleef, and al the world quaved"—all of these emphasize the divinity of Christ and the paradox of the death of God. It is absolutely characteristic of Langland that one side of the paradox never swallows up the other: man and God, tenderness and awe, grief and wonder together are part of the intellectual toughness of lines that require the reader to look squarely at mystery, at what cannot be fully understood.

The characteristic styles and themes of the two poets as seen in these two passages (i.e., Chaucer's use of pathos and emphasis upon women and

---

[29] Charles Muscatine, *Poetry and Crisis in the Age of Chaucer* (Notre Dame, IN: University of Notre Dame Press, 1972), 94.

[30] Langland "reduces rather than inflates the gospel narrative" (Bennett, *Poetry*, 106). See James Simpson, *Piers Plowman: An Introduction to the B-Text* (London: Longmand, 1990), 211. But Elizabeth Kirk also points out that this passage presents the "events as witnessed," and surrounds the crucifixion with "a kaleidoscope of superimposed images...and contexts" ("Langland's Narrative Christology," in Robert R. Edwards, ed., *Art and Context in Late Medieval English Narrative* [Cambridge: D. S. Brewer, 1994] 17–35), 23 and 30.

[31] David Aers, "Christ's Humanity and *Piers Plowman*: Contexts and Political Implications," *Yearbook of Langland Studies* 8 (1994): 107–126; 117.

[32] Matt. 27–45, 51–54; Mark 15.38; Luke 23.44–5.

Langland's biblical, liturgical language and focus upon mystery) seem to provide no basis for comparison or contrast. But a distinction made by Walter Ong some fifty years ago in a study of Latin hymnody seems to provide such a basis and to touch upon some of the foregoing elements.[33] Ong divides Latin hymns of the Middle Ages into two groups: affective poetry, like the *Dies Irae* and the *Stabat Mater*, and poetry of wit, like the *Pange Lingua* and the *Adoro Te*. Affective religious poetry, begun perhaps by Bernard and made popular by the Franciscans, features, he says, "tender and haunting melancholy,...awesome and plaintive foreboding...plangent pathos;" it "generally finds the source of its rhetoric in the commonplaces of ordinary life—the love of son for mother, of mother for child, of brother for brother" or of knight for lady, "calling up familiar blocks of feeling and transferring them to a higher plane."[34] The purpose of this affective or emotional poetry is not so much understanding as feeling, the evocation of emotion.[35] Ong calls the other kind of medieval Latin hymnody "wit poetry," comparing it to the metaphysical poetry of the seventeenth century. In it, "interest in word-play and witty conceit go hand-in-hand with preoccupation with genuinely distinctive 'mysteries' of Christianity,"[36] those beliefs that can never be fully explained, like the Trinity and the incarnation.

At least in a general way, this distinction seems useful in a contrast of the religious works of Chaucer and Langland, for Chaucer is a great artist of religious affectivity, including pathos, and Langland of wit as a way to probe mystery. The distinction harmonizes with observations that many scholars have made about each of the writers individually. Robert Frank, for example, says of Chaucer's tales of pathos, "There is little or no complexity. Characters are generally one- or two-dimensional, motivated by a single virtue....Chaucer's principal artistic concern...is to produce a strong emotional effect."[37] David Benson notes Chaucer's "appeal to the common experience of a general audience," his "affective piety"[38] and, in contrast, *Piers Plowman*'s "poetic and intellectual density. Langland's intricacy of argument and richness of imagery often resemble metaphysical poetry...This concentration of ideas and images is very different from

---

[33] Walter Ong, S.J., "Wit and Mystery: A Revelation in Mediaeval Latin Hymnody," *Speculum* 22 (1947): 310–341.

[34] Ong, "Wit," 311, 321, 322.

[35] See, for example, Douglas Gray, "Popular Religion and Late Medieval English Literature, " in Boitani and Torti, eds., *Religion*, 1–28; here 7. Ong's use of the term "affective poetry" is different from James Simpson's use of "affective knowledge" in Simpson's "From Reason to Affective Knowledge: Modes of Thought and Poetic Form in *Piers Plowman.*" *Medium Ævum* 55 (1986): 1–23. Simpson distinguishes between two modes of knowing in *Piers Plowman*: *scientia* or intellectual knowledge, and *sapientia* or affective knowledge. The latter resides in the will and is deeper than the feelings to which Ong's "affective poetry" appeals.

[36] Ong, "Wit," 323.

[37] Frank, *The Canterbury Tales*, 143.

[38] Benson, "Aesthetic," 109 and 110.

Chaucer's usual conversational style...the looser poetry of Chaucer."[39] R. A. Waldron writes that Passus 18 of *Piers Plowman* "as a whole is not a single-minded stimulus to devotion, but rather, in its poetic and logical complexity, a challenge to the imagination and intellect."[40] George Kane comments that "Langland's style functions as a mode of meaning...by intellectual engagement rather than imaginative suggestion,"[41] and Bennett, that "Langland's piety is spare, restrained, not affective."[42]

Chaucer's religious affectivity may be seen, for example, at the end of *The Prioress's Tale* when the dead child speaks:

> "And after that thus seyde she to me:
> 'My litel child, now wol I fecche thee,
> Whan that the greyn is fro thy tonge ytake.
> Be nat agast; I wol thee nat forsake.'"
> (*PriorT* 666–669)

The situation is full of pathos and wonder, the voice that of a "litel child" who has suffered innocently and been marvelously saved. The voice of Mary is heard through the voice of the child[43] who repeats the words she spoke to him as she called him "My litel child" and reassured him as any mother would reassure a child, "Be nat agast, I wol thee nat forsake." Mary is seen as merciful and powerful enough to do miracles. Both she and the child are simple characters, perfect and single-minded, isolated from the horror around them. The poetry is affective; it appeals to the emotions of ordinary human relationships, and, if readers do not advert to what is happening to the Jewish people outside the chapel, it leaves them with a feeling of comfort about Mary's relationship with her children.

If they do advert to it, of course, they may feel the intense satiric and moral force of the whole tale, the absurdity and obscenity of antisemitism among those who pray to Rachel, Mary, and Jesus, and perhaps become aware that "Chaucer is touching something true here...about the kinship of pathos and violence as extremes of feeling....The poem can be read both as successful pathos and as an exposure (conscious or unconscious) of the brutality which lies beneath it."[44]

A passage from the end of Passus 5 in *Piers Plowman* will serve as a contrasting example:

---

[39] Benson, "Frustration," 7–8.
[40] Waldron, R. A., "Langland's Originality: The Christ Knight and the Harrowing of Hell," in Kratzmann and Simpson, eds., *Medieval*, 66–81; 67.
[41] George Kane, *Chaucer and Langland* (London: Athlone Press, 1989), 143.
[42] Bennett, *Middle*, 438.
[43] Carolyn P. Collette, "Chaucer's Discourse of Mariology: Gaining the Right to Speak," in Edwards, ed., *Art and Context*, 127–147; 145.
[44] Muscatine, *Poetry*, 140.

> 'Ac ther are seven sustren that serven Truthe evere
> And arn porters over the posternes that to the place longeth.
> . . . .
> And but if ye be sibbe to some of thise sevene,
> It is ful hard, by myn heed, any of yow alle
> To geten ingong at any gate but grace be the moore!'
> 'Now, by Crist!' quod a kuttepurs, 'I have no kyn there.'
> 'Ne I,' quod an apeward, 'by aught that I knowe.'
> 'Wite God,' quod a wafrestere, 'wiste I this for sothe,
> Sholde I never ferther a foot for no freres prechyng.'
> 'Yis,' quod Piers the Plowman, and poked hem alle to goode,
> 'Mercy is a maiden there, hath myght over hem alle;
> And she is sib to alle synfulle, and hire sone also,
> And thorugh the help of hem two—hope thow noon oother—
> Thow myght gete grace there—so thow go bityme.'
> (B.5.618–619, 627–638)

The passage is partly comic and satiric; it is without pathos. Piers has delineated a difficult road to Truth, and ends by declaring that unless a person
is "sibbe" to the seven virtues, "It is ful hard...any of yow alle / To geten
ingong..." Kinship, relationship to the austere virtues seems entirely out of
the question to the cutpurse, wafer seller and apekeeper: "I have no kyn
there," and they are ready to give up. But Piers intervenes, not with a new
course of penance, but with an astounding alternative:

> 'Yis', quod Piers...
> 'Mercy is a maiden there, hath myght over hem alle;
> And she is sib to alle synfulle, and hire sone also'
> (B.5.634–6).

Mary here is, if anything, more majestic than in *The Prioress's Tale*, but she
does not act out of pity (as for the "litel child"); rather, bound as she is by
a permanent, objective bond to humankind as a woman of flesh and blood,
and therefore our sister, she embodies an improbable, astonishing mercy.
The bond of kinship, it seems, can be called upon and will not fail. The
poet's emphasis is on paradox rather than pathos, the paradoxes of a maid-
en with a son and of two innocents who are brother and sister precisely to
sinners. This is not affective, emotional poetry, but wit poetry, spinning out
literal implications of the incarnation in paradox; an astringent passage,
not a direct appeal to feelings,[45] it nevertheless touches the heart through

---

[45] A. J. Minnis judges that "the poem was directed primarily at the *affectus* or will and not the intellect,"
quoted in Anne Middleton, "The Audience and Public of *Piers Plowman*," in David Lawton, ed., *Middle
English Alliterative Poetry and Its Literary Background* (Cambridge: D. S. Brewer, 1982), 153 n36; it is not
a logical disquisition but metaphors and paradoxes which get to the will through the mind. As James
Simpson says of Patience's poetry, "it is intellectually demanding, but its intellectual force is designed to
move the will" (*Piers*, 156). "Nothing...associates it with speculative theology" (Middleton, "Audience,"
109); as A.C. Spearing says, the poem progresses "not on the level of propositions linked by logic but on
that of images linked by action" (*Readings in Medieval Poetry* [Cambridge: Cambridge University Press,

a new understanding of the solidarity of Christ with everyone at all times. "The emancipatory force of this solidarity is not only eschatological; it is also always present."[46] The passage offers neither abstract theology nor simple emotion, but what Middleton calls "'heart-ravishing' knowledge"— a *kynde knowyng*.[47]

Besides this basic difference between poetry of feeling and poetry of wit, a second point of contrast between the religious writing of Chaucer and Langland lies in their relationships with their audiences. Both poets involve their audiences deeply, but in very different ways. Chaucer or the Chaucerian narrator frequently speaks to the reader: inside and outside the fiction, both as narrator and as the speaker in the "Retractions,"[48] Chaucer declares himself to be concerned about audience reaction. That is, from inside the text, Chaucer speaks to those who are outside the text, addressing reader or audience as "Yow." Amused or touched, readers or hearers are aware of their position outside the poem and their freedom to "Turne over the leef and chese another tale" (*MilPro* 3177). Within the tales, some of Chaucer's narrators also speak to their audience, astutely or foolishly, so that several layers of fiction separate the audience from the events of the narrative.

Paradoxically, all of this emphasizes a gulf between poet and reader; "the fictional nature of the performance is ever more forcefully stressed."[49] This gulf does not nullify the emotional power of the performance. Indeed, "Chaucer appeals to the power of pity to work on the reader...obliterating distance in an intense identification of feeling."[50] "The aim is to involve the audience and persuade them to an empathetic posture...to evoke pity and compassion." Each reader responds "empathetically to the scene...[and is] told to step into the scene...[;] tears [are]...ardently sought from the reader."[51] The pity and pathos *do* touch us, but *as readers* observing a pathetic figure within the narrative.[52]

Unlike Chaucer, Langland rarely calls his audience "yow," rarely addresses it directly at all after the first passus. His characters frequently address all people, or "yow rich" or "alle cristene" but not as audience.

1987], 228). Middleton also notes that "neither specifically mendicant learnedness, nor the affective meditations particularly associated with mendicant spirituality are closely associated with the poem" ("Audience," 109).

46 Aers, "Christ's," 122.

47 Middleton, "Audience," 115. "The modes of poetry seem to me to be consistently designed to produce a sapiential, experiential, 'kynde' knowledge of God" (Simpson, "From Reason," 14); (he is speaking here of text from Passus 16.74 to the end of the poem.)

48 Dieter Mehl, "The Audience of Chaucer's *Troilus and Criseyde*," in Beryl Rowland, ed., *Chaucer and Middle English Studies* (Kent, Ohio: Kent State University Press, 1974), 173–189; 186.

49 David Lawton, *Chaucer's Narrators* (Cambridge: D. S. Brewer, 1985), 13.

50 Jill Mann, *Geoffrey Chaucer* (New York: Harvester Wheatcheaf, 1991), 140.

51 Frank, *Canterbury Tales*, 144, 145–6, 158.

52 See also Gerard Genette, *Narrative Discourse*, trans. Jane E. Lewin (Ithaca: Cornell University Press, 1980), 260–61, and Walter Ong, "The Writer's Audience is Always a Fiction," *PMLA* 90 (1975): 9–21; 17.

Nothing, therefore, emphasizes the gulf between "inside" and "outside" the poem. Rather, as readers, we seem to be inside it; we are part of "us alle," or of the "riche" or the "Cristene" or the "feeld ful of folk" (Prol. 17). Lawton distinguishes "two key patterns of narratorial voice in the poetry of the later fourteenth century: the non-Chaucerian, and Chaucer's. The first and older type of narratorial voice addresses itself "'as if' to the entire community:"[53] Anne Middleton has described it as "the idea of public poetry," and Langland's poetry is certainly public. But the distinction I am trying to make goes further than that, to the way Langland causes readers to perceive themselves as part of the community rather than as readers or audience. "It is not simply that he makes no attempt to present the poem as a performance or book, but that in his declining to do so the composition as such vanishes: it becomes indistinguishable from the experiencing of it by the audience. The literary fiction is that there is no fiction..."[54]

Tone and style complement these relationships to audience. Chaucer is a supreme ironist, and this, as well as the Canterbury frame and his direct appeals to audience, seems to distance him from his own text and to allow the reader distance. Also his mastery of the high art of rhyme and meter increases awareness of his art. Langland's "natural" use of the alliterative line conceals art, allowing the audience perhaps to be unaware of his style, and although he is quite capable of irony, his most characteristic tone is what Richard Barnes calls his "inconsolable sensitivity to the world's pain [which] has a kind of pure anger as one of its elements," and which pulls the audience in.[55]

In addition, the puns, paradoxes, and shifts of scene in *Piers Plowman*, like puzzles, demand effort from the reader to bring meaning together in the mind, to see multiple meanings together in a single word; in some sense (though not in an arbitrary or licentious one) the reader "creates" the meaning of the poem by wrestling with it, playing the "game" inside the poem. In so doing, the reader begins to struggle with Will to see into the mysteries of Christian faith.[56] Langland "offers an interactive text, as Iser might call it."[57]

The difference in the effects of Chaucer's and Langland's works upon the reader can, of course, be felt. Personally, as a reader I have a varying distance and range of reactions to the Pardoner, the Summoner, even to Custance and Cecilia. I judge them, admire them, laugh at them or weep for them. When, however, I read the passus of the Seven Deadly Sins in *Piers Plowman*, I become implicated. What the penitents say is funny but

---

[53] Lawton, *Chaucer's*, 12–13.

[54] Middleton, "Audience," 113.

[55] Richard Barnes, "Stance and Style," *Yearbook of Langland Studies* 9 (1995): 19–31.

[56] See Benson, "Frustration," 12, Bennett, *Middle*, 452, and Mary Clemente Davlin, O. P., *A Game of Heuene: Word Play and the Meaning of Piers Plowman B* (Cambridge: D. S. Brewer, 1989), 122.

[57] Benson, "Frustration," 12.

at the same time I find it painful, not with pathos, but because somehow
they begin to speak for me, to confess my frailties. I feel, not sympathy, but
contrition: as Waldron says, "One of the effects of the confessions of the
sins *is* to convict the reader of sin."[58]

A good place to look at Chaucer's relationship with his audience is at
the end of *Troilus and Criseyde*:

> O yonge, fresshe folkes, he or she,
> In which that love up groweth with youre age,
> Repeyreth hom fro worldly vanyte,
> And of youre herte up casteth the visage
> To thilke God that after his ymage
> Yow made, and thynketh al nys but a faire,
> This world that passeth soone as floures faire.
>
> (*TC* 5.1835–1848)

This is gentle poetry; simple diction evokes deep emotion with words of
family ("Repeyreth hom"), of "love" and "herte." Here, Chaucer speaks
tenderly to his doubtless fictional audience as to the very young, in a direc-
tive way: "Repeyreth hom." "Thynketh," he says, that everything in this
world is only "a faire...that passeth soone as floures faire." (1840–41).
There is less pathos here, yet this is affective, emotional poetry, using
"familiar blocks of feeling"[59] with lovely fresh diction and metaphor. The
rime riche on "faire" suggests that the world is not to be despised in its
beauty, but neither is it to be depended upon, because it will pass as surely
as fair flowers do. Instead, the young listeners are urged,

> And loveth hym the which that right for love
> Upon a crois, oure soules for to beye,
> First starf, and roos, and sit in hevene above;
> For he nyl falsen no wight, dar I seye...
>
> (*TC* 5.1842–45)

"For he nyl falsen no wight...." Here is the tie to the narrative in which
Criseyde "falsed Troilus" (1053), and to Chaucer's comment shortly before
this passage that often women "bitraised be / Thorugh false folk"
(1780–81). Chaucer is moving his readers from grief for Troilus—through
the experience of the eighth sphere where Troilus holds "al vanite / To
respect of the pleyn felicite / That is in hevene above" (1817–19)—"hom"
to an awareness of Jesus who "best to love is, and most meke" (1847). His
attempt to move the audience is overt, his aim the remarkable feat of
swinging a whole worldview into synthesis with Christianity. The audience
he addresses is so well-defined that if we are not "yonge, fresshe folkes,"

---

[58] Waldron, "Langland's," 66.
[59] Ong, "Wit," 322.

we are perhaps doubly distanced. Part of our pleasure is imagining them being influenced by the speaker.

The last stanza begins as wit poetry:

> Thow oon, and two, and thre, eterne on lyve,
> That regnest ay in thre, and two, and oon,
> Uncircumscript, and al maist circumscrive,
> Us from visible and invisible foon
> Defende, and to thy mercy, everichon,
> So make us, Jesus, for thi mercy, digne,
> For love of mayde and moder thyn benigne. Amen.
>   (*TC* 5.1863–69)

The first three lines are Dante's, for Chaucer here is "reproducing," as Kean says, "some of the greatest religious poetry he knew."[60] Yet, in doing so, Chaucer makes only what Ong calls in another context "a loose gesture toward the mysteries as such,"[61] here the mystery of the Trinity. Chaucer uses Dante's paradox but does not probe it, turning away from any further consideration of what the first three lines mean, to end with a prayer to Jesus and his mother, calling to mind their tender human relationship. Chaucer does something similar in *The Second Nun's Tale*, when Cecilia, asked about the Trinity, gives one analogy and starts immediately "bisily to preche / Of Cristes come, and of his peynes teche" (342–3). In both passages, Chaucer evokes the Trinity but does not find it artistically compelling, as Langland does, for example, in the Samaritan's long treatise in Passus 17. Instead, at the end of *Troilus*, the audience has the affective delight of coming "hom" to the Christian universe and divine love.

Langland's relationship to his audience is quite different. In Passus 11, Will cries out:

> For Crist cleped us alle, come if we wolde—
> Sarsens and scismatikes, and so he dide the Jewes:
>   *O vos omnes sicientes, venite...*
> And bad hem souke for synne save at his breste...
>   (B.11.119–121)

This passage immediately implicates "us alle," not as audience, but as those called in the passage from Isaiah: "*O vos omnes*," "O all you who thirst, come." The invitation, since it is to everyone, includes the reader, who is not mentioned or adverted to except insofar as she or he is one of "us alle."

---

[60] P. M. Kean sees this stanza as a "newer synthesis of intellectual argument and illuminating image which Chaucer developed to best effect under the influence of Dante" (*Chaucer and the Making of English Poetry*, 2 vols., [London: Routledge and Kegan Paul, 1972], 2:201).

[61] Ong, "Wit," 323.

This, too, might have been affective poetry, comparing, as it does, Jesus to a nursing mother,[62] and "us alle" to her/his babies, but instead it is wit poetry, its diction leading not directly to emotion, but to thought, which in turn leads to wonder and love. There is no description, there are no diminutives, but instead, the evocation of the Isaian passage, "Come and drink," paraphrased by Christ in John 7.37. The metaphor of nursing with which Langland interprets the passage may evoke in the reader a pre-conscious memory of one of the earliest needs and most intimate relationships of "us alle," as human beings, not as readers. The passage thus involves and moves us, not through explicit appeals to feeling, but through a witty metaphor.[63] It involves us in much the same way that liturgical poetry involves us, not eliciting our admiration so much as our prayer.

Despite these two major differences, the two poets share significant religious understandings. One would expect this, since both are late fourteenth-century English Catholics, although both were claimed by the Reformers.[64] Several of the religious views they share, in particular, are part of their alterity, and therefore sometimes a stumbling block for readers, because whatever our personal religious affiliations, we twenty-first-century persons from the Western world tend to be deeply affected by our culture's Puritan or Jansenistic bias and by the economic presumptions of our time, both of which are easy to read back unconsciously into medieval religious literature.

One of their shared views is the paradox that they saw the church as a community of sinners destined for heaven. Not that they believed in total depravity or negative predestination. But they did believe that human beings are sinners. Thus Reason quotes Cato, "*Nemo sine crimine vivit!*" (*PPl* B.11.402) and the Parson says, "For soothly oure sweete Lord Jhesu Crist hath spared us so debonairly in oure folies that if he ne hadde pitee of mannes soule, a sory song we myghten alle synge" (*ParsT* 315).[65] This is the traditional Catholic self-understanding, even now: "All members of the Church, including her ministers, must acknowledge that they are sinners...the Church gathers sinners, already caught up in Christ's salvation but still on the way of holiness."[66]

In this Catholic view, which sometimes shocks others, the church is a society of imperfect persons whom the Parson, in *The Canterbury Tales*, and Repentaunce, in *Piers Plowman*, address, whose sins the irony, satire,

---

[62] On nursing mothers as analogous to Christ see, e.g., Caroline Bynum, *Holy Feast and Holy Fast* (Berkeley, CA: University of California Press, 1987), 30; and Aers's comment in "Christ's," 119.

[63] Aers notes the spareness of this metaphor ("Christ's," 119).

[64] Burrow, *Ricardian*, 5.

[65] Nigel Thompson calls *The Canterbury Tales* a "web of transgressions to show what is wrong with the world" in "'Boys Behaving Badly': Male Infamy in the *Decameron* and *The Canterbury Tales*," paper delivered to the International Medieval Conference, Kalamazoo, MI, 1995.

[66] *Catechism of the Catholic Church* (New York: Doubleday, 1995), #827.

and invective of the two poets scourge—not in a despairing mode, but in a curative—or in Bennett's word, "sanative," way.[67] The awareness that Chaucer and Langland had of evil among church people—the skill of the Pardoner and Mede in perverting justice and religion; the corrosive, even if unconscious, antisemitism of Chaucer's Prioress and Langland's Feith;[68] the misuse by their friars of great talents in order to gain money—these are not signs of disillusion or despair in the poets, though they cause great anger; they are rather signs of what they would have regarded as healthy clarity of vision. Chaucer and Langland believed that if humans had not been sinners, they would not have needed a savior, and so they cried out with the church at each Easter vigil, "O happy fault! O necessary sin of Adam that merited...so great a redeemer!", a passage quoted (in Latin) by Langland at B.5.484a.[69] Sinners need the poets' satire as well as the Parson's "meditacioun" as a call to repentance.

A second similarity between the poets is a biblical belief: their pre-capitalist or anti-capitalist view of poverty as a painful state chosen by Christ and worthy of great respect. A similar view was expressed in *Newsweek* by a Cuban-American doctor who makes "house calls to the homeless," saying, "I've had the privilege of treating the sick and the honor of working with the poor."[70] This is a common Judeo-Christian perception; Vivian Paley says of Yiddish stories she heard as a child: "Very, very often it was the odd person, the poor person, the cast-aside person who ends up in the role [of] 'best-loved by God.'"[71] Thus Psalm 34 says, "The Lord hears the cry of the poor," and Mary cries out in Luke 1:53, "He has filled the hungry with good things and has sent the rich away empty."

For Langland, and later, for Chaucer, this view appears in the fact that they choose the plowman as exemplar and symbol of holiness (*GP* 529–541 and *PPl* B.5.537–555). It is a view dramatically different from the "new ethos" of the late middle ages, a "work ethos" condemning the poor in favor of "aggressive individualism,"[72] and also from that sixteenth-century view that Max Weber called "The Protestant Ethic,"[73] where materi-

---

67   Bennett, "Chaucer's," 324.

68   Middleton reminds the reader that we must not "ignore the possible fictiveness of the main voices in [*Piers Plowman*]" ("Audience," 119).

69   Aers seems to feel Langland close to despair at the sins of church people. My position is closer to that of Przemyslaw Mroczkowski, who notes that "Chaucer felt as free as any other clerk of his pre-Tridentine epoch to...lay bare their duplicity where undeniable" ("Faith," 95).

70   "Making House Calls to the Homeless," *Newsweek* (May 29, 1995): 34.

71   "The Only Kindergarten Teacher...Vivian Paley," *Chicago Tribune Magazine* (June 25, 1995): 10: 12–19, 28–29.

72   David Aers, *Community, Gender, and Individual Identity* (London: Routeldge and Kegan Paul, 1988), 34, 55, 59. Anna Baldwin argues: "By centring his poem on a plowman, Langland is, in effect, reversing the [feudal] model" ("The Historical Context," in John A. Alford, *A Companion to Piers Plowman* [Berkeley, CA: University of California Press, 1988], 68).

73   *The Protestant Ethic and the Spirit of Capitalism* [1904–5]. Trans. Talcott Parsons. (N.Y.: Scribner, 1958).

al success was proof of hard work demanded by God, and therefore a sign of election. For Langland, material success is dangerous rather than desirable: "The heighe wey to heveneward ofte riche letteth—" as Patience says (14.212): both Piers and Chaucer's Parson are wrathful with "wastours," who are guilty of what we might call conspicuous consumption, precisely because the waste could have helped the poor (*ParsT* 418; cf. 444; *PPl* B.5.374).

There are differences in sensibility between the poets on this matter. Langland writes with "unsentimental loving compassion and...raw truth" about the real poor and their experiences;[74] as Christopher Dawson wrote many years ago, *Piers Plowman* "is the first and almost the only utterance in literature of the cry of the poor."[75] Chaucer is more distanced from the poor; he does not represent their anguish or suffering, although he satirizes some of them, creates comedy with some, and offers pure description of others.[76] Both poets regret the commercialization of life, as *The Shipman's Tale* and the story of Mede show.[77] Even if both poets are politically conservative, respecting and supporting the structure of feudal society, and even if in their plowmen they advocate a traditional gospel ideal, not a social revolution, it is still startling and significant that in the period of what has been called the Peasants' Revolt, each "idealized the peasantry" by making the plowman a religious ideal.[78] Such idealization was "a point-by-point reversal of the almost universal contemporary criticism of laborers."[79]

In *Piers Plowman*, Passus 14 is the best place to study this attitude to poverty (e.g., 156–64, 173–79), but there is a pertinent passage in Passus 9, as well:

---

[74] Derek Pearsall, "Poverty and Poor People in *Piers Plowman*," in E. D. Kennedy, R. Waldron, J. S. Wittig, eds., *Medieval English Studies Presented to George Kane* (Cambridge: D. S. Brewer, 1988), 167–85; 180.

[75] Christopher Dawson, *Medieval Essays* (London: Sheed and Ward, 1953), 250.

[76] "Chaucer's portrayal of the poor widow at the beginning of *The Nun's Priest's Tale* is like something from a different world—a genre-portrait of rural poverty, and a masterpiece of patrician condescension" (Pearsall, 180). "For us, poverty will remain perhaps an economic problem with sociological implications: for Langland a religious mystery, which continues to ask diffuse and complicated questions" (Geoffrey Shepherd, "Poverty in *Piers Plowman*," in T. H. Aston et al eds., *Social Relations and Ideas* (Cambridge: Cambridge University Press, 1983), 169–189; 177. See also Bennett, *Middle*, 434, and Christopher Dyer, "*Piers Plowman* and Plowmen: A Historical Perspective," *Yearbook of Langland Studies* 8 (1994): 155–176. Henrik Specht notes a contrast in the convention of "calendar pictures" (and some literature of the period) "equivocal in...attitude to the peasantry" (*Poetry and the Iconography of the Peasant, Anglica et Americana* 19 (Copenhagen: University of Copenhagen Press, 1983), 72 and 89.

[77] See David Aers, "Justice and Wage-Labor After the Black Death: Some Perplexities for William Langland," in Allen J. Frantzen and Douglas Moffat, eds., *The Work of Work: Servitude, Slavery and Labor in Medieval England* (Glasgow: Cruithne, 1994) 164–190; here 177–181.

[78] Dyer, "*Piers*," 173. See also Anne Hudson, "*Piers Plowman* and the Peasants' Revolt: A Problem Revisited," *Yearbook of Langland Studies* 8 (1994): 85–106, especially 101.

[79] Elizabeth Kirk, "Langland's Plowman and the Re-creation of a Fourteenth-Century Religious Metaphor," *Yearbook of Langland Studies* 2 (1988): 1–21; 7.

> Sholde no Cristene creature cryen at the yate
> Ne faille payn ne potage, and prelates dide as thei sholden.
> A Jew wolde noght se a Jew go janglyng for defaute
> For alle the mebles on this moolde, and he amende it myghte.
> 'Allas that a Cristene creature shal be unkynde til another!
> Syn Jewes, that we jugge Judas felawes,
> Eyther helpeth oother of hem of that that hym nedeth.
> Whi nel we Cristene be of Cristes good as kynde
> As Jewes, that ben oure loresmen? Shame to us alle!
> The commune for hir unkyndenesse, I drede me, shul abye.
> 'Bisshopes shul be blamed for beggeres sake;
> Than Judas he is wors that yyveth a japer silver
> And biddeth the beggere go, for his broke clothes...'
>   (B.9.80–92)

Such passages, "without any sentimentalization...force readers to shift outside the ethos in which able-bodied vagrants are swiftly classified as drunken scroungers, drones, wasters."[80] The "beggeres" with "broke clothes" who "faille payn" and "potage" are yet "Cristene creature[s]," persons with dignity, part of the community, to whom the rest of "us alle" owe "kyndenesse": kindness, which means the way people ought to treat one another as opposed to "vnkyndenesse," which is monstrous behavior.

Care for the poor is thus not a matter of unusual charity but of justice:

> The commune for hir unkyndenesse, I drede me, shul abye.
> Bisshopes shul be blamed for beggeres sake...
>   (B.9.89–90)

The poor have a *right* to "payn" and "potage" and "silver," a right as "Cristene creature[s]" not to be excluded, not to be left to "cryen at the yate." Thus, against the worldly mores of his time and ours, Langland gets to the heart of Christian doctrine, implicating the whole community: "Shame to us alle." This attitude is subversive, not of the church, but of oppressive wealth; it is precisely the kind of teaching about human dignity that has called out the death squads in El Salvador and Guatemala.[81]

Another subversive perception in the passage is the example of kindness Langland gives: the care of the Jewish community for one another. Langland is as aware as Chaucer of antisemitic feeling. The adjectival clause, "that we jugge Judas felawes," sounds as if the speaker identifies with such feeling. But this judgement itself is judged a few lines later: Christians who are spendthrifts, bishops contemptuous of the poor, are worse than what they falsely judge Jews to be—"wors than Judas." And of

---

[80] Aers, *Community*, 61.

[81] Aers also sees such passages as "*political* theology" ("Christ's," 120) and points out their power "against the assimilation of the church in contemporary networks of power." If the church, however, is a community of sinners in need of repentance, then attacking sin within the church is an act of loyalty to the church, subversive though it may be to particular power groups among sinners.

course, the use of the example at all suggests that the Jews who enact love and "kyndenesse" are not only not "Judas felawes," but are kin to Kynde/Caritas, for whom their virtue is named.

Sometimes Langland goes beyond the question of social justice to the promise of perfect justice for the poor in heaven:

> Ther the poore dar plede, and preve by pure reson
> To have allowaunce of his lord; by the lawe he it cleymeth:
> Joye, that nevere joye hadde, of rightful jugge he asketh,
> And seith, 'Lo! briddes and beestes, that no blisse ne knoweth,
> And wilde wormes in wodes, thorugh wyntres thow hem grevest,
> And makest hem wel neigh meke and mylde for defaute,
> And after thow sendest hem somer, that is hir sovereyn joye,
> And blisse to alle that ben, bothe wilde and tame.'
> 'Thanne may beggeris, as beestes, after boote waiten,
> That al hir lif han lyved in langour and in defaute.
> But God sente hem som tyme som manere joye
> Outher here or elliswhere, kynde wolde it nere...'
> (B.14.108–119)

The comparison of human life with that of birds, beasts and "wilde wormes in wode" emphasizes its poverty and suggests the universal relationship of all creation, birds and beasts and worms and people, with the Creator, who, in another part of the poem, is called "Kynde." In line 119, "kynde" demands joy for all beings; the first meaning, of course, is that nature demands this, but a second meaning is hard to avoid; the God of nature, who is kindness itself (*deus caritas*), would not be kindness if any creature were totally deprived of joy. As throughout *Piers Plowman*, ultimately it is the nature of God, the natures of Christ, that are the basis of human hope. "The scrupulousness of Langland's record of reality can end only, for him, in the necessity of raising the eyes to a higher reality."[82] Is such a passage as this an opiate for the people, a support for oppression? On the contrary, Langland's statement about heaven is daring, not escapist: "the poor dar plede, and preve by pure reson / To have allowaunce of his lord; by the lawe he it cleymeth" (108–9). "Here the anxious and competitive pleading of beggars is transformed into a gesture of confident, energetic request"—indeed, a demand of God.[83] The poor have dignity and rights. Poverty, painful and evil as it is, is a claim upon God's justice, guaranteed both by the divine nature and by the human nature of Christ.

And this leads to the final and most obvious way in which both *Piers Plowman* and *The Canterbury Tales* are religious, in the world-view they share of a stable universe: "that larger theological landscape within which, for medieval...[people], all human activity is played out and ultimately

---

[82] Pearsall, "Poverty," 185.
[83] Simpson, "From Reason," 164.

judged";[84] that is, heaven above (or to the right), hell below (or to the left), and the world between, though, unlike Dante, both are more interested in *this* world than in the next.

Langland makes this cosmology explicit at the beginning:

> 'The tour up the toft...Truthe is therinne...'
> (B.1.12)
> 'That dongeon in the dale that dredful is of sighte—
>
> . . . .
> That is the castel of care....
>
> . . . .
> Therinne wonyeth a wight that Wrong is yhote,
> Fader of falshede'
> (B.1.59, 61, 63–4).

In *The Second Nun's Tale*, Cecile tells Tiburce, "But ther is bettre lif in oother place..." (323), and several of Chaucer's tales end with benedictions and warnings based on this world-view: "And brynge us to his heighe blisse! Amen" says the Nun's Priest, for example (3446), and the Friar warns, "Disposeth ay youre hertes to withstonde / The feend, that yow wolde make thral and bonde" (1659–60).

This world, between heaven and hell, is temporary. Langland says, "for hennes shul we alle" (11.210), and Chaucer says in his little poem, "Truth": "Her is non hoom, her nis but wildernesse" (17). Both poets create imaginatively an earth that is precious but transitory, open to the influences of heaven and hell, redeemed by Christ.

Sometimes Chaucer deliberately experiments with alternate world views and allows us to forget the Christian one posited most clearly at the end by the Parson. But occasionally, an angel (as in *The Second Nun's Tale*) or a devil (as in *The Friar's Tale*) slips in, where Chaucer "create[s] an explicitly theological image of the world in which the Canterbury pilgrimage takes place—the world of *real powers* in which his pilgrims (both in the tales they tell and in the framing fiction they inhabit) move and speak and intend and determine their eternal destiny."[85]

Langland, like Julian, seems to say that no one will go to hell. He mentions heaven over fifty-five times, though he never tries to describe it at length as Chaucer and the Pearl-poet do. His concept of heaven is living in and with God:

> Lord, who shal wonye in thi wones with thyne holy seintes
> Or resten on thyne holy hilles?—This asketh David.
> (B.3.235–6).

---

84 V. A. Kolve, "'A Man in the Middle': Art and Religion in Chaucer's *Friar's Tale*," *Studies in the Age of Chaucer* 12 (1990): 5–46; 24.
85 Kolve, "Man," 23.

And this concept of heaven is in harmony with his view throughout the poem, based on John, that those who live in love, live in God and God in them. Twice (B.5.487b; B.9.64a) he quotes John's lines, "*qui manet in caritate, in Deo manet et Deus in eo,*" and uses images of Treuthe in the heart (B.5.605–608); of all creation in the hand of God (B.17.161-2); of the folk called into Unite (B.20.74–5); of Christ found in oneself (B.15.161-2a) and in others (B.11.184–186; 241-2); of eating and drinking Christ (as the milk from his breasts, and the eucharist). He even uses images of God living within God: "*Ego in Patre et Pater in me est*" (John 14:11, B.10.245a), Truthe "in Trinitee" (B.1.133). Thus those who already live in truth and "enden...in truthe...mowe be siker that hire soule shul wende to hevene, / Ther Treuthe is in Trinitee and troneth hem alle" (B.1.131-3).

One of the ironies of not taking Chaucer's religious writing seriously is that the end of *The Parson's Tale* is the most beautiful attempt at a description of heaven in English. The Parson speaks in exquisitely rhythmic prose, solemn in the way each phrase comes to rest accentually, the simple *sermo humilis* structured in parallels and antitheses.

> Thanne shal men understonde what is the fruyt of penaunce; and, after the word of Jhesu Crist, it is the endelees blisse of hevene, ther joye hath no contrarioustee of wo ne grevaunce; ther alle harmes been passed of this present lyf; ther as is the sikernesse fro the peyne of helle; ther as is the blisful compaignye that rejoysen hem everemo, everich of otheres joye; ther as the body of man, that whilom was foul and derk, is moore cleer than the sonne; ther as the body, that whilom was syk, freele, and fieble, and mortal, is inmortal, and so strong and so hool that ther may no thyng apeyren it; ther as ne is neither hunger, thurst, ne coold, but every soule replenyssed with the sighte of the parfit knowynge of God. This blisful regne may men purchace by poverte espiritueel, and the glorie by lowenesse, the plentee of joye by hunger and thurst, and the reste by travaille, and the lyf by deeth and mortificacion of synne.
>
> (*ParsT* 1075–1080)

Chaucer expresses here that "grand and final...eschatological faith" that Charles Muscatine notes in the "Retraction," the epilogue to *Troilus*, and *The Nun's Priest's Tale*.[86] In the Parson's view, heaven is the place for sinners, repentant sinners, represented by the pilgrims whom he has lectured and reprimanded for a thousand lines in order to show them "the wey, in this viage/ Of thilke parfit glorious pilgrymage / That highte Jerusalem celestial" (X. 48–50). His emphasis is not on worldly metaphors of thrones and jewels, power and honor, as it so often is in medieval descriptions and artistic conceptions of heaven, but on the redemption of the body and the comfort of the soul. Strongly influenced by the Book of Revelation, the passage is full of pity and tenderness for the sufferings of a body nearing death,

---

[86] Muscatine, *Poetry*, 113.

"foul and derk...syk, freele, and fieble, and mortal," as well as the poverty of "hunger, thurst" and "coold." All of this earthly pain is contrasted with the radiance of heaven, its "endelees blisse...joye...blisful compaignye...glorie"; earthly suffering is given meaning by what it "purchases," so that the passage is glorious with a profound hope in the comforting that God has in store. Chaucer's heaven, like Langland's, and like Fra Angelico's a few decades later, is a social place where "the blisful compaignye...rejoysen hem everemo, everich of otheres joye." For the Parson, joy is the ultimate reality, as, for Langland's Patience it is the right of every creature: "endelees blisse...the plentee of joye."

Both Chaucer and Langland are great religious writers. For both, God is comfort and protector, not threat; Christ the evidence and incarnation of relationship with God; life consequently precious, sometimes comic, never totally tragic; love its greatest value (though Langland sometimes calls it *treuthe*); and although a number of Chaucer's pilgrims imagine villains damning themselves, heaven, "Jerusalem celestial," is its appointed end, an end inconceivably more wonderful than the greatest joys of earth. Langland is more interested than Chaucer in who and what God is, although Jill Mann in her analysis of *The Clerk's Tale* has suggested convincingly that Chaucer was interested as well.[87] Implicit in the whole of *Piers Plowman*, though it appears on the surface to be inconclusive and incoherent, is an entirely coherent perception of the nature of God and God's relationships with creation, based upon insistent probing of what the church believes. All sorts of relationships and connections between God and human beings are implied or dramatized throughout the text, such as kinship through the blood of Christ who is "sib to alle sinful," mutual indwelling, effective likeness to God (as, for example, in Trajan, who lives in *treuthe* and is given salvation by the God who is *Treuthe*), the likeness of Christ to all other humans because of *humana natura*, the armor he wears; poverty, the "secte" in which Christ won us, transforming the basic poverty of the human condition. Langland retells biblical and apocryphal stories which dramatize the mystery of evil over which God triumphs by bringing good, as when Longeus pierces Christ's heart and instead of being struck dead, is healed by the blood that flows from the wound. The poem, powerful in its alliterative line, is a tissue of minute revelations of the nature of the Christian God. No wonder Bennett calls it "the supreme English testament of Christian faith and practice."[88] Its purpose, I think, is to bring the reader gradually to a *kynde knowyng* of *Treuthe*.

---

[87] Mann, *Geoffrey Chaucer*, 146-64.
[88] Bennett, *Poetry*, 85.

Chaucer's body of religious poetry is smaller, and has different purposes: *sentence and solaas*. It is easier to read, urbane, sensuous and musical, varied in tones, filled with pathos, comedy, and the triumph of miracle over evil. Chaucer's religious writings, of course, are short individual stories and lyrics, each with its own brilliant, clear texture. "*The Canterbury Tales* is a book about the world,"[89] and most of us, I think, search them for a deeper understanding, not of God, but of the vagaries of human event and character in God's universe.

Each is a treasure that is endless.

---

[89] Donald Howard, *The Idea of the Canterbury Tales* (Berkeley, CA: University of California Press, 1976), 380.

Through the Lens of Theory

The Power of Impropriety: Authorial Naming in *Piers Plowman*

James Simpson

The desire to find the author of *Piers Plowman* will not go away. Proponents of multiple authorship earlier in the century may have dispersed authorship, and resisted putative authorial signatures as convincing.[1] And since then various movements may have tried to dislocate the narrator's represented life from the author's "real" life, or to deny that the represented life is in any case a "life."[2] For all that, the need to recover the author is visible in the poem's earliest reception, and continues to resurface. It is already apparent in the early fifteenth-century C-Text explicit that reads *Explicit liber Willielmi de Petro le Plowghman*.[3] Based, presumably, on no more evidence than the narrator's name "Will," this assumes both that the narrator is the author, and that the personification "Will" should be personalised to produce a proper name. The note in Dublin, Trinity College, MS 212 (D.4.1), also dateable to the early fifteenth century, goes further and offers a name for the poet ("Willielm[us] de Langlond"), along with his father's name, status, location and landlord.[4] Robert Crowley's 1550 edition of the poem offers a name "Robertus Langland,"[5] and his contemporary John Bale, whose bibliographical work

---

[1] See, for example, J. M. Manly, "The Authorship of *Piers Plowman*," *Modern Philology* 7 (1909): 83–104 (p. 97 for resistance to the authorial signature at B.15.148).

[2] For a strong statement dislocating the represented life from the "real" life, see George Kane, *The Autobiographical Fallacy in Chaucer and Langland Studies*, Chambers Memorial Lecture, March 1965 (London: H. K. Lewis, 1965); for the denial that Will's experience represents a life, see, for example, David Lawton, "The Subject of *Piers Plowman*," *Yearbook of Langland Studies* 1 (1987): 1–30.

[3] See Ralph Hanna III, *William Langland*, Authors of the Middle Ages 3 (Aldershot, Hants. G.B.: Variorum, 1993), 5. Letter forms have been modernized here and throughout this essay.

[4] For the text of the note, see, for example, Vincent Di Marco, *"Piers Plowman": A Reference Guide* (Boston: G. K. Hall, 1982) 1; George Kane, *"Piers Plowman": The Evidence for Authorship* (London: Athlone Press, 1965), 26; and Hanna, *William Langland*, 2.

[5] For the Crowley ascription, see Di Marco, *"Piers Plowman,"* 4–5.

was resolutely author-centred, reproduces the same name and guesses at a life (where Bale's only certainty is that Langland was among the first disciples of Wyclif).[6] Although no one after Bale or Crowley pretends to offer substantial information about Langland's life outside what is represented in the poem, successive editors (as John Bowers has recently demonstrated) have each implicitly, and sometimes explicitly, presupposed a life, often curiously close to the practice or ideals of the editor's own life.[7] Such presupposition, as Charlotte Brewer argues in her reply to Bowers's article, is by no means incidental to the project of editing itself. Many scholars earlier this century had originally argued that the question of single or multiple authorship could not be settled until the question of the text had been settled. As Brewer points out, this turned out to be fallacious, since (as was recognised by E. Talbot Donaldson in 1968), questions of establishing the text turn out to be dependent on understandings of authorship.[8] And in that debate, single authorship (and, therefore, a single life) gained control of the field.[9]

Editorial practice, along with hermeneutics more generally, cannot (in my view) escape circularity of a kind: readers certify interpretation of a text by reference to an understanding of intention; understanding of that presumed intention, however, is at least initiated by the same text whose meaning is to be sought. It is perhaps for this reason that interpretation of the poem has also proceeded on the basis of implied or explicit understandings of the poet's life and person. In any case, textual disputes themselves have produced interpretative responses: E. Talbot Donaldson's book on the C-Text, for example, was designed to demonstrate the excellence of that version of the poem, and its coherence with the B-Text. The conviction of single authorship behind this project also produces a putative life as the last chapter of that book.[10] Proponents of multiple authorship aside, all the major strands of interpretation this century before the 1960s were premised on an understanding of the poet outside the work, whether the critic regarded the poet as, for example, either lettered or inspired, either

---

[6] For Bale's author-centred practice as a bibliographer, see Anne Hudson, "*Visio Baleii*: An Early Literary Historian," in Helen Cooper and Sally Mapstone, eds., *The Long Fifteenth Century: Essays for Douglas Gray* (Oxford: Clarendon, 1997), 313–29. For Bale's references to Langland, see Di Marco, "*Piers Plowman*," 3–4; 6.

[7] John M. Bowers, "*Piers Plowman*'s William Langland: Editing the Text, Writing the Author's Life," *Yearbook of Langland Studies* 9 (1995): 65–90. For the history of editing *Piers Plowman* more generally, see Charlotte Brewer, *Editing "Piers Plowman": The Evolution of the Text*, Cambridge Studies in Medieval Literature 28 (Cambridge: Cambridge University Press, 1996).

[8] Charlotte Brewer, "Response", in John M. Bowers, "*Piers Plowman*'s William Langland," 91–4; here, 92.

[9] The case for single authorship has been almost universally accepted since Kane, "*Piers Plowman*": The Evidence for Authorship*.

[10] E. Talbot Donaldson, "*Piers Plowman*": The C-Text and Its Poet*, Yale Studies in English 113 (New Haven: Yale University Press, 1949).

concerned with personal salvation or social regeneration.[11] Since George Kane's essay of 1965, and since structuralism and post-structuralism after that, readers have been wary of connecting the life and the work, and have restricted themselves to what Ralph Hanna prudently calls "the represented life."[12] Despite the power of those movements, however, already we can see (particularly in the work of J. A. Burrow and Anne Middleton) subtle attempts to reassimilate a biography from within the poem's represented life, and to connect that with the poet's "real" life.[13]

In this article I do not wish to arbitrate between proponents of, respectively, the life and death of the author. Instead, I do want to suggest how deeply these issues are built into the poem itself, and especially the question of communal authorship. In particular, I want to focus on the logic of naming actants as common nouns (i.e., personification); I argue that "Langland" (a name I use for convenience) has "Will" evade the stabilities and neutralities of proper naming by entering increasingly anonymous discursive territory. Even if it is true that "William Langland" really was the poet's name,[14] the logic of the poem insists on repeatedly thematizing

---

[11] For recent surveys of Langland scholarship, see Di Marco, "*Piers Plowman*"; Anne Middleton, "*Piers Plowman*," in Albert E. Hartung, ed., *A Manual of the Writings in Middle English, 1050–1500*, Vol. 7 (New Haven: The Connecticut Academy of Arts and Sciences, 1986), 2211–34, 2419–48; Derek Pearsall, "*Piers Plowman* Forty Years On," in Helen Phillips, ed., *Langland, the Mystics and the Medieval English Religious Tradition: Essays in Honour of S. S. Hussey* (Cambridge: D. S. Brewer, 1990), 1–9; and Derek Pearsall, *An Annotated Critical Bibliography of Langland,* Harvester Annotated Critical Bibliographies (New York: Harvester Wheatsheaf, 1990).

[12] Kane, "*Piers Plowman*," 1965; Hanna, *William Langland,* 17.

[13] J. A. Burrow, "Langland *Nel Mezzo del Cammin*," in P. L. Heyworth, ed., *Medieval Studies for J. A. W. Bennett* (Oxford: Clarendon Press,), 21–41; J. A. Burrow, *Langland's Fictions* (Oxford: Clarendon, 1993), ch. 4; and Anne Middleton "William Langland's 'Kynde Name': Authorial Signature and Social Identity in Late Fourteenth-Century England," in Lee Patterson, ed., *Literary Practice and Social Change in Britain, 1380–1530,* The New Historicism 8 (Berkeley: University of California Press), 15–82. As I am in this article, Middleton is sensitive to the limits of "the common and the proper," arguing that in *Piers Plowman* they "blur and fail to sustain themselves as useful heuristic distinctions" (18); her central argument in this dense article, however, is that "Langland's signature methods...encourage the reader's sense that the author's social, vocal, and even physical presence is also somehow 'in' the text, that the words on the page represent a person as well as his product, and that it is his coherence as intelligible actor and the paradigmatic and exemplary form of his life...that secures its value to the user" (36). My concern in the present article is to articulate more exactly what it is to be a "person" for Langland, and in particular to show how his sense of ideal personhood resists propriety of name. For a more recent attempt to locate the "real" Langland, see Kathryn Kerby-Fulton, "Langland and the Bibliographic Ego," in Stephen Justice and Kathryn Kerby-Fulton, eds., *Written Work: Langland, Labour and Authorship* (Philadelphia, PA: University of Pennsylvania Press, 1997), 66–143.

[14] The arguments in favor are fully developed in Kane, "*Piers Plowman*", ch. 4, and summarized by Hanna, *William Langland,* 1–6. Attempts to find records of William Langland (or of other named individuals who may have written the poem) have been both strenuous and fruitless; see, for example, O. Cargill, "The Langland Myth," *PMLA,* 50 (1935): 36–56; Lawrence M. Clopper, "Need Men and Women Labor?: Langland's Wanderer and the Labor Ordinances," in Barbara Hanawalt, ed., *Chaucer's England: Literature in Historical Context, Medieval Studies at Minnesota* 4 (Minneapolis: University of Minnesota Press, 1992), 110–29; Hanna, *William Langland,* 4–6.

"Will" (and occasionally "long" and "land") in such a way as to efface the boundaries between author and reader. Not only is the word "Will" given common force throughout Will's educative experience, but the very fulfillment of Will is itself improper, or common. Foucault's point that the "author is...the ideological figure by which one marks the manner in which we fear the proliferation of meaning" is strikingly perceptive.[15] By putting it that way, however, Foucault suggests that there is an alternative to authors. In fact many anti-authorial hermeneutic movements simply personify authors in the "person" of forces that act through human agents (e.g. Language, Power), thereby camouflaging what is in fact an unacknowledged commitment to authorship. But even if there may be no alternative to authors, that leaves the question wide open as to what constitutes authorship: the author is not necessarily the fully-formed subject of liberal ideology. My focus in this article is on the personification of will, and on the way in which the developing logic of that personification, particularly between Passus 8 and 15 of the B-Text, creates a communal authorial position.[16]

I

Chaucer's *Squire's Tale* begins with a brief yet subtle account of narratorial "entente." The Host's invitation itself concedes an authorial "wille," to which the Squire replies by submitting to the will of the Host:

> "Squier, com neer, if it youre wille be,
> And sey somwhat of love, for certes ye
> Konnen theron as muche as any man."
> "Nay, sire", quod he, "but I wol seye as I kan
> With hertly wyl, for I wol nat rebelle
> Agayn youre lust; a tale wol I telle.
> Have me excused if I speke amys;
> My wyl is good, and lo, my tale is this."[17]

This small passage succinctly outlines the structure and strategy of narratorial "entente": the Squire does have a will, but that is activated only in response to another will, or "lust" (that of the Host). The projected attempt to satisfy the desire of a commanding audience opens the possibility of failure, or of speaking "amys;" at the same time, the very desire to please also excuses failure, since the underlying posture is benevolent. In

---

[15] Michel Foucault, "What is an Author?," in David Lodge, ed., *Modern Theory and Criticism, A Reader* (London and New York: Longman, 1991), 197–210; 209.

[16] I do not broach the implication of my argument for the editing of *Piers Plowman*. See Tim William Machan, *Textual Criticism and Middle English Texts* (Charlottesville: University Press of Virginia, 1994), for an argument that most Middle English authors cannot be described as authors in the humanist sense of that word, and cannot, therefore, be used as the pretexts for textual criticism (43–4).

[17] Citation from Larry D. Benson (ed.), *The Riverside Chaucer*, 3rd edition (Oxford: Oxford University Press, 1987), *Canterbury Tales* V. 1–8, 169.

this essay I apply these observations on the structure and strategy of narratorial will to the much more unruly text of *Piers Plowman*, whose very narrator is itself the "good wyl." For in *Piers*, too, a represented narratorial and authorial will only comes into being in response to larger, more powerful "ententes," and (in a much more extended way) the narratorial will can excuse itself by its underlying posture of well-willing. Passus 8–20 of *Piers Plowman*, indeed, could be described as a massively expanded version of the topos of an author declaring his will to be good.[18] What is striking and distinctive about *Piers Plowman*, however, is the fact that the poem's acts of narratorial submission are also, finally, claims to a kind of authorial power, a power that derives from the poem's refusal to settle into propriety of authorial name.

Personification analyzes force, isolating as it does the powers that govern particular fields of action. The governing agents of economic practice are not, Langland's allegory in Passus 2–4 of the B-Text would have it, individuals, but rather the desire for profit itself, figured as Mede. To personify Mede already concedes that the phenomenal world can be grasped only in conceptual terms, terms that recognize the presence and impersonal force of systems that drive individual action. As deployed in satirical texts, personification is diagnostic, isolating the pathological forces that invade the body politic.[19] Not only is personification diagnostic, but it is also (in Langland's hands, at any rate) therapeutic, designed to control and disperse those pathological forces. Passus 2–4 of the B-Text not only isolate Mede as the force governing corrupt economic practice; the narrative logic of those passus is equally driven by the need to reinstate a normative political order, within which economic practice is governed by ethical constraints. Unequivocally corrupt figures, such as Falsnesse and Lyere, are easily dispersed (2.211–221), while Mede more successfully resists the attack of Conscience precisely because she is equivocal. The word "mede" is already ambiguous, covering many different kinds of reward, and Mede proliferates her applications, camouflaging her corrupt activity by confusing it with a spectrum of perfectly legitimate kinds of payment (3.170–227). As long as she remains ambiguous, she survives in the narrative; the moment

---

[18] See, for example, Passus 1. 76–81 of *Richard the Redeless* (1400), in Helen Barr ed., *The Piers Plowman Tradition* (London: J. M. Dent, 1993), 104:

> My souereyne, that suget I shulde to be,
> I put me in his power and preie him, of grace,
> To take the entent of my trouthe that thoughte non ylle,
> For to wrath no wyght be my wyll neuere,
> As my soule be saff from synne at myn ende.

See also *Mum and the Sothsegger*, ll. 72–102, in Barr, *The Piers Plowman Tradition*, 140–41.

[19] Personification has been associated with pathological states in theoretical formulations of the figure; see James J. Paxson, *The Poetics of Personification*, Literature, Culture, Theory 6 (Cambridge: Cambridge University Press, 1994), 29, 41.

that Conscience defines her analytically, and distinguishes earthly "mede" from legitimate earthly reward (3.230–58), the way is prepared for her dismissal in Passus 4. Analysis of name is the prelude to and premise of therapy. The double action of the whole narrative (both analytical and therapeutic) is neatly encapsulated in Conscience's response to the equivocal figures of Wisdom and Witty, who follow in the train of Reson to the King's court in Passus 4: on the one hand it it said at line 32 that "Conscience knew hem wel" (the analysis); only nine lines later Conscience himself, warning Reson, says that "Conscience knoweth hem noght" (the therapy). The therapeutic end of such narrative is to neutralize pathological forces, to render them incapable of controlling further narrative by driving them from it.[20]

The analytical definition and neutralisation of pathological forces applies not only to actants within fourteenth- and fifteenth-century texts. In more fundamental ways, it also applies to the fictional representation of authorship itself. Authors in this period very often represent themselves not simply as deficient and debilitated in some way, but as taken over, possessed by a force whose power is pathological. In the prologue to Hoccleve's *Regement of Princes* (1412), for example, Hoccleve represents himself as being possessed by the almost vampiric figure of Thought (here meaning "anxiety, distress"):[21]

> What whyght that inly pensif is, I trowe,
> His moste desire is to be solitarie;
> That this is soth, in my persone I knowe,
> For evere whil that fretynge adversarie
> Myn herte made to hym tributarie,
> In sowkynge of the fresschest of my blod,
> To sorwe soole, me thoght it dide me good.[22]

"Thoght" is, by Hoccleve's account, a serious danger to the body politic, since rebellion can erupt from suppressed and melancholy obsession: Thoght's "violence is ful outrageous" (269). It was "thought" that provoked the heretic Badby (267–371),[23] just as it is "irous thought" that produces treacherous, false peace (5055–89). By representing himself as subject to the very force that threatens the state, Hoccleve's strategy is to create a kind of dangerous vacuum at the centre of the text, a vacuum that

---

[20] For the logic of personification in *Piers Plowman*, see Lavinia Griffiths, *Personification in "Piers Plowman,"* Piers Plowman Studies 3 (Woodbridge, Suffolk: Brewer, 1985); for this action of Passus 2–4 in particular, see James Simpson, "From Reason to Affective Knowledge: Modes of Thought and Poetic Form in *Piers Plowman*," *Medium Ævum* 55 (1986), 1–23 (especially 9–13).

[21] See *MED*, sense 5 (b).

[22] Citation from, *faute de mieux*, Frederick J. Furnivall, ed., *The Regement of Princes*, EETS, e.s. 72 (London: Kegan Paul, Trench, Trübner, 1897), ll. 85–91, 4. Letter forms have been modernised; "soole" in line 91 has been emended from Furnivall's reading "soule."

[23] See Anthony J. Hasler, "Hoccleve's Unregimented Body," *Paragraph* 13 (1990): 164–83.

draws another voice into it. The dialogue with the old man that follows serves to reconstitute the narrative of Hoccleve's life, and to redirect Hoccleve's energies. By the end of the Prologue, Hoccleve's "thought" is assuaged by the old man's suggestion that he write a text for Henry (then Prince of Wales), at which point the old man asks him his name:

> "What schal I calle the? what is thi name?"
> "Hoccleve, fadir myn, men clepen me"
> "Hoccleve, sone?" "Iwis, fadir, that same."
> (1863–65)

This heavily-underlined signature marks the point, then, at which Hoccleve recovers himself. This recovery of name is the precondition of addressing a tract of political advice to the king, since it insists that the authorial position is not itself symptomatic of a dangerous political pathology. Beyond that, it offers a direction of sorts to Henry: by accepting the text, Henry preserves the benevolent stability of his subject author; "thoght" is neutralised both by the old man, and implicitly by Henry himself. Hoccleve communicates to the future king not only the point that subjects with proper names are locatable, constructive, and payable, while subjects (particularly authorial subjects) under the control of disruptive forces are dangerous. He also suggests that if Henry's own power is properly conducted, then his subjects will remain within the legitimate discursive limits of their proper name.

Gower's *Confessio Amantis* (1390–93) equally traces a movement from improper authorial subjection under a disruptive power, to "proper" authorial subjection to a king (in the first version of the *Confessio*, at any rate). Precisely insofar as Cupid gains control of Amans in the *persona* of all lovers "whom love binds," so, too, does Amans effectively gain control of the text.[24] Although he is ostensibly subject to Genius, *Amans* governs the flow of narrative, commissioning Genius as he does to satisfy his narrative desire. Given the inherently constructive psychology within which Gower is working, however, the movement of the poem reinstates Amans, and Genius for that matter, within the larger person to which they belong: by the end of the poem Amans, still apparently subject to Venus, returns to his proper name and political identity:

> Sche caste hire chiere upon mi face,
> And as it were halvinge a game
> Sche axeth me what is mi name.
> "Ma dame," I seide, "John Gower."
> "Now John," quod sche, "in my pouer

---

24 The gloss to Book 1, line 61 makes the point explicitly: "*Hic quasi in persona aliorum, quos amor ligat, fingens se auctor esse Amantem, varias eorum passiones...scribere proponit.*" Cited from G. C. Macaulay, ed., *The English Works of John Gower*, 2 vols. EETS e.s 81–2 (London: Oxford University Press, 1900, 1901), 37.

Thou most as of thi love stonde."
            (8.2317–2323)

Gower might still seem to be subject to Venus here—he even rhymes "Gower" and "pouer" to make that point. The effect of Venus's moving speech here is, however, to provoke in Gower a graceful repudiation of his subjection to Venus; as "John Gower" (8.2908), he should now return, says Venus, "ther vertu moral duelleth, / Wher ben thi bokes, as men telleth, / Whiche of long time thou hast write" (8.2925–28). This recovery of a biographical and authorial self is equally, as in Hoccleve, the prelude to Gower's reaffirmation of a political self, as he ends the first recension of the *Confessio* by offering the work to Richard. The "Simplesce of mi poverte / Unto the love of my ligance / Desireth forto do plesance" (8.3046–8), and it is this desire, "in myn entente," that incites him to present the book to the king. The recovery of proper name from the predations of a tyrannical desire also reestablishes proper relations of subjection and desire between subject and king: it is Richard who finally commissions and activates the text, not Amans.

Both Hoccleve and Gower, then, generate their works by personifications of a diminished authorial self, a self which has been taken over by pathological forces that distort relations of true benevolence between subject and king. In the *Confessio*, the subversive power that gains control of the author is explicitly linked with "will." In Book 3, Amans complains to Genius of an internal and apparently irresolvable debate between his will and his wit, figured as belonging to two opposed factions of courtiers within the internal court of the psyche. The faction of Wit, Resoun, and Conseil demand that Will be put "out of retenue" (3.1166),

> For as thei sein, if that he mote
> His oghne rewle have upon honde,
> Ther schal no witt ben understonde.
>   (3.1168–70)

Amans, of course, is provisionally identifiable with this dominant will; as long as he governs the soul, then relations of true desire between subject-counsellor and king are obstructed. The movement back into that benevolence, or well-willing, is coterminous with a return to a proper name. In a sense the Prologue to the *Regiment* and the entire body of the *Confessio* enact the recovery of the proper conditions of political dialogue between subject-counsellor and king. Of course the recovery of a position from which to deliver advice also itself masks advice: in the *Confessio*, for example, the pathological disruption in Amans figures the same potential disruption in the king and in the body politic. To talk about Amans is also to talk about, and to, the king, and the absorption of Amans into "John Gower" is a model for the king's own will, just as it models relations in the body politic at large. The normative situation for *all* these areas of political application is the subjection of will to wit, or, in scholastic terms, the transformation of a cupidinous and sensual desire into a rational desire.[25] Proper willing, which in these cases produces proper naming, is the primary condition of political counsel.

Even if improper willing may be given different colorations (Thought, Drede, Amans), the opposition between will and wit is unquestionably the master code of such distortions. In both political and ethical discourse throughout the later medieval period, improper and dangerous assaults on personal or political integrity are frequently described in terms of will gaining power over wit, or of sensual, singular, and "privy" desire gaining control over the common profit of rational order.[26] Langland, along with Hoccleve and Gower, works within this same opposition, since his authorial narrator is also, clearly enough, called "Will." And the narrative of *Piers Plowman*, like those of the *Regement* and the *Confessio*, traces the movement whereby a distempered authorial will is absorbed into a larger order. There, however, the resemblance ends, for two interconnected reasons: on the one hand, Langland's Will is not contained within the rational bounds

---

[25] For Aquinas' distinction between sensual and intellectual appetite, see St. Thomas Aquinas, *Summa Theologiae*, 61 vols. (London: Blackfriars, 1964–81), la, 80, 1, art. 2, Vol 11, 200–203.

[26] Examples are legion. For the necessity of controlling will by wit in political discourse, see, for example, the early fifteenth-century political poem from which the following stanza is drawn:

> In kingdom, what maketh debate,
> Riche and pore both anoyyed?
> Yong counseil, and prevey hate,
> And syngulere profit ys aspiyed,
> Highe and lowe men abyyed;
> Echone wayte other for to kille.
> That kyngdom mot nede be striyed,
> That leveth wit and worcheth by wille.

Cited from J. Kail, ed., *Twenty-Six Political and Other Poems*, EETS, o.s. 124 (London: Kegan Paul, Trench, Trübner, 1904), ll. 25–32, 23.

The "Record and Process" of Richard II's deposition also thematizes Richard's faults as the product of uncontrolled will; see Chris Given-Wilson, ed., *Chronicles of the Revolution, 1397–1400: The Reign of Richard II* (Manchester: Manchester University Press, 1993), 168–89. The document records a sermon by Archbishop Arundel, in which the king's childish will is personified: "*Cum igitur puer regnat, Voluntas sola regnat, Ratio exul.*" Latin text from J. Strachey, ed., *Rotuli Parliamentorum*, 6 vols. (London, 1783), 3:415–53.

For the theme of will gaining control over the self, see, for example, Gower's *Confessio Amantis*, 3.1158–92, and 8, passim; or *Pearl*, whose psychological action is one of reason gaining control over will:

> A devely dele in my herte denned,
> Thagh resoun sette myselven saght.
> I playned my perle that there watz spenned
> Wyth fyrce skyllez that faste faght
> Thagh kynde of Kryst me comfort kenned,
> My wreched wylle in wo ay wraghte.

Text cited from E. V. Gordon, ed., *Pearl* (Oxford: Clarendon Press, 1953), ll. 51–56.

of any "wit"; on the other, Will refuses the discursive stability promised by a proper name. Instead, so I will argue, he occupies increasingly inclusive and anonymous discursive spaces, whereby the poem's authorship ideally becomes its readership, written as it is by a common will, or *voluntas communis*.

II

In a striking article of 1987, David Lawton revealed the ways in which earlier criticism had been misguided in treating "Will" as a continuous "character," whose development provided a focus and rationale for the narrative. Not only did such an approach iron out the serious discontinuities of *Piers Plowman*, but it also had the correlative effect of domesticating the poem's heterodoxy. Formal disruptions in the text, that is, are absorbed within a narrative of individual confusion and search; the institutional and doctrinal authority that Will seeks to instantiate are not in themselves questioned when we read the narrative as the account of Will's difficulties. Lawton argued that "Will" is better understood within a more recent account of the subject, according to which the "subject is a collection of discourses, unable to escape from division yet impelled by the desire for unity, 'a single Truth,' for that desire is the lack that constitutes the subject."[27] According to Lawton, there is no "name more potent than Will in activating the greatest number of such discourses,"[28] and however much Will seeks a single Truth, "his consciousness is itself plural and split: necessarily so, for it is constituted by the discourses that divide it. If Truth cannot be seen as single or stable, the seeker cannot be either."[29]

Lawton's perception resolves at a stroke a deep tension in *Piers Plowman* scholarship, between scholars who see the poem as being about Will's salvation, and those who see it as a poem of social regeneration.[30] If, that is, "Will" is himself constituted by authoritative institutional discourses, then it becomes impossible to discuss "Will" without at the same time confronting the wider institutional context out of which he arises as a visible subject. "Will" is already implicated in institutions, and *vice-versa*, rather than being separable from them, as liberal criticism would have it (with its enabling notion of the fully-formed subject, and its dislike of personification).[31] The subject of *Piers Plowman*, or what the poem is

---

[27] Lawton, "Subject," 6.

[28] Lawton, "Subject," 6.

[29] Lawton, "Subject," 4.

[30] The work that brought this opposition most clearly to the surface (coming out in favor of social regeneration) was Morton W. Bloomfield, *Piers Plowman as a Fourteenth-Century Apocalypse* (New Brunswick, NJ: Rutgers University Press, 1961).

[31] Dislike of personification as practiced in *Piers Plowman* is already apparent in the introduction to Whittaker's 1813 edition; Whittaker describes allegory (by which he means personification) as "the most insipid for the most part and tedious of all vehicles of instruction." Political caution is the only possible

"about," is, then, the "subject" itself, and this equally marks an engagement with institutions. It is precisely for this reason that "Will" should be a common noun, an English translation of Latin *cupiditas, sensualitas, affectus*, and *voluntas*, since these words are the key counters in a wide range of institutional discourses (e.g. political, legal, penitential, educational, hermeneutic).[32] The completed movement from personification to person observed in Hoccleve and Gower implies a separation of institution and speaker, since what a properly-named person says does not of itself necessarily implicate institutions; what a personification of institutional discourse says must also implicate the institution that gave rise to the personified concept, and that is responsible for absorbing that disruptive concept.

The most striking confirmation of Lawton's point is that both God and the soul are represented in the poem as being divided. These two most apparently unitary sources of authority are provisionally split by the variety of their names and the variety of functions designated by those names. God is known as Truthe and Kynde, names that designate different operations of God, and his different historical instantiations. The variety of Christ's own names, too, is resolved by accounting for the different institutional functions he has. In Passus 19, Will asks Conscience why Christ has two different names: "'Why calle ye hym Crist' quod I, 'sithen Jewes called hym Jesus?'" (19. 15). Will argues that the prophets had foretold that all creatures would kneel as soon as the name "God Jesu" was uttered.

> *Ergo* is no name to the name of Jesus,
> Ne noon so nedeful to nempne by nyghte ne by daye.
> For alle derke develes arn adrad to heren it,
> And synfulle aren solaced and saved by that name.
>   (19.19–22)[33]

This is surely a reference to the devotional tradition of reflecting ardently on the holy name "Jesus"; Richard Rolle (d. 1349), for example, encourages his addressee in *The Comandment* to "forgete noght this name Jhesu, bot thynk it in thi hert, nyght and day, as thi speciall and thi dere tre-

---

explanation of such a mode: "the satirist was compelled to shelter himself under the distant generalities of personification" (cited in Walter W. Skeat, ed., *The Vision of Piers the Plowman*, 2 vols. [Oxford: Oxford University Press, 1886], l: xl–xli). For the nineteenth-century dislike of personification more generally, see Paxson, *The Poetics of Personification*, 28.

[32] For an account of scholastic theories of will as applicable to *Piers Plowman*, see John M. Bowers, *The Crisis of Will in "Piers Plowman"* (Washington, D.C.: The Catholic University of America Press, 1986), ch. 2. For the hermeneutic implications of will as reader, see James Simpson, "Desire and the Scriptural Text: Will as Reader in *Piers Plowman*," in Rita Copeland, ed., *Criticism and Dissent in the Middle Ages* (Cambridge: Cambridge University Press, 1996), 215–43.

[33] Citation from *Piers Plowman*, unless otherwise stated, is from A. V. C. Schmidt, ed., *William Langland, The Vision of Piers Plowman*, second edition (London: J. M. Dent, 1995). C-Text citation is from Derek Pearsall, ed., *"Piers Plowman" by William Langland: An Edition of the C-text* (Berkeley, CA: University of California Press, 1978).

sowre...For it chaces devels."[34] If Langland refers to this tradition, however, he does so in order to distinguish his own spiritual program from that of the likes of Rolle. Reflection on the proper name "Jesus" can be contained within penitential and devotional discourses; Langland's interests are institutional, and Conscience goes on to spell out the institutional implications of the name "Christ." The one person, he says, can be knight, king and conqueror; as king, Jesus taught the faith, but as conqueror he defeated death (19.26–62). Conscience then goes on "to carpe moore of Crist, and how he com to that name" (19.69), in the course of which exposition he gives a summary of Christ's life, ending with Christ's act of Dobest, when he "yaf Piers power, and pardon he graunted" (19.184). To understand the names of Jesus Christ is to recount the whole life, a life that resolves into its immediate, institutional upshot in the England of a newly-made papal figure, Piers Plowman. Reflection on the name of Jesus in this poem produces not so much penitence as a reimagining of the historical and institutional sources of penitence. The same is also true of the authorial name "Will": understanding this name might provisionally produce personal penance, but the name's consequences continue to drive the narrative until in Passus 19 a whole society is imagined acting, within a renewed Church, with one will, at which point "Will/will" becomes invisible, as it must.

The point at which Will is most visible, and most fully "himself," as it were, is when he encounters the figure known as "*Anima*" in criticism. "*Anima*," in fact, covers many other names, and Will's encounter with him marks a point of a psychosynthesis, after the psychoanalysis of the preceding passus from Passus 8 forwards. This very moment of unitary regrouping serves, however, to underline the potential fissures in the soul and in Will himself. Like God, and possibly for identical reasons, the soul has multiple allegiances. In Passus 15 Will encounters a figure who declares that he is a member of Christ's "court" (15. 17). Will asks him to name himself, at which point Will's interlocutor offers no fewer than nine names:

> "The whiles I quykke the cors," quod he, "called am I *Anima*;
> And whan I wilne and wolde, *Animus* ich hatte;
> And for that I kan and knowe, called am I *Mens*, "Thoughte";
> And whan I make mone to God, *Memoria* is my name;
> And whan I deme domes and do as truthe techeth,
> Thanne is *Racio* my righte name, "Reson" on Englissh;
> And whan I feele that folk telleth, my firste name is *Sensus*—
> And that is wit and wisdom, the welle of alle craftes;
> And whan I chalange or chalange noght, chepe or refuse,
> Thanne am I Conscience ycalled, Goddes clerk and his notarie;

---

34 Cited from Hope Emily Allen, ed., *English Writings of Richard Rolle* (Oxford: Clarendon Press, 1931), 81. For the tradition of devotion to the holy name "Jesus," see Rosemary Woolf, *The English Religious Lyric in the Middle Ages* (Oxford: Clarendon Press, 1968), 172–9.

> And whan I love leelly Oure Lord and alle othere,
> Thanne is "Lele Love" my name, and in Latyn *Amor*;
> And whan I flee fro the flessh and forsake the careyne,
> Thanne am I spirit spechelees—and *Spiritus* thanne ich hatte."
> (15.23–36)

This may not be one of Langland's more elevated poetic flights, and even as pure exposition one may have wished for a more systematic fit between this sequence of names and the preceding action of the poem from Passus 8. For all that, the passage is working hard: not only does it translate a complex Latin psychology into English, but it also reveals the complex set of jurisdictions within the soul.[35] What justifies this multiple figure's membership in the institution of Christ's "court" is the proper functioning of the soul's many sub-categories. Within the involuntary actions of *Anima* and *Spiritus* (mere animation and the flight of the disembodied soul at death respectively), lie a complex set of potentially conflicting powers. Each of these fits the soul for a specific social or religious operation, whereby the soul can participate in institutional life by being itself like a complex institution, with different offices. Each of these offices requires the participation of will, or desire, here labelled "*Animus*," and as such the passage effectively recapitulates much of the action of the poem from Passus 8 forwards: Will has encountered versions of all these figures or functions except *Amor* and *Spiritus*. To say that is, however, to insist on the partitions of "Will" himself: the will is constituted differently in each of these functions of the soul, whether the function be mere thinking, penitential remembrance, legal judgement, sensual apprehension, or ethical discrimination. The first person pronoun is the repeated subject of this passage, subliminally implying the soul's coherence, and the very fact of being able to survey the operations of the whole soul itself marks a kind of achieved coherence. On the other hand, the very formulation of the soul's partition cannot help but put that coherence, along with the notion of "individuality," under pressure.

The passage does, nevertheless, *promise* a fullness of self. The one figure Will has not yet encountered is *Amor*, and this is precisely the subject of Will's dialogue with *Anima* (named *Liberum Arbitrium* in the equivalent C-Text passage), to whom he poses the question "What is charite?" (15.149). To say that Will is discontinuous is true, but that is not to say that the poem cannot conceive of an integrated will. Like many other late medieval poems, *Piers Plowman* is a "person-shaped" narrative.[36] If, how-

---

35 The source of this passage (Isidore, *Etymologiae* 11.1.13) is given in John A. Alford *"Piers Plowman": A Guide to the Quotations*, Medieval and Renaissance Texts and Studies 77 (Binghampton, New York: Medieval and Renaissance Texts and Studies, 1992), 92. One might add, as a possible intermediary source, the pseudo-Augustinian *Liber de spiritu et anima*, PL 40.780–832 (col. 803).

36 The term "person-shaped" narrative is taken from James Simpson, *Sciences and the Self in Medieval Poetry: Alan of Lille's "Anticlaudianus" and John Gower's "Confessio amantis,"* Cambridge Studies in Medieval Literature, 25 (Cambridge: Cambridge University Press, 1995), 272. The literary form of certain

ever, Will's integration is achieved only in the act of loving "leelly Oure Lord and alle othere," that integration comes only by effacing his differences from others; Will's fulfilment, that is, comes not as an "individual," but only by his indivisibility from the corporate body of the Church.

Will names himself in his encounter with *Anima*, in a line that provides the strongest internal evidence for the poet's proper name: "'I have lyved in londe,' quod I, 'my name is Longe Wille" (15.152). Understanding this line is critical to our sense of Will's identity as author, and I shall return to it. By way of putting it into focus, however, we should consider some moments in the process by which Will is empowered to name himself.

III

The problem of wilfullness is certainly at the heart of the action of the first two visions of *Piers Plowman* (Prologue and Passus 1–4, and Passus 5–7 respectively), though it is only fleetingly apparent that this problem has anything to do with the narrator. In the political and economic action of Passus 2–4, the King promises to forgive Mede if "she werche bi my wit and my wil folwe" (3.7); the possibility of this offer being accepted is immediately put into doubt by the justices' promise to Mede that they will "thi wey shape / To be wedded at thi wille and wher thee leef liketh" (3.17–8), or the clerics' adjacent promise to Mede to "werche thi wille the while thow myght laste" (3.28). The action of these passus is, indeed, a competition of factional wills, which is resolved only by the King's acceptance of Reason and Conscience as his counsellors at the end of Passus 4. This acceptance of rational and ethical principles of law as his counsellors renders the King's own will a rational will.

The political resolution of those passus calls forth the penitential discourse of Passus 5–7, a discourse that subtends, in Langland's view, the political. Reason provokes a communal repentance, whose individual instantiations are contained within the master code of repentance provoking will: "Thanne ran Repentaunce and reherced his teme / And gart Wille to wepe water with hise eighen." (5.60–1). Only once, in a remarkable moment, does the narrator (who has not yet been named in the B-Text) suggest that his own *persona* overlaps with that of the sinners. In the absolution of Wrath, the confessor Repentance warns Wrath against excessive drinking, "that thi wille by cause therof to wrathe myghte turne" (5.183). The next lines (which clearly baffled at least one scribe),[37] break the fictional frame by suggesting that Wrath and the narrator are identical, or at

medieval (and post-medieval) works is correlative with the form of the psyche whose integration is imagined in those works: as the soul comes to its own fullness, so too does the narrative end. Langland's psychological narrative, however "discontinuous," does work progressively through higher sources of perception.

[37] See the variant "hym" for "me" in CrM, in George Kane and E. Talbot Donaldson, *Piers Plowman: The B Version* (London: Athlone Press, 1975), 317.

least overlap: "'*Esto sobrius!*' he seide, and assoiled me after, / And bad me wilne to wepe my wikkednesse to amende" (5.184–5). This single suggestion that the narrator's *persona* might be fluidly identifiable with actants in the represented world of the poem is in no way sustained at this point. Instead, the confession scene as a whole remains within the standard ethical topos of will conforming itself to wit. It is Reason, after all, who provokes the repentance, and this rational containment of an obstreperous will is recapitulated in Piers' directions to the shrine of Saint Truth, which is located in a manor, whose "walles ben of Wit to holden Wil oute" (5.587). If Passus 2–4 work within a standard political topos of reason containing a socially disruptive will, Passus 5–7 elaborate a standard moral topos that uses exactly the same counters to define the tensions of ethical life.

However much Langland is working with the standard topos of the conflict of will and wit in Passus 2–7, in the narrative of Passus 8 forwards it is remarkable just how soon Wit is left behind, subject as he is to the coruscating attack of his wife Study. In however self-effacing a way, Will moves decisively beyond Wit very early on in his interrogation of parts of the soul to which he belongs. It is true that Will only comes into focus as Will in his encounter with Wit. Thought calls Will by his "kynde name" (8.71), but we do not hear what that name is; only as Will is introduced to Wit is Will named (for the first time in the B-Text):[38]

> Wher Dowel and Dobet and Dobest ben in londe
> Here is Wil wolde wite if Wit koude teche him;
> And wheither he be man or no man this man fayn wolde aspie,
> And werchen as thei thre wolde—this is his entente.
>
> (8.125–28)

This little passage brims with the self-reflexivity of personification: the verbs sandwiched between the actants in line 126 ("wolde" and "wit") allude to the mental processes that have produced the surrounding hypostases Will and Wit in the first place; and to say that this is Will's "entente" is playfully to allude to what drives the narrative in any case— that Will *is* "entente." Above all, the passage would seem to concede Will's dependence on Wit: he only comes into definition in Wit's presence, named as he is for the first time as "Will," a rational desire.[39] As with the texts by Gower and Hoccleve discussed above, the narratorial "I" of this poem has been taken over by one aspect of his psyche. The very act of bringing that desire into definition by Wit would equally seem to promise its resolution, since a will obedient to a rational wit together form an integrated psyche. To name Will seems, in this formulation, to imply that the solution to Will's desire for "kynde knowynge" necessarily reposes in Wit; and this, in turn,

---

[38] For a complete conspectus of authorial signatures in each version of the poem, see Middleton, "William Langland's 'Kynde Name,'" Appendix, 79–82.

[39] For wordplay on will and wit of this kind, see Janette Dillon, "*Piers Plowman*: A Particular Example of Wordplay and its Structural Significance," *Medium Ævum* 50 (1981): 40–48.

implies Langland's apparent acceptance of the standard psychological limits for the instruction of the laity. Both those inferences turn out to be wrong.

Study's attack on Wit is couched in apparently conservative terms: Study is, after all, Wit's wife, and Langland presents her as an archetypal scold, before the ferocity of whose tongue the husband Wit "bicom so confus he kouthe noght loke / And as doumb as deeth, and drough hym arere" (10.138–9). Equally conservative, apparently, is Study's fierce attack on secular theological speculation of all those lay people who "wilneth to wite the whyes of God almyghty" (10.124). This flurry of reactionary gestures is, however, disguising the very unusual move in vernacular texts of criticizing Wit. Texts before and after Arundel's *Constitutions* of 1409 stress the importance of the laity resting within the bounds of "reason."[40] Here, however, Study not only makes the point that Wit can be "carded with coveitise" (10.18), but her very critique of lay theological speculation is a kind of passport for Will's own progression to specifically theological learning with Clergy. The logic of the narrative is quietly revealing the radical nature of Will's call for "kynde knowynge": it is a self-knowledge that Will/the will requires, and this drives him/it beyond the limits of reason. If Will is somehow at fault here, his error cannot be one of lay desire for theological learning (since Study does send him onto Clergy); the problem can only be with the quality of desire itself, and, more seriously, the institutional contexts in which that desire can be contained. Certainly at this stage in the poem Will remains unabsorbed by the psyche of which he is a part, or by any institution that promises to offer him "kynde knowynge." Instead, he continues at large in, and driving, the narrative, and he continues therefore (by the logic of personification) to remain a common noun, resisting the integration implied by proper naming. He may be brought into definition by his submission to psychological or institutional figures, but his surviving these figures equally implies his continued power over the narrative. If the psychological resources and educational institutions Will meets are incapable of absorbing him and satisfying his desire, this is not only a critique of Will, but also of those sources of authority themselves.

The incapacity of institutions to contain the will/Will is everywhere apparent in the passus that follow. This incapacity is partly to do with the shortcomings of institutions, and partly with Will's own correlative wilfullness. Clergy (who, in my view, represents university theological learning) is unable to satisfy Will's doubts about salvation (Passus 10); the friars refuse to accept Will for burial (Passus 11). The most powerful account

---

[40] For the development of English vernacular theology and its interruption by Arundel's *Constitutions*, see Nicholas Watson, "Censorship and Cultural Change in Late-Medieval England: Vernacular Theology, the Oxford Translation Debate, and Arundel's Constitutions of 1409," *Speculum* 70 (1995): 822–864. For an example of a post-Arundel text that stresses the bounds of "reason," see Nicholas Love's *Mirrour of the Blessed Lyf of Jesu Christ*, passim.

of the will's own refusal to participate in communal life is made in the description of the coat of Christendom worn by Will's *alter ego*, Haukyn, or *Activa Vita*. Haukyn is

> so singuler by hymself as to sighte of the peple
> Was noon swich as hymself, ne noon so pope holy;
> Yhabited as an heremyte, an ordre by hymselve.
>   (13.283–85)

This singularity is produced especially by an intellectual arrogance: Haukyn's coat declares that he is "wilnynge that men wende his wit were the beste" (13.292). Other versions of uncontrolled will are also visible in the coat's stains: it is "bidropped with wrathe and with wikkede wille" (13.321); and "with likynge of lecherie as by lokynge of his eighe...Til eitheres wille wexeth kene" (13.344–48). Haukyn himself declares that he is unable to keep the coat of his flesh clean for an hour, without soiling it "thorugh werk or thorugh word, or wille of myn herte" (14.14).

Haukyn's solitary wilfulness might suggest that he should be reabsorbed in institutions by the exercise of "reason" and "wit". In fact, however, Haukyn's narrative environment pushes him even further beyond institutions; and his conversion is produced not through any acceptance of what is reasonable, but instead by submission to a larger will. It is Conscience and Patience who provoke Haukyn's moving conversion. Conscience himself is first moved by Patience's speech at the academic feast of Passus 13, in which Patience declares the lesson of his "lemman" Love:

> "With wordes and with werkes," quod she, "and wil of thyn herte
> Thow love leelly thi soule al thi lif tyme."
>   (13.141–42)

The very source of Haukyn's problem ("wil of...herte") is equally the source of his solution. When Conscience leaves the feast in response to Patience's exhortation to long-sufferance, he formulates this positive version of will in terms of a communal desire. He provisionally abandons Clergy, and the institutions of academic learning, by disclaiming intellectual understanding of what Patience has said:

> For al that Pacience me profreth, proud am I litel;
> Ac the wil of the wye and the wil of folk here
> Hath meved my mood to moorne for my synnes.
> The goode wil of a wight was nevere bought to the fulle:
> For ther nys no tresour therto to a trewe wille.
>   (13.190–94)

The prelude to Haukyn's conversion, then, is itself produced by a communal will that drives the conscience beyond institutional boundaries. Conscience's definition of the boundlessness of will both underwrites the "partyng" from Clergy, and effectively predicts the challenge posed to any

institution that tries to contain the will. Certainly the immediate effect of
Conscience and Patience on *Activa Vita* is radical: "Haukyn the Actif
Man" grieves at his very being as the active life, that "evere he hadde lond
or lordshipe, lasse other moore, / Or maistrie over any man mo than of
hymselve" (14.327–28). At the heart of this conversion is the exhortation
to submit to a higher will, and to "eat" that will "whan the hungreth":

> But I lokede what it liflode it was that Pacience so preisede;
> And thanne was it a pece of the *Paternoster—Fiat voluntas tua.*
>   (14.48–9)

The text is poised on a paradox here: precisely by accepting the centrality
of patience, the capacity of institutions to contain Will/the will is questioned. And that challenge is founded on the boundlessness of a will that
submits itself to the divine will, and in so doing equally submits itself to a
communal will. This act of submission produces radical effects.

The notion of a communal will is implicit in the dispersal of Will's self
across the action of these passus: Conscience is Will's conscience; Patience
is an ideal for Will; and the conversion of Haukyn (whose own *persona* is
dispersed across a wide range of occupational types) clearly implicates
Will. The conversion of *Activa Vita*, furthermore, is equally a conversion of
society more generally. And this conversion is the prelude and premise of
Will's encounter with *Anima/Liberum Arbitrium*, to which I now return in
conclusion of this article. Will asks *Anima* the simple question: "What is
charite?", after which the dialogue follows in this way:

> "...A childissh thyng," he seide—
> "*Nisi efficiamini sicut parvuli, non intrabitis in regnum celorum—*
> Withouten fauntelte or folie a fre liberal wille."
> "Where sholde men fynde swich a frend with so fre an herte?
> I have lyved in londe," quod I, "my name is Longe Wille—
> And fond I nevere ful charite, bifore ne bihynde."
>   (15.149–53)

Critics have seen in line 152 the strongest internal evidence for the poet's
proper name, if we read the line as a cryptogram, producing "Wille
Longelonde." Ralph Hanna, for example, suggests that Will's reference to
the Pauline verse on identity a few lines further on ("*Hic in enigmate, tunc
facie ad faciem*" (15.162a), renders probable the claim that line 152
encodes the author's name.[41] One could also add that the word *aenigma*
has a specifically rhetorical sense, meaning "obscure, riddle-like allegory."[42] I suggest that the line is more powerfully read as a riddling preser-
vation and extension of the common force of "Will." Because we have (and

---

[41] Hanna, *William Langland,* 4.

[42] For which see James Simpson, "'Et vidit deus cogitaciones eorum': A Parallel Instance and Possible
Source for Langland's Use of a Biblical Formula at Piers Plowman B.XV.200a," *Notes and Queries,* ns 33
(1986): 9–13.

only because we have) external evidence that William Langland was the poet's name, are we persuaded to read this as a cryptogram for the poet's proper name. In doing so, however, we miss its much greater force as a riddle for Will's/the will's new identity as an authorial "long wille," a *longanimis* common will, the locus of long-suffering charity who speaks for the whole land.[43] If "Jack Upland" is unquestionably a satirist's pseudonym, "Will Long-land" goes one better: Long Will can speak as a long-suffering desire not only because he comes from "opelond," but more powerfully because he is himself the will, or common voice, of that land.[44]

Certainly Will himself misses the key to his name "Wille" in saying that he has never seen charity "bifore ne bihynde," since the whole point is that charity is located within the "liberal wille." This forgivable blind spot, however, gives way to a statement by Will that is closer to breaking the riddle of self-knowledge: he has never seen Christ, he says, "but as myself in a mirour." (15.162). Anima goes on to resolve the riddle by emphasising the centrality of will and suffrance in any account of charity. Piers Plowman knows charity more profoundly than clerics, since

> ...Piers the Plowman parceyveth moore depper
> What is the wille, and wherfore that many wight suffreth:
> *Et vidit Deus cogitaciones eorum.*
>
> (15.199–200a)

Will cannot know charity by "colour ne by clergie," but

---

[43] The suggestion that "Longe Wille" might translate *longanimis* ("long suffering") was first made, to my knowledge, by Howard Meroney, "The Life and Death of Long Wille," *ELH* 17 (1950): 1–35; 4; the suggestion is also found in John Norton-Smith, *William Langland* (Leiden: Brill, 1983), 88; and Schmidt, *The Vision of Piers Plowman*; there "Longe Wille" is glossed as both "Tall Will" and "Perseverance itself." The suggestion gains strength from the fact that the word *longanimitas* appears in the Pauline epistles (the main source for 15.149–175): see 2 Corinthians 6:6, and Galatians 5:22; *MED* cites the first instance of "longanimite" as an English word at 1400. For a discussion of B.15.152 that also marks its difference from contemporary examples of proper naming, see Helen Barr, *Signes and Sothe: Language in the "Piers Plowman" Tradition*, Piers Plowman Studies 10 (Cambridge: Brewer, 1994), 6.

[44] For "Jack Upland" as a satirist's pseudonym, see P. L. Heyworth, ed., *Jack Upland, Friar Daw's Reply and Upland's Rejoinder* (Oxford: Oxford University Press, 1968); the first two of these texts were written between (?) 1389 and 1396. Langland himself says that Will has lived "yn London and opelond bothe," at C.5.44. The pose of the rude, uplandish satirist is exploited in *Mum and the Sothsegger*, ll. 44–57. The equivalent of B.15.152 in the C-Text is "I haue yleued in Londone monye longe yeres" (C.16.286) [Citation from Derek Pearsall, ed., *Piers Plowman by William Langland*, York Medieval Texts, second series (London: Edward Arnold, 1981)]. With the prompting of the B-Text cryptogram, we could see "Longelond" here too. Although this is admittedly more specific than "in londe," it is still true that (if it is a cryptogram) Langland's proper name is built into a communal space. For discussion of C.5.44 consonant with the lines of this article, see Anne Middleton, "Acts of Vagrancy: The C Version 'Autobiography' and the Statute of 1388," in Steven Justice and Kathryn Kerby-Fulton, eds., *Written Work: Langland, Labour and Authorship* (Philadelphia: University of Pennsylvania Press, 1997), 208–317; 253–4: "By claiming that his regular 'place' is not single but multiple, Will in the first instance attempts to defeat the determination of a proper 'place' to which he can be committed if found indigent."

> ...thorugh wil oone,
> And that knoweth no clerk ne creature on erthe
> But Piers the Plowman—*Petrus, id est, Christus.*
> (15.210–12)

This mysteriously circular, Pauline account of knowing by being known, then, places the will's own capacity to suffer at the heart of an understanding of charity.[45] This, however, equally implies the communal nature of the practice of charity: *Anima*'s description of Charity is of a "dispersed" figure, a quality instantiated in different places and historical moments (15.165–194a; 220–67); and if Charity can only be found in Will through *Piers Plowman*, that implies that it can only be found through the communal practice that Piers characteristically initiates in this poem. If Will is to find himself, that is, he is to do so through and in others. This fluidity of name, and of selfhood, is already implicit in the typological association of Piers and Christ, where the highest potential of a proper name produces another: *Petrus, id est, Christus.* And just as Christ's pun on the proper name Petrus is exploited in *Piers Plowman*, so, too, does William Langland exploit the full range of his name: just as *Petrus/petra* is the foundation of an institution, so, too, is Langland's creation of a common will.

It is because Will can only become himself through communal practice that Passus 15 also focuses on the church as an institution. Whereas Holy Church had instructed Will in Passus 1, here it is the integrated soul, speaking in the voice of all Christians, who addresses the Church. After *Anima* itemizes his several names, Will jokingly likens him to bishops, since they, too, "bereth manye names" (15.40). Will's comparison of the soul's many names to those of a bishop is possibly strategic, since *Anima* is about to act precisely as a bishop, addressing the problems of the Church as an institution. The intimate connection between the will's search for charity and the institution of the Church is more explicit in the C-Text. Will asks *Liberum Arbitrium* for a definition of "holy churche":

> "...Charite," he saide;
> "Lief and loue and leutee in o byleue and lawe,
> A loue-knotte of leutee and of lele byleue,
> Alle kyne cristene cleuynge on o will,
> Withoute gyle and gabbynge gyue and sulle and lene."
> (C.17.125–29)

Langland is here adducing, I think, a standard monastic notion of the "common will," or *voluntas communis*, sometimes found in accounts of monastic obedience. The monk is to resist the temptations of the "proper will," or *voluntas propria*, and submit himself to the common will of the monastery.[46] Langland's translation of this concept from the monastery

---

[45] For the probable Augustinian source of line 15.200a, see Simpson, "*Et vidit deus cogitaciones eorum.*"

[46] The notion of *voluntas propria* is frequently attacked in the *Rule of Saint Benedict* (PL 66), ch. 3 (col. 288); ch. 4 (col. 297); ch. 5 (col. 349); and ch. 7 (col. 371), for example. For one of many possible later

involves much more than a vernacularization of the idea, since its deployment in a vernacular context gives the idea an entirely new force: here obedience to the common will involves the establishment of a reimagined
English church with *Piers Plowman* at its head. This Church has not only
been imagined in the poem, but the poem itself (decidedly not a book of
"privy counselling") has been written by a common will.[47] It is the desire
of a common will that enables Will's dynamic reading of Scripture from
Passus 16–19, a reading that finally produces a newly imagined institution
that can contain the common will evoked by this poem. The act of submission to a common will paradoxically produces results that are anything
but submissive.

---

examples, Bernard of Clairvaux, *In tempore resurrectionis, ad abbates, Sermo 3*: "*Voluntatem dico propri-
am, quae non est communis cum Deo et homonibus, sed nostra tantum: quando quod volumus, non ad
honorem Dei, non ad utilitatem fratrum, sed propter nosmetipsos facimus, non intendentes placere Deo et
prodesse fratribus, sed satisfacere propriis motibus animorum. Huic contraria est recte fronte charitas, quae
Deus est....Etiam nunc, cum frigus aut famem aut aliquid tale patimur, quid laeditur nisi propria voluntas?
Quod si voluntarie sustinemus, ipsa iam voluntas communis est.*" (*PL.* 183.289–290). The notion was
available in the vernacular contemporary with Langland; see the little tract "Propyr Wille," possibly by
Walter Hilton, in C. Horstmann, ed., *Yorkshire Writers: Richard Rolle of Hampole*, 2 vols. (London: Swan
Sonnenschein, 1895–6), I.173–4.

[47] A posture of common authorship is cultivated by other writers in the late fourteenth and early fifteenth
centuries; see Christina von Nolcken, "A 'Certain Sameness' and Our Response to It in English Wycliffite
Texts," in Richard G. Newhauser and John A. Alford, eds., *Literature and Religion in the Later Middle
Ages: Philological Studies in Honour of Siegfried Wenzel*, Medieval and Renaissance Texts and Studies 118
(Binghamton, New York: Medieval and Renaissance Texts, 1995), 191–208: "We are dealing with authors
who want to present themselves as writing both as and from a group" (200). For the anonymity of the
poem, its manuscripts and Lollard material, see also John M. Bowers, "*Piers Plowman* and the Police:
Notes Toward a History of the Wycliffite Langland," *Yearbook of Langland Studies* 6 (1992): 1–50; 17–18.

Measurement and the "Feminine" in *Piers Plowman*: A Response to Recent Studies of Langland and Gender

Elizabeth Robertson

> "The road of excess leads to the palace of wisdom"
>
> *The Marriage of Heaven and Hell*
> William Blake

Feminist medievalist critics, who have for some time been engaged in Chaucer studies, rarely turn their attention to William Langland's *Piers Plowman*. Despite recent valiant attempts to open up the discussion about gender in the poem, in most conference sessions devoted to exploring gender issues in late fourteenth-century England, Langland has been dismissed as conventional, conservative, and uninteresting when it comes to his representations of women. At first glance, vivid, theoretically-challenging female characters from Langland's poem do not leap to our attention as they do in Chaucer's work: no lively economically independent woman rages against generations of anti-feminist diatribes as does the Wife of Bath; no ineffable suffering religious heroines tease our imagination as do Constance and Griselda. A closer look, however, makes us realize that there are indeed many female figures in Langland who are powerful, articulate, well-educated, and challenging—Holi Chirche, Dame Study, Lady Mede, to name a few. Indeed, in one of the first essays to consider Langland's representations of women, Terence Dolan concludes that Langland "seems to be friendly towards women much more consistently than Geoffrey Chaucer."[1]

It may be that the most provocative lack in Langland's work is not that of female figures, but rather that of anti-feminism itself. As Helen Cooper observes, "the poem is...remarkably free of the misogyny or the hatred of

---

[1] Terence Dolan, "Langland's Women," in *A Wyf Ther Was*, ed. Juliette Dor (Liege: Liege Language and Literature, 1992), 128.

sex that stalk so many medieval homiletic works."[2] Despite his inheritance of a literary and a theological tradition marked by its condemnation of women, Langland repeatedly avoids anti-feminist polemic or even anti-feminist images. Not even in his portrait of Adam and Eve, where calumny of the feminine is traditional, does he let slip a single word of condemnation or criticism of women. And surprisingly, Langland shows no special interest in one of the most central topics of the period concerning women: the cult of chastity. Perhaps it is hard for the feminist critic to write about women in Langland because, in the end, female characters are treated just about the same way as are male ones.

Given Langland's avoidance of the most obvious misogynistic diatribes of his age and given the variety of his female figures from the historically mimetic to the allegorical, Langland's poem in fact offers fertile ground for feminist explorations. As yet, this territory has been virtually uncharted. In recent years, there have been a handful of essays that consider gender issues, but few take explicitly feminist stances (although admittedly, in an age of feminisms it is difficult to articulate a single feminist position.) Most recently, the *Yearbook of Langland Studies* devoted a portion of a volume of essays to a consideration of gender issues.[3] The general view of those essays, however, is that gender, while of more interest than hitherto acknowledged, is, in the end, as Morrison and Baker put it, a "luxury," something subordinated to the poem's more pressing concerns with social, political and theological issues: "Langland privileges the exigencies of human necessity over a concern for the burdens of gender."[4]

Rather than view gender as peripheral to the poem's major concerns with social exigencies, I propose that we view it as a central mode of analysis for Langland. The nature of social needs are explored in the poem primarily in terms of measurement, limits, or the containment of excess, the transgressions of which come to be explored in Langland through the feminine. From Holi Chirche's opening admonitions to Nede's penultimate lessons, the poem anxiously explores the nature of sufficiency. Holi Chirche explains that God has prescribed exactly the contours of human need—food, clothing and shelter—and yet the society of the poem has not yet found a way to apportion such necessities to each individual. As a result, excess rules on one side, and want on another. The nature of proper allotment—a topic explored in almost every arena of the poem—extends ultimately to the theological question of the nature of just reward. The

---

[2] Helen Cooper, "Gender and Personification in *Piers Plowman*," *Yearbook of Langland Studies* 5 (1991): 44.

[3] Volume 12 (1998) of the *Yearbook of Langland Studies* includes a special section on gender and *Piers Plowman*. This essay was originally written before this volume appeared and I have not been able to engage with the essays as fully as I might have liked in this revision. Of these, the only essay to take an explicitly feminist stance is that by Stephanie Trigg.

[4] Joan Baker and Susan Signe Morrison, "The Luxury of Gender: *The Merchant's Tale and Piers Plowman*," *Yearbook of Langland Studies* 12 (1998): 33; reprinted in this volume, pp. 41-67.

poem repeatedly stresses the necessity of limits, of "mesure," as well as the salvific possibilities found in exceeding those limits. A crucial means of exploring the nature of such limits is the poem's engagement with a cultural predisposition to associate the feminine with features specifically concerned with measurement, especially the dilatory and the excessive. Furthermore, the excessive and the dilatory challenge measured boundaries, even of definitions themselves. As we shall see, gender, or more precisely the "feminine," as it was understood in late fourteenth-century England, is indeed a "luxury," but it is its very luxuriousness that opens up possibility and possibilities in the poem.

That women are associated with excess is a medieval commonplace that grows out of commentaries on Eve, condemned both for her excessive garrulity and for her excessive carnality. Both female speech and female sexuality demanded containment, constraint enacted both theoretically and practically in theology and law. Furthermore, female copiousness, as Lee Patterson has shown us, came to be associated with writing itself, for guides to rhetoric asked the writer to engage in a process of feminine excess, that is, to dilate their prose.[5] Dilation was frequently and variously associated with the feminine during the Middle Ages and the Renaissance. As Patricia Parker explains, the word "dilation" was understood as a translation of Rahab, a figure who comes to stand for both the expansion and the deferral of stasis or resolution that is inherent to dilation, and, ultimately, for the openness of the Church:

> The Church figured as female is that other redeemed harlot who in the space between the First and Second Coming of another Joshua, Christ—that is, between the disappearance and final triumphant return of the Master of Creation, Time and History—expands or dilates in order, so to speak, to take in more members, before that ultimate apocalyptic end.[6]

Associated also with the spreading of the Word, "The dilation of Rahab or of the Church, then, involves symbolically two orifices: expansion to take in a multiplicity of members...and the propagation, through the mouth, of the Word, again an activity not unexpectedly linked with a Church figured as symbolically female."[7]

Dilation (as both openness and delay) and excess pervade the poem in a variety of ways. The structure of the poem is itself dilatory in that it never reaches an end, and incidents within the poem explore the consequences of the dilatory and the excessive. Moreover, these two principles are seen as both terrifying and liberatory in just the ways women—or more precisely

---

[5] Lee Patterson, "'For the Wyves Love of Bath': Feminine Rhetoric and Poetic Resolution in the *Roman de la Rose* and *The Canterbury Tales*," *Speculum* 58 (1983): 656–695.

[6] Patricia Parker, *Literary Fat Ladies: Rhetoric, Gender, Property* (London and New York: Methuen, 1987), 9.

[7] Parker, 9.

"woman"—were understood to be in the Middle Ages. While dilatoriness and excess are typically embodied in female characters, these categories, with their inevitable associations to the feminine, inhabit other spheres of concern in the poem.[8] They may be embodied in male characters. Given the often observed association between the dangerous pleasures of the feminine and rhetoric, dilatoriness and excess also occur in the structures and the poetics of the poem itself.[9] Since women are representative of linguistic tropes and figures in the poem, the feminine inevitably calls into question not only the poem's use of figures, but the very idea of poetry.[10]

Such associations open up large arenas of concern for the feminist critic, but I will focus here mainly on the tropes of excess and dilation as Langland relates them to the feminine. The theories of Irigarayan mimicry and feminine fluids as well as those of the Kristevan feminine semiotic or abjection can help us understand the ways in which this poetry makes use of these attributes. We shall see that notions of the feminine play both negative and positive roles in the unfolding of the poem's lessons. Langland, in my view, adapts the concepts of women that inform medieval notions of rhetoric itself to explore existing social formations and to envision new ones. His use of gender, therefore, plays with, rather than reinscribes, essentialist notions of the feminine while at the same time repeatedly asserting the complexity and contradictions of fourteenth-century social conditions of men and women alike. I shall first review gender studies that have been made of *Piers Plowman* and then, with a primary focus on Langland's representations of Gluttony and Mede, I shall offer some new directions we might pursue through the lens of such feminist theories.

Perhaps one reason why feminists have yet to grant much attention to the work of Langland is that the handful of women who do appear in *Piers* are most often gendered personifications of abstract concepts rather than mimetic representations of fourteenth-century women. Chaucer's characters afford greater analysis and interest precisely because they are characters; gendered personifications, on the other hand, seemingly resist analysis. *How*, or even *if*, gender signifies in these representations is problematic. In her careful and informed early analysis of gender and personification in *Piers*, Helen Cooper directs our attention to the problem of assessing the gender of a character who is assigned a gender grammatically; a feminine

---

[8] Other "feminine" attributes such as pregnancy also inform the theology of the poem. Andrew Galloway explores, for example, "a medieval species of finding the 'feminine' in medieval male spirituality, and its contrast with a more directly feminine form of late-medieval vernacular piety." See his essay, "Intellectual Pregnancy, Metaphysical Femininity and the Social Doctrine of the Trinity in *Piers Plowman*," *Yearbook of Langland Studies* 12 (1998): 117–152. The quotation is from page 3 of his Introduction to *YLS* 12.

[9] See Paxson's discussion of this association in James J. Paxson, "Gender Personified, Personification Gendered, and the Body Figuralized in *Piers Plowman*," *Yearbook of Langland Studies* 12 (1998): 65–96.

[10] See Paxson's discussion of the implications of the relationship between rhetoric and the feminine ("Gender Personified," 65–96).

noun in Latin, such as *philosophia* will often appear as a female figure in classical and medieval allegories; the question then becomes what signification that gender has beyond the accident of grammar. She shows that a ninth-century commentary on Boethius's *Consolation of Philosophy* reacts to the character, Lady Philosophy, in terms of her femininity as both maternal and seductive. Such responses to gendered representations were typical of the late classical period, Cooper argues, and she concludes, therefore, that, gender does signify in these early texts. Langland inherits this tradition, but because linguistic change had loosened the hold of grammatical gender, personifications no longer needed to be gendered by necessity. However, Cooper determines, although the gender of his personifications are finally unrelated to grammar, the "genders Langland gives his personifications are not casual."[11] In her final assessment, Langland's use of gender is, nevertheless, conservative.

Cooper's essay argues that "[m]ost often…women are seen in one relation only: the sexual. They are the mistresses of hermits, priests or beggars; they are prostitutes; they are chaste only for lack of opportunity, they are victims of rape."[12] We might further explore the origins of this relational understanding of women. Do women in medieval culture have an identity outside of (sexual) relationship? Nuns seem the figures most likely to have forged identities outside their roles as the property of men. Yet, even nuns are encouraged to think of themselves first and foremost as brides of Christ. Women did sometimes function in medieval society free of relationship. The legal category of *femmes soles* allowed married women to act as independent legal agents, and, as Judith Bennett and Sharon Farmer have recently discussed, single women who were outside of relational roles either by circumstance or choice, although almost invisible in the historical record, troubled the system that categorized women only as virgins, married or widowed; charitable organizations, for example, resisted counting such women among the deserving poor.[13] Single women were excessive to the system.

In *Piers Plowman*, not all female characters are defined principally in terms of their relational status. Holi Chirche, for example, appears relatively independent of her sexual status. Langland also gives us fragmentary images of other women not defined first and foremost by their relationship to men. Women earning a living selling beer or goods such as Beton the Brewster or Rose the Regrator, although married (Beton is described as a "breuh-wif" in C.6.354 and Rose is married to Coveitise), are not obviously defined by their gender roles, although admittedly Beton's work falls clearly under the patriarchal umbrella of the domestic household where

---

11 Cooper, "Gender," 33-34.

12 Cooper, "Gender," 44.

13 See Judith Bennett, Sharon Farmer and others in *Single Women in the European Past, 1250–1800*, ed. Judith Bennett and Amy Froide (Philadelphia: University of Pennsylvania Press, 1999).

most women's brewing historically took place and Rose's work is intertwined with that of her husband.[14]

Even if we grant that Langland primarily tends to represent women relationally, this tendency is not necessarily misogynistic. The family, as M. Teresa Tavormina has recently argued in her thorough analysis of marriage and family in *Piers*, lies at the heart of Langland's idealized society.[15] To be in correct relation at all levels, either grammatically, sexually, morally, or spiritually, is key to the right operations of society. Furthermore, while female characters may be represented relationally, so, too, are male characters, and women are not always presented in subordinate relation. This is an unusual departure from tradition that signals Langland's more radical vision of the relationship between the sexes than is commonly espoused in exegetical tradition. Correct marriage, as we shall consider in more depth later in this essay, thus becomes not only a central social practice for Langland, but one that reflects and predicts the integration of the Trinity into daily life.

Cooper's second major point about Langland's use of gender in personification is that, more often than not, Langland will change an abstraction usually gendered female in the classical tradition to male. *Luxuria*, for example, in a departure from tradition, appears as male in the confession scenes. Cooper also notes that sometimes a character will appear as multiply-gendered or hermaphroditic. The character Wrath, for example, slides from male to female, and Envy's gender identification is not clear. On the whole, however, male personifications predominate. Cooper concludes that Langland's choice to personify grammatically female abstractions as male is ultimately a reflection of the male consciousness of the dreamer and a sign of Langland's acceptance of "structures of patriarchal dominance."[16]

But perhaps these choices aren't as conformist as Cooper seems to suggest.[17] As she herself writes, "The genders [Langland] chooses for the characters...have to do with his entire conception of language, the world, human behavior, above all, with rhetorical strategies for expressing his comprehension of the world to his readers...Personification takes precisely that step of shifting discourse beyond the rational and conceptual to the poetic, the imaginative, and the moving."[18] While he certainly does not

---

14   Quotations from the C-Text of *Piers Plowman* are taken from *Piers Plowman by William Langland: An Edition of the C-text*, ed. Derek Pearsall (Berkeley: University of California Press, 1978). Passus and line numbers will be given within the body of my text.

15   M. Teresa Tavormina, *Kindly Similitude: Marriage and Family in Piers Plowman* (Cambridge: D.S. Brewer, 1995). This meticulously researched book offers much useful information for feminist scholars.

16   Cooper, "Gender," 46.

17   In his essay in the *Yearbook of Langland Studies*, Paxson offers a more complex theoretical critique of the limits of Cooper's analysis than I am offering here. What my argument shares with his is an interest in the "slippage" between grammar/logic and rhetoric that is enacted by a feminine personified abstraction. In addition, I share his interest in the "paralogical" effects of this slippage.

18   Cooper, "Gender," 38.

challenge patriarchal structures of dominance from a feminist viewpoint, Langland's imaginative range, like that of many great poets, still allows for the faultlines of social structures and gender stereotypes to be exposed. That is, he includes analysis of a wide variety of social formations, including those of "patriarchal dominance." Langland's use of ideas about the feminine becomes the means, not the ends, of exploring the conditions, simultaneously of both a particular marginalized group, and, more importantly, of cultural configurations generally.

Even choosing to ignore grammatical gender by personifying a feminine Latin noun as a male character can have complex gender signification. Langland's representations of the Seven Deadly Sins offer a rich and varied set of examples. Changing gender attributions that have been naturalized by grammatical attributions especially draws our attention to the assumptions that unconsciously underlie gender constructs. This is most obvious in those representations of sins that go against the gender attributed to the sin by tradition. A straightforward example is the one already mentioned, Langland's unexpected personification of *Luxuria* in the B-Text as male. Surprisingly, Langland glances only briefly at this sin which usually receives extensive commentary. It is also unusual to see Pride, that sin associated with Lucifer, as female, here Pernele Proud-herte. It is notable that Langland feels free to change that gender later in the poem where Pride appears as male (B.14.216–17).[19] Gender shifting also occurs outside of the representations of the sins. Paxson has analyzed, for example, one of the more complex of these shifts, the dual representation of *Anima* as female in Passus 9 of the B-Text and as male in Passus 15.[20]

These shifting genders make it possible for us to view these characters in terms of Judith Butler's theory of gender performance: that is, each personification can be seen as acting a role and taking on gendered attributes rather than enacting gendered behavior springing from an essential source.[21] As in the early performances of a Shakespeare play—where boys dressed as female characters then cross-dressed to portray male characters—here Langland clothes a grammatically gendered female concept as male and then presents that character as transgendered; it is thus difficult to identify the figure clearly in terms of gender. As Cooper points out, the gender of each sin seems to bear the attributes of the other gender or to slide uneasily from one set of gendered characteristics to another. R. W. Frank argues that Langland chooses to represent characters such as Envy and Sloth as "now a man, now a woman" in order to illustrate the ways in

---

[19] Dolan sees this shift in gender as a sign that Pride's earlier representation as female is insignificant. I would argue to the contrary that this shows precisely how significant gender is to Langland because his shifts in gender draw our attention specifically to the different associations gender attributions carry. See Dolan, "Langland's Women," 127.

[20] See Paxson, "Gender Personified," 82–89.

[21] Judith Butler, *Gender Trouble: Feminism and the Subversion of Identity* (London: Routledge, 1990).

which these sins are "at work among men and women."[22] Paxson suggests, on the other hand, that "the cases of gender-shifting could be construed as extended enactments of anthimeria," and that such gender shifts in their disruption of the logic of grammar disturb and unsettle the reader.[23] It is this disturbance of order, one achieved by blurring categories of gender, especially those that define the feminine, that I shall look at more closely through the example of the figure of Gluttony.

Langland's personification of Gluttony allows the poet to utilize received notions about the feminine in order to explore the poem's thematic concern with measurement, for Gluttony is, of course, the embodiment of excess measure. Although grammatically female, the poet chooses to represent Gluttony as male. Yet, as we shall see, in performance and excessiveness, this personified abstraction can be described as culturally female.[24] The most significant description of Gluttony in these terms is the following:

> There was laughynge and lourynge and 'Lat go the cuppe!'
> [Bargaynes and beverages bigonne to arise;]
> And seten so til evensong, and songen umwhile,
> Til Gloton hadde yglubbed a galon and a gille.
> His guttes gonne to gothelen as two gredy sowes;
> He pissed a potel in a *Paternoster*-while,
> And blew his rounde ruwet at his ruggebones ende,
> That alle that herde that horn helde hir nose after
> And wisshed it hadde ben wexed with a wispe of firses!
> He myghte neither steppe ne stonde er he his staf hadde,
> And thanne gan he to go like a glemannes bicche,
> Som tyme aside and som tyme arere,
> And whoso leith lynes for to lacche foweles.
> And whan he drough to the dore, thanne dymmed his eighen;
> He [thr]umbled on the thresshfold and threw to the erthe.
> Clement the Cobelere kaughte hym by the myddel
> For to liften hym olofte, and leyde him on his knowes.
> Ac Gloton was a gret cherl and a grym in the liftyng,
> And koughed up a cawdel in Clementes lappe....
> With al the wo of this world, his wif and his wenche
> Baren hym to his bed and broughte hym therinne.
>   (B. 5. 337-359)[25]

---

22 R. W. Frank, "The Art of Reading Medieval Personification Allegory," *English Literary History* 20 (1953), 247, discussed in Paxson, "Gender Personified," 81.

23 Paxson, "Gender Personified," 72.

24 I am grateful to my students for discussions about Gluttony's feminine qualities, especially to Katherine Millersdaughter who is completing her own essay on this topic.

25 *The Vision of Piers Plowman: A Critical edition of the B-Text*, ed. A. V. C. Schmidt, 2nd edition (London: Everyman, 1995). All further references to the B-Text will be taken from this edition. Passus and line numbers will be given in parentheses within the body of my text.

David Aers has shown the important ways in which this scene illuminates fourteenth-century labor conditions.[26] Citing Bakhtin, Aers writes, "However hostile the aim, the poetry includes the projection of a profane, counter-culture in which the body, as Gloton's performance displays, is present and open."[27] Gluttony is a perfect example of a Bakhtinian grotesque body; one that is "unfinished, outgrows itself, transgresses its own limits," and one "not separated from the world by clearly defined boundaries."[28] Aers demonstrates how the carnivalesque meeting in the tavern, with its alternate Mass, comments on orthodox church culture, although one might disagree, as Derek Pearsall does, with viewing this commentary as celebratory rather than condemnatory.[29] In a footnote, Aers suggests that we need to consider "the unexamined assumptions about the maleness of the body in Bakhtin's work."[30] This point is developed by Peter Stallybrass who argues that in the early periods a woman's body in its carnality was in itself understood to be grotesque.[31] He further considers the subversive potential of such a body: "The female grotesque could indeed interrogate class and gender hierarchies alike, subverting the enclosed body."[32] While Stallybrass considers the ways in which the feminine body is "naturally" grotesque, he does not address how the grotesque body is naturally feminine.

I and others propose that the disruption of social order enacted through the grotesque is furthered precisely through the feminine. Commenting on Tertullian's famous description of women as "the Devil's gateway," Paxson argues that medieval commentators saw a woman as a "violator" or "agent of transgressed margins."[33] The age's correlation between the grotesque and the feminine both informs and complicates the gender identity of Gluttony's obviously grotesque body. There are a number of ways in which Gluttony might be described as feminine. Despite his name, "Sire Gloton," Gluttony carries the echo of the feminine in his female gendered Latin name, *Gula*. Furthermore, he is feminized in his

---

[26] David Aers, *Community, Gender, and Individual Identity: English Writing 1360–1430* (London and New York: Routledge, 1988), 40.

[27] Aers, *Community*, 40.

[28] Quoted in Peter Stallybrass "Patriarchal Territories: The Body Enclosed" in *Rewriting the Renaissance: The Discourses of Sexual Difference in Early Modern Europe*, ed. Margaret Ferguson, Maureen Quilligan and Nancy J. Vickers (Chicago and London: University of Chicago Press, 1986), 124, from M. Bakhtin, *Rabelais and His World*, trans. Helene Iswolsky (Cambridge, Mass: MIT Press, 1968), 26.

[29] Pearsall writes, "Something of the pullulating life of the city comes over, though I cannot, hard as I try, agree with David Aers in admiring the vitality of the scene as a kind of celebration of an anti-establishment counterculture...I am sure that Langland regarded Glutton's tavern as the very sump of the den of iniquity." See Derek Pearsall, "Langland's London," in *Written Work: Langland, Labor, and Authorship*, ed. Steven Justice and Kathryn Kerby-Fulton (Philadelphia, PA: University of Pennsylvania Press, 1997), 191–2.

[30] Aers, *Community*, 189 n60.

[31] Stallybrass, "Patriarchal," 126.

[32] Stallybrass, "Patriarchal," 142.

[33] Paxson, "Gender Personfied," 75.

behavior, becoming passive, unable to enact his own will, and ultimately controlled physically by women, as when his wife and a wench see him home. More importantly, Gluttony is feminized in his bodily excesses.

The much-debated psychoanalytic theories of Luce Irigaray and Julia Kristeva also can shed light on Langland's manipulation of such medieval ideas about feminine excess.[34] Langland's figure of Gluttony is a perfect example of the Kristevan theory of the abject. Describing the corpse as the ultimate abject, Kristeva writes "refuse and corpses *show me* what I permanently thrust aside in order to live. These body fluids, this defilement, this shit are what life withstands, hardly and with difficulty, on the part of death;" and later, "It is thus not lack of cleanliness or health that causes abjection but what disturbs identity, system, order. What does not respect borders, positions, rules. The in-between, the ambiguous, the composite."[35] These characteristics can be applied to Gluttony, a sinner who has no respect for borders or rules. What should be inside Gluttony is outside. His body has exceeded the boundaries that mark the identity of self from other. Like the corpse, Gluttony, as the abject, produces an abject response in the reader (in Kristeva's terms, the reader becomes a "deject"). By viewing Gluttony's excesses, the reader learns to avoid the sin that produces that shattering of identity. Gluttony's inability to contain what is inside results in a regression of his identity as he becomes increasingly passive and controlled by women. His masculine identity has disappeared, and from a Kristevan point of view his identity as either subject or object has vanished—he has become the abject. The abject is culturally associated with the feminine, especially in the Middle Ages, where women's bodies, as mentioned above, were deemed both seductive and repellent.

Irigaray also explores the association of grotesque, exuding, bodily excess with the feminine. Her theory applies within a medieval context since Aristotelian physiology described the female as made up of excess fluids that must be purged regularly through menstruation. In Irigaray's theory of mimicry, women can challenge these essentializing attributions by exaggerating them to the point where they unravel the logic that produced them. As Irigaray writes of mimicry:

---

[34] Kristeva and Irigaray are useful for the feminist reader because of their utopian ability to imagine systems outside the hegemony, an imaginary process not dissimilar to the effect produced by visionary poets such as Langland. Irigaray and Kristeva's theories are based on the belief that all human beings, whatever their historical circumstances, share the same psychic structures—although both Kristeva and Irigaray do recognize that those structures may be socially produced. Recent critics tend to reject these theories as both essentialist and ahistorical and therefore of little use to an analysis of medieval literature. Kristeva and Irigaray can be useful, however, in considering medieval texts because both theorists demonstrate how gender identity is formed culturally. For a discussion of the subtlety of Irigaray, see Naomi Schor, "This Essentialism Which is Not One: Coming to Grips with Irigaray" in *The Essential Difference: Another Look at Essentialism in Differences* 1, no. 2 (Summer, 1989): 38–58.

[35] Julia Kristeva, *The Powers of Horror: An Essay on Abjection*, trans. Leon S. Roudiez (New York: Columbia University Press, 1982), 3, 4.

> One must assume the feminine role deliberately. Which means already to convert a form of subordination into an affirmation, and thus to begin to thwart it. Whereas a direct feminine challenge to this condition means demanding to speak as a (masculine) "subject" that is, it means to postulate a relation to the intelligible that would maintain sexual indifference.

> To play with mimesis is thus, for a woman, to try to recover the place of her exploitation by discourse, without allowing herself to be simply reduced to it. It means to resubmit herself—insomuch as she is on the side of the "perceptible," of "matter"—to "ideas" in particular to ideas about herself, that are elaborated in/by a masculine logic, but so as to make "visible" by an effect of playful repetition, what was supposed to remain invisible.[36]

Carolyn Dinshaw has shown how, through mimicry, the Wife of Bath, both in her manipulation of texts and in her excessive behavior, draws our attention to the system that produced the category of woman in medieval culture.[37] Karma Lochrie has made a similar case for Margery Kempe, one whose behavior is not only excessive but also often abject and grotesque.[38] I suggest that Langland's poem shows similar aspects. As we shall see, the figure in Langland who arguably engages most in mimicry is Lady Mede; she makes visible to the reader the position of women in aristocratic society and its expectations of her mobility and role. Because Gluttony is male, we cannot describe him as an Irigarayan mimic whose mimicry unravels cultural stereotypes about women. His hyperbolic purging of excess, however, challenges the very notion of excess as a defining quality of identity, whether male or female, and the exaggeration of gendered attributes more commonly associated with the female body challenges the essentialism of such notions. Furthermore, the example of Gluttony's excesses asks the reader to contemplate how and why such excess, culturally coded as feminine, can be challenging to the social order.

Gluttony's feminization is furthered in this scene by his dilatoriness. In Parker's terms, Gluttony is a feminized dilatory "fat" body. Gluttony can never get to church to confess because he will always be delayed by his desires for food and drink. His habit of delay and the dilatory misuses of language by himself and those around him are to Langland the essence of his sinfulness—he can not reach the proper end, repentance. Parker

---

36 Luce Irigaray, *This Sex Which is Not One*, trans. Catherine Porter (Ithaca, NY: Cornell University Press, 1985), 76.

37 Carolyn Dinshaw, *Chaucer's Sexual Poetics* (Madison, WI: University of Wisconsin Press, 1989), 113–131. See also Elaine Tuttle Hansen, *Chaucer and the Fictions of Gender* (Berkeley, CA: University of California Press, 1992), who makes a similar argument about the Wife of Bath and mimicry (26–57).

38 Karma Lochrie, *Margery Kempe and Translations of the Flesh* (Philadelphia, PA: University of Pennsylvania Press, 1991).

describes such dilatoriness and the misogyny associated with it with reference to the Wife of Bath:

> As one recent reading of this excessive 'Dame' puts it, Alisoun of Bath ameliorated the harsh polarizations of apocalyptic judgment and eschatology and opens up a space of dilation in which what we have come to call literature can have its place. Her 'increase' however, is verbal rather than generational, and from this more judgmental perspective, as a form of sterility or fruitless activity, it is finally preempted by the teleological framework in which there is no—or no longer—'essoin' [the Parson's word from Chaucer's *Parson's Tale* referring to legal delays in judgment.][39]

In Langland's vision, dilatoriness that diverts the sinner from the lessons of the future Judgment Day is natural to sin. Furthermore, Gluttony mirrors the dilatoriness of Will and even of the poem itself.[40] Thus while dilatoriness is negative in its sinfulness, it is also positive as the means to learn about the nature of salvation. What is significant for the feminist reader are the ways in which Langland here manipulates a cultural predisposition to associate dilatoriness with the feminine in order to further his exploration of the nature of sin and salvation.

Woven into these manipulations of essentialized notions of identity in this portrait of Gluttony, as elsewhere in the poem, are powerfully mimetic female characters reflecting the actual social conditions of women in the fourteenth century. Langland utilizes both ideological notions about women and actual women's lived experiences to fashion his female characters, and it is just as important for us to attend to history as to the history of ideas. An opposite point of view is voiced by Marina Warner, who warns us against reading allegorical figures as if they were accurate representations of historical women. She observes that, "often the recognition of a difference between the symbolic order, inhabited by ideal, allegorical figures and the actual order of judges, statesmen, soldiers, philosophers, inventors, depends on the unlikelihood of women practicing the concepts they represent."[41] Nonetheless, a number of Langland's representations grant us insight into the historical conditions of women in the period. In a recent essay, Aers urges us to consider Langland's representations of both gender and class in a historically responsible way.[42] Aers's earlier analysis

---

[39] Patricia Parker, "Literary Fat Ladies and the Generation of the Text," in *Literary Fat Ladies*, 16.

[40] I am grateful to Teresa Nugent for suggesting the role dilatoriness plays in a poem that apparently "delays" its readers.

[41] Marina Warner, *Monuments and Maidens: The Allegory of the Female Form* (London: Weidenfeld and Nicolson, 1985), xx, as cited in Colette Murphy, "Lady Holy Church and Meed the Maid" in *Feminist Readings in Middle English Literature: The Wife of Bath and All Her Sect*, ed. Ruth Evans and Lesley Johnson (London and New York: Routledge, 1994), 140–64.

[42] David Aers, "Class, Gender, Medieval Criticism, and *Piers Plowman*" in *Class and Gender in Early English Literature: Intersections*, Britton J. Harwood and Gillian R. Overing, eds. (Bloomington, IN: Indiana University Press, 1994), 59–75.

of the Gluttony scene recognizes one of the most unusual features of
Langland's work—that is, his representation of women of a variety of classes. Langland's poem is one of our few sources of images of medieval working women—women as brewsters, prostitutes, seamstresses, retailers, and
the like, and women who drink side by side as equal wage-earners in the
pub with Gluttony. The famous C-Text passage on poverty offers a moving
portrait of the material circumstances of poor women in fourteenth-century England:

> Ac þat most neden aren oure neyhebors, and we nyme gode hede,
> As prisones in puttes and pore folk in cotes,
> Charged with childrene and chief lordes rente;
> þat they with spynnyng may spare, spenen hit on hous-huyre,
> Bothe in mylke and in mele, to make with papelotes
> To aglotye with here gurles that greden aftur fode.
> And hemsulue also soffre muche hunger,
> And wo in wynter-tymes, and wakynge on nyhtes
> To rise to þe reule to rokke þe cradel,
> Bothe to carde and to kembe, to cloute and to wasche,
> And to rybbe and to rele, rusches to pylie,
> That reuthe is to rede or in ryme schewe
> The wo of this wommen þat wonyeth in cotes;
> And of monye oþer men þat moche wo soffren,
> Bothe afyngred and afurste, to turne þe fayre outward,
> And ben abasched for to begge and wollen nat be aknowe
> What hem nedeth at here neyhebores at noon and at eue.
>   (C.9.71–87)

More fragmentary glimpses of other mimetic figures are sprinkled throughout the poem—Rose the Regrator, Wrong's rape victims, Rose and
Margrete in Passus 4, and Beton the Brewster, to name a few.

When analyzing these historically mimetic representations, the critic
must remember that they occur within a poem, appearing first and foremost as part of the poet's large concerns. However realistic the above passage seems to be, it also has much in common with a long tradition of commentaries against marriage known as the *molestiae nuptiarum*.[43] While it
is important to keep literary convention and poetic concerns in mind before
analyzing a passage as a reflection of the condition of women in fourteenth-century England, it is also crucial for the feminist reader to keep theoretical feminist questions foremost in mind while searching for an accurate rendering of women's lives. The Bennett-Hanna debate over how to
understand Beton the Brewster from a feminist perspective is a case in

---

[43] Critics for some time argued for the realism of *Hali Meidenhad*'s harsh portrait of marriage, childbirth,
and childraising before Bella Millett located the sensitive portrait's source in a letter by Hildebert of
Lavardin to the recluse Athalisa on the woes of marriage. See Bella Millet's discussion of this source and
other sources that may have shaped the "realistic" portrait of marriage painted in the text in the introduction of her edition, Hali Mei®had for the EETS o.s. 24 (Oxford: Oxford University Press, 1982), xiii–lviii.

point. Judith Bennett, in her encompassing historical study of women brewers in medieval England, cites Langland's representation of Beton the Brewster as an example of fourteenth-century hostility to women in the brewing trade.[44] Ralph Hanna, reacting to an early formulation of Bennett's thesis, argues that this scene is not misogynistic and actually tells us little about women in brewing and a lot more about Langland's view of sins in the food trade more generally, sins associated equally with men and with women. He warns us not to read these characters mimetically as a direct reflection of fourteenth-century life. Instead, Hanna argues that if we consider Beton both as part of the scene within which she appears and within the context of the poet's larger concerns, it is hard to find misogyny here; Langland's primary concern is not to attack women making money, but rather to criticize abuses among the victualers in general.

Hanna's warning is an important caveat for those seeking historically mimetic examples in any literary text. Nonetheless, in situating this scene within the poem's larger concerns, Hanna may have overlooked some details that could have motivated some of Bennett's concerns and that are of interest to the feminist reader. Why do we see here a woman who makes money, perhaps by manipulating measure, as a facilitator of sin? Is this Langland's covert way of criticizing women who enter the world of business, as Bennett suggests? Or is it Langland's way of turning the kaleidoscope one more time on the issues of proper measurement that permeate the poem as a whole? Like Lady Mede and Mercy, in Beton we have yet another female character who elicits ideas about measurement, and, in Beton's case, historically resonant questions about women who were sometimes arraigned for measuring drink unfairly.[45] In some ways this scene, as Hanna argues, does not seem especially misogynistic, since men and women do share equally in dilatory behavior—and thus, appear to be equal as sinners. Perhaps, however, the apparently historically mimetic vision of society glimpsed here, in which men and women participate as drinkers and revellers and sinners together, might actually be Langland's critique of sin—that is, the fact that sin equalizes gender roles may be itself a sin. If so, then we would have to conclude that hierarchy rather than equality might be more consonant with Langland's vision of a just society.

At the very least, we should question the gendering of space itself in this scene. Sin is represented here in terms of a feminized space—a woman,

---

[44] Judith Bennett, *Ale, Beer, and Brewsters in England: Women's Work in a Changing World, 1300–1600* (New York and Oxford: Oxford University Press, 1996), 126–144. An earlier formulation of this argument appears in "Misogyny, Popular Culture, and Women's Work," *History Workshop* 31 (Spring, 1991): 166–88, to which Ralph Hanna responds in "Brewing Trouble: On Literature and History—and Alewives" in *Bodies and Disciplines: Intersections of Literature and History in Fifteenth-Century England,* Barbara A. Hanawalt and David Wallace, eds., *Medieval Cultures* 9 (Minneapolis and London: University of Minnesota Press, 1996), 1–18.

[45] See Bennett's book for a discussion of these charges.

Beton, entices Gluttony in. (Of course this is countered later by a woman who gets him out, Gluttony's wife.) Furthermore, Beton acts as the gate-keeper of excess and invites Gluttony to the feminization of the masculine, a feminization or gender-blurring that seems part of Langland's under-standing of what sin is. While issues other than misogyny may well be oper-ating in this representation of Beton, Langland is at least drawing on a cul-tural conception of women as seductive and negatively excessive. Furthermore, Langland uses gender here to explore many aspects of sin from the historical sin of unfairly measuring food and drink to the more abstract sin of losing one's sense of self by losing one's sense of one's gen-der. That sin makes a man more womanly is in keeping with the hierarchi-cal gendering of sin in the Christian tradition which, on the one hand, emphasizes the inherent sinfulness of all humanity, but, on the other hand, especially associates sin with the female (Adam is the head; Eve the willful body, etcetera) Whatever his ultimate position concerning the relationship between gender and sin, by upsetting the reader's expectations of gendered behavior, Langland challenges the essentialism of these notions. In his rep-resentation of Gluttony, then, Langland draws on negative stereotypes about the feminine in order to explore the nature of sin; these negative qualities of excessiveness and dilatoriness do have the potential, however, if not to challenge social injustice, at least to call attention to the social def-initions of gender roles. Elsewhere in the poem, the potential of the femi-nine to be liberatory as well as disruptive is more fully articulated.

Langland's personification of women as abstract ideas affords even greater range of play concerning limits. Dame Study, for example, offers a particularly rich instance of a personified abstraction who undermines our expectations of typical feminine behavior and who furthermore offers an avenue of complex cultural critique. She first surprises us with her unusu-al position of mastery over her husband, Wit. Traditionally Wit, as in the thirteenth-century allegory of the household of the soul, *Sawles Warde*, curbs the excesses of an unruly wife called Will; here, in *Piers*, however, the wife, Study, curbs the behavior of those who presume to know. While urg-ing Will to pursue education through training in the seven liberal arts, Study, at the same time, exposes the dangers of such education. Presumptions of knowledge can lead to a range of abuses including those of language (bad minstrels) and of food (drunkenness), both of which must be measured.

Dame Study may at first glance seem to embody repression, the bind-ing or linking of the impulse to education. But in fact her cautionary posi-tion would serve to make education more efficacious and available to a greater range of the population. As Louise Bishop has argued, Langland here engages with the vexed questions raised by Lollardy of the dangers and liberatory potential of vernacular theology itself.[46] Study thus engages

---

[46] Louise Bishop, "Dame Study and Women's Literacy," *Yearbook of Langland Studies* 12 (1998): 97–116.

historical female educators in a number of ways. First, she may well reflect the historical fact that most students received their early education from female teachers who both intellectually and physically liberated and restrained the child. Study sends Will on to her cousin, Clergy—appropriately male, reflecting the fact that clerical education was taught by men for men only. Clergy, himself, is overmastered, however, by the feminine in his wife, Scripture. Second, Study may well reflect the Lollard female preacher who possesses a dangerously limited understanding of theology. More metaphorically, she can be said to stand for the limits and potential of the very medium within which Langland works, vernacular theology. By drawing on the double association of the "feminine" with limit and freedom, therefore, Langland is able to capture the heart of his anxieties and hopes for his poetic enterprise.

The personification who most fully embodies the extremes of liberation and constraint is Lady Mede, a character who has received attention from gender critics interested in the issue of the nature of female subjectivity and agency. Numerous critics have responded to what Aers has described as her "overflowing sexuality," her "voracious, ever-open, all-consuming sexual body,...which flows everywhere and is fixed nowhere," qualities like those of Gluttony that challenge notions of limit or containment.[47] Furthermore, like the Wife of Bath, Lady Mede's behavior mimics the very categories that define women in the period both theoretically and in practice, especially the commodification of women on the marriage market. Her openness and overflowing excesses also have potentially positive aspects, however, as we shall see. The question that has dominated critical study of Mede to date is the degree of subjectivity she exhibits. What it means to be a female subject has been an ongoing concern of feminist scholarship. For the medievalist, that question has necessarily been considered in the broadest terms—is there such a thing as a subject at all in the Middle Ages?[48] Most recently medieval feminists have turned their attention to a more graspable question: What does it mean for a woman to act in the Middle Ages, that is, what kind of agency do women in the Middle Ages demonstrate and what kind of information about female agency can be gleaned from literary sources?

Three recent essays by Clare Lees, Colette Murphy and Elizabeth Fowler raise first the question of why it matters that Mede is portrayed as a woman, and second the question of female agency her portrait inspires.[49]

---

[47] Aers, "Class, Gender," 67, 69.

[48] See David Aers's discussion of subjectivity in the Middle Ages in "A Whisper in the Ear of Early Modernists; or, Reflections on Literary Critics Writing the 'History of the Subject'" in *Culture and History: 1350–1600: Essays in English Communities, Identities and Writing*, ed. David Aers (New York: Harvester Wheatsheaf, 1992), 177–202. For a discussion of theories of subjectivity from a variety of perspectives including feminism see Paul Smith, *Discerning the Subject* (Minneapolis, MN: University of Minnesota Press, 1988).

[49] Clare Lees, "Gender and Exchange in *Piers Plowman*" in *Class and Gender in Early English Literature,*

All three essays explore the significance of Mede's marriageability, noting the importance of Will's initial reaction to her when he wonders, "whos wif she were." (B.2.18.) This query highlights the period's understanding that a woman's identity must be established relationally. The characters who surround Mede are engaged in the business of identifying just what that relationship will be. As Murphy points out, Conscience is particularly anxious to fix Mede's meaning. And Fowler argues, "Conscience argues that Mede's incompleteness is vicious in itself and incapable of remedy."[50] Mede's fluid identity at all levels as a daughter (whose?), as a wife (whose?), as Alice Perrers, as the Whore of Babylon, and as money, teases our desires as readers. As Lees puts it, "Langland's personification generates a powerful desire to fix her, to close her."[51] In her discussion of the nature of allegory in general, Maureen Quilligan argues with reference to Lady Mede that it is only when we let go of this desire for one meaning and learn to read multiply that we can begin to understand how to read Langland's poem as a whole.[52]

The circulation of money and the anxiety produced by excessive payment are linked in this portrait of Mede to the circulation of women on the marriage market and the urgent need of the society to contain female sexuality. The questions Langland explores about the nature of reward are inextricably linked, so all three critics argue, with Lady Mede's status as a woman, that is, as both an object of exchange on the aristocratic marriage market and as an object of desire (as wife and whore). As Lees writes, he displaces "the newly pressing issues of the social circulation of money onto the issues of the more traditional institutions of the patrilinear family and patriarchal marriage."[53] Fowler explores the analogy between money and marriage in more depth. She writes, "The uncontrollable nature of this surplus circulation of payment is portrayed as feminine, and the text claims through this portrayal that the economy must be morally analyzed and socialized by strict controls, just as marriage controls women and sexuality."[54]

All three critics conclude that the fact that Lady Mede's identity is formed by marriage makes it difficult for the feminist reader to view her as a self-determining subject. Fowler explains that marriage in the Middle Ages resulted in a woman's erasure of her legal identity, in what is termed civil death or "coverture," an erasure of the female required under the doc-

---

112–130; Colette Murphy, "Lady Holy Church and Meed the Maid"; and Elizabeth Fowler, "Civil Death and the Maiden: Agency and the Conditions of Contract in *Piers Plowman*," *Speculum* 70 (1995): 760–792.

[50] Fowler, "Civil Death," 774.

[51] Lees, "Gender and Exchange," 114.

[52] Maureen Quilligan, *The Language of Allegory: Defining the Genre* (Ithaca, NY and London: Cornell University Press, 1979), 13–79.

[53] Lees, "Gender and Exchange," 116.

[54] Fowler, "Civil Death," 780.

trine of unity of person in marriage.[55] This doctrine theoretically presupposes mutuality of relationship, but in practice, under the law, the wife disappears altogether. Lees focuses on Mede as a product rather than a producer, a figure denied any subjectivity and desire of her own. She concludes, "As a result, Mede says nothing about women, though much about the attitudes that men have toward women. It comes, therefore, as no surprise to me that Mede is not married. Unmarried, she comes finally to represent all that men fear and desire most—the whore."[56] Similarly Murphy sees Mede most often as not "self-determined, a broker of herself," and thus as a "victim of the desires of the men who surround her and subject her to their misuse and their reading (unlike Lady Holy Church, Meed is not an active interlocutor in the opening frames of her story)."[57] Rather than seeing Mede as lacking in agency, to the contrary, Fowler argues that Mede is all agency, but agency without intention. She writes, "Mede embodies action loose from its intention or subjective source—femininity in need of masculinity."[58] It takes marriage to either False or Conscience to determine what kind of agent she will be. Her free floating agency is threatening to the system, but also exposes to us the contours of the system. Despite this disruptive potential, in the end, like Murphy and Lees, Fowler concludes that Lady Mede cannot be described as a subject.

Lady Mede's unmarried state, however, is precisely where Mede does trouble the system that wishes to contain her. While the text pushes us to fix her meaning as whore, her unmarried state allows for many possibilities. Murphy writes of the potential subversiveness of the position Lady Mede occupies as "an unclaimed woman who lurks in the system as a threat to the truth of husbands."[59] She is both a "destabilising dynamic (seductive materialism) which may disrupt the reproduction of feudal society and the hierarchical ordering of the Church (she circulates freely in the Pope's court) and the product of this destabilising dynamic: a female bastard-heir who excites the attention and attraction of many men whose eligibility excites the anger, and to a certain extent the jealousy, of her 'better bred' female rival."[60] Mede potentially destabilizes the system in other ways, not just as an unmarried woman, but as a potentially incestuous daughter and a possible bastard. Her indiscriminate sexuality is potentially most disruptive. Like Gluttony, it is her open body that disturbs. There are places in the text where she might be said to engage in Irigarayan mimicry: her eagerness to marry all comers, for example, or even her cleric-like reading practices (like the Wife of Bath, she chooses the part

---

55 In his explorations of the legal notion of coverture, Christopher Cannon urges us to recognize the complexity of medieval female agency under the law in "The Rights of Medieval English Women: Crime and the Issue of Representation," *Medieval Crime and Social Control,* ed. David Wallace and Barbara Hanawalt (Minneapolis: University of Minnesota Press, 1999), 156-185.

56 Lees, "Gender and Exchange," 125.

57 Murphy, "Lady Holy Church," 153.

58 Fowler, "Civil Death," 779.

59 Murphy, "Lady Holy Church," 150.

60 Murphy, "Lady Holy Church," 151.

of the Latin she wants—and like Will, she is an untrained reader). In these ways, Lady Mede enacts the very fears and desires evoked by ideas of the feminine.

Lady Mede also disturbs the reader because of her reflection of the actual legal agency sometimes afforded women historically in the fourteenth century. From this perspective, Stephanie Trigg warns against a too easy dismissal of Mede's agency.[61] She asks us to consider the ways in which the representation of Lady Mede draws on contemporary cultural debates about Alice Perrers, a woman who did exhibit agency. Historically, she herself manipulated her status in terms of marriage, choosing to act as a *femme sole* when she wished to disengage herself from her husband's legal obligations, and as a *femme couvert* when she wished to disengage herself from her own potential legal obligations. She was charged in the Good Parliament of 1367 with inspiring the King to spend too much money on her, for engaging in bribery and maintenance, and for having too much influence on royal policy, all activities also enacted by Lady Mede. Perrers is an example of the contradictory powers afforded to women under the law in medieval England. These contradictory subject positions are embraced in the figure of Mede, who as Trigg points out is represented as a speaking subject when she argues her case with Conscience before the King. Furthermore, Trigg continues, she exhibits a degree of agency in her material donations, in her advice to the King and in her depiction as a reading subject, however limited that reading activity is.

Women in medieval culture did escape the limits of society's prescribed definitions when they became *femmes soles* and as single women, and, as the historical record suggests, clearly women whose sexual potential was not clearly circumscribed were threatening to the system. Lady Mede, like Alice Perrers, offers an example of the ways in which women historically exceeded the boundaries that sought to contain and delimit them. Mede's unruliness unravels the very concept of rule—a disruption at once frightening and liberating in the sense that it questions the existing social formations and offers the possibility of envisioning new ones. Furthermore, as Fowler points out, the allegorical marriage plot is transferred at the end to two men in an alliance that itself disrupts the heterosexual economy of the poem.[62] Mede's dilatory doubleness is captured in the King's condemnation of her, "Mede overmaistreth Lawe and muche truthe letteth" (B.4.176), where the primary sense of "let," from "letten," to prevent or delay, dominates the phrase, but its echo of the other verb "leten," "to allow," hints at other possibilities.

In urging us to acknowledge the contradictions of the historical record, Trigg warns that we be careful not to reinscribe misogynistic categories of

---

[61] Stephanie Trigg, "The Traffic in Medieval Women: Alice Perrers, Feminist Criticism and *Piers Plowman*," *Yearbook of Langland Studies* 12 (1998): 5–30.
[62] Fowler, "Civil Death," 787.

women in our analyses of Langland's representations of women and that we recognize that women in the past were not necessarily governed by the essentializing notions articulated in the culture. It is indeed important to recognize that the period itself held contradictory and complex views of women even in theory and that these views had only partial influence on how women acted in practice. Another historical contradiction that might complicate our understanding of Mede's potential agency in marriage is the fact that historically, from the point of view of the Church rather than secular law, marriage both in theory and in practice did allow women agency. While the above critics have explored Lady Mede's status as a commodity on the marriage market, they have failed to appreciate fully the contradictory understandings of the female subject that underlie medieval marriage practices in the two different arenas of the Church and the state. Under canon law, mutual consent was required for marriage. From a theological point of view, marriage requires that a woman verbally assent to her marriage. Fowler questions whether the theological requirement that both men and women mutually consent to marriage, a requirement that did at least nominally inform secular marriage practices, did actually grant women self-determination:

> If women are brought up to be agents of other principals, to be obedient to the will of others, then with what free will do they consent? Their consent is impoverished by being produced by an endless consent they are brought up to give. Further, consenting to marriage is, in this model, consenting permanently: consenting to give up the capacity to consent, consenting to life in a constant condition of what, as we have seen, the chancellor Robert Stillington calls coercion and dread.[63]

And while the doctrine of mutual consent to marriage implies an equality between the sexes, the civil death that results for women because of marriage contradicts that idea. As Fowler explains, "despite the equal footing of their consent, the parties to a marriage contract do not consent to the same thing, whether in the twelfth or the twentieth century."[64]

While Fowler offers an important caution to our understanding of the potential power of consent, it is nonetheless important to recognize that the doctrine of consent comes from an ecclesiastical discourse only imperfectly consonant with the desires of the state. Mede's potential refusal of the King's choices offers a possible challenge to the King's control—although Mede does not avail herself of this—a possible challenge reflected in the historical record where women did succeed in overmastering the desires of their King. Joan, the Fair Maid of Kent, who married Edward the Black Prince against the wishes of his father, is a case in point. Furthermore, the doctrine of consent powerfully asserts the legitimacy of women as subjects rather than the objects secular, aristocratic, and feudal marriage practices made of them.

---

63 Fowler, "Civil Death," 785.
64 Fowler, "Civil Death," 768.

As someone who consents to all-comers, Lady Mede might be said to parody, in an Irigarayan sense, the imperfections of the doctrine of consent. One might argue that the cultural problem that Langland has uncovered here is the conflict between an ideal of mutuality that springs from consent and a social practice in which a woman's consent has little real meaning. If Mede could say no, and if women's refusal to marriage had social power, then the theological ideal might become socially realizable. Mede's ability to consent is at the heart of her potentiality as a subject, but the ways in which that consent can be manipulated by others of greater power shows that female subjectivity cannot be granted only theoretically but must be rooted socially. This gap between the theoretical and the practical concerns Langland throughout the poem; for the feminist reader, that gap is particularly acute when it comes to the question of female agency.

Lady Mede's marriageability is thus a crucial aspect of her meaning both as a person and as an abstraction. I mentioned above the centrality of marriage in Langland's poem as a concept and practice that for Langland most fully binds together the theological and the social. Considering marriage less in terms of its implications for an understanding of female subjectivity and more within the context of fourteenth-century marriage practices, Tavormina elucidates marriage's key role in the poem. Like Lees, Murphy, and Fowler, Tavormina considers how marriage operates as a metaphor in the Lady Mede sequence; Mede's commodification on the marriage market becomes the locus of financial corruption. Elsewhere in the poem, marriage is treated literally. The key to the proper functioning of marriage is mutual consent, as we see in this passage in Passus 9:

> Trewe wedded libbynge folk in this world is Dowel,
> For thei mote werche and wynne and the world sustene.
> For of hir kynde thei come that confessours ben nempned,
> Kynges and knyghtes, kaysers and cherles
> Maidenes and martires—out of o man come.
> The wif was maad the wye for to helpe werche,
> And thus was wedlock ywroght with a mene persone—
> First by the fadres wille and the frendes conseille,
> And sithenes by assent of hemself, as thei two myghte acorde;
> And thus was wedlok ywroght, and God hymself it made;
> In erthe the heven is—hymself was the witnesse.
> (B.9.108–118)

Dolan suggests that Langland tends to take "the supremacy of the male partner" in marriage for granted.[65] While the poem does at times assert male dominance (sometimes even physical dominance) in marriage, Langland's more common image of marriage is one of mutuality rather than subservience. And in some of his examples of married couples, the marriage of Dame Study to Wit and Dame Clergy to Scripture, the wife

---

[65] Dolan, "Langland's Women," 125.

occupies the dominant position in the marriage. In the above passage, the mutual assent of the couple to marriage is asserted as essential to marriage; they marry "by assent of hemself, as thei two myghte acorde" (116). The originary married couple is Adam and Eve, who are presented in the A-Text version of this discussion of marriage as mutual in their sin: "Aftir þat adam & heo eten þe appil" (A.10.141).[66] There follows in all three versions a list of the wrong motivation to marry—for lust or for money, generally—the only right motivation being love. As Langland writes, "For no londes, but for love, loke ye be wedded" (B.9.177). Not only does Langland here satirize the abuses of the age concerning marriage and the wrong uses of money, but also he disrupts the misogynistic trope that Eve was the cause of the downfall of mankind. Here it is not Eve that needs correction, but a social bond from which all other social bonds emerge that needs to be secured—a bond that ultimately reflects God's love for the soul. Maintaining a proper marriage is one definition of Do-Wel and Do-Best; and, as Tavormina writes, "By bringing about universal and mutual affection, and well-ordered, supportive relationships, Do-Best ideally can create a society in which all interactions would in fact be familial, based on shared love and law. The Christian message, which the Church should be preaching to all nations, holds out hope for social harmony as well as for individual salvation."[67] For the feminist reader, in his ideal of marriage, Langland radically undermines the basis for medieval misogyny and offers a vision of a subtly restructured society—one in which theological ideas of mutuality and equality in marriage become socially real. The episode concerning Mede's marriage crystallizes a social order in disarray. Things can only be set right if Mede (and all women) becomes a figure of both agency and subjectivity, one whose consent is validated within the social order, and one whose excesses when positive are embraced rather than repressed.

Mede offers a rich point of comparison with other female personifications who also engage questions of limits as she does. Murphy and Fowler both consider Mede's contrast with Holi Chirche, which at the most general level is one that reinscribes the typical medieval Eve/Mary dichotomy. Langland develops a medieval commonplace of the Church as a woman, yet the figure he presents is a stern and unforgiving mother. To Murphy, Langland chooses to represent the Church as feminine because Langland wishes to separate the Church from institutional power. He wants Will "to communicate with a figure of the Church who is apart from the male-dominated body of the Church as it manifests itself to him in actual social practice in his waking world."[68] Her very femininity exceeds the bounds of a

---

66 Citations of the A-Text of *Piers Plowman* are from the edition by George Kane, *Piers Plowman: The A Version*, rev. ed. (Berkeley, CA: University of California Press, 1988). Passus and line numbers will be given in the body of my text.

67 Tavormina, *Kindly Similitude*, 71-72.

68 Murphy, "Lady Holy Church," 146.

male-dominated contemporary social institution. Fowler goes further by exploring not the differences, but the similarities between Holi Chirche and Lady Mede, such as their sexual promiscuity and their sexual competitiveness, and the way in which each defines herself by lineage, Holi Chirche claiming superior parentage.[69] Furthermore, both characters act as mediators through which the limits of "mesure" are tested.

Lady Mede and Holi Chirche, as women, also initiate the lessons Will learns by first generating desire in him. Will first responds to Holi Chirche's face seeing "A lovely lady of leere"(B.1.3), and later he says, "I was afered of hire face, theigh she fair weere"(B.1.10). Will is dazzled by Mede's rich clothes and jewels and tells us, "Hire array me ravysshed" (B.2.17). Women's beauty, for good or ill, radiates magnetic power. In each of these scenes, Will is drawn to image first, then to words and lessons. It might even be argued here that Langland uses images of female beauty and the idea of the male gaze to engage with the debates of his age on the powers and dangers of imagery as tools for the unlettered.

Most importantly, Lady Mede's excesses anticipate those of Mercy.[70] Not only does Lady Mede share attributes with Holi Chirche, but she also, as David Benson has suggested, shares surprising affinities with Langland's representation of Mercy and Jesus Christ. Arguing for a typological reading of Mede as on one level prefiguring Langland's representation of Christ, Benson outlines the surprising similarities between Mede and Christ.[71] Like Mede, Christ is associated with payment: he buys mankind. Christ offers amends for mankind's sins; Mede's mother is Amends. Christ is indiscriminately generous just as is Mede, who "grants her favors easily to one and all in a spirit of generosity" and "what Meed does for lecherous folk with money is exactly what Christ has done for all mankind with his life."[72] Benson argues further that the interrogation of Lady Mede by an earthly court raises questions about the nature of earthly justice that are not dissimilar to those raised in the debate between the Four Daughters of God in Passus 18. Like Truth and Righteousness, who are equally incomplete in understanding, Conscience and Reason are limited in their understanding of Mede because they seek only earthly justice. We learn from the debate of the Four Daughters of God that justice is not sufficient and must be balanced with mercy; as Benson writes, "justice does not suffer a breach but an expansion with mercy."[73] The Law, Old Testament Law, that is, is

---

[69] Fowler, "Civil Death," 784.

[70] James Simpson illuminates the way the poem develops from notions of strict and delimiting justice to an embracing mercy in his *Piers Plowman: An Introduction to the B-Text* (London and New York: Longman, 1990).

[71] C. David Benson, "The Function of Lady Meed in *Piers Plowman*," *English Studies* 61 No. 3 (June, 1980): 193–205.

[72] Benson, "Function," 197 and 198.

[73] Benson, "Function," 205.

fulfilled through Christ's ability, not to subvert the law, but to go beyond it.

That women must and will find various ways to subvert or go beyond the "law of the father" is a basic tenet of much psychoanalytically-oriented feminist criticism. Mercy goes beyond the law of men, offering a new law that challenges the logic of earthly, secular, and patriarchal law. Like many of the female characters we have encountered, Mercy exudes excess—excess love that must be modulated by truth and righteousness, but an excess that can unravel the relentless logic of the law of the father, that is, the law of men, and save humankind. This excess operates from the margins; it cannot be at the center where power resides because it is outside of the hegemony. Thus, Langland offers a broader vision of God's power, one that comes from without, rather than from within: one that operates outside logic, being arational rather than rational. It is not part of a binary system, but like the abject (Gluttony, Mede, and, ultimately, the suffering Christ), it occupies a third position that is neither subject nor object. Finally, God and God's mercy are infinite, uncontainable by names and ultimately unknowable.

The image of Christ offered by Langland in Passus 18—Christ as Piers, Christ as dressed in the arms of humanity—is a deeply human Christ. When understood within the context of the debate of the Four Daughters, he is also a feminized Christ. Mercy and Justice operate equally in Christ's enactment of God's power, and both of these attributes, along with truth and fortitude, are cast as specifically feminine in Langland's account of the harrowing of hell. This suggests that Langland's vision of God is one in which male and female qualities are in balance, a vision that is not dissimilar to the feminized Christ posited by Julian of Norwich and analyzed by Caroline Bynum.[74] The feminine is an important mediator in this poem of Christianity not only through the figures of Christ and the Four Daughters of God, but also through other figures such as Holi Chirche and Dame Study, all of whom display Langland's varied understanding of the feminine, from the stern to the forgiving.

In Lady Mede and Dame Study, Langland utilizes cultural anxieties about the fearful seductiveness of women to explore the necessity and limitation of boundaries. By exploring the nature of limits through representations of the feminine, Langland questions the very nature of such definitions. Gluttony also draws on misogynistic assumptions about the feminine, but by enacting feminine attributes in a male body, the essentialism of the ages's notions about women are challenged. Thus, varieties of not only the feminine, but also the masculine are played out in the poem. With the exception of Paxson's recent essay, virtually no attention has as yet been

---

[74] See Caroline Bynum, *Jesus as Mother: Studies in the Spirituality of the High Middle Ages* (Berkeley: University of California Press, 1982) and *Holy Feast and Holy Fast: The Religious Significance of Food to Medieval Women* (Berkeley: University of California Press, 1987).

given to gay and lesbian issues in Langland. Paxson argues that the representation of Elde presents him in a homosexual relationship to Will. More
ambitiously, he proposes that the complex implications of shifts in gender
in the personifications of the poem, and further the relationship of these
shifts to the anthimeria or "paralogical" implications of the gendering, not
only of personifications but of rhetoric itself, is itself a "queering" of the
poem. As he writes,

> The queering of Elde, and indeed my whole reading which at this point
> queers *Piers*, therefore convey the notion that personification and
> body-centered allegory can be viewed as queer semiotic enterprises.[75]

Such readings of Langland's poem from the perspective of queer theory will
have to contend with the fact that Langland's vision of a just society has at
its base an ideal of heterosexual marriage. That heterosexism, however,
does not exclude the kind of bending and blending of gender that we see in
the vision of the Seven Deadly Sins and perhaps, ultimately, as we shall consider in a moment, in the figure of Will himself.

At the urging of JoAnn McNamara, feminists have begun to turn their
attention not only to queer theory, but also to the representation of heterosexual men in literature.[76] Ralph Hanna recently considered precisely
how male identity is constructed in Langland's poem.[77] Following a careful exposition of educational practices in medieval England in which boys
are taught through physical punishment, Hanna explores the regulatory
practices of Will's identity formation as a pupil of Dame Study and others.

The character who most suggests the multiple gender positions a subject can occupy is Will himself. Such gender roles have as much to do with
men as with women, and it is crucial to attend not only to the various constructions of femininity in the poem, but also to the poem's construction of
masculinity. A question that has yet to be considered is how Will comes to
be a male character in the first place. As is well known from works such as
Sawles Warde, a typical allegory of the household of the soul, the attribute
of the Will is normally gendered as female. Will is the unruly wife who
must be controlled by the husband and *paterfamilias*, Wit. In this poem,
Wit is indeed personified as male, but appears as the husband of the more
forceful and central character, Dame Study. By representing the central protagonist of the poem, Will, normally identified as female, as male, one
might argue that Langland offers finally Virginia Woolf's androgynous
vision of the self, one in which male and female are in balance.[78] And when

---

[75] Paxson, "Gender Personified," 91.

[76] JoAnn McNamara made a special plea to feminists to consider this topic in her summary remarks at a
conference organized by the North Carolina Research Group on Medieval and Early Modern Women. Ruth
Karras is currently completing a book on this topic.

[77] Ralph Hanna, "School and Scorn: Gender in *Piers Plowman*," *New Medieval Literatures* 3 (1999), 213-227.

[78] See Virginia Woolf, *A Room of One's Own* (San Diego, New York and London: Harcourt Brace
Jovanovich, 1929).

Will is in balance, Will can achieve what Lady Mede cannot: agency as a subject.

To conclude, I believe it would be a mistake to argue that Langland is a proto-feminist, just as it is a mistake to argue for Chaucer's feminism. As I said at the beginning of this essay, the traditional reading of Langland has found that the female presences in the poem are not particularly significant. This alone makes it difficult to consider Langland a feminist since Langland does not demand rights and conditions for women that they do not have. Yet, the studies I have surveyed suggest that Langland's visionary exploration of his culture is one that seeks a more just society under the sanction of religion, one in which neither the poor nor women are oppressed. Langland's complex engagement with issues of interest to the feminist reader springs not, in my opinion, from his unorthodoxy, radical politics, or proto-feminism, but rather from the social critique that is inherent in the kind of visionary poetics he embraces. His poem is not a critique of patriarchy, but his probing and comprehensive analysis of society necessarily includes a consideration of the mechanisms of patriarchy. The mimetic (in an Irigarayan sense) association of the feminine with excess and the dilatory frees women from the constraints of such esssentialism. Feminine excess and dilatoriness as embodied in historically realistic characters (e.g. Rose the Regrator) or in personified abstractions (e.g. Gluttony and Mede) become the means to explore the strengths and limits of social formations in their legal, ecclesiastical, and educational institutional manifestations, as well as in the moral, theological, and psychological structures that underpin those formations. Although Langland makes use of misogynistic tropes, he nonetheless repeatedly avoids the persistent misogyny of his age and refuses to lay originary blame on Eve. In his representation of that bond that is fundamental to his reformulation of society, marriage, he posits a relationship between men and women that is one of mutuality rather than subservience. That relationship based on mutual interdependence reflects not only the Trinity, but the nature of God's love for the soul. Langland seeks a means to make his vision of God's love not only theologically, but also socially, imminent, a goal that benefits men and women alike.[79]

---

[79] Elizabeth Kirk delivered a far-ranging and provocative paper on gender in Langland and in Chaucer for the 1995 National Endowment for the Humanities Institute on Langland and Chaucer in Boulder, Colorado that shaped my thoughts on this topic. I would also like to thank Mark Amsler, C. David Benson, Gerda Norvig, and Karen Palmer for their comments on an early draft of this essay. Teresa Nugent urged me to develop my interest in the significance of dilatoriness in the poem. Deborah Uman developed a paper written in a class on Lady Mede that has informed my reading. I am especially grateful to James Simpson and Jeffrey Robinson for their thoughtful responses to this essay.

Allegory Reconsidered

Inventing the Subject and the Personification of Will in *Piers Plowman*: Rhetorical, Erotic, and Ideological Origins and Limits in Langland's Allegorical Poetics

James J. Paxson

Partaking really of two categories that shape this current volume of Langland essays—Through the Lens of Theory and Allegory Reconsidered—my essay must speak to our poet's unique power as an allegorist, or rather to criticism's longstanding productivity that has met that power; it must also speak to the impasse which that productivity has finally put us in. The impasse comes from a general exhaustion with or from allegory. Like Will at the end of Passus 20 of the B-Text, we are worn out—*forbeten*, one might say—by allegory's persistence in the critical academy. But the impasse comes too from the tenuous hold contemporary theory yet has on Langland studies.[1] *Piers Plowman* more than ever seems a text dominated by critical historicism. This has made for a productive state of affairs, as few would dispute. Never before has historical knowledge of the poem been at so maximal a point. Yet much of the strangeness in the strangest of great Middle English poems still beckons. That strangeness, I maintain, consists in the poem's rhetorical, erotic, psychic, and ideological contouring. And this contouring continues to enrich the historical picture of Langland's narrative world.

It is, however, critically intransigent—even deviant, one might say—for a reader to try and articulate a sexual poetics in the margins of *Piers*

---

[1] Though it still serves as the most important guide for theoretical work in Langland studies—indispensably so for this essay—David Lawton's "The Subject of *Piers Plowman*," published signally as the lead article in the inaugural issue of *Yearbook of Langland Studies* (1 [1987]: 1–30]), does not represent the field's trajectory in 2000. Lawton's call for our application of postmodern models of subject formation to the fragmented and discontinuous, textual invention of Will/will in the poem warrants applause. With alacrity, he suggests Bakhtinian, Althusserian, Lacanian, and Greimasian formulas for supplementing the historical model treating Langland's representation of the "plurality of voices" (11) expressed via the "character" Will; his historical model in turn depends on the thematic correspondences between Will's experience and materials in late Middle English penitential manuals.

Plowman, the most ascetic of the great didactic, Middle English allegories, though I own up to insisting on this in my recent work. In a recent article on personification and gender in *Piers Plowman*, I concluded by arguing that the gender poetics energizing Langland's personificational system—a system cognate at base with the classical rhetorical tradition of embodying personified characters as women in accord with various patristic proto-cols—yields to the "queer" or same-sex scenario of the male figures Elde and Will as potential sodomists.[2] The masculine coupling imagined at the conclusion of the poem's B-Text ironizes and deconstructs the traditional and normative paradigms of embodied feminine personification constitu-tive of earlier medieval allegory.

This conclusion, though provocative, sought not merely to inflame. It proceeded, as I will further show in this essay, from the semiotic forces at work in the signal rhetorical tropes and figures upon which Langland's alle-gorical poetics (and all figures of rhetoric, for that matter) rely. As some innovative work in criticism and the philosophy of rhetoric has recently shown, formalism and historicism by themselves have failed to account for the strangest of interactions among rhetorical tropes and figures as well as the imaginary "histories" within those figures.[3] The psychic and erotic dimensions of rhetoric can be seen to produce in its figures and master tropes a metafigural energy or vitality that could be well conceived as bod-ily and indeed sexual, certainly to the point of aesthetic excess. My work on *Piers Plowman* has begun to show how sexualized rhetorical figures undergird the allegorical poetics constitutive of much medieval thought and literature, with prosopopeia or personification above all revealing the energies and drives of figures—of *figurae*, or bodies—as well as rhetorical devices of eloquence so conceived.

But such a turn in understanding Langland's allegorical poetics also enables a new way of theorizing the ideological and political implications of maleness, monarchical rule, and social identity in late fourteenth-

---

[2] See James J. Paxson, "Gender Personified, Personification Gendered, and the Body Figuralized in *Piers Plowman*," *Yearbook of Langland Studies* 12 (1998): 65–96.

[3] See Shirley Sharon-Zisser and James J. Paxson, "Rhetorical Copulas/Bodily Copulations in Medieval and Renaissance Rhetoric: Introduction," *Exemplaria* 11 (1999), 109–110 for an overview of work under this aegis. I owe a debt to Shirley Sharon-Zisser who has been the first scholar, to my knowledge, to formulate the relations among tropes and figures, the grammatical and ontological copula central to this essay, and the erotics of rhetoric and narrative. In sum, Sharon-Zisser's procedures follow strict Lacanian models as well as the influential psychocritical paradigm offered in Nicolas Abraham and Maria Torok, *The Shell and the Kernel: Renewals of Psychoanalysis*, Nicholas T. Rand, trans. (Chicago: Chicago University Press, 1994). A less informed and devoted follower of these procedures, I am aware, too, that I depart from the stricter economy represented in Sharon-Zisser's use of the key terms "trope" and "figure"; admittedly, my employment of these terms makes them interchangeable at times, a move more in the tradition of Poststructural rhetoric and in tension with the finer distinctions used in both the traditional history of rhetoric and in Sharon-Zisser's Lacanian analysis. Both of our treatments, however, challenge the complete flattening out of the concept "trope" that results in New Historicist writing, which recklessly assimilates traditional rhetoric's terms "trope," "figure," "scheme," "analogy," "enthymeme," and even "topos."

century England. The personal and authorial signature of "Will Langland" so thoroughly documented by Anne Middleton[4] enjoys intimate connection with the rhetorical semiotics that motorize Langland's master tropes of allegory. As I will show, Will personified—a status not at first clear in that it must be shown whose or what's "will" our narrator *is*—exists as a narrative, cognitive, and political entity through the erotics of unconscious rhetorical structures and through the social implications of male homosociality or same-sex imaging, an effect that must be allegorically signaled and then cordoned off in the implied political making of a nation's collective and corporatist "will."

I will go forward in this speculative argument, then, by first addressing the promises for contemporary criticism of the queer poetics seen, by way of methodological example, in the recent work of Carolyn Dinshaw. Specifically, I will borrow her tactic of articulating the ways in which our own, contemporary culture of media-driven consumerism invents or interpolates an *idea* of the Middle Ages—a strategy Dinshaw calls "getting medieval"—in order to figure out its own national and social project of containing queerness or promoting masculinity in the service of a probative will-building. Whereas Dinshaw's stimulating book, *Getting Medieval,* hinges on the "juxtaposition" of late Middle English narratives and didactic writings treating sodomy and dissenting behavior (mainly Lollardy) with the cultic 1994 film *Pulp Fiction*,[5] I shall bring together narrative moments from *Piers Plowman* B.20 with the 1998 film *Meet Joe Black.* If the most stunning feature of this strange movie is its personification of Death in uncannily medieval undertones, it occults the gendered triangulations among its main characters and especially the tacit picture of queerness governing Death's relations with his human "subjects," while it places in question Death's status as a real though personified and incarnate abstraction whose ultimately defining acts involve corporatist (and commercial) politics. I will, at the same time, account for a check placed against Dinshaw's queer theory by looking at Allen Frantzen's call for a "legitimizing" and not merely "liberationist" queer or same-sex commentary.[6] The counterbalance is significant here partly for the reason that Frantzen's powerful book, *Before the Closet,* proceeds on a tactical course similar to Dinshaw's in *Getting Medieval* and to mine in "Inventing the Subject and the Personification of Will in *Piers Plowman*": all three studies use a con-

---

[4] "William Langland's 'Kynde Name': Authorial Signature and Social Identity in Late Fourteenth-Century England," in *Literary Practice and Social Change in Britain, 1280–1530*, Lee Patterson, ed. (Berkeley and Los Angeles, CA: University of California Press, 1990), 15–82.

[5] Carolyn Dinshaw, *Getting Medieval: Sexualities and Communities, Pre- and Postmodern* (Durham, NC and London: Duke University Press, 1999). For introduction of the practice of critical "juxtaposition" or "touching," see 12, et passim.

[6] Allen J. Frantzen, *Before the Closet: Same-Sex Love from Beowulf to Angels in America* (Chicago and London: University of Chicago Press, 1998), 24.

temporary popular American document (for Frantzen, Tony Kushner's *Angels in America*) about the homosocial or same-sex male imaginary in order to show how our modern culture appropriates, defines, misreads, intersects with, and projects onto things medieval its own narrative myths of subject formation and public (or corporative) activity.

The conjunction of Death personified and the queer I take to be a structural projection and amplification of psychic and tropological process-es seen in the allegorical poetics of *Piers Plowman* B.20; it is a conjunction I likewise take as the node for enabling the larger political and cultural sur-veillance and understanding of masculinity and power—both feudal and capitalist, respectively—in late fourteenth-century England and in late twentieth-century America.

Finally, I will show how the semiotic disposition of personification as a narrative power and the personification of Will as a character dramatizes Louis Marin's semiological theory of state-formation as the dispersal and embedding of the king's numinous image via various public media—didac-tic allegorical narrative for the late Middle Ages and popular film for 1990s America. If Will is the will of the nation (see James Simpson's "The Power of Impropriety" elsewhere in this volume)[7] as well as the will of an indi-vidual human consciousness, such an ideological and politically significant projection outward of allegorical materials that had evolved in the service of sacramental and psychological poesis shows decisively that Langland's poetics of personification owes its vitality to a series of psychic, erotic, and tropological effects evident at the micro-level of figures appreciable in no minor part through Freudian and Lacanian generative models (though it would be more accurate to say that my procedure will highlight discursive and imagistic prefigurations of Lacanian discourse in the literalizing and sensuous discourse of late medieval personification allegory). This dis-course defines the self and the masculine, two concepts essential to the establishment of imaginary relations between the individual and the national state, the latter being a corporate personification of the king.

Along the way, this procedure will of course involve the structural articulation of tropes that will draw on their classical and canonical iden-tities in classical rhetoric; it will engage in my own personificational (meta)narrative of the sexed and social "bodies" of rhetorical figures, artic-ulating how the grammatical and rhetorical structures of the grammatical and ontological *copula* that inhabit and enable the four elocutionary cate-gories—personification, *transumptio*, metaphor, and simile—allegorize human sexuality in Langland's heretofore "straightly" read poem of dog-matic gravity; and it will even resort to the phonological underpinnings of one master figural maneuver, paranomastic juxtology, which animates two

---

7 I am thankful to Kathleen Hewett-Smith and James Simpson for letting me read in advance James's essay, "The Power of Impropriety: Authorial Naming in *Piers Plowman*." It has helped me greatly in formulat-ing a critical model of Will's personification in the poem.

of the most important semantic or lexical terms in *Piers Plowman*—the cognitive and political expressions "kynde" and "kyng," respectively.

I begin by noting that the provocative commentary coming towards the conclusion of my 1998 essay "Gender Personified" began as the hermeneutic response to something overwhelmingly literal, straightforward, even flat in its frankness: reading the interchange between the personification of old age, Elde, and the narrator Will in passus 20 of the B-Text, I was seeking to better understand the already overdetermined representation of one of the few sexually explicit moments in Middle English literature. We get not only the most frank description to date of a husband and wife in bed at night—something unexpected in Langland's austere social landscape—but perhaps one of the still scarcer Middle English poetic representations of sodomy. The incident feels gratuitous, to be sure; but as Carolyn Dinshaw says, queer analysis should be "always interested in what seems gratuitous in a narrative, since these are the things that, for some reason, the author simply cannot leave out."[8] Will first complains of Elde's pugilistic assault: "He buffetted me aboute þe mouþ [and bette out my wangteeþ]; / And gyued me in goutes" (B.20.191–92);[9] he then goes on to lament the sexual impotence brought on by old age by defining that impotence as the failure of his penis to "be made to do his wife's will" any longer. If Will's ambulatory or manual limbs swell from the gout, his manly member can ironically no longer do so. The failure has resulted from Kit's simply having worn out Will's member after many, many nights. Yet such sexual failure may have been incurred not just by the natural overstimulation and exercise in heterosexual copulation between Will and his wife Kit, but by stimulation "enacted" by the personification Elde as well.

> And of þe wo þat I was Inne my wif hadde ruþe
> And wisshed ful witterly þat I were in heuene.
> For þe lyme þat she loued me fore and leef was to feele
> On nyghtes namely, whan we naked weere,
> I ne myghte in no manere maken it at hir wille,
> So Elde and [heo] hadden it forbeten.
> (B.20.193–98)

I will more fully identify and discuss the range of figures and tropes at work in this passage later on—a passage that serves as target for almost all of this essay's exhaustively close readings. (The tropes of allegory exhaust theorists, and so my discussion will follow suit.) For now, the syntactical designation of Will's "lyme," his penis, as the grammatical object of Elde *and* Kit's "forbeating" (note that she's listed *second* to Elde as part of the sen-

---

8 Dinshaw, *Getting Medieval*, 186.
9 Citations to the B-Text are from *Piers Plowman: The B Version*, George Kane and E. Talbot Donaldson, eds. (London: Athlone, 1975). Subsequent citations shall be noted parenthetically.

tence's third-person-plural grammatical subject) makes for a humorous quibble, a raunchy anacoluthon or sloppiness in sentence execution that comically puts the three actors—Will, Kit, and Elde—in the same nuptial bed together throughout the years. The amusing *ménage a trois* implies as well the unnatural coupling of Elde and Will. Might this be taken as a moment of same-sex intimacy, perhaps a queer encounter? If so, it seems only the consummation of an already semiotically strained relationship between Elde and Will; even so epistemologically normative a book of criticism as Pamela Raabe's 1990 study of allegory in *Piers Plowman*—a book that decries the "hermeneutics of suspicion," to use Paul Ricoeur's ubiquitous designation, entrenched in modern allegory theory in general and in Langland studies in particular—cannot resist branding the encounter between Elde and Will as flatly "odd."[10] The adjective *odd*, never innocent given its parallel usage in modern English as the (now passé) synonym for "gay" or "queer," discloses something surely excessive or overdetermined in the text's presentation of the personification of old age. Will's tormenter, who exacts his toll on our narrator's pate, teeth, and genitals, comes across as an intrusive and violent, and potentially overly-intimate, male figure. The poem's discourse might be said to queer Elde in one of the final images of the life history of narrator Will.

I am of course reading this sex scene literally, even hyperliterally. As Robert Sturges has brilliantly shown, medieval narratives of masculine sexual desire often plant a ruse in their demand that we read them allegorically; Gottfried von Strassburg's *Tristan* lures us with the desire to understand the famous love potion in that poem as an allegorical sign, whereas our efforts are best rewarded, if we are to understand the homosocial engine of the poem as well as the eclipsed theme that even heterosexual relations are actually social *constructions*, once we appreciate the very literal sense of King Mark's desire for Tristan and the literal dictates that spur Tristan and Isolde to become mutually infatuated.[11] Such a bold hermeneutical protocol countermands Augustine's doctrine of charity since hyperliteralization, the primatizing of *lettera* over *spiritus*, seems to openly subvert one kind of allegory, the allegory of heteronormative patristic exegesis.[12] Indeed, queer readings or the commentary upon homosocial and same-sex poetics must embrace the canonically cupidinous in order to interrogate or deconstruct it. The queering of Elde and Will thereby begins as a concentrated effort at "remembering the literal."[13]

---

10 Pamela Raabe, *Imitating God: The Allegory of Faith in* Piers Plowman B (Athens, GA, and London: University of Georgia Press, 1990), 97.

11 Robert S. Sturges, "The Construction of Heterosexual Desire in Gottfried von Strassburg's *Tristan*," *Exemplaria* 10 (1998), 245.

12 St. Augustine, *On Christian Doctrine*, D. W. Robertson, trans. (Indianapolis: Bobbs-Merrill, 1958), 3.5.9, 83–84.

13 Sturges, "Construction," 246.

This marks a basic qualification, then, fashioned to subvert normative allegory. A further qualification is thus required at this point. What I am designating "queerness" in Elde and Will's same-sex encounter indicates the historically and theologically definable category of sodomy as it was understood in late medieval society. Most concise for purposes here is Allen Frantzen's definition of the term: sodomy comprises all "unnatural" sexual exchange (i. e., not heterosexual copulation) in fourteenth-century literary representation and social coding.[14] As Carolyn Dinshaw, drawing on the dicta of John Mirk, emphasizes, sodomy means any "mode of coupling" that is "'aȝeynes kynde'."[15] But in complementary terms, Dinshaw has also drawn on the Middle English *Book of Vices and Virtues* to show that sodomy could also comprise excessive heterosex between a husband and wife if its end was pleasure alone, not reproduction.[16] The syntactical consolidating of Elde, Will, and Kit makes them into a trio of sodomists. Although some contemporary queer theory has sought to divide sodomy from the queer—just as it has distinguished queerness from the concept of gayness[17] or from same-sex love[18]—sodomy still serves as the most viable indicator or index of the queer, particularly in the context of pre-modern sensibilities. The impeccable historical work of Mark Jordan, an authoritative voice on the theological and exegetical importance of sodomy in late medieval culture, well demonstrates this essential association.[19]

The links between sodomy, queerness, and allegorical personification make for further interesting resonances. As Jordan shows, the very design of a great, cosmic allegory such as Alan of Lille's *De planctu naturae* itself presents a deep anxiety about the inherent twistedness of natural history, sexuality, logical and grammatical taxonomy, and the mechanisms of didactic allegory in medieval thought.[20] Alan's allegorical treatise can be said to show signs of discursive and cognitive "stammering" in that it cannot avoid advertising the sociosexual queerness of the personification Nature's grand zoological scheme itself: beavers and bats are less curiosities of a complex animal world and moreso queer creatures—non-human sodomists who throw a wrench into the Plinian scheme that they inhabit.[21] This oddness recapitulates the in-built problem voiced on the first few pages of the *De planctu*: troping amounts to a kind of sodomy, a grammatical unnaturalness since sodomitical relations must always be configured as gross grammatical violations—the switching of active and passive

---

14 Frantzen, "The Disclosure of Sodomy in *Cleanness*," *PMLA* 111 (1996), 454–55.
15 Dinshaw, *Getting Medieval*, 3.
16 Dinshaw, *Getting Medieval*, 6; see also Augustine, *On Christian Doctrine*, 3.19.28, p. 96.
17 See Donald Morton, "Birth of the Cyberqueer," *PMLA* 110 (1995), 372–73.
18 Frantzen, *Before the Closet*, 1–4, 22–23, et passim.
19 See Mark D. Jordan, *The Invention of Sodomy in Christian Theology* (Chicago: University of Chicago Press, 1997).
20 Jordan, *Invention*, 70–87.
21 Jordan, *Invention*, 84.

voices, or subjects and predicates in sentences, standing equivalently for the sexual violations characterizing much human sexual commerce. Nowhere has Alan of Lille better formalized these ideas than in the famous and oft-cited opening exhortation from Meter 1[22] or the catalogue of grammatical-ontological violations in Prose 4.[23] His disquisition thus plants a land mine for all future allegories: the nature of trope or figure evokes the queer; per-sonification itself, the motor of the *De planctu*'s very narrative vitality, is threatened by association to queer sodomy.

If B.20 in *Piers Plowman* evokes this association too (for, any kind of sodomy or same-sex union conjures the idea of grammatical violation or rhetorical troping), then the existential inspection of Elde's *being* and his sexuality are at the heart of Langland's self-referential allegorical poetics. Indeed, "desire for [same-sex sexual relations] is natural and presumably innate, but seems unnatural as well and can be taught, or even caught."[24] Built into *natura*, into "kynde," and its corollary *grammatica* are the pro-clivities of queerness and thus the need for their policing. The ultimate source of semiosis for Langland may be divine, but the temporal instantia-tion of it in historical process or lived fact records all the gradations of fal-lenness and error.[25]

To emphasize: queerness in medieval literature may be yoked to alle-gorical personification itself. The claim would seem counterintuitive on the face of things, since allegory served medieval writers as an authoritative tool for expressing cosmic or divine order, transcendent power, or the ineffabili-ty of God's presence in the world (via the orthodox Augustinian principle of *adcommodatio*). The yoking of allegory to queerness as a conceptual maneuver bespeaks its own queer motive, its own appetite for illuminating the strangeness or surreality in medieval literature that indeed marks itself as such, though even a transgressive reading must be careful not to tram-ple on the official record that would prove that Church, government, and public or ecclesiastical readerships sought to effectively police sexual transgression in medieval society or in literature.[26] The broad rhetorical

---

22 For example: "The active sex shudders as it sees itself degenerate into the passive sex. A man turned woman blackens the fair name of his sex. The witchcraft of Venus turns him into a hermaphrodite. He is subject and predicate: one and the same term is given a double application. Man here extends too far the laws of grammar. Becoming a barbarian in grammar, he disclaims the manhood given him by nature. Grammar does not find favour with him but rather a trope"; *Plaint of Nature*, James J. Sheridan, trans. (Toronto: Pontifical Institute of Medieval Studies, 1980), 67–68.

23 The various grammatical solecisms map only asymmetrically onto varieties of sodomy ranging from continuous male-male same-sex coupling and serial bisexuality to what I would interpret as the practice of frottage ("Others, disdaining to enter Venus' hall, play a deplorable game in the vestibule of her house"); see 136–37.

24 Dinshaw, *Getting Medieval*, 11.

25 Anne Middleton, "Two Infinites: Grammatical Metaphor in *Piers Plowman*", *English Literary History* 39 (1972), 169–88.

26Such is Frantzen's important critique of much queer scholarship in medieval studies; see his sobering "Straightforward," *Before the Closet*, 1–29.

picture I've filled in thus far charges that the actual, textual *presence* of an allegorical personification may be a *queer effect*; queerness predicated on sodomy (both male-male and male-female) may open up a semiotic field that helps generate a narrative personification.

I noted a moment ago that contemporary queer theory often seeks to distinguish queerness from sodomy. For Donald Morton and others, the former represents a larger cognitive category that seeks to throw into question whole epistemological notions including taxonomy, categorization, hierarchy, and identity; the latter signifies the violation of an established sexual code (i. e., legal or juridical code) in a society.[27] It is thus curious that in modern allegory theory a similar taxonomic reconstruction has long been underway: theorists continually remind themselves—and this is so for *Piers Plowman* criticism, especially—of a paradox: that personification not only should be thought of as an essential component in that mode known as allegory, but simultaneously that personification and allegory are intrinsically at odds.[28] This analogy I hope to exploit as a productive departure point in my re-seeing of sexuality, tropes, and gender in *Piers Plowman*: personification:allegory as sodomy:queerness.

Conservative, albeit anti-literal, responses to the Passus 20 scene would foreclose the whole reading I am proposing. The actuality of Will's queer encounter should be challenged. Correlatively, the "personification" of Elde might stand on shaky ground, too. The playful syntax of B.20.198 engages a number of tropes (see below), but personification of course dominates. Yet it dominates the rhetorical scene in that its ontic *gradations*, ranging from mere discursive ornament through full-scale actantial *presence*, emerge as a tacit theme in Langland's self-reflexive poetics. Elde's "appearance" in the scene rests on a fundamentally poetic, or formalist, quandary: we wish to take some of the figural utterances in *Piers* "merely" as animate metaphors, while other utterances or descriptions involve the deployment of actual personified character. Should Elde at this point be taken as old age or Old Age? But this formalist quandary has never found resolution in *Piers Plowman* criticism let alone in the theory of allegorical literature *in toto*. As Lavinia Griffiths has nicely shown, much of the poem's dynamism arises from the "oscillation" or vacillation in ontological or characterological designation: we are too often quite uncertain about whether we are faced with actual allegorical personifications or with what

---

27 See Michael Warner, "Introduction," in Michael Warner, ed., *Fear of a Queer Planet: Queer Politics and Social Theory* (Minneapolis, MN and London: University of Minnesota Press, 1993), xxvi–xxvii, for a brief sketch on varying definitions of queerness.

28 See for instance John M. Steadman, *The Lamb and the Elephant: Ideal Imitation and the Context of Renaissance Allegory* (San Marino, CA: Huntington Library, 1974), 75; Howard H. Schless, "The Backgrounds of Allegory: Langland and Dante," *Yearbook of Langland Studies* 5 (1991), 131; and most recently and emphatically, Thomas E. Maresca, "Personification vs. Allegory," in *Enlightening Allegory: Theory, Practice, and Contexts of Allegory in the Late Seventeenth and Eighteenth Centuries*, Kevin L. Cope, ed. (New York: AMS Press, 1993), 21–39.

Morton Bloomfield once called a "simple animate metaphor."[29] To be
sure, this kind of lectorial oscillation explains much of the omnipresent
ambiguity felt in Langland. The poet's method of allegorical personification goads the reader with its wavering feel, its referential instability. And
in the larger scheme of things, the effect marks even postmodern allegory's
global "unreadability," as Paul de Man eventually declared,[30] serving in
turn as an instance of Derridean *différance* (differing/deferring) in general[31]
and of the cognitive inconsistency characteristic of the non-characterized
subject familiar to readers of *Piers Plowman* in particular.[32] Therefore we
should not merely dismiss the narrative image, however offensive or incred-
ible, of an Old Age (capital O, capital A) who has worn Will out sexually—in whatever graphically combinatory manner possible—through the
years.[33]

To recapitulate, two formalist questions in the reading of passus B.20
enable a queer reading: is Elde an actual "character" present in this scene;
and does the grammar of line 198 represent sodomy? The ontological
implications of presence (vs. absence), of sodomy (vs. heterosex), and of lit-
eralism (vs. grammatical troping), program the poetics of personification
that seems to be coming to some kind of summary treatment once the apocalyptic actions of Passus 20 have gotten underway. Will's final ontic, spiritual, and psychic status takes shape in relation to a trio of ontologically
fundamental personifications—Elde, Death, and Kynde or Nature, who
emerge following the petitions of Conscience (in response to the destruc-
tiveness of Antecrist) and well consequent to the activity of the personification Nede, who seems to spur this biological parable of last things:

> Kynde Conscience þo herde and cam out of þe planetes
> And sente forþ his forreyours, Feueres and Fluxes...
> There was 'harrow!' and 'help! here comeþ kynde
> Wiþ deeþ þat is dredful to vndo vs alle!'...
> Elde þe hoore; [he] was in þe vauntwarde
> And bar þe baner bifore deeþ;
>   (B.20.80–81, 88–89, 95–96)

---

[29] Lavinia Griffiths, *Personification in* Piers Plowman (Cambridge: D. S. Brewer, 1985), 4; Morton W.
Bloomfield, "A Grammatical Approach to Personification Allegory," *Modern Philology* 60 (1963), 164.
See, too, William C. Strange, "The Willful Trope: Some Notes on Personification with Illustrations from
Piers (A)," *Annuale Medievale* 9 (1968): 26–39.

[30] Paul de Man, *Allegories of Reading: Figural Language in Rousseau, Nietzsche, Rilke, and Proust* (New
Haven and London: Yale University Press, 1996), 201–202.

[31] Jacques Derrida, *Margins of Philosophy,* Alan Bass, trans. (Chicago: Chicago University Press, 1982),
3–27.

[32] Lawton, "Subject," 6 and 10.

[33] The combinatory "grammar" of three bodies in this imaginary *ménage a trois* suggests a range of
sodomitical practices: mutual masturbation emerges as an image (see Thomas Tentler, *Sin and Confession
on the Eve of the Reformation* [Princeton: Princeton University Press, 1977], 89; cited in Dinshaw, *Getting
Medieval,* 8), since Elde/Kit has worn down Will's "lyme"—that which Kit "leef was to feele"—manually;
so too does Will as passive receiver or Elde as receiver.

This pageant of personifications accumulates energy as it shuffles these three, seemingly interchangeable allegorical *prosopa*—Nature, then, Death, then Old Age—the last two serving as the ultimate delimiters of Will/will and as his own narratologically final allegorical shadows.

In an effort to think together the semiotic horizons of the apocalyptic moments in Passus 20 and the contemporary limits, in postmodern thought, of queerness and allegorical character ontology, I find that the juxtaposition of a contemporary personification fable from popular, *fin de siècle* American film with the end of *Piers Plowman* B can help us to hear a number of uncanny resonances and get also a glimpse of the semiosis central to another transhistorical, Anglo-Saxon/Anglo-American expression—potentially parallel, that is, to Frantzen's progression from the Old English penitentials to *Angels in America*—of subject formation and psychosexual legislation.

The fitting film is the 1998 romance *Meet Joe Black*, a putative "remake" of the 1934 fantasy *Death Takes a Holiday*,[34] though a film expressing much greater philosophical ambition and aesthetic depth. *Meet Joe Black* proffers as its main plot a traditional romance in which Death takes on the body of a recently dead young lawyer (Brad Pitt), enters the life of news and publishing magnate William Parish (Anthony Hopkins) whom he insists serve him as a guide and tutor in the fine details of human life, and who eventually falls in love with Parish's daughter Susan (Claire Forlani), a medical resident. The plot hinges on a predictable device: Death, who alone knows that the great man's angina grows fatally worse by the night, will accompany Bill Parish for an allotted time at the end of which the kindly, virtuous corporate patriarch will depart with his mysterious guest for good.

Much of the film's slow-paced action details the amusing, quotidian things Joe Black (as Death introduces himself publicly) experiences in the course of trying to take meals, get dressed, make his way about a house, or mix with Parish's wealthy family members or his corporate associates. For a cosmic personification, Joe Black lacks the most basic social knowledge, making him ingenuous and dependent on a mildly comical scale: in the vast kitchen manned by Parish's servants, Joe takes to the mystery of peanut butter served on a teaspoon, which he cherishes like a small boy who won't let go of a prized lolly pop.

Bill Parish's new charge and omnipresent sidekick remains virtually silent in every social encounter, Parish each time nervously standing by while awkwardly talking around the handsome man's presence. And so the ubiquitous Joe Black draws the comments of the curious. "Who is he? What's his relationship to Bill?" asks Drew (Jake Weber), Parish's future

---

[34] *Meet Joe Black*, Martin Brest, dir., Ron Osborn, Jeff Reno, Kevin Wade, Bo Goldman, screenplay (Universal Pictures, 1998). See, too, *Death Takes a Holiday*, Mitchell Leisen, dir., Maxwell Anderson, Gladys Lehman, Walter Ferris, screenplay (1934).

son-in-law, betrothed to Susan, who also serves as a member of the corporate board of directors for Parish Communications. Curiosity multiplies
mainly because Joe acts so odd and dumb, so uninformed and out of place,
at every turn. Parish acts embarrassed at each turn, too. The gravest example of this social dynamic comes at a corporate board meeting set for the
discussion of the company's takeover by an aggressive competitor tycoon.
Clearly not welcome, Joe Black, who sits at his earthly tutor's side, all the
while drawing suspicious glances from the board members, tops himself
when he asks, "Do you have any more of these delicious cookies—the jelly
ones? And a cup of tea—with milk"? Parish winces and squirms, while we,
the film viewers, know the look given by the board: who *is* this odd young
man?

Joe's ingenuousness throughout the film—the basis of the film's light-
comedy dimension for us since *we* know the plot's vast incongruity (Death
wants to learn about life by bungling the most banal of social moments)—
conflicts with the character's true nature. Death is a tyrant, as despotic as
if he'd escaped from a Renaissance revenge tragedy. In private, he orders
Bill Parish to bring him here or there; his initial attendance at a family dinner where he'll be awkwardly introduced by Bill as "an...associate" comes
after he decrees, "It's not open for discussion, Bill. Nothing is." We viewers keep a tab on these moments of incongruity, waiting, waiting for a final
moment when Bill, probably during the upcoming celebration of his sixty-
fifth birthday, will be taken by Death; or when Death will unmask himself
for Susan; or when Death might smash the "Machiavellian" usurper Drew
who (predictably) also happens to have been planning all along to help a
rival tycoon in his bid for a hostile corporate takeover.

All of this amounts to the cliché of romance, with compositional gestures drawn from the few other Hollywood productions presenting a personified Death in a modern American setting (Frederic March in *Death
Takes a Holiday* aside, Brad Pitt's supremely handsome Death hearkens back
to an old *Twilight Zone* episode in which Robert Redford played a blond-
haired, blue-eyed, irresistible Death dressed as a policeman; Joe Black's
self-introduction at the Parish late-night dinner recalls the uproarious scene
in Monty Python's *Meaning of Life* in which the Grim Reaper has insinu-
ated himself into an upper-class dinner party "through the salmon"; we're
reminded as well of movies like *On Borrowed Time*). But featured as a
nearly invisible aspect of *Meet Joe Black* is the pattern of character relations taken from varying points of view: personified Death + dying William
Parish (things as they *really* are) vs. Joe Black + corporate boss at the climax of worldly power (things as the suspicious board and Parish family *see*
them). What *is* the relation, folks must be asking, between this young, gor-
geous upstart and the Old Man? Whoever Joe Black may be, he exerts
astonishing control over Parish. On what's to be done after the board meeting, Parish's faithful son-in-law Quince (Jeffrey Tambor) informs Drew that

Bill insists all "things are up to Joe." Drew: "It's up to Joe? That's what he said? That's very interesting." And later: "What exactly is the relationship of Joe Black to Bill Parish"?

The film offers a feeble hint as to "what's interesting" when Susan confronts Joe on his presence: "What are you doing here in this house with my father?" *In this house*: the formulation suggests a locus just *outside* the Closet, but not yet all the way out. Yet the frank inquiry nets nothing. We then hear from Susan the litany of queries about Joe's *mysterioso* status: "Are you married...got a girlfriend?" And then—a question not even formulated as a sentence, an aposiopesis from both ends of syntax: "Gay"? To each of these, Joe answers an emphatic "no." But the invisible, indeed unspeakable, possibility lurking in the minds of the story's characters has revealed itself partially. Joe may not *be* "gay," but—the nature of Joe Black's relationship to Bill Parish, as Drew speculates more than once, may be closer than any of them all could wish to know.

The only plausible explanation for this character relationship—stunning-to-look-at Joe Black and sixty-five-year-old billionaire (note that the film overdetermines the two semiotic categories, beauty and wealth)—would be that Joe serves as Bill's same-sex lover. Why else the tolerated inanities, the awkwardness, the embarrassment? In his dotage, Bill Parish has taken up with and been taken in by a beautiful young male companion who could turn out to be more than just a fling or whim (and who of course *is* more than that, though William Parish is certainly Death's *whim*). Made in the conservative late 1990s, however, the film could not possibly *voice* the suspicion presumably held by its onlooking characters.

Nor is it that, in the world of Hudson River manor houses, corporate helicopters, and penthouse offices in art deco Manhattan skyscrapers, a billionaire couldn't be allowed a walk on the wild side as he turned sixty-five. But the Machiavellian animal Drew senses the danger: Joe enjoys inordinate power in the decision-making process of the corporate body politic; Joe Black is too much in the body politic's head, Bill Parish. He threatens the process of control, power regulation, and alliance, for the promised merger with the intruding company, run by the ruthless aggressor tycoon John Bontacue, is just such an alliance intended to extend the life and power of Parish Communications.

If the presumably queer relationship between Joe Black and Bill Parish exists as an unspeakable presence in the film—already a film about ontologically compromised presence since the main character starts out as an allegorical personification who must secondarily incarnate himself into the body of a recently dead man—the film inextricably mixes the phantom quality of same-sex male desire with the perpetuation of power relations as it is realized in a corporative body politic. For Renaissance culture, sodomy is, according to Jonathan Goldberg,

anything that threatens alliance—any sexual act...that does not promote the aim of married procreative sex...[and that] emerge[s] into vis-
ibility only when those who are said to have done [such acts] also can
be called traitors, heretics, or...disturbers of the social order that
alliance—marriage arrangements—maintained.[35]

This configuration the usurper Drew understands: he had been slated to
marry Parish's daughter Susan so that, at one stroke, he would lay claim to
Parish's empire and fortunes, ascending the corporate ladder as a result of
both a nuptial merger and a corporate one. But this double alliance wished
by Drew is threatened by the presence, the decision-making privilege, of
Bill's "ubiquitous" minion Joe Black. A Machiavellian dilemma to be sure!

And if there are actual Renaissance or medieval romance precursors
for this threat-effect in a film already dominated by the shadow of neo-
medievalism (for what else might one brand a story about Death personified in a media age in which personification allegory is all but dead?), they
would include precisely the crux in power genealogy and queer desire
evinced in a monument such as Gottfried's *Tristan*, where King Mark's
inordinate desire for the hero threatens stability and makes for a "particular transmission of power [that] proves unacceptable" in "the specifically
heterosexual ideology of Mark's society";[36] yet we are more likely to recognize both a distinctively English historical cast to the hidden thread in
Meet Joe Black as well as that thread's mythographic instantiation: Bill
Parish stands as a latter-day antitype for King Edward II and Joe Black is
his minion Piers Gaveston (at least in the Marlovian take on things); likewise, Parish would be Jove to Joe Black's Ganymede. This confluence of
subtextual or allusive English history, epic literature, and mythography
adds density to the film's ideological template projected into a medieval
imaginary: queer relations imply a "sensitive register precisely for delineat-
ing relationships of power and meaning, and for making graphically intelligible the play of desire and identification by which individuals negotiate
with their societies for empowerment."[37]

Meet Joe Black ends by catering to popular taste, as one would expect:
Joe does "unmask" himself for Drew and the board of Parish
Communications—but only as another performance, as "IRS agent Joe
Black," assigned to investigate John Bontacue's corporate maneuvering.
(This ruse had occurred to Joe owing to the fact that he actually determines
some of his actions by processing clichés, dead metaphors, uttered by other
characters in the film—most prominently Drew's early claim that the Deal
coming down the corporate pike is "as certain as death and taxes"; and so

---

[35] Jonathan Goldberg, *Sodometries: Renaissance Texts, Modern Sexualities* (Stanford: Stanford University Press, 1992), 19.

[36] Sturges, "Construction," 253.

[37] Eve Kosofsky Sedgwick, *Between Men: English Literature and Male Homosocial Desire* (New York: Columbia University Press, 1985), 27.

we get the joke.) Susan has already fallen in love with Joe, so by the film's final scene, we are ready to see Death release the reanimated body he'd borrowed as a cosmic walk-in, a body that, once he is restored to his original identity as the brash Young Lawyer, can now share a life with Susan. Bill Parish has gone off with Death following the celebratory and very satisfying climax of his lavish birthday party on the lawn of his Hudson River estate, and unquestionably order is restored.

Two semiotic platforms emerge from the whole mix of romance, light comedy, and pretentious, conservative, predictable (however satisfying) cinematic moralizing that adds up to *Meet Joe Black*: the designation of a potentially queer relationship (male/male) as a refraction of other category transgressions (age/youth, rich/poor, bourgeois/aristocrat, crooked/honest, ruthless/merciful, cultured/ignorant) and secured power alliances in the corporatively controlled ethos of late American capitalist society; and the linkage of the very *presence*, the linguistic utterability, of an allegorical personification to that triggering but unspeakable or unmentionable queer, same-sex male relationship. It is astonishing that the film correlates the mandate by Death that Bill not divulge the *true* nature of their "relationship" at any time with the implicit speculation that Joe and Bill are sexually linked in private. One might say that the link between William Parish's body and soul, a link severable at death and by Death personified, corresponds in the film's layered social coding to the imagined, and thus imaginary, link between the bodies of two men in a scene of abjection that really causes anxiety because of its threat to heteronormative power relations and flows of capital. In psychoanalytical terms, the anxiety of genealogy's possibility—alliances and reproductions in the family and in its analogue, the corporate body politic—depends on an imaginary rhetoric of copulations. Which bodies will link with which? How does soul unlink from body and when? How does an abstraction, or a cosmic force, enter into a body both ontologically and epistemologically—that is, in and as an agency *in a discursive field*, the linguistic field of character communication and knowledge constitutive of the text's whole "action"?

Perhaps it is no coincidence that Anthony Hopkins's character has the name "Will." He reminds us of Langland's Will in *Piers Plowman*, who must interact with an array of demanding personifications, acting of course not as tutor to them but as bungling protégé. (And who wouldn't manage to bungle around Study and Scripture—intimidators of their own personificational husbands?) *Piers Plowman*, however, presages the popularist entertainment of *Meet Joe Black* in fundamentally semiotic ways that I have only begun to make clear: both texts present allegorical personification in terms of its linguistic or structural limits given the enfolding poetic discourse of the respective texts. In *Piers Plowman*, personifications "waver" or "oscillate" regarding their ontological statuses in general (as has been discussed by Griffiths, Strange, Bloomfield, and Lawton), though

Elde's actual presence as a narrative personification character hinges directly on his syntactical function in a fugitive poetic line about Will's sex life.
In *Meet Joe Black*, Death's social presence or his epistemological disclosure
equates to the ontological "limit" of the film's protagonist, Bill Parish and
his biological-temporal span, while it doubles as half of a suspectedly secret
same-sex relationship with that protagonist. These homologies are more
than a coincidence.

I will show, in the remainder of my discussion, how the semiotic conflation of imagined bodily copulation—potentially queer copulation—with
the textual generation of rhetorical effects, such as allegorical personifications, draws its vitality from the deep structure of tropes and figures at
erotic and unconscious levels. I will then show how these erotic subfigura-
tions, these rhetorical copulas, find projection outward into the superordi-
nate semiotic zone of ideology. Herein will we see the consummation of
power relations concomitant upon subject formation, a formation that
regards the allegorical ratio between individual personality and national
state. If *Meet Joe Black* holds up, as its central collective concern, the health
of the corporate body (represented in Parish Communications or the
genealogy of the Parish clan) in late capitalist America—a health that must
proceed from the policing of potentially queer threats to heteronormative
alliances—then perhaps *Piers Plowman* charges that its central consciousness, Will, can be configured as an ideological and rhetorical entity constructed out of erotic materials that must be publicly projected and sanctioned. If, as James Simpson argues in "The Power of Impropriety,"
Langland's poem personifies "Will" as a collective quantity, what then are
the microstructural processes upon which Will, both personal and collective, are built? This is a question never before pursued in Langland studies,
though it is one that I believe can vastly illuminate Langland's astonishing
allegorical poetics.

As Carolyn Dinshaw reminds us, sodomy or queerness remained
unnameable more often than not in official discourse of the later Middle
Ages. The silence parallels the unspeakability of those relationships that
might be suspected in *Meet Joe Black*. I would submit further that the
graphic frankness of the imagined copulatory moment bears an intense aesthetic weight correspondent to the aesthetic representation of death—and
thus to the figurative mimesis of Death, the moment or process of dividing
the soul from the body, in narrative personification. *Meet Joe Black* in fact
represents "death" in a completely novel and shocking cinematic way:
early in the film, the Young Lawyer played by Brad Pitt meets his end in
one of the most graphic dramatizations of a traffic accident put on film.
The character crosses a busy New York City street, thoroughly distracted
by thoughts of the beautiful Susan whom he's just met, only to be struck
by a speeding car, thrown into the air, and then struck again by a taxi cab

before landing on asphalt. The visual sequence, made possible by the technology of image-generating computer software (no dummies were harmed in the making of the scene, we might be assured), sickens the viewer in its realism. We can be reminded of the culture of the Middle Ages on this point, one accustomed to public enactments of death but that reached its own sickeningly technical maximalization of death's artistic representation in, say, the work of Pierre Remiet, the late medieval French illuminator.[38] How does an artist technically "represent death"? Personification is one kind of hyperliteralization. But the sickening literalization, something like painterly hyperrealism, of the Young Lawyer's death scene functions as an aesthetic foil to the phantom reality of Death personified in the film's coding, while it animates for a modern viewership a process virtually invisible, something that must overcome or subvert, as Dinshaw notes regarding the effect of Remiet's art, "the thousands of horrifyingly superficial, simulated deaths we see on television."[39] But *Meet Joe Black* supplies at that crucial moment the eye-bite of images that *couldn't* be simulated, right down to the accelerated spinning of Brad Pitt's solid torso and the dust raised off the pavement when he strikes it at high speed. One commentator on the cinematic representation of death strikes a chord of synthesis that this essay has been making more and more palpable:

> Nudity and explicit sex are far more easily available now than are clear images of death. The quasi-violence of movies and television dwells on the lively acts of killing—flying kicks, roaring weapons, crashing cars, flaming explosions. These are the mortal equivalents of old-time cinematic sex. The fictional spurting of gun muzzles offer flirtation and seduction but stop a titillating instant short of *actual copulation*. The results of such aggressive vivacity remain a mystery.[40]

The commentator's metaphorical mixing of coitus and death restages that psychoanalytical synthesis now grown cliché in Freudian studies. But it more importantly describes the technical achievement actually made in *Meet Joe Black*'s staging of literal death, a narrative event aesthetically antipodean, one might say, to the film's staging of Death personified and his queer imaginary vitality in the story's social landscape. Indeed, allegorical personification bespeaks both violent and erotic registers, recording itself thusly as the persistent "problem of the presence of abstraction in the world."[41] *Meet Joe Black* implies a macabre trebling of queer union, allegorical personification, and graphic demolition of the living body in full public light. If allegory is a spectacle of the civil *agora*, as Gordon Teskey

---

[38] See Michael Camille, *Master of Death: The Lifeless Art of Pierre Remiet, Illuminator* (New Haven and London: Yale University Press, 1996).

[39] Camille, 245; cited in Dinshaw, 36.

[40] Sean Tejaratchi, ed., *Death Scenes: A Homicide Detective's Scrapbook*, Katherine Dunn, text; Jack Huddleston, photo. (Portland, OR: Feral House, 1996), 29; my emphasis.

[41] Gordon Teskey, *Allegory and Violence* (Ithaca and London: Cornell University Press, 1996), 14.

reminds us, and if the despot, personification of the State (*lo stato* in the Romagna of the Renaissance), commands the speaking space of allegory, his power finds exercise in the triune subjugational act of torture, sodomy, and murder; "the male bodies of his subjects are [figuratively] sodomized by the prince, violated at the opposite end to the voice."[42]

Meet Joe Black, then, can be said to meditate allegorically upon the limits of representation—limits to the text's medial substrate (which it seeks to overcome using technological virtuosity and thereby also staging a public execution in the city streets), limits to the social representation of queerness, limits to personification allegory's sheer presence. Such at-odds limits invoke the microstructural origins, also embedded in discourses of unspeakability and ineffabilty, that characterized both medieval allegorical writing and philosophical speculation of a cosmic cast. After all, and as Alexandre Leupin has so decisively shown, the writing of human sexuality in medieval culture, especially that of female desire and female sexual climax, equates to the writing of theology and cosmic ineffability; the abjection of sexual desire matches the abjectness of theology's discursive negativity.[43] Coordinate with these discourses of ineffability is psychoanalysis, a discourse invested in the rhetorical urge "to isolate and clarify"[44] but which advertises its structural or cognitive origins and limits. The unspeakability of queerness in medieval didactic writing as well as in the "straight white male imaginary" seen in some queer theory to circumscribe medieval poetry and contemporary Hollywood filmmaking,[45] respectively, echoes the discursive depths of theological writing testable, for Leupin, through psychoanalysis and structural semiotics.

As I have already begun to explain, the presence of Elde, or Old Age, as a narrative personage implies the copulatory linking together of two (or three) bodies by a penis that was, but then no longer is, present. Elde's being depends on a matter of syntax and at the same time a potentially queer copulation that he, as the enactor of it in the first place, disables. Any formulation of this imaginary, ontological, and grammatical relationship in critical language seems to defeat itself, for whether the relationship is ultimately a grammatical or syntactical side-effect, or an imaginary process, cannot be specified.

Yet as a grammatical action, Kit and Elde's conjoint "beating down" of Will's "lyme" in the frankest of formulations amounts, one might say, to an absenting of that limb or *membrum*. This erasure bears significant tropological weight. In rhetoric, the literal effect of penile depletion sug-

---

42 Teskey, *Allegory and Violence*, 135.
43 Alexandre Leupin, *Barbarolexis: Medieval Writing and Sexuality*, Kate M. Cooper, trans. (Cambridge, MA, and London: Harvard University Press, 1989), 6 and 14.
44 Leupin, *Barbarolexis*, 5.
45 Dinshaw, *Getting Medieval*, 187

gests a metafigural anapodoton—that is, metafigural in the customary metalanguage used by rhetorical theorists to enhance understanding of the tropes and figures as if those devices were often themselves personages. The figure by which a locution is "wanting one member" in the words of Henry Peacham's *Garden of Eloquence*[46]—members being the organic segments of an oration that are successfully or unsuccessfully "eyther coupled or uncoupled"—connotes a de-erection, perhaps a castration. "Will," long recognized as the cryptonym for the tumescent male member[47] and thus as a powerful pun word, dematerializes in a moment of irony. Future copulations are prohibited owing to a literalized anapodoton, the figure that marks the failure in the "coupling" of discursive or oratorical segments— failures being marked down as aporias, *errores*, solecisms, anacolutha of the sort glimpsed in B.20.198. Anapodoton perhaps would serve as the fittingly eroticized metadiscursive sign of fragmented or sputtering subject formation in *Piers Plowman*; it marks a narrative node or foreclosed characterological coalescence "forever in search of [its] missing term."[48]

Taken under the strictly Freudian view, the quasi-figural anapodoton elicits the so-called (if overworked) idea of the castration complex, in which fear of the loss of the male member generates sexual consciousness as well as a massive boost in the subject's ego formation.[49] Yet the literalized anapodoton ironically marks the end for Will (and for *the* will) of his sexual life. So Will's life as a sexual being, his very presence in the erotic social arena, so to speak, finds definition in an anapodoton triggered by another imaginary being, one who's very presence or ontological density must be put under question.

But the business of interrogating Elde's presence or being calls up a more elementary drill in classical psychoanalysis. The traditionalist reader of *Piers Plowman* B.20 would insist that the eccentric reading at the heart of this essay makes too much of a metaphorical comment made by the narrator off the cuff: old age (small "o," small "a") has metaphorically taken away Will's ability to have an erection and enjoy intercourse, leaving Will to carry on once again in his well-known register of grumbling. At most, the traditionalist might allow that a *slip* in the poet's syntax arising from hasty composition has occurred: "Anyway—old age and she had beaten it down." Yet what could be a more telling departure point for a psychoanalytical reading than the "mere slip of the pen," the error, or parapraxis, that unexpectedly emerges in writing in spite of concentrated revision, as Freud had so convincingly argued.[50] Penned errors, however, which take on the

[46] Henry Peacham, *The Garden of Eloquence*, 1577; facs. ed. (Menston: Scolar Press, 1971), n.p.

[47] Paxson, "Gender Personified," 91–92.

[48] Lawton, "Subject," 26.

[49] Sigmund Freud, *Introductory Lectures on Psychoanalysis*, standard ed., James Strachey, trans. and ed. (New York and London: W. W. Norton and Company, 1966), 317–18.

[50] See Freud, *The Psychopathology of Everyday Life*, Alan Tyson, trans., James Strachey, intro. and ed. (New York and London: W. W. Norton and Company, 1960), 116–33; and *Introductory Lectures*, 69–70.

status of significant parapraxes in the Freudian psychoanalytical schema, might just as well be construed as "metaplasms"—or indeed as figures or tropes in the categorical sliding-scale of medieval rhetorical taxonomy.[51] Such supercharging of the discursive field by potential figures and tropes invites other candidates.

A more precise description of line 198's anacoluthon, parapraxic or willed—though the displacement or loss of will(s) does seem to characterize the moment—is the figure zeugma: the sentence sports a lightly bungled arrangement of two nouns in its plural subject, a pluperfect tense main verb, and the single direct object. In explaining zeugma, George Puttenham employs a subsidiary, discursive analogy that bears more fruit for this analysis: "But if it be to mo clauses then one, that some such word be supplied to perfit the congruitie or sence of them all, it is by the figure Zeugma we call him the single supplie because by one word we serue many clauses of one congruitie, and may be likened to the man that serues many maisters at once."[52] Though Puttenham's analogy may suggest the biblical two masters served by one man (Matt. 6:24), the social picture of power and mastery fortuitously characterizes the internal logic of figures in general. As Grant Williams observes of Peacham's political agenda, the figures are to be deployed in order to secure their "promise to confer upon the writer the ability to control the other, whether person or book."[53] The zeugma leading to Will's anapodoton inscribes a contest of mastery, of will applied and will displaced.[54]

But the paramount figure of rhetorical "mastery," according to Grant Williams's Lacanian reading of early modern rhetorical theory, must be personification.[55] The figure, or metafigure, whose very presence comes into question in the B.20 passage I've been scrutinizing so closely, serves the orator or poet as a mirroring mechanism for constitutive maneuvers in self-identity. Although figure or trope understood as merely exoticizing or "alluring" ornament seems to feed into the formalist view of figural language as defamiliarization, use of figures effects a more radical change. Williams writes,

---

[51] Ernst R. Curtius, *European Literature and the Latin Middle Ages*, Willard R. Trask, trans. (Princeton: Princeton University Press, 1953), 44.

[52] George Puttenham, *The Arte of English Poesie*, 1569, Gladys Doidge Willcock and Alice Walker, eds. (Cambridge: Cambridge University Press, 1936), 163–64.

[53] Grant Williams, "Disarticulating Fantasies: Figures of Speech, Vices, and the Blazon in Renaissance English Rhetoric," *Rhetoric Society Quarterly* 29 (1999), 45.

[54] Compare the zeugma of B.20.198 with its counterpart in the C-Text: "So Elde and hue hit hadde a-feynted and forbete." The revision defuses the zeugmatic co-mastering of the direct object by the dual subject ("Old Age and she") because of the C-Text's superadded dual verb that possibly distributes physical effects in a more normative and less queer manner: Old Age "had made faint/had made a feint at" Will's member, while Kit still "had forbeaten" it. "A-feynted" records a pun, but the dual sense conveyed still minimizes Elde's actantiality in the scene: he's either weakened Will's limb, or 'made a false move to beat on it, pretending instead to withdraw.'

[55] Williams, "Disarticulating," 43.

> Whereas the device of defamiliarization encourages the reader to encounter the big Other, that is, language in its radical alterity as the symbolic order, the figure of speech projects onto language the little other, the ego's imaginary counterpart. The subject fails to realize that the little other is not really other at all, but quite literally his "subject complement." It is only a version of himself dialectically propping up his equally imaginary identity.[56]

For Williams, personification is always already the name of this metarhetorical unconscious process. And uncannily, the Lacanian *objet petit a* that orthographizes the ego's imaginary counterpart—the "little other" complementary yet again to the Real or the big Other—shadows the actual state of affairs in B.20.198: old age (small "o" and "a") contends with Old Age (big "O" and "A"), though the former is all that's ever virtually constructed in the linguistic scenario of the text.

The deep structures, inner histories, and imaginary lives of the constitutive tropes and figures of allegory inscribe imagery of complementarity, proximity, solidity. As imagined bodies, figures have potentially erotic lives, as it were, that would, in the classical rhetorical picture, equate to what we might deem their own unconscious, their own Real and Imaginary orders. For Quintilian, the term figure "is applied to any form in which thought is expressed, just as it is to bodies [*sicut in corporibus*] which, whatever their composition, must have some shape [*utique habitus est aliquis*]" (9.1.10).[57] Prior even to the narrative invention of a sprawling allegory like *Piers Plowman*, rhetorical figures disclose structure and vitality that can be projected upwards, through successive systemic levels, into the world of narrative action (and beyond, into the presumed ideological field that expresses itself poetically as a range of political and social themata—the constitution of the kingdom and its relationship to the self or subject, as we'll see in my conclusion below). The narrative bodies in the main action of the poem adumbrate effects at the imaginary systemic level of constitutive, localized through "bodied" tropes and figures.

The meta-allegory of rhetorical copulas—mirror versions or microforms of the narrative copulatory bodies we've just begun to analyze—hinges on the psychic structures of the two paramount and programmatic figures of all rhetoric: simile and metaphor.[58] The phenomenological and semiotic central ground of sexual drive and rhetorical troping, as recent studies in the philosophy of rhetoric demonstrate,[59] subsist in what is known as the grammatical copula along with its analogous narrative image, the copulating human body. In his stunning essay on metaphor,

---

[56] Williams, "Disarticulating," 44.

[57] Quintilian, *The Institutio Oratoria of Quintilian*, vol. 3, H. E. Butler, trans., Loeb Classical Library (Cambridge, MA: Harvard University Press, 1920), 353.

[58] For this segment of my discussion, I draw on my article "Queering *Piers Plowman*: The Copula[tion]s of Figures in Medieval Allegory," *Rhetoric Society Quarterly* 29 (1999): 21–29.

[59] See above, footnote 3.

"The Solar Anus," Georges Bataille emphasizes that "the *copula* of terms is no less irritating than the *copulation* of bodies," while he goes on to exult: "And when I scream I AM THE SUN an integral erection results, because the verb *to be* is the vehicle of amorous frenzy."[60] As Shirley Sharon-Zisser has argued, Bataille's conceptual source for phallicized metaphor is Aristotle's prolonged meditation on the structural and ontological distinction between metaphor and simile in the *Rhetoric*, which parallels conceptualizations of sexuality in the philosopher's *Generation of Animals* and the *Metaphysics*.[61] For Aristotle, simile was "equal to metaphor in all but its copula," which designated it as inferior, as ill-formed, as less attractive. Aristotle transcodes this formulation with his designation in the *Metaphysics* that the female is a "defective" male marked by inferior organs of procreation.[62] In classical Greek, the gendered differences between male and female biology and their transcodings in semantic or lexical root verbs as well as in the two paramount figures of rhetoric may have involved the contrast between the copulative, essential verbs *eikaso* and *eimi*, "to resemble" and "to be,"[63] while the famous distinction has continued to take form, in modern English rhetoric and composition, as the stylistic preference for metaphor's "is" over simile's inferior "is like"—the latter materializing often as the *-ly* prefix in the stylistically weak adverb. Aristotle's whole structural distinction in terms of male and female gendered bodies therefore marks metaphor as superior, better formed, whole, while simile is an imperfect version of the former—a state of affairs visible in male and female sex organs themselves, as Aristotle emphasizes. The Aristotelian relationship between phallically endowed metaphor and phallically lacking simile, Sharon-Zisser continues, marks the complementary terms as "isomorphic."[64] In Aristotle's words, simile "is a metaphor differing only by the addition of a word [*metaphora diapherousa prosthesei*], wherefore it is less pleasant because it is longer."[65] That is, the graphic or phonic *prosthesis* of simile marks, ironically and isomorphically, the figure's truly ontological lack or hole, a hole that thus expresses itself

---

[60] Georges Bataille, *Visions of Excess: Selected Writings, 1927–1939*, Allan Stoeckl with Carl R. Lovitt and Donald M. Leslie, Jr., trans., Allan Stoeckl, intro. and ed. (Minneapolis: University of Minnesota Press, 1985), 5.

[61] Sharon-Zisser, "Re(De)-Erecting Collatine: Castrative *Collatio* in *The Rape of Lucrece*," *Rhetoric Society Quarterly* 29 (1999), 56.

[62] *The Basic Works of Aristotle*, Richard McKeon, trans. (New York: Random House, 1947), 1055b.

[63] Henry George Liddell and Robert Scott, *A Greek-English Lexicon*, Henry Stuart Jones with Roderick McKenzie, supp. ed., rev. and aug. (Oxford: Clarendon Press, 1968), 484, 487–88.

[64] "'Illustrer nôtre langue maternelle': Illustrative Similes and Failed Phallic Economy in Early Modern Rhetoric," *Exemplaria* 9 (1997), 401–402.

[65] Aristotle, *Art of Rhetoric*, J. H. Freese, trans., Loeb Classical Library (Cambridge, MA: Harvard University Press, 1975), 3.10.3.

as metaphor manque—metaphor being that imaginary *figura*/body that, as a mark of superiority, possesses phallic status and power.[66]

The Aristotelian sexualization of these grammatico-lexical relations inheres, of course, in Lacan's claim that the verb "to be" or the logical copula "is" carries phallic resonance, functioning as the signifier of a woman's "own desire in the body of him to whom she addresses her demand for love."[67] For Lacan, the phallic signifier serves as "the most tangible element in the real of sexual copulation, and also the most symbolic in the literal (typographical) sense of the term, since it is equivalent...to the (logical) copula."[68] Commentators on this psychoanalysis of grammar have adduced it as the uncanny reflex of certain poetic scenes or images built upon the anapodota of sexual loss, romantic frustration, and the end of amatory exchange.[69] Such a psychoanalysis of grammar may well lie at the base of Langland's narrative scene of queer copulation as I've begun to describe it in this argument.

Taking this argument further, we can see that the binarizing of metaphor and simile—rhetoric's key figures characterized by grammatical-ontic plenitude and by lack, respectively—could be taken as structural twins of the traditional distinction made by Morton Bloomfield, Lavinia Griffiths, William Strange, and myself, between what might be thought of as "primary personification" and "secondary personification." Primary personification offers the plenitude of actual, characterological presence; secondary personification involves those "simple animate metaphors" first identified by Bloomfield as imperfect versions of "real" personification. In narratological terms, primary personification exists on the level of narrative *story*, while secondary personification exists on the level of narrative *discourse*.[70] To apprehend a secondary personification as a primary per-

---

[66] Offering an argument that depends on the phenomenal, bodily, and narrative representation of Will's physical penis, this essay does take note of the ongoing theoretical investment in the counter-term phallus, a purely conceptual, abstract, and legislative category for Lacan—see *Écrits: A Selection*, Alan Sheridan, trans. (New York and London: W. W. Norton and Company, 1977), 282–91—that it does not always conflate automatically with the penis (a purely bodily thing nameable not just in the Lacanian realms of the Real or the Imaginary, but in the Symbolic order of narrative). Nonetheless, the Lacanian phallus may be allegorically prefigured in the poetic and oneiric anxieties voiced by Will over the loss of his personificational penis, his personified body's masculine sign in narrative actuality as well as a reification of his own putative identity, will, itself.

[67] Lacan, *Écrits*, 290.

[68] Lacan, *Écrits*, 287.

[69] Shirley Sharon-Zisser, "'Similes Hollow'd with Sighs': The Transferential Erotics of the Similaic Copula in Shakespeare's 'A Lover's Complaint'," *Exemplaria* 11 (1999), 206–210.

[70] In *The Poetics of Personification* (Cambridge: Cambridge University Press, 1994), I tried to cobble together a shorthand or calculus that would designate the "two personifications": I used the symbol p1 for what I am *here* calling secondary personification or local, animate metaphor; and I used p2 to designate a fully narrative personification character (see 161). I'm only reversing the meta-metaphors of primariness and secondariness here in order to underline the plenitude sought in the ontically superior personification. The absence of full narrative personification seen in the de-erection of Will and the non-being of Elde expectedly registers erasure of the ontological copula, yielding the broad textual idea of "absence itself" (Derrida, 201). See of course Derrida's important essay, "The Supplement of Copula: Philosophy Before Linguistics," 175–205.

sonification means the misunderstanding of the existence of an ornamental figure existent on the level of narrative discourse not story.[71] This formal distinction mirrors, I believe, the same order of ontological differentiation glimpsed in the gendered guises of Aristotle's similaic and metaphorical copulas. As another formal analogy would have it, secondary personification:primary personification as simile:metaphor. An imaginary copula divides primary and secondary personification, just as it divides metaphor and simile, for surely simple animate metaphor and full character personification differ in terms of an increased ontological density in the latter, though true allegorical personification still involves a kind of epistemological error—a sort of forgetting, or parapraxis, of the textual status rightly belonging to animate metaphor or secondary personification.

Since, in the Lacanian understanding of the unconscious as something "structured like a language" (a language often articulable as a repository of rhetorical figures), key figures such as metaphor indicate not just occluded phallic presence but also the narrative creation of an actual subject (the cognitive bonus of the onto-logical copula), the masterly status of personification gives us new critical direction. To repeat, the very "is-ness" of literary personification—"is there a personification in this scene or isn't there?"—finds metaallegorization at the end of *Piers Plowman* revealing rhetoric or tropology's bodily inner history in that it advertises the play of the phallic signifier's presence. Whether Elde is Old Age or old age— whether Elde is or is not—de-pends (who, like Lacan, could resist so bad a pun?) on the presence of Will's penis, which serves as two main signs: as (1) literal penile copula between same-sex lovers or between husband and wife; and as (2) reification of Will as will, or erotic drive, *sensualitas, cupiditas*, etc. Not only does will get allegorized at this point in the text, but so does the psychic motor of tropology's erotic semiotics as well. Perhaps moreso than simile and metaphor, full-scale narrative personification enables the semiological meditation on ontic-linguistic lack and phallic plenitude. It truly enjoys status as the master trope, the trope of rhetorical and semiotic mastering.[72]

The "increasing density" of ontological copulas might be extended still further through the inventory of classical tropes and figures (central to Langland's allegorical poetics). If the prefiguration of the Shakespearean topos, will-as-penis (well described by Joel Fineman),[73] caps off the narrator's life experiences in the B-Text of *Piers Plowman*, it might have its architectonic analog or imaginary bodily Other, as I've recently argued,[74] in Langland's most cryptic character—the personification *Anima* in Passus

---

[71] Paxson, *Poetics*, 41–42.

[72] Williams, 43.

[73] *Shakespeare's Perjured Eye: The Invention of Poetic Subjectivity in the Sonnets* (Berkeley and Los Angeles: University of California Press, 1986), 22–25.

[74] Paxson, "Gender Personified," 81–89.

15. (*Anima* of course means "Soul" as well as "Will" when it is gram-
maticized now as a feminine noun, now as a masculine noun—*animus*; see
Simpson in this volume). The main figure at work in the invention of
Anima, I believe, is *transumptio* or metalepsis. Upon meeting *Anima* inside
an inner dream, Will describes the entity according to a cryptic iconography that seems sexualized:

> ...and in þat folie I raued
> Til reson hadde ruþe on me and rokked me aslepe,
> Til I seiȝ, as it sorcerie were, a sotil þyng wiþ alle.
> Oon wiþouten tonge and teeþ tolde me whider I sholde
> And wherof I cam...
>
> (B.15.10–14)

In an allegory that projects outward into narrative space the psychic and
erotic components of rhetoric's microstructure—into the realm of the narrative Symbolic the elements of the Other, the Real—one complement to
this "defaced" entity might well be Will as he's "beaten" by Elde upon their
initial encounter: "And Elde...ouer myn heed yede / And made me balled
bifore and bare on þe croune /...He buffetted me aboute þe mouþ [and
bette out my wangteeþ]" (B.20.183–84, 191). Elde, the figure whose presence hangs on his own de-erection of a penis, a literalized anapodoton, and
on syntactical zeugma, legislates the biological and biographical end of
Will's sexual life; yet his actions strangely reduce Will to the pre-form of
such a life—a stylized *infans*, a rebus of a baby with its toothless mouth,
bald head, and pre-sexual masculinity. *Anima* becomes the small "other"
of Will's subject-self (*anima/animus*).

But this particular epigenetic irony presupposes a corollary Freudian
precept: it takes little imagination to see in the toothless and even tongueless *Anima*—who even first generalizes Will's origin together with his end
("whider I sholde / And wherof I cam")—a plausible rebus of the abjection
of the vagina as described by Freud,[75] and a prefiguration of the *vagina
dentata* (ironically without teeth in this case) discussed by Luce Irigaray.[76]
If will can be reified as a penis, it can also be *transumpted* as a vagina, the
conceptual isomorph of the penis in medieval physiology.

The text's vaginal transumption functions ever more cryptically, and
through the logic of the copula. A *transumptio* or metalepsis, as Quintilian
explains, is a kind of metafigure in which metaphorical predication is completely encrypted or "passed over," making the *transumptio* akin to the

---

[75] Freud, *New Introductory Lectures on Psychoanalysis*, standard ed., James Strachey, trans. and ed. (New
York and London: W. W. Norton and Company, 1965), 90.
[76] *Speculum of the Other Woman*, Gillian C. Gill, trans. (Ithaca: Cornell University Press, 1985), 243–300;
see also E. Jane Burns, *Bodytalk: When Women Speak in Old French Literature* (Philadelphia: University of
Pennsylvania Press, 1993), 53–55.

vicious mixed-metaphor shunned in the cult of writing style. Quintilian finds little favor with the difficult trope himself, shoving it to the end of his discussion on the tropes and figures. This repression warrants citation of his succinct passage on the trope (whereas well-advertised metaphor and simile, which I addressed above, I let speak for themselves):

> There is but one of the tropes involving change of meaning which remains to be discussed, namely, metalepsis or transumption, which provides a transition from one trope to another [*quae ex alio tropo in alium velut viam praestat*]. It is (if we except comedy) but rarely used in Latin, and is by no means to be commended, though it is not infrequently employed by the Greeks, who, for example...substitute the epithet θοαι (swift) for οξειαι in referring to sharp-pointed islands. But who would endure a Roman if he called Verres *sus* or changed the name of Aelius Catus to Aelius *doctus*? It is the nature of metalepsis to form a kind of intermediate step [*medius quidam gradus*] between the term transferred and the thing to which it is transferred, having no meaning in itself [*nihil ipse significans*], but merely providing a transition. It is a trope with which to claim acquaintance, rather than one which we are ever likely to require to use. The commonest example is the following: *cano* is a synonym for *canto* and *canto* for *dico*, therefore *cano* is a synonym for *dico*, the intermediate step being provided by *canto*. We need not waste any more time over it. I can see no use in it except, as I have already said, in comedy.[77]

According to the conceptual scheme of this essay, metalepsis or *transumptio* works by eliding the *gradus* linking the terms of a complex metaphor; that "step" might be taken as a logical or grammatical copula, one that would be putatively more attractive still in the Aristotelian metaphysical picture because it "shortens" that much more the cognitive work expendable in the form of linearly disposed language or coupled discourse. That is, a *transumptio* is a "final" metaphor in which a middle metaphor in a chain of metaphors gets dropped out—the whole middle metaphor functioning like the "is like" of simile, the figure "longer" than metaphor and thus uglier than it. (Here again, too, appears Lawton's "missing term," so characteristic of syntagmatic structures in *Piers Plowman*.) Thus, one more classical analogy: simile:metaphor as metaphor:*transumptio*, owing to the occultation and therefore the amelioration of the copula.

Anima of Passus 15 would thus be a transumptive or metaleptical vagina in that it materializes as the orifice of simultaneous abjection and desire. It is the locus of heterosexual male erotic drive while it at the same time signifies heterosexual female drive in the guise of the lack of that "signifier of [woman's] own desire in the body of [man]"[78]—that is, in the phallus, which is conveniently allegorized in B.15.13 as an absented phallic *tongue*.

---

77 Quintilian, *Institutio*, 8.9.38–39.
78 Lacan, *Écrits*, 290.

I can not stress the importance, incidentally, of such lack as a synonym for abjection, for indeed the violent image of exlinguation, doubled as the grotesque prosopopeia of bodily pudenda, would even find historical expression in demonological writing in the late Middle Ages and early modern period (which covers the theme of tongueless persons and speaking vaginas.)[79]

The *Anima* scene thus serves as a structural counterpart, one likewise arising out of psychic and erotic potentials at the micro-level, to the baroque and queer narrativizing of personification in Passus 20. Some rehashing of the semiotic scenario should be welcome: the literal mouth lacking tongue doubles as an icon of the failed power of speech, of eloquence or oral linguistic production, thus making it thematize the very motor of prosopopeia itself (*prosopon poiein*, "to make a face or mask or speaker");[80] yet it also serves as the icon of the phallus *manque* according to Lacan, and in so doing, it works as another micro-allegorical sign of the phallic copula seen by Aristotle, Bataille, Lacan, and Derrida, to instantiate the psychic and rhetorical potential of self-reflective human consciousness itself at all systemic levels. Such is the upshot of David Lawton's reading of *Anima*'s representation in B.15 as he catalogues encrypted signs of subject formation, or cognitive liminality, and images of the "fall into the Symbolic order" throughout *Piers Plowman*.[81]

Now, to return to Will's spent organ: Is the flaccid penis the workable equivalent to the phallic lack implied in the Passus 15 transumptive vagina/mouth? This almost goes without saying (but let us not let Langland's allegorical *phantasmata* speak too much for themselves). Will's ontic presence as literary character, as ethical quality, as male possessor of the penis, as penis itself, finds absolute compromise in his impotence, his state of "de-erection," as Shirley Sharon-Zisser would put it. The compromise finds double inscription by Elde's queer actions. Here might be a fictional and literalized effigy of the Phallic Father, a father who is himself a personification of male potency always figured in its shadow self, male impotence, for in Western literature, old age often entails post-sexuality axiomatically. In his own self-assertion, the Phallic Father threatens to enact a castrational "taking away" of the vital and literal male penis belonging to the poem's narratorial consciousness. And it is Elde's queerness that further fortifies this semiotic state of affairs: the penis-immolating personification can be thought of as a quasi-copulator since sodomy, achieved anally or through chiro-manipulation and when conceived according to the most regulatory

---

[79] See Ambroise Paré, *Des Monstres et prodiges*, 1560, Jean Céard, ed. (Geneva: Libraire Droz, 1971), 83, for discussion of how possessed persons, who have had their tongues cut out, still manage to speak from their bellies or from their *genitals* ("Ceux qui sont possedez des Demons parlent la langue tiree hors las bouche, par le ventre, *par les parties naturelles*" (my emphasis).

[80] Paxson, *Poetics*, 68–69.

[81] Lawton, "Subject," 7.

of social schemes, could be understood as a simulacrum of heterosexual intercourse.[82] It is, in short, the *simile* of it, the figure of it, in which an erect penis profanes the ethical valorization of bodily commerce scrutinized in heteronormative and regulatory social practice characteristic of the late Middle Ages.

To partially summarize at this point: *Piers Plowman* B presents an imaginary categorical progression from metaphor through animate metaphor (one of Aristotle's "proportional metaphors" in *The Rhetoric*) through full personification, a progression structured on the presencing of an imaginary grammatical and ontological copula. The progression parallels Aristotle's, which, we should recall by comparison, charts the evaluative progression from simile to metaphor, predicting in turn Quintilian's discussion of that figure called *transumptio* or metalepsis. This structural progression, really a spectrum, has its most salient expression in the text's ontological distinction between personification "characters" in the fullest, actantial narrative sense of the term and ornamental or discursive personifications once called, by Bloomfield, simple animate metaphors or personification metaphors; yet the density or consistency of full-scale personification itself varies throughout the poem's narrative line, as David Lawton and James Simpson insist. In addition, a catalogue of corollary binaries shadow the grades of this spectrum: old age as animate metaphor/Old Age as mock-copulator, natural copulation/unnatural copulation, *Anima* as personified man/*Anima* as reified vagina, penile presence/penile lack, eloquence/*infans*, etcetera. In *Piers Plowman*, the *dispositio* of tropological forces and mechanisms, taxonomically dependent upon varied deployments of grammatical copulae, can indeed be glimpsed in the allegory of sexualized bodies—in particular the occulted, allegorical, transumptive representation of female and male genitals that serve as the counter-vehicles of psychic repression and as the icons of conscious and unconscious erotic drives.

So if *Piers Plowman* can be read as a metanarrative about the semiotic making of prime figures and tropes, it also narrates the erotic energies invested in those figures. Such is the language of allegory, the unsurpassed discourse of desire, embodiment, and gender. And it can be a discourse of the queer, not merely the normative, the normative being that with which allegory has always been aligned. Personification, allegory's most insistent sign, itself reveals what might be thought of as the queerness of allegory because, as I have shown, the sheer presence of personified "character" is finally made to hang on the ambiguous but same-sex stimulation of a penis.

---

82 See James A. Brundage, *Law, Sex and Christian Society in Medieval Europe* (Chicago: University of Chicago Press, 1987), 533; cited in Dinshaw, 22, n20. Let us take note, too, that this heteronormative comparison evokes the "tyranny of the penis" and the reign of heterosexual copulation; for relevant discussion, see Guy Hocquenghem, *Homosexual Desire,* Daniella Dangoor, trans. (Durham, NC: Duke University Press, 1990).

David Lawton's observation that the personification of Will in the poem lacks consistency or permanence finds specification in the narratological, structural, and psychoanalytical turns I have tried to describe. Indeed, Lawton's acknowledgement that a Lacanian model of subject formation holds promise for understanding the (often thwarted) "growth" of Will in the poem almost requires the copulatory rhetoric and poetics I have tried to articulate.[83] In contemporary literary theory, allegory has been equated to everything from the grotesque or the baroque to the cognitive in general. Yet it might also be equated, in some analytical cases, to the queer itself, another of the intersecting and disruptive discourses that Lawton might see as being essential to the formation of Langland's allegory in his generous prognostication.[84]

I want to register that I offer this generalization with caution. Before moving on to my conclusion, which makes speculations about the part played by *Piers Plowman*'s semiology of erotics and rhetoric in the larger ideological patterns of the late fourteenth century, I must return to Allen Frantzen's polemic against the sort of queer theoretical enterprise that admittedly undergirds so much of this essay. Frantzen has certainly put limits on queer theorization, which he opts to call "queer commentary," following Lauren Berlant and Michael Warner,[85] and which he sees as not well-served by its inflammatory label ("same-sex" should replace "queer," for starters)[86] or its obsession with genital sex alone.[87] On many of these counts this essay would stand guilty, though I must affirm that the large theoretical armature of the essay should be seen as an attempt not to argue that a "liberationist" Middle Ages existed historically, but to meet Frantzen's charge that, since queer theory "passes" as the production of historical knowledge about the late Middle Ages,[88] a "legitimist queer theory"[89] might try to account for ostensibly same-sex literary images on some historical grounds. For this essay, that ground has been the history of rhetoric, a history of tropes and figures imagined as actantial agents or bodies endowed with psychic and erotic lives or internal histories of their own. I add too that Frantzen's own macrometaphor for legitimist queer theory, the image of the Shadow that must replace the Closet,[90] engages its own allegory of allegorical hermeneutics: after all, "shadow" or *umbra* served as a paramount sign for allegorical significance itself in medieval poetics;[91] my own document, an exercise in neo-allegorical discourse, can't

---

83   See Lawton, "Subject," 5.
84   Lawton, "Subject," 25.
85   Frantzen, *Before the Closet*, 20–21.
86   Frantzen, *Before the Closet*, 3.
87   Frantzen, *Before the Closet*, 21–22.
88   Frantzen, *Before the Closet*, 16–17.
89   Frantzen, *Before the Closet*, 24.
90   See Frantzen, *Before the Closet*, 14 and 24.
91   See Erich Auerbach's discussion of the term in his monumental "Figura," *Scenes from the Drama of European Literature*, Paolo Valesio, foreword (Minneapolis, MN: University of Minnesota Press, 1984), 48.

resist taking up shadows or grades (recalling, I guess, Nabokov's contra-
puntal characters John Shade and Gradus in his own neo-allegory, *Pale
Fire*) of tropological spectra, continua, taxonomies. In an allegory such as
Piers Plowman, a poem invested in the narration of its own allegorical
codes, the appearance of Elde in B.20 involves a sort of shadow play: Elde
shadows Kit as Will's co-copulator; Elde shadows Will as Kit's co-copulator; old age indeed seems the shadow version of one's earlier, vital sex life,
just as the film *Meet Joe Black* divulges its protagonist's feeling that, at the
signal age of sixty-five (vulnerable now for mandatory retirement by the
board's fiat), he's a shadow of his vital self who's now being shadowed by
an omnipresent sidekick, a fellow who takes as a surname the chiaroscuro
word "black." It is uncanny that Frantzen's allegory of the Shadow—legitimist queer theory's polemical image—verily shadows out or palimpsizes
the recalcitrantly theorized insistence on the imaging of genital sex that
Frantzen views as the obsession of liberationist queer theory and upon
which this essay about rhetorical shadows builds its entire theoretical
superstructure.

The better part of my analysis, powered by Lacanian psychoanalytical
tactics and deep-structural semiotics, mustn't be seen only as the apparatus
for disclosing a preemptive turn inward made possible through Langland's
allegorical poetics. The psychic, erotic, and structural contours of the master tropes metaphor, simile, *transumptio*, and personification (as well as
anapodoton and zeugma) that constitute *Piers Plowman* no doubt rehearse
a psychology or phenomenology of the individual human consciousness
that *could* be made to stand apart from larger, global political and historical considerations that such allegories tend to project outward. But the history of medieval allegory had mandated this synthesis of inner and outer
realms. After all, Prudentius' *Psychomachia* furnished the template for
exploring, first, the securing of the inner arena of the heart (the combat
between six Virtues and six Vices in epic fashion); and consequently, the
building of a holy, public, and cosmic *templum*, a New Jerusalem, to be
commanded by *Sapientia*.[92] With Allen Frantzen's caveat in mind, I cannot
pass off this synthetic study, one bringing together insights from semiotics,
rhetoric, narratology, psychoanalysis, philosophy, and queer theory, as an
historical statement. But I see the need to make some broad claims about
how the rhetorical and poetic models so far assembled adumbrate what
certain historical investigators and ideological projects *have* uncovered
about subjectivity and the formation of the late medieval or early modern
national state.

---

[92] *Prudentius*, H. J. Thomson, trans., vol. 1, Loeb Classical Library (Cambridge, MA, and London:
Harvard University Press, 1969), ll. 875–76.

The allegorical tropes paranomasia and syllepsis, or rather, their compositional practice *juxtology*,[93] situates Langland's cognitive allegory in the context of the poet's social and political obsession—the subject's role in the formation, vitality, and growth of the national state, in the *vita communis*, as we shall see in a moment. The poet's pun-built name and historical identity commands this yet one more rhetorical juncture in my argument.

Anne Middleton ponders the dilemma in *Piers Plowman* criticism of balancing the "external" materials of the presumed (and ultimately constructed) literary author's life with the literary construction, using rhetorical and poetic materials, of character and psyche within the poem:

> How...might such a relentlessly "external" regimen [as Langland's intertextual process of composition] be assimilated and given back as the "internal," as the apparent constituents of a subject located in space and time? And even more puzzling, why?[94]

Middleton projects farther outward into history the inquiry into subject formation that characterized Lawton's study (and which, for Simpson in this volume, involves our articulation of a collective *voluntas communis* that resembles the "monastic will" known historically from house charters and meditative writings). Here lies the route to joining the deep-structural with the historical that I have urged.

The ideological relation between subjected individual and subjectifying nation in Langland's England has been nowhere more deeply analyzed than in Middleton's influential 1990 study of authorial signature in *Piers Plowman*. Technically, her procedure hinges on recognition and decoding of the text's presumed puns that reveal phonic, anagrammatic, and distributed versions of William Langland's "kynde name," his true, legitimate, and naturally nominated identity. The Langlandian pun, of course, has been seen as the motor of the very crisis in subject formation traced by Lawton.[95] Middleton frames the project of determining the import of authorial signature and biographical presence—that is, the inscription of a "life" rather than a narrative "role"[96]—precisely as a metafigural quandary, one that foregrounds any sense of the "proper" (which in rhetoric, by the way, also presumably opposes the "figural"):

> Text and context, "external" and "internal" information, narrative progression and digression, the generic and the specific, the common and the proper, blur and fail to sustain themselves as useful heuristic

---

[93] See R. A. Shoaf, "The Play of Puns in Late Middle English Poetry: Concerning Juxtology," in *On Puns: The Foundation of Letters*, Jonathan Culler, ed. (Oxford: Oxford University Press, 1988), 44–61.

[94] "'Kynde Name'," 24.

[95] On Langland's punning, see Mary Clemente Davlin, *A Game of Heuene: Word Play and the Meaning of* Piers Plowman (Cambridge: D. S. Brewer, 1989), 10.

[96] Middleton, "'Kynde Name'," 24.

distinctions in stabilizing either Langland's "authorship question" or ours.[97]

This appreciation of figural self-reflexivity (which foregrounds the structuralist bases of such an inquiry) will call up the function of the pun as yet another master trope in Langland's poetics. As a "grammatical and ontological rather than economic" propriety,[98] Langland's signature primarily exists in *Piers Plowman* manuscripts as an inscription of linguistic play—a play utilizing either the obvious "monosyllable Will"[99] or the "occulted technique of anagram" that "anatomizes" the author's name.[100] But all such methods key on phonetic resemblance, on paranomastic or pun-like operations of the poet's name under a variety of transformations. The "self-personification" of authorial naming in *Piers Plowman*[101] thus hangs on juxtology.

Will Langland's "biographical" identity understood according to these lexical or phonic distributions and transformations, from "longe wille" who'd "lyued in londe" (B.15.152) to the "lond of longynge" (B.11.8—and Middleton has exhaustively catalogued and analyzed them all), enshrines certainly the complex pun as well as the most elementary phonic (or syllabic) particle in Langland's paranomastic code, *will*, from which all anagrammatic and signatory formulations arise or enucleate, as it were. That is to say, "will" itself functions as the copular link between paranomastic language and presumably "proper," neutral language. To be sure, the word in itself always resonates or self-multiplies. "Will," taken as penile tumescence, as an icon of success at literal copulation and the fulfillment of sexual drive (as Joel Fineman delineated it in Shakespeare criticism), enjoys primacy as the linguistic sign of erotic and figural dimensions folded into the poem. "Will" signifies, as James Simpson remarks in "The Power of Impropriety" and elsewhere, a marker in the text's (and its culture's) ethical code—*voluntas* configured as *sensualitas* or *affectus*.[102] No other semantic place-holder enjoys the prominence of "will," isomorph of the Lacanian phallus, in the text's semantic and semiotic fields.

I have two observations to add to Middleton's (or Simpson's) analysis of will, land, and things long. First, the juxtological or paranomastic energy of the process appropriates *especially* the most literalized markers of erotic pulsion. In language so frank that it could be drawn from the register of Anglo-Saxon penitential writing (as Allen Frantzen might agree concerning the narrativizing of same-sex activity in medieval writing), *Piers*

---

[97] Middleton, "'Kynde Name'," 18.

[98] Middleton, "'Kynde Name'," 27.

[99] Middleton, "'Kynde Name'," 43.

[100] Middleton, "'Kynde Name'," 32.

[101] Middleton, "'Kynde Name'," 29.

[102] Simpson, "Desire and the Scriptural Text: Will as Reader in *Piers Plowman*," in *Criticism and Dissent in the Middle Ages*, Rita Copeland, ed. (Cambridge: Cambridge University Press, 1997), 217.

Plowman B presumes to nominate female sexual desire just prior to the damning zeugma that implicates Elde in what was putatively only a heterosexual relationship: "For þe lyme þat she loued me fore and leef was to feele" (B.20.195). The traditional Saxon word (OE, *lim*) designates Will's penis; but it might also be read as a pun on the presumed, and biographically marked, full Christian name of our poet: William = Will + li[a]m. The phonetic component of the full name's second syllable (which is still better perceived in the Gaelic "Liam," a form cognate to Anglo-Norman "Willem") can be seen as another distributed or dispersed monosyllable, one severed, via the adjunct trope apheresis, from the full Christian name's initial syllable. Phonetically dismembered and scattered, the poet's name "William" maintains its semantic status as marker of the phallus. If in Langland's culture, as Middleton asserts, "to disavow the *paternal* surname is to *sever* one's connection to a "kynde" ancestral place,"[103] the subjectivizing complement of that surname, the Christian name Will, in our poem's case, can also be said to contain the occulted inscription of paternal, phallic power that perforce records its own immanent severance, dismemberment, erasure. That Christian name, the indicator of the subject's "spiritual identity" as opposed to his "civil identity,"[104] still constructs him as a "self-personification" emergent from the phallic enterprise of the Symbolic order, the order presided over by the metaphysical Father, the medieval Christian God, or by the civil Father, the King and/as his state.

The fathering of semantic identity and rhetorical or tropological self-constitution in the individual subject implies that the energies and structures I have been identifying should exist at the level of the state's semiotic constitution. They should exist at the level of that ultimate personification, the medieval body politic with its sacramental sign, the king.

James Simpson suggests that in *Piers Plowman*, Will indeed becomes the "will of the long land"—the will of his nation, England, in a word. If this is so, the medieval king, a duplex entity possessing, as Ernst Kantorowicz once brilliantly showed, "two bodies,"[105] must be thought of as the tropologically constituted subject par excellence. He possesses his own, natural and personal human body; and he possesses the collective, eternal, corporate body of the commonwealth, an entity both geographical and social. The king is himself a super-personification that allegorizes all constituent persons, faculties, resources, localities, or institutions as "scattered" or distributed aspects of himself. Will, the narrator of *Piers Plowman*, therefore exists as the subject of the king and kingdom and as a component of that imaginary body politic's cognitive apparatus. He may

---

103 Middleton, "'Kynde Name'," 62; my emphasis.
104 Middleton, "'Kynde Name'," 62.
105 See Ernst H. Kantorowicz, *The King's Two Bodies: A Study in Medieval Political Theology* (Princeton, NJ: Princeton University Press, 1957).

well signify the collective *voluntas* of the state itself, a state seen in the poem to be internally threatened by sin and folly and in need of willed, moral correction. Nowhere can we see a better example of R. A. Shoaf's concept of poetic juxtology than in the nominatory dimension of this state of affairs. Our narrator Will, who serves as will for the "long land"— England—indeed spells the allegorical office in his name "Will Langland," for "Will[l] Angland" = Will England. The film *Meet Joe Black* allegorized the life of its willful protagonist, one Will Parish, as a male-bonding sketch between a Joe and Bill. How would, say, Kurt Vonnegut or Thomas Pynchon have branded an allegory about the life and times of a personified Will England? *Billy England*, I should think.

The second supplement I wished to add a moment ago to Middleton's anagrammatical analytics was in fact further juxtological meditation on Langland's favorite trigger words. The juxtological code of *Piers Plowman* underwrites the semantic identity of those very important markers we call "king" and its phonic echo "kind"; and "long" and its echo "land." These four Middle English words comprise a minimal lexicon out of which the poem generates an entire universe of identity treating both subject formation and the image of political power or social order. The final phonemes in "king," "long," "kind," and "land," represent close, almost indistinguishable, phonemic echoes. We might say that the four words represent mutual polyptota and homeoteleuta (*ki-* and *la-*, and *-ng* and *-nd*, can be recombined four ways via the two tropes of sound repetition). Such phonic, semantic, and semiotic wordplay also works for the pair "Kit" and "Wit" (both figures serving as the allegorical counterparts of Will, the first in terms of the poem's sociosexual code and the second in terms of the poem's ethical code, as James Simpson nicely shows in "The Power of Impropriety") and for the pair "Wit" and "Will."

But the quaternary array of words, king + long + kind + land, might also rehearse a certain phonological disquiet about their philological emergences. The "competing" phonemes [nd] and [ng], in fact, serve as the cliché basis for a grammatical distinction made in how we territorialize fourteenth-century Middle English geography: present participles and gerunds ending with *-and* signify and indicate the West Midlands dialect (the culturally peripheral locale of the Malverns, William Langland's true Fatherland) as opposed to those participles or gerunds ending with *-ing*, signifying the East Midlands dialect (the culturally central locale of London's Chaucer, Father of English literature).[106] Surely this records a long-appreciated thematic tension in fourteenth-century English geo-politics.

By the logic of this acoustical play, with its regional and dialectal ramifications for fourteenth-century English culture, the semantic marker

---

106 For review of the historical -ing/-and formations, see Tauno Mustanoja, *A Middle English Syntax, Part 1* (Helsinki: Société Néophilologique, 1960), 547–8; 566–78.

"*langland*" functions as an instance of echolalia—verbal babble or stammer of the sort one might expect in the epigenetic development of a speaker, as Lacan might say, just about to enter the Symbolic order once he's acquired his teeth and "found" his tongue. "Langland" becomes "long-long" becomes "longing" or "longand." The crucial term "kingdom"—where [ng] and [nd] phonically merge in the still more impossible allophone cluster [ngd]—might just as well reverberate as *kyndom* or perhaps *kyndnom*, that is to say, as the poem's most significant of phrases, "kynde name." The same goes for the immensely powerful trigger word "London," the locus where Will has dwelt biographically but that echoes his "longing" and in turn his "longland."

In laying out this bare minimum of acoustic or phonic juxtologies in *Piers Plowman*—and they can be dizzying, owing to the poem's foundational device of word alliteration—I've only hinted at tropological as well as structural foundations, though I have all along contextualized the imaginary process driving such acoustic effect as a Lacanian psychic process. The work of structuralizing the acoustic proliferations of allophones and phonemes programmatic to allegorical narrative first appeared in Joel Fineman's notorious Jakobsonian reading of the *General Prologue* to *The Canterbury Tales*.[107] If Fineman's innovative though neglected achievement in that essay holds any water, we might conclude that Langland's allegorical poetics similarly keys on acoustic juxtology and echolalia. These juxtological effects underwrite the function of key words in the poem's political and cognitive spheres, programming the invention of subject formation and collective, even geographical, identity. They inform a range of personificational registers working at the phonic, epigenetic, personal, and national levels; and they are isomorphic with the erotic and structural fabrics of a number of master tropes lifted by Langland's text from the body of rhetoric.

So far, we have covered a lot of ground in the semiotization of Will understood as a personification. It remains for me to finish my remarks on the collective personification of the king/state. The personification of the state or nation as the king, as Ernst Kantorowicz so well demonstrated, presupposes what Louis Marin labels a *body semiotic*.[108] It is the "third" imaginary body of the king, the sum total of dispersed or scattered public representations of the king's omnipresence.[109] Although Marin's materials and arena of discussion are early modern—seventeenth-century France and the government of the Sun King—I believe that the dispersional semiotics of *Piers Plowman* presages the kingly body semiotic charted in Marin's

---

[107] Fineman, "The Structure of Allegorical Desire," in *Allegory and Representation*, Stephen J. Greenblatt, ed. (Baltimore, MD and London: Johns Hopkins University Press, 1981), 26–60.

[108] *Portrait of the King*, Martha M. Houle, trans., Tom Conley, foreword (Minneapolis, MN: University of Minnesota Press, 1988).

[109] Marin, *Portrait*, 14.

study. Methodologically, Marin proceeds in his semiological construction of early modern polity from Lacan's description of the social Imaginary, a semiotic ground diffused through omnipresent, *visual* images of power and potentiality that circumscribe the public representations of the king.[110] This circumscription amounts to "a ploy of the king's simultaneous absence and presence [through which] spectators are forced to *divide their faculties....*"[111] A predictable weakness in Marin's picture is his phenomenological distinction between the value of visual and literary media. But in the realm of allegory, especially of the sort seen in *Piers Plowman*, verbal and narrative forms partake of the Imaginary, pre-Symbolic order. The inner histories of tropes and figures do so, as I've shown all along in this essay, with verve. The initial achievement of the monarchical semiotic Imaginary is, no doubt, a sort of universal prosopopeia, a making the dead present and "speaking." Marin writes:

> The first effect of the [king's] representational framework and the first power of representation are the effect and power of presence instead of absence and death; the second effect and second power are the effect of subject, that is, the power of institution, authorization, and legitimation as resulting from the functioning of the framework reflected onto itself.[112]

The king's portrait—for our purposes, an allegorical picture of the nation or society or land as his projected person—can seem more real: the images "are his *real presence.*"[113] The pan-prosopopeia (for what more could be made of the body of representation since it has the cognitive power to "reflect onto itself" the "effect of subject") of the king's third body matches well, in power, attribute, authority, and agenda, the allegorical picture of the distributed or scattered consciousness or personality with *Piers Plowman*'s will/Will, ultimate isomorph of kingly phallic presence, as its most important aspect. Rooted in the *kynde name/kingdom*, Will persists through the end of B.20 as the poem's touchstone in a projected, grand, body semiotic, the king's "most real" body. His final encounters with that trio, Kynde, Death, and Elde—figures of abjection, to be sure—mark well the tension between the body semiotic's will and the absence or death it always overcomes by virtue of the power of representation, moment to moment. And the same-sex, the potentially queer episode produced by the intransigent language of B.20 signifies yet a more extreme irruption of abjection in the legitimizing, alliance-forging, genealogically invested personification of the king called in this poem the Long Land. Marin summarizes nicely how the biographical and historical sort of man William

---

110 Marin, *Portrait*, xv.
111 Marin, *Portrait*, xv; my emphasis.
112 Marin, *Portrait*, 6.
113 Marin, *Portrait*, 8; emphasis in original.

Langland was would be transformed into an effigy redesigned to fit into the "machine" of the king's semiotic apparatus.

> Thus do historical actors become portraits or characters, through reduction in the narrative of what they are in History. Again we must understand that these portraits are processes, microsystems of inverted effects of augmentation and expansion, little simulating machines, frameworks of transformation of the forces of the history not only into characters of the narrative but also—and that is indeed the goal of the operation—into manners of its reception, in a word, into simulacra.[114]

The systemic levels of trope and figure, in this fine specimen of Marin's hermetic writing, can be understood to fill all levels of expression—the narrative poem *Piers Plowman*, its aberrant and episodic scenes (such as the B.20 episode), and the national fiction of the king's regulatory and eternal body semiotic. Indeed the "land of longing/londand" understood as London would take on special status, since a kingdom's capital city is the cartographic, and thus juridical, head of "the eminent body of the king."[115]

In closing, I return us to *Meet Joe Black*, that contemporary fantasy that is as much about the perpetuation of corporate hegemony (embodied both in the narrative fiction of Parish Communications and in the film's media producer, Universal Pictures) as it is about the structurally imbricated elements of same-sex male relations and the medievalistic personification of Death. Personificational narratives, and all allegory indeed, play out corporatist or collective wills of astonishing power and realness. Langland's poem goes far with this truth. I hope that my project of "looking at the contextualization of real and contradictory discourses of power, not [just] at literary characterization," helps us to "learn more about, and from, the subject of *Piers Plowman*."[116]

---

[114] Marin, *Portrait*, 69.
[115] Marin, *Portrait*, 175.
[116] Lawton, "Subject," 28.

"Nede ne hath no lawe": Poverty and the De-stabilization of Allegory in the Final Visions of *Piers Plowman*

Kathleen M. Hewett-Smith

This study will examine the ways in which the pressures of circumstantial history, most vividly expressed in the figure of Nede, de-stabilize the idealizing, hierarchizing power of allegory in the final visions of *Piers Plowman* by forcing our attention to an historically immediate material world, to the literal level of the sign—by advertising the disparity between real and ideal, signifier and signified. I have argued elsewhere that the subject of poverty in *Piers Plowman* involves the poem in an intense confrontation with its own modes of referentiality; that in the vision of Hunger in particular Langland exploits the deep medieval ambivalence toward the problem of need in order to expose the limits of allegorical understanding.[1] The present study will suggest not only that Nede, like Hunger, advertises the allegorical instability that results from the pressures of circumstantial history upon faith, but also that, in its figuration of God's need for us as a kind of mutual devouring, Nede provides a means for reaching at once through and beyond the rift within allegory; that is, rather than exposing the inevitable and irreparable failure of the sign, the de-stabilization of allegory provoked by Nede is, finally, a means of redeeming the mode, of providing significance *within* the epistemological void constitutive of allegorical discourse.

Considering allegory in *Piers Plowman* can be an experience akin to that of reading the poem for the first time. One is confronted with many discrete, and at times conflicting, "visions" of the mode, overwhelmed by the varied narratives of its history and, finally, bewildered by the manifold arguments over its meanings and purposes. Critics of *Piers Plowman* have

---

[1] See Kathleen Hewett-Smith, "Allegory on the Half-Acre: The Demands of History," *Yearbook of Langland Studies* 10 (1996), 1–22, and "'Lo, here lyflode ynow, yf oure beleue be trewe': Poverty and the Transfiguration of History in the Central Visions of *Piers Plowman*," *Chaucer Yearbook* 5 (1998), 139–62.

dealt bravely and extensively with the allegorical mode of the poem. In the past, many of these studies were based upon the assumption that the goal of all medieval allegory is (and should be) the representation of spiritual truths. As a result, such scholars as D. W. Robertson and Bernard F. Huppé read Langland's poem as a spiritual allegory exclusively.[2] Now, however, critics have begun to view *Piers Plowman* as a poem that exploits both the move toward complete abstraction intended by allegory and the impossibility of that move which the effort to allegorize reveals.[3] This study will begin with a brief consideration of the (sometimes surprising) affinities between medieval conceptions of allegory and contemporary theories of the mode, focusing in particular upon the anxiety (both medieval *and* modern) over the final goal, the destination if you will, of allegorical discourse.[4] Then, through a close reading of the final visions of *Piers Plowman*, particularly of the figure of Nede, I will show that a deeper understanding of Langland's allegorical poetics illuminates the significance of the theme of poverty in the poem.

In its most potent guise medieval allegory incorporates material reality into a spiritual or intellectual design, its goal to interpret the palpable and physical in immaterial, celestial or eschatological terms, to reveal the translucency of the things of world to the logos—its project one of containment, idealizing, hierarchizing.[5] As Augustine observes in *On Christian Doctrine*, successful allegory requires the sublimation of "reality."

> Thus in this mortal life, wandering from God, if we wish to return to our native country where we can be blessed we should use this world and not enjoy it, so that the 'invisible things' of God 'being understood by the things that are made' may be seen, that is, so that by means of corporal and temporal things we may comprehend the eternal and spiritual.[6]

---

2 See D. W. Robertson and Bernard F. Huppé, *Piers Plowman and Scriptural Tradition* (Princeton: Princeton University Press, 1951).

3 See for example James J. Paxson, *The Poetics of Personification* (Cambridge: Cambridgue University Press, 1994), particularly Chapter 5, "Personification, Dreams, and Narrative Structures in *Piers Plowman* B," 114–138; James Simpson, "The Transformation of Meaning: A Figure of Thought in *Piers Plowman*," *Review of English Studies* 37 (1986): 161–83; and Maureen Quilligan, *The Language of Allegory: Defining the Genre* (Ithaca: Cornell University Press, 1979), especially pages 58–79.

4 This segment of the discussion draws in part upon my article, "Allegory on the Half-Acre."

5 See Thomas Aquinas, *Summa Theologiae: Latin Text and English Translation*, ed. Thomas Gilby, 61 vols., (London: Blackfriars, 1963–80), 1.1.9 and 1.1.10, and Dante's *Convivio* for prominent medieval notions of fourfold allegoresis. See particularly Erich Auerbach, "Figura," in his *Scenes from the Drama of European Literature*, Theory and History of Literature 9 (Minneapolis: University of Minnesota Press, 1984), 11–76, for a discussion of figural allegory.

6 Augustine, *On Christian Doctrine*, D. W. Robertson, trans. (New York: Macmillan, 1986), 1.4.4; cf. 2.10.15.

Allegoresis makes possible what our fallen natures disallow—the revelation of divine mysteries within the objects of the material world. In this formulation, the things of sense are unimportant in and of themselves; instead, they become merely the "means" of attaining divine understanding.[7] For Augustine, the central (and inevitable) Christian tension between visible and invisible, temporal and eternal, corporal and spiritual is resolved by imagining a hierarchy in which we ascend toward truth, by the idealizing power of allegory.

For contemporary theorists the very need for allegorical expression draws attention to the impossibility of representing transcendent truths in limited human language. As Gordon Teskey observes, allegory "evokes a schism in consciousness—between a life and a mystery, between the real and the ideal, between a literal tale and its moral" by "forc[ing] on our attention the difference between what it refers *to* and what it refers *with*."[8] Post-Structuralist discussions of allegory see in such an imaginative rift *only the failure* of signification—'rupture,' 'void,' 'gap'. Theirs is a potent response to what they might consider a kind of delusional confidence—on the part of earlier theorists of the mode—in allegory's ability successfully to figure abstract truths. In one of the milder formulations of this perspective, J. Hillis Miller observes:

> The possibility that the allegorical representation is a human fancy thrown out toward something which is so beyond human comprehension that there is no way to measure the validity of any picture of it is the permanent shadow within the theory [of allegory].[9]

For Miller, the allegorical representation itself is immaterial, an idea, a "fancy," which attempts to recover meaning by moving beyond its material embodiment toward something that is ultimately unknowable. The only way to speak of allegory is to acknowledge its fundamental instability, its "permanent shadow," to accept the impossibility of fusing abstract and concrete modes of understanding. Rather than confidently asserting the union of the sign, contemporary theorists recognize the irrecoverable rupture within it.[10]

Paul de Man suggests that the space for allegory is precisely *within* its epistemological gap: "Allegory designates primarily a distance in relation to its own origin, and, renouncing the nostalgia to coincide, it establishes

---

[7] In fact, Augustine suggests that to seek physical satisfaction from material objects, to "enjoy" them, is to endanger spiritual fulfillment (*On Christian Doctrine*, 1.4.4).

[8] Gordon Teskey, *Allegory and Violence* (Ithaca: Cornell University Press, 1996), 2, 11.

[9] J. Hillis Miller, "The Two Allegories," in Morton W. Bloomfield, ed., *Allegory, Myth and Symbol* (Cambridge: Cambridge University Press, 1981), 362–363.

[10] Cf. Walter Benjamin, "The false appearance of totality is extinguished. For the *eidos* disappears, the simile ceases to exist, and the cosmos it contained shrivels up" ("Allegory and Trauerspiel," in his *The Origin of German Tragic Drama*, John Osborne, trans. [London: New Left Books, 1977], 178).

its language in the void of this temporal difference."[11] Allegory signifies within the "void of temporal difference," through the inevitable confrontation with what it denies. For de Man, we must not look to either side of abyss, toward neither the union nor the failure of the sign, but rather *into* that tension—there we will find the "truth" within the language of allegory.[12]

Perhaps surprisingly, Post-Structuralist views of allegory are implicit in medieval theories of representation. According to Augustine, "A sign is a thing which causes us to think of something beyond the impression the thing itself makes upon the senses."[13] Although, as we have seen, Augustine assumes the direct referentiality of the sign, he at the same time oberves that the signified follows, is "beyond," the signifier, thereby acknowledging the presence of absence in language.[14] Indeed, in *On Christian Doctrine* Augustine questions the very basis of representation itself:

> Have we spoken or announced anything worthy of God? Rather I feel I have done nothing but wish to speak: if I have spoken, I have not said what I wished to say. Whence do I know this, except because God is ineffable? If what I said were ineffable it would not be said. And for this reason God should not be said to be ineffable, for when this is said something is said. And a contradiction in terms is created, since if that is ineffable which cannot be spoken, then that is not ineffable which can be called ineffable. This contradiction is to be passed over in silence rather than resolved verbally.[15]

As Laurie Finke observes, "Augustine's frustration at the task of representing the divine is evident in the convoluted language of the passage."[16] Like contemporary theorists, he recognizes the impossibility of successfully representing abstract truths allegorically and yet, unlike the Post-Structuralists, Augustine suggests not that we accept and even exploit this "contradiction," but that we "pass over [it] in silence"—the silence of

---

[11] Paul de Man, "The Rhetoric of Temporality," in his *Blindness and Insight: Essays in the Rhetoric of Contemporary Criticism*, 2nd ed. (Minneapolis: University of Minnesota Press), 207.

[12] In "Pascal's Allegory of Persuasion" de Man famously asks, "Why is it that the furthest reaching truths about ourselves and the world have to be stated in such a lopsided and referentially indirect mode?" (in Stephen J. Greenblatt, ed., *Allegory and Representation* [Baltimore: Johns Hopkins University Press, 1981]. 2). In one of the most recent studies of the mode Gordon Teskey seeks to articulate the de Manian void, arguing that "at the root of the motives for allegorical expression is instrumental meaning, meaning not as a representation of what already is but as the creative exertion of force"—in Teskey's configuration, violence (*Allegory*, 5).

[13] Augustine, *On Christian Doctrine*, 2.1.1.

[14] For a useful discussion of Augustine's relation to Post-Structuralist theories of allegory see Laurie A. Finke, "Truth's Treasure: Allegory and Meaning in *Piers Plowman*," in Laurie A. Finke and Martin B. Schichtman, eds., *Medieval Texts and Contemporary Readers* (Ithaca: Cornell University Press, 1987), 51–68.

[15] Augustine, *On Christian Doctrine*, 1.6.6.

[16] Finke, "Truth's," 54.

faith. For Augustine, the act of faith can fill the de Manian void at the heart of allegory for it allows us to believe that there is something beyond human comprehension. In some ways then (at least to the medieval mind), a belief in the possibility of successful allegory is a confirmation of belief itself. Allegory both makes faith possible and requires faith to succeed.

Langland's images of poverty and economic necessity in the final visions of *Piers Plowman* make faith possible by reaching through the rift within allegory. In the figure of Nede Langland at once exposes the limits of an allegorical understanding of the material world and offers a means of redeeming the fissure within that understanding; for rather than seeing an unbridgeable gulf in that space between human and divine, Langland, like Augustine, articulates a space for divine figuration that not only acknowledges but embraces our humanity. For Langland, we must not "pass over" difficult historical truths "in silence," but must confront them if we are to have the smallest hope of reaching "beyond" them to a responsible position of faith. Before we consider the figure of Nede himself, however, we must examine the disruption of allegory at the end of the poem's central visions that allows him to appear.

I have argued elsewhere that in the central visions of *Piers Plowman* Langland objectifies poverty, disentangles it from the web of historical circumstance that so endangers the proper spiritual understanding of need in the poem's early visions, as a means of stabilizing the mode of allegory itself, of containing and finally recuperating the palpable and physical within an intellectual or spiritual design.[17] Following the discourse of Patience in Passus 15 and 16 the poem moves through a long series of formal, deeply detailed spiritual allegories: the Tree of Charity, the allegories of the palm and taper, Hope and the Good Samaritan, Jesus' joust, his crucifixion and the Harrowing of Hell, and the founding of Holy Church.[18] There is little narrative progress in this part of the poem—almost a sense of stasis. The dreamer himself is more a witness to than a participant in these visions, saying and *doing* less than he has at any other point. Indeed, narrative interest in Will's quest has been subsumed by an attention to the adventures of Christ, and Piers. The discourse of material actuality so prominent in the *visio*, and present still even in the pardon from Truth, has

[17] Hewett-Smith, "Lo, here lyflode ynow." Derek Pearsall also briefly explores this shift in focus in the central visions in his "Poverty and Poor People in *Piers Plowman*" in *Medieval Studies Presented to George Kane*, ed. Edward Donald Kennedy, Ronald Waldron, and Joseph S. Wittig (Wolfeboro: D. S. Brewer, 1988), 167–85.

[18] C.18–21. Because it presents the most extensive discussions of the poor and the problem of poverty I refer in this essay specifically to the C version of *Piers Plowman* and cite *Piers Plowman by William Langland: An Edition of the C–text*, ed. Derek Pearsall (Berkeley: University of California Press, 1978). Subsequent citations will be noted parenthetically. Any reference to the B version will be explicit and will follow the text found in George Kane and E. Talbot Donaldson, eds., *Piers Plowman: The B Version*, rev. ed. (Berkeley: University of California Press, 1988).

been replaced, in a move reminiscent of Augustine's *Confessions*, by the
discourse of allegory and biblical narrative.

What I wish to emphasize about these final moments of *Piers
Plowman*'s central visions is that abstract truths are now conveyed not by
experiential allegory—that is, not by plowing, seeking, or even feasting—
but instead by a more powerfully intellectualized (and intellectualizing)
form of the mode. The Tree of Charity, the palm, the taper; these are
schema for organizing, defining, and thereby for containing, the most complex spiritual notions. These images are not only referentially dense, they
in fact expose, even advertise the process of signification:

> For god þat al bygan in bigynnynge of the worlde
> Ferde furste as a fuste, and 3ut is, as y leue,
> > *Mundum pugillo continens,*
> (...)
> The paume is the pethe of the hand and profereth the fyngeres
> To ministre and to make þat myhte of hand knoweth,
> And bitokeneth trewly, telle ho-so liketh,
> The holy goest of heuene: he is as þe paume.
> The fyngres þat fre ben to folde and to cluche
> Bitokneth soethly the sone þat sente was til erthe,
> Touchede and tastede, at techynge of the paume,
> Seynte Marie, a mayden, and mankynde lauhte.
> > *Natus est ex Maria virgine.*
> The fader is thenne as þe fuste, with fynger and with paume
> To huyde and to holde as holy writ telleth...
>   (C.19.111–125)

The image lays bare the workings of metaphor. In it we *see* (both in the verbal text and in the visual image it elicits) the dynamics of allegorical signification as each vehicle is assigned a direct, spiritual referent. Furthermore,
we are assured that this performance of signification "bitokeneth trewly,"
"bitokneth soethly," "telle ho-so liketh," its success ensured by "holy writ"
and, most powerfully and fundamentally, by the incarnation itself. In the
early visions of *Piers Plowman*, as I have argued elsewhere, exposing the
act of representation results in the failure of the sign.[19] Uncovering the
process of metaphor at this point in the poem, however, seems only to re-
invigorate its power. As allegories, these images are utterly stable, utterly
translucent, their literal levels dissolving into the logos. Furthermore, the
biblical narratives that surround them are themselves heavily, and unusu-
ally for Langland, explicitly typological.[20] Indeed, Langland would seem to
be doing all that he can to ensure the spiritualizing of the things of sense,

---

[19] Hewett-Smith, "Allegory on the Half-Acre," especially 15–20.

[20] Derek Pearsall observes that Langland's reworking of the parable of the Good Samaritan (Luke 10:
25–37) "is one of the few instances where Langland's allegorical technique can be analysed usefully in terms
of the traditional four levels of scriptural exegesis" (*Piers Plowman*, 308, note to B.19.47).

to bring his dreamer, and reader, to the point of spiritual revelation and renewal through the recuperative therapy of orthodox allegorical interpretation.

The allegories of the central visions culminate in the founding of Holy Church and the appearance of Grace, who brings the gifts of the Holy Spirit to Conscience, Piers, and "[t]o alle kyne creatures þat can his fyue wittes" (C.21.216):[21]

> Som men he ȝaf wyt with wordes to shewe,
> To wynne with treuthe þat the world asketh,
> As prechours and prestes and prentises of law:
> They leely to lyue bi labour of tonge
> And bi wit to wissen oþere as grace hem wolde teche.
> And somme he kende hem craft and konnynge of syhte,
> With sullyng and buggynge here bileue to wynne.
> And som he lered to laboure a londe and a watre
> And lyue by þat laboure a leele lyf and a trewe.
> And somme he tauhte to tulye, to þecche and to coke,
> As here wit wolde when þe tyme come.
> And somme to deuyne and to deuyde noumbres,
> To kerue and to compace and coloures to make.
> And some to se and to saye what sholde bifalle
> Bothe of wele and of wo and be ywaer bifore,
> As astronomens thorw astronomye, and philosopheres wyse.
> And somme to ryde and somme to rekeuere that vnrihtfulliche was wonne;
> (...)
> And somme he lered to lyue in longyng to be hennes,
> In pouerte and in pacience to preye for alle cristene.
> And al he lered to be lele, and vch a craft loue oþere,
> Ne no boest ne debaet be among hem alle.
>
> (C.21.229–51)

Grace's gifts allude to the seven gifts of the Holy Spirit distributed to the Apostles: "To one indeed, by the Spirit, is given the word of wisdom; and to another, the word of knowledge, according to the same Spirit; to another faith in the same Spirit; to another the grace of healing in on Spirit; to another, the working of miracles; to another, prophecy; to another the discerning of spirits; to another, diverse kinds of tongues; to another, interpretation of speeches."[22] In the biblical account, the Holy Spirit extends to the disciples primarily intellective and spiritual skills and does not articulate the ends to which those gifts should be put. In Grace's formulation, however, the "tresor"of the Holy Spirit includes not only the enhancement of mental and devotional faculties, but also the physical skills necessary to

---

[21] Cf. 1 Cor.12:4, "Now there are diversities of graces, but the same Spirit." (*Divisiones vero gratiarum sunt, idem autem Spiritus.*) Citations of the Vulgate are from *Biblia Sacra* (Paris: Desclée, 1927). Translations are from *The Holy Bible*, Douai-Rheims version, (New York: P. J. Kenedy, 1914.)
[22] 1 Cor. 12:8–10.

mundane life: the means to "laboure," "tulye," "þecche," "coke," and "ride." Furthermore, Grace prescribes what should be done with both sets of capabilites: they are to be put to very practical ends—to respond to what "the world asketh" of the good Christian. Finally, his gift is stunningly inclusive for the mediation of the Holy Spirit covers not only to those in religious life but people of all vocations, religious and secular—even the poor, whose only "vocation" is "to lyue in longyng to be hennes." This passage reconfigures biblical discourse in an effort to redeem and even transfigure matters of material concern. But for Langland, as we shall see, such an interest in the demands of historical actuality is dangerously de-stabilizing to an allegorical understanding of life in the world.

Grace's description of the ideal Christian community, with its repetition of "somme" and its enumeration of "laboure[s]" and "craft[s]," overtly and, I would argue, intentionally, recalls both the dreamer's depiction of the field of folk (C.Prol.22–94) and Piers's establishment of the social system on the half-acre (C.8.7–18)—particularly in its emphasis on faithful work, communal order, and social concord.[23] Those earlier communities, however, were described primarily in literal, material terms, their allegorical significance apparent only obscurely. In contrast, Grace's social order, though agriculturally based like that of the half-acre, is presented in explicitly spiritual terms:[24]

> Grace gaf Peres a teme, foure grete oxen:
> That oen was Luc, a large beste and a lou-chered,
> And Marc, and Mathewe the thridde, myhty bestes bothe,
> And ioyned til hem oen Iohan, most gentill of all,
> The pris neet of Peres plouh, passynge alle opere.
>   (C.21.262–66)

In this allegory of the founding and life of the Christian community under the dominion of the Church, Piers tills the field of Truth with the plough of the Scriptures pulled by the oxen of the four evangelists.[25] He then cultivates the soil with the horses of the Church Fathers—Augustine, Ambrose, Gregory, and Jerome—and the harrows of the Old and New Testaments (C.21.267–73). Finally, in an attempt to "naturalize" the four cardinal

---

[23] Critics have often compared the "Do-Best" section of *Piers Plowman* to the *visio*, particularly to the plowing of the half-acre. The first study to note the connection between the two episodes is Henry W. Wells, "The Construction of *Piers Plowman*," *PMLA* 44 (1929): 123–40, repr. in *Interpretations of Piers Plowman*, ed. Edward Vasta (Notre Dame: University of Notre Dame Press, 1968), 1–21. Other useful studies that compare the two scenes include Mary Carruthers, *The Search for St. Truth: A Study of Meaning in Piers Plowman* (Evanston, IL: Northwestern University Press, 1973), 152–73; Elizabeth D. Kirk, *The Dream Thought of Piers Plowman* (New Haven: Yale University Press, 1972), 190–205; and Stephen A. Barney, *Allegories of History, Allegories of Love* (Hamden, CT: Archon Books, 1979), 89–101.

[24] Carruthers, *Search*, 154–56; and Wells, "Construction," 7–12.

[25] Stephen Barney notes that the association of oxen with the apostles was traditional in the agricultural imagery of the commentators ("The Plowshare of the Tongue: The Progress of a Symbol from the Bible to *Piers Plowman*," *Medieval Studies* 35 [1973], 267–8). See also Derek Pearsall, *Piers Plowman*, 352 n262.

virtues, he plants "in mannes soule" (C.21.175) the "graynes"of *spiritus prudencie, temperancie, fortitudinis,* and *iusticie.*

At this point in the poem we are almost overwhelmed by the density of allegorical representation. As in the earlier metaphors of the Tree of Charity, the palm, and the taper, each piece of the literal narrative is assigned an overt, privileged, spiritual referent. Every signifier is merely the vehicle of its signified. Carruthers observes, in a discussion of the B version of *Piers Plowman,* that in some ways this spiritual plowing might be understood to contain the figural fulfillment of the agricultural activity of the poem's second vision:

> ...these scenes from Passus XIX, the culmination of the *Vita,* are intended to reveal the meaning of passus VI–VII, the culmination of the *Visio,* through a relationship which binds the two parts of the poem in an explicitly figural way. Passus XIX redeems Passus VII, as the life of Christ redeems that of the men of the Old Law....It is a redemption not only of mankind and human society, but of the poem's allegory and of its language.[26]

As I have already suggested, since the breakdown of the plowing of the half-acre in C.9, Langland has emphasized the need for a moral and spiritual understanding of life as it is lived in the world. He asks that we see working poverty, for example, not only as a sign of physical distress but also, and more importantly, as a means of moral strengthening. In this sense, Grace's spiritual plowing might usefully be considered the "redempt[ive]" figural fulfillment of the historically-based plowing of the half-acre, the culmination of the central visions' movement from material to spiritual concern. I wish to argue, however, that although the poem might attempt this intellectualizing move toward figural abstraction (which is, after all, invited by the explicitly allegorical nature of Grace's field) it does not, finally, succeed; for upon revisiting the half-acre we are reminded of the discourse of material "reality" that allegory, because it must always suppress the literal in some measure, cannot hope adequately to contain or represent. While the agrarian society of *Piers's* second vision failed because it lacked "filial loue," because its attention was turned solely toward a literal understanding of material needs, the spiritual plowing of Passus 21 is concerned exclusively with charity and lacks any sort of recognition of the legitimate demands of economic actuality.

Langland himself seems to recognize that Grace's allegory of the Christian life has become impossibly absolute, for as soon as Piers begins to plow, indeed within the same poetic line, he and his fellow laborers are attacked by Pride (that figure who in his C-Text confession, borrowed from Haukyn, exhibits all the economic and social sins of one who lives in the world) and the agricultural allegory falters, "Now is Peres to the plouh—

---

[26] Carruthers, *Search,* 155.

Pryde hit aspiede / And gadered hym a grete oeste" (C.21.336–7). The fearful Christians take refuge in the Barn of Unity and defend themselves by
digging a moat of Holiness around the structure. Some members of the
community, however, apparently disenchanted by this overwhelming spiritual display, suddenly rebel against Grace's complete intellectualization of
worldly activity:

> 'ʒe? bawe!' quod a breware, 'y wol nat be yruled,
> By Iesu! for al ʒoure iangelyng, aftur *Spiritus iusticie*
> Ne aftur Consience, bi Crist, while y can sulle
> Bothe dregges and draf and drawe at on hole
> Thikke ale or thynne ale; and þat is my kynde
> And nat to hacky aftur holinesse—hold thy tonge, Consience!
> Of *Spiritus iusticie* thow spekest moche on ydel.'
>   (C.21.396–402)

The brewer's interruption is striking, even unsettling, not only in its sud-
denness, but in its rudeness ("bawe!"). His unmannered discourse explodes
not only the passus's spiritual narrative, but even the construct of civility
presumed by the poem—a move we will see again in the figure of Nede.
The brewer's stubborn insistence on the primacy of material desires echoes
the remarks of the cutpurse and the apeward in Passus 7 who were too
busy pursuing worldly gain to bother about the pursuit of grace through
pilgrimage.[27] Like the thievery and fraud engaged in by those earlier busi-
nessmen, the brewer's practices, too, are immoral and unethical, his interests, solely economic.[28] He cheats his customers for personal gain by selling the lees of the ale and by watering down his thickest brew.
Furthermore, and again like those earlier figures who insisted in understanding Piers's allegory of the pilgrimage to Truth only in literal terms
(C.7), the brewer finds that the preceding spiritual discourse is irrelevant
"iangelyng," "ydel" words which have no significance to the literal-mind-
ed merchant. The brewer's retort is followed by the equally self-interested
claims of a "lewed vicory," a lord, and a king, each of whom perverts the
meaning of the cardinal virtues with an eye to his position in the world
(C.21.409–81).[29] Although Langland makes clear the moral dubiousness
of each of these figures' interest in material gain, like the pickpocket and
the apekeeper they serve to remind us of the undeniable presence of a material reality that cannot, and I would argue *should* not, finally, be contained
within a spiritual or eschatological design. As Robert Frank so aptly
observes, in the midst of Grace's spiritual community, "there is still the

---

27 C.7.283–86. Carruthers suggests that the brewer's retort recalls Avarice's confession in B.5.188–295
(*Search*, 157).
28 Unlike the cutpurse, the apeward, and the pickpocket, however, the brewer is not a wanderer, nor is his
economic activity inherently immoral or unstable. He chooses to corrupt his business practices.
29 On the relation of these figures to the cardinal virtues they subvert, see Robert Worth Frank, *Piers
Plowman and the Scheme of Salvation* (New Haven: Yale University Press, 1957), 103–6.

world."[30] By the end of the central visions of *Piers Plowman* the demands of history have once again threatened the stability of allegorical abstraction.

The final passus of *Piers Plowman* begins in this climate of allegorical instability. After he hears the disruptive arguments of the brewer, the vicar, the lord, and the king the dreamer's spiritual vision ends. Upon awakening, he is overcome by "heuy-chere" and hunger and wanders the countryside looking for a place to eat (C.22.1–3). Near noon, he meets a figure named Nede who accosts and berates him, calling him "foule" and "faytour." Nede then offers the dreamer some advice concerning, as we might expect, the legitimate urgency of need (C.22.6–50). He begins by suggesting that the destitute person has the absolute right to steal what he needs in order to survive—food, drink and clothing—as long as that need is measured by the virtue of temperance; for temperance, according to Nede, is the virtue closest to God. He then supports these claims by observing that Christ himself became man and was poor; therefore, one should not be ashamed to beg and be needy since he who created the world was voluntarily destitute. Indeed, no one ever died more poor or more needy.

Critical response to Nede's speech has fallen generally into two groups.[31] Some scholars argue that Nede's advice to the dreamer is both morally and ethically sound. For these critics Nede represents the "regulating principle of temperance" and embodies the culmination of the poem's teaching on the virtues of patient poverty.[32] Others suggest that his words are suspect and "slippery," that we must "convict" him of distorting the virtue of temperance, of promoting greed and "petty thievery" for personal gain.[33] Each of these interpretations, however, is based upon the

---

[30] Frank, *Scheme of Salvation*, 105.

[31] There are actually few detailed studies of the Nede episode. The best discussion of (and only complete article devoted to) the scene is still Robert Adams, "The Nature of Nede in *Piers Plowman* XX," *Traditio* 34 (1978), 274–301. Several book-length studies of *Piers Plowman* treat Nede in some detail. They include Lawrence M. Clopper, *'Songes of Rechelesnesse': Langland and the Franciscans* (Ann Arbor: University of Michigan Press, 1997), 71–72, 93–99, 294–304; Wendy Scase, *'Piers Plowman' and the New Anti-clericalism*, Cambridge Studies in Medieval Literature 4 (Cambridge: Cambridge University Press, 1989), 64-83; David Aers, *Community, Gender, and Individual Identity: English Writing 1360–1430* (London: Routledge & Kegan Paul, 1988), especially 62–66; Morton W. Bloomfield, *Piers Plowman as a Fourteenth-century Apocalypse* (New Brunswick, NJ: Rutgers University Press, 1962), 135–43; Carruthers, *Search*, 160–66; Frank, *Scheme of Salvation*, 110–18; Robertson and Huppé, *Scriptural Tradition*, 223–31; and Penn R. Szittya, *The Antifraternal Tradition in Medieval Literature* (Princeton: Princeton University Press, 1986), especially 268–73. Geoffrey Shepherd also treats Nede briefly in his "Poverty in *Piers Plowman*," in *Social Relations and Ideas: Essays in Honour of R. H. Hilton*, ed. T. H. Aston, P. R. Cross, Christopher Dyer, and Joan Thirsk (Cambridge: Cambridge University Press, 1983), 187–89.

[32] Bloomfield, *Apocalypse*, 135. See also Robertson and Huppé, *Scriptural Tradition*, 228.

[33] Those critics who find Nede suspect include Frank who finds that "the purpose of Nede's speech is to expose the [corrupt] philosophy of need which motivated the friars" (*Scheme of Salvation*, 113); Carruthers, *Search*, 160–62; Adams, "Nature of Need" 273–301; and Szittya, *Antifraternal Tradition*, who finds that "Nede...is a dangerous state to be in," 275.

assumption that Nede is a figure of moral authority, like Holy Church or even Hunger, sent to instruct the dreamer in the lesson of temperance. I wish to argue, however, that Nede presents the *experience* rather than the authority of need.[34] That is, rather than presenting in his speech to the dreamer a kind of doctrine that must be measured against Christian standards of morality and ethics (and thus judged either suspiciously lacking in integrity, or consistent and worthy of praise), Nede escapes discursive formulation altogether, and provides instead a portrait of the fact of necessity and want. In his study of the figure, Penn Szittya places Nede beyond the reach of such labels as "good" or "bad" by suggesting that Nede's "semantic ambiguity" blurs the "many moral degrees," legitimate to illegitimate, of need presented in *Piers Plowman*.[35] I would suggest, however, that for Langland, Nede is in fact broadly, constitutively, *amoral*, outside, beyond the reach of those social, religious, and even literary constructs that hope to contain him: manners, law, christian doctrine, and allegory.[36]

Nede's appearance is sudden, his manner abrupt. He has not been summoned, as was Hunger, nor has he come to instruct the dreamer as to the moral significance of his vision, as did Holy Church or Patience. In fact, this meeting with Nede does not seem to be a vision at all; rather, it appears to take place in the dreamer's waking life. There are only two other extended "waking episodes" in the poem in which the dreamer interacts with personified figures—the so-called "autobiographical" passage that initiates the series of confessions in C.5, and Will's meeting with the friars at the beginning of his search for Do-Well—but neither so overtly confuses the boundaries between allegorical vision and fictive reality.[37] In the first instance, for example, though the dreamer is apparently awake, his extravisionary encounter with Reason occurs not in the "real" world of Cornhill where he dwells with his wife, but within his own mind as he composes verse:

---

[34] Cf. Pearsall, *Piers Plowman*, 363 n37. Paxson notes that Nede does not identify himself to the dreamer "using the exclusive formula 'I am x'—a formula that characterizes all the initial verbal declarations made by all the instructional personifications...whom Will meets face to face" (*Poetics of Personification*, 123).

[35] Szittya, *Antifraternal Tradition*, 269. See also Carruthers, *Search*, 160–1, on Nede's contribution to the verbal "disintegration of meaning" at the end of *Piers Plowman*.

[36] And probably even literary criticism!

[37] C.5.1–108; C.10.1–60. A useful study of the waking episodes may be found in John M. Bowers, *The Crisis of Will in Piers Plowman* (Washington, D. C.: Catholic University of America Press, 1986), 129–89. See also David Mills, "The Rôle of the Dreamer in *Piers Plowman*," in *Piers Plowman: Critical Approaches*, ed. S. S. Hussey (London: Methuen & Company, 1969), 180–212. Most recently Steven Justice and Kathryn Kerby-Fulton have edited a volume of penetrating essays focused upon the so-called "autobiographical passage" (*Written Work*: Langland, Labor and Authorship [Philadelphia: University of Pennsylvania Press, 1997]).

Paxson has argued recently that personification figures "seem to be present in the diegetic level of the narrator's waking life" because of a "general confusion between literal reference and local figurative ornament" (*Poetics of Personification*, 122).

Thus y awakede, woet god, whan y wonede in Cornehull,
Kytte and y in a cote, yclothed as a lollare,
And lytel ylet by, leueth me for sothe,
Amonges lollares of Londone and lewede ermytes,
For y made of tho men as resoun me tauhte.
For as y cam by Consience with Resoun y mette
In an hot heruest whenne y hadde myn hele
And lymes to labory with and louede wel fare
And no dede to do but to drynke and to slepe.
In hele and in inwitt oen me apposede;
Romynge in remembraunce, thus Resoun me aratede.
(C.5.1–11)

The dreamer does not actually encounter Conscience and Reason on the field "in an hot heruest" but instead conjures them within his "inwitt" as he "ma[kes]" poetry. Allegorical vision does not intrude upon the dreamer's actual life but is manifest in his thoughts, like a dream, through the act of writing verse.

The second waking episode occurs after the dreamer has heard the lesson of Truth's Pardon, and, having awakened from his vision, begins to "rome aboute" in search of Dowel. Along the way, and after inquiring of "mony men," he meets with a pair of friars who reveal that Dowel resides pre-eminently with them (C.10.1–19). The dreamer disputes their claim and is offered an exemplum in response (C.10.20–55). He then leaves the friars and, wearied from walking "wyde-whare," falls asleep to experience his next vision. Unlike the autobiographical passage, this episode provides no overt allegorical references. Though they speak metaphorically of Dowel, the friars themselves are not clearly personifications and do not disrupt the integrity of the dreamer's extra-visionary experience. Rather, they are part of it.[38]

While the first two waking scenes maintain the line between allegorical vision and fictive reality, the Nede episode transgresses that boundary. At its opening Will is not dreaming but is awake and hungry for he "ne wiste where to ete ne at what place" (C.22.3). This emphasis on the dreamer's actual physical state, his hunger for food at "noen" opposes and demystifies the spiritual food offered by Conscience to satisfy the Christians who labored on Grace's allegorical field in the preceding vision.[39] As he searches for sustenance the dreamer meets with Nede: "And hit neyhed neyh þe noen and with Nede y mette / That afrounted me foule and faytour me calde" (C.22.4–5). There is little here to suggest that Nede is merely a projection of Will's imagination, as were Reason and Conscience in the ear-

---

[38] That the dreamer apparently treats Dowel as a noun (and thus, in a sense, as a personification) does not, I think, contradict my notion that allegorical vision is not confused with fictive reality in this episode. On the dreamer's misunderstanding of Dowel, see especially Mills, "Rôle," 194–96.

[39] Conscience's offering "godes body" to the famished workers in turn recalls Patience's offering to Haukyn a "pece of þe Paternoster" for his "liflode" (B.14.49).

lier waking scene.[40] Nede interacts in and with the dreamer's "real" world. We are startled by his appearance for it challenges our understanding of the conventions of dream allegory which have it that these realms, though perhaps influencing one another, are finally separate. The dreamer, too, is surprised. Indeed, he is apparently so astonished that he simply accepts Nede's accusations passively, without uttering even a word—a unique response for the outspoken Will. "Whenne Nede hadde vndernome me thus, anoen y ful aslepe" (C.22.51). As the brewer's retort, with its insistence upon an acknowledgment of the world of economic necessity, deconstructed the completely spiritualized understanding of Christian life represented in Grace's field, so the appearance of Nede explodes the bounds/bonds of allegorical discourse not only by blurring the line between the visionary and mimetic, but also, as we shall see, by thrusting before us the undeniable actualities of indigence.

In the first section of his speech, Nede argues that the needy person has a right to the necessities of life, even if they must be acquired by theft, for "nede ne hath no lawe."

> 'Couthest thow nat excuse the, as dede the kyng and oþere,
> That thow toke to lyue by, to clothes and to sustinaunce,
> Was bi techyng and by tellyng of *Spiritus temperancie*
> And þat thow nome no more then nede the tauhte?
> And nede ne hath no lawe ne neuere shal falle in dette
> For thre thynges þat he taketh his lyf for to saue:
> That is mete, when men hym werneth for he no money weldeth,
> Ne wyht þat now wol be his borwe ne no wed hath to legge;
> And he cacche in þat caes and come therto by sleithe
> He synegeth nat sothlich þat so wynneth his fode.
> And thow he come so to a cloth and can no bettere cheuesaunce,
> Nede anoen-riht nymeth hym vnder maynprise.
> And yf hym lust for to lape the lawe of kynde wolde
> That he dronke at vch a dysch ar he deye for furste.
> So nede at greet nede may nyme as for his owne
> Withouten consail of Consience or cardinale vertues,
> So þat he sewe and saue *Spiritus temperancie*.'
>   (C.22.6–22)

Nede argues in these lines that the experience of material distress is beyond not only legal and social construction, but also beyond the purview of the moral dictates of conscience and the spiritual and institutional demands of

---

[40] Paxson notes that the Middle English verb "meten" in line 4 can mean both 'to encounter or meet' and 'to dream' (*Poetics of Personification*, 122), though the latter meaning is difficult to accept in conjunction with the line's prior "wiþ". While I acknowledge that there *may* be punning ambiguity in Langland's use of the verb, I am not persuaded that such usage indicates clearly that Nede cannot be present within the poem's mimetic frame. In any case, what I wish to emphasize about the scene is that Langland *confuses* the boundaries of allegory and fictive reality, thereby disrupting the organizing and containing impulse of figural representation.

the cardinal virtues. The needy person is "excused" from such communal covenants—an exception to their systems for understanding and regulating human experience. He "taketh,"[41] an action at once transgressive and presumptive, without consent. Nede's position responds not to some abstract doctrine concerning dearth but, rather, to the lived demands of material necessity, "a lyf for to saue." The situations that he describes to illustrate the validity of his claims are powerfully mundane, deeply individual, and insistently unidealized: "he dronke at vch a dysch ar he deye for furste." What we do *not* find in his remarks is any gesture toward recognizing the spiritual rewards of being poor, the more typical medieval response to indigence and the one promoted in the central visions of *Piers*,[42] instead, we see an insistence upon the immediacy of dire necessity and the physical burdens of distress. For Nede, these burdens are subject only to the "lawe of kynde." They cannot and should not be circumscribed within discursive formulations, like allegory, which would hope to idealize and sublimate the experience of poverty.

Discussions of the problem of necessity in the Middle Ages acknowledge the constitutive a-morality of need.[43] The traditional model of communal social relations is provided in Acts 2:44–45 in the description of the life of the apostles: "And all they that believed were together, and had all things in common. Their possessions and goods they sold, and divided them to all, according as everyone had need."[44] There is nothing inherently sinful in the possession of property as long as that property is distributed when necessary. By the thirteenth century, canonists emphasized that while ownership of property was not immoral, the accumulation of excess riches beyond reasonable need was both sinful and anti-social. Ambrose had asked in indignation: "Who is as unjust and avaricious as the man who hoards the food of many people which is of no use to him? Therefore it is

---

[41] Forms of "taketh" and "nymeth" are repeated five times in the passage.

[42] There are now several general studies of poverty in the Middle Ages. Those most relevant to my argument are Scase, *Anti-clericalism*, Janet Coleman, "Property and Poverty," in *The Cambridge History of Medieval Political Thought c.350–c.1450*, ed. J. H. Burns (Cambridge: Cambridge University Press, 1989); Lester K. Little, *Religious Poverty and the Profit Economy in Medieval Europe* (Ithaca: Cornell University Press, 1978); Michel Mollat, *The Poor in the Middle Ages: An Essay in Social History*, trans. Arthur Goldhammer (New Haven: Yale University Press, 1986); *Études sur l'histoire de la pauvreté*, ed. Michel Mollat, 2 vols. (Paris: Sorbonne, 1974); Miri Rubin, *Charity and Community in Medieval Cambridge* (Cambridge: Cambridge University Press, 1987); and Brian Tierney, *Medieval Poor Law: A Sketch of Canonical Theory and Its Application in England* (Berkeley: University of California Press, 1959).

[43] The literature on medieval property, and particularly on the rights of the poor, is vast. The most useful studies are Gilles Couvreur, *Les pauvres ont-ils des droits?: Recherches sur le vol en cas d'extrême nécessité depuis la concordia de Gratien (1140) jusqu'à Guillaume d'Auxerre (1231)* (Rome: Università Gregoriana, 1961); Tierney, *Poor Law*, 22–44; John Gilchrist, *The Church and Economic Activity in the Middle Ages* (London: Macmillan & Company, 1969), 76–82; and Coleman, "Property and Poverty," 607–25. For a study of canonist formulations as well as those of popular sermons and religious instruction, see Rubin, *Charity*, 54–98.

[44] *Omnes etiam qui credebant erant pariter, et habebant omnia communia. / Possessiones et substantias vendebant, et dividebant illa omnibus, prout cuique opus erat.*

no smaller crime to take from him who has than, having, to deny the needy what you can give them in abundance."[45] To "hoard" one's superfluous food is not only "unjust" but also criminal. Ambrose introduces a social dimension to the moral dilemma of the distribution of community property. While he does not suggest that the needy have a legal right to steal from the "avaricious," Ambrose does point out that the poor, too, if not given assistance, might be considered victims of theft. In a sense, his equating these two "crimes" increases our sympathy for the plight of the indigent.

Aquinas extends the logic of Ambrose's argument to suggest that the destitute, in cases of extreme need, may rightfully steal food:

> Nevertheless, if the need be so manifest and urgent, that it is evident that the present need must be remedied by whatever means at hand (for instance, when a person is in some imminent danger, and there is no other possible remedy), then it is lawful for a man to succor his own need by means of another's property, by taking it either openly or secretly: nor is this properly speaking theft or robbery.[46]

Aquinas acknowledges the primacy of the actualities of physical distress. Indeed, he defines just activity not in terms of some "proper," abstract legal or doctrinal definition of destitution, but in response to the undeniable experiences of bodily need.

By the fourteenth century, Richard FitzRalph places theft due to need outside the law altogether:[47]

> If someone suffering need not caused by his own wrongdoings should desire his neighbor's property, as long as that property is a necessity to him, he desires, as it were, his own property, since under those circumstances his necessities are owed to him from the things possessed by his neighbor, according to the law of God and men....It can be said that a case of necessity does not come under the law, but is understood as excepted from the law.[48]

---

[45] *Quis enim tam iniustus tam avarus quam qui multorum alimenta suum non usum, sed habundantiam et delicias facit? Neque enim minus est criminis habenti tollere, quam,cum possis et habundas, indigentibus denegare* (J. -P. Migne, ed., *Decretum Gratiani, Patrologiae Cursus Completus*, Latin Series, vol. 187 [Paris, 1891], D. 47, c. 8).

[46] *Si tamen adeo sit urgens et evidens necessitas ut manifestum sit instanti necessitati de rebus occurrentibus esse subveniendum, puta cum imminet personae periculum, et aliter subveniri non potest, tunc licite potest aliquis ex rebus alienis suae necessitati subvenire, sive manifeste sive occulte sublatis; nec hoc proprie habet rationem furti vel rapinae* (Thomas Aquinas, Summa *Theologiae*, Blackfriars edition, II.II.q. 66, a. 7.)

[47] For a more detailed discussion of the ideas of FitzRalph see particularly Katherine Walsh, *A Fourteenth-century Scholar and Primate: Richard FitzRalph in Oxford, Avignon, and Armagh* (Oxford: Clarendon Press, 1981); also W. A. Pantin, *The English Church in the Fourteenth Century* (1955; repr. Toronto: University of Toronto Press, 1980), 151–65; and Penn Szittya, *Antifraternal Tradition*, Chapter 3, "The Antifraternal Ecclesiology of Archbishop Richard FitzRalph," 123–51.

[48] *"Si quis necessitatem habeat non provenientem ex culpa, non tunc rem sibi necessariam proximi sui cupit, sed suam, cum eo casu id quod necessarium extat ei de possessis a proximo debeatur sibi de lege dei et hominum....Dici potest quia casus neccessitatis non venit sub lege, sed intelligitur a lege exceptus"* (Quoted and translated in Szittya, *Antifraternal Tradition*, 269).

For FitzRalph, true necessity "hath no lawe," as Nede states in the common proverb. It requires an *other* context for interpretation. From the standpoint of dire material need, what might be considered a "neighbor's property" must be redefined as one's own. Poverty cannot rightly be understood except on its own terms. For FitzRalph, as for Langland, the reality of need (and Nede) stands outside the doctrinal mandates of charity.

Nede's advice to the dreamer provides an alternative to the failed spiritualized society of Grace's field. Indeed, the latter part of Nede's speech seems to be a kind of revision in "realistic" terms of Grace's ideal social order.

> For is no verte be ver to *Spiritus temperancie,*
> Noyther *Spiritus iusticie* ne *Spiritus fortitudinis.*
> For *Spiritus fortitudinis* forfeteth wel ofte;
> He shal do more þen mesure mony tymes and often
> And bete men ouer-bitere and som body to litel
> And greue men grettore then goed faith hit wolde.
> And *Spiritus iusticie* shal iugen, wol he, nel he,
> Aftur þe kynges conseyl and þe comune lyke.
> And *Spiritus prudencie* in many a poynt shal faile
> Of þat he weneth wolde falle yf his wit ne were.
> (C.22.23–32)

Before the spiritual plowing, as we have seen, Grace distributes the gifts of the Holy Ghost to the members of Christian society: lawyers, who are to live "bi labour of tonge / And bi wit to wissen oþere as grace hem wolde teche"; philosophers and diviners, who "se and...saye what sholde bifalle / Bothe of wele and of wo and be ywaer bifore"; and protectors of the people, who are..."to ryde and...to rekeuere that vnrihtfulliche was wonne." In his speech, Nede exposes the limitations of Grace's idealized society by refiguring each of these groups of professions not in terms of how each *ought* to function but in terms of how it *does* function, in response to the demands of actual life. Lawyers subvert the notion of justice by deeming arbitrarily, "wol he, nel he," in accordance not with the dictates of conscience, but "after þe kynges conseyl and þe comune lyke." They are influenced by personal and political gain. Philosophers undermine the virtue of prudence by using their "witte" to ensure that what they "weneth wolde falle" and by suggesting that they might be able to foresee what only God can know. They are motivated by pride and arrogance. Finally, protectors become strong-men as they push the meaning of *fortitudinis* beyond "mesure" and "bete men ouer-bitere and som body to litel / And greue men grettore then goed faith hit wolde." Nede articulates a view of the *reality* of earthly life that cannot adequately be contained by Grace's allegorical understanding. Indeed, these lines criticize the pretensions of such organizing schemes as somehow comprehending the processes of good actions. When enacting the cardinal virtues these vocations respond logically, if imperfectly—as Nede would suggest they inevitably must—to the demands of life in the world. Their activities, therefore, are beyond the scope of moral or social judgement.

The final image of Nede's speech is a representation of the poor. It, too, has its counterpart in Grace's spiritualized social order. In that society, the poor are taught by the Holy Ghost to live "in longyng to be hennes, / In pouerte and in pacience to preye for alle cristene" (C.21.248–9). In Grace's formulation, we do not see the suffering of the poor, only the sublimation of their misery. These are the patient paupers of the central visions of *Piers Plowman*. Living with no interest in the things of this world, their thoughts turned only "hennes," to the kingdom of heaven promised them in the Beatitudes. Nede's figuration of poverty begins with a radicalizing of the conventional image of the ennobling powers of indigence:

> And Nede ys nexst hym, for anoen he meketh
> And as louh as a lamb for lakkyng þat hym nedeth,
> For Nede maketh neede fele nedes louh-herted.
> Philosopheres forsoke welthe for they wolde be nedy
> And woneden wel elyngly and wolden nat be riche.
>   (C.22.35–39)

According to Nede, poverty is nearest God ("hym," as well as Christ, the "lamb") in its capacity to induce meekness and humility, the authority of the discourse of cardinal virtues having proved inadequate to the task of shaping un-idealized human activity. Here, the needy are morally enhanced not by the transcendence of suffering—as traditional configurations of the "blessed poor" would have it—but within the experiencing of lived misery: "For Nede maketh neede fele nedes louh-herted." The passage dwells in need, as it were, repeating some form of the term six times in only five lines. In a sense, and in spite of powerful medieval theological and allegorical impulses that would have it otherwise, poverty signifies because it has become powerfully materialized, literally embodied, incarnate in the needy human being, and, as the slippery personificatory term in line 35 would suggest, in Nede himself, thus underpinning the radical notion with which the passage began—need is next to God, and therein finds significance.

Langland ensures that we see in need the instantiation of the gap between real and ideal, human and divine, by ending Nede's speech with an explicit evocation of the ultimate site of such tension, the incarnation itself:

> And god al his grete ioye goestliche he lefte
> And cam and toek mankynde and bicam nedy.
> So he was nedy, as saith the boek in mony sondry places,
> That he saide in his sorwe on þe sulue rode:
> 'Bothe fox and foule may fle to hole and crepe
> And þe fisch hath fyn to flete with to reste,
> There nede hath ynome me þat y moet nede abyde

And soffre sorwes ful soure, þat shal to ioye torne.'
Forthy be nat abasched to byde and to be nedy
Sethe he þat wrouhte al þe worlde was willefolliche nedy,
Ne neuere noen so nedy ne porore deyede.
(C.22.40–50)

Upon first glance the passage seems to recall the conventional theological argument for the special status of poverty that dominates the central visions of *Piers:* in becoming man, Christ chose to be poor; therefore, poverty itself is redeemed, "as saith the boek in mony sondry places."[49] Of course, such a view of indigence requires a transcendence of the actualities of material distress, a formulation that Nede has already demonstrated is not only morally untenable, but figurally unsuccessful. As the speech continues, however, the emphasis shifts to a consideration of the nature of Christ's need. Again, the passage seems at first straightforward. Nede recalls the words of Christ in Matthew 8:20: "The foxes have holes, and the birds of the air nests: but the son of man hath not where to lay his head." Nede omits, however, Christ's conclusion that he "hath not where to lay his head," suggesting instead that Christ's "home" is constituted within the experience of need—"There nede hath ynome me þat y moet nede abyde." Clopper and Scase demonstrate persuasively that this section of Nede's speech recalls the volatile contemporary debates surrounding Franciscan discussions of poverty.[50] I wish to argue, however, that while the reference here to Christ's poverty doubtless bespeaks these debates, Langland's seemingly redundant use of the term "nedy" in C.22.50 to indicate Christ's distress ("Ne neuere noen so nedy ne porore deyede") suggests that the *metaphor* of need, as figured in the Nede episode, is not circum-

---

[49] The homilies of the Church Fathers, preached in such cities as Antioch and Constantinople, were often forceful commentaries on those passages of the Bible that dealt specifically with the special status of the poor. See the discussion of poverty in the homilies of Clement of Alexandria, John Chrysostom, Basil, Gregory of Nyssa, and Ambrose in Mollat, *Poor in the Middle Ages,* 18–24.

[50] Clopper, '*Songes of Rechelesnesse,*' 93-97; Scase, *Anti-clericalism,* 64-83. In its earliest phases, the fierce conflicts between the friars and the Parisian secular masters over poverty and religious mendicancy centered around the conflicts between the Spiritual wing of the Franciscans and its more conservative element, the Conventuals. In an effort to remain true to St. Francis's teachings, the Spirituals claimed that to emulate the life of Christ was to live in actual poverty, without possession or ownership. This claim to "absolute" poverty opposed directly the established church's acceptance of, and practical need for, property. The Conventuals, on the other hand, in attempting to recognize the material demands of a growing order, submitted to Papal authority and acknowledged the necessity of the use of material goods. As a result of this schism within the Franciscan movement, the question of the degree and quality of poverty itself came to be seen as disruptive of social and religious order.

Later phases of the controversy, beginning in 1321, focused upon the theological implications of the doctrine of Christ's absolute poverty. These were intellectual debates that sought to discredit altogether the notion of complete indigence. The rejection of the Franciscan principle of the absolute poverty of Christ in John XXII's Bull *Cum inter nonnullos* (1323) signalled the defeat of the radical fraternal notion of need. By denying that Christ and the Apostles had always lived without possessions and that what they had used had been of necessity and not of right, John, in assuming dominion and ownership of property, in effect repudiated both propertylessness and poverty.

scribed by historical definitions of mendicant poverty. It remains outside such discursive formulations. What is it, precisely, that Christ needs?

In this image of the incarnate Christ, Nede reminds us that our need for God is underpinned by God's need for us. From the beginning of *Piers Plowman*, the incarnation is figured not only as the merciful redemption of fallen humanity, but also as the necessary fulfillment of divine lack. Indeed, as early as Passus I, in the poem's first ruminative discussion of the nature of God's love, Holy Church counsels the dreamer:

> Loue is plonte of pees, most precious of vertues,
> For heuene holde hit ne myghte, so heuy hit first semede,
> Til hit hadde of erthe yȝoten hitsilue.
> (C.1.148-50)

Heaven cannot contain the weight of Love, which seems to spill downward, toward Earth, "til" it is at last taken in, and satisfied, as God begets himself ("yȝoten") within a human body. Later in the poem, the impulse behind Christ's incarnation is described as God's desire to experience *what he is not*: "creatour weex creature to knowe what was boþe" (B.16.215). Again, in Passus 20, Pees argues that God "toek Adames kynde" in an effort to know what God cannot: human suffering:

> And aftur, god auntred hymsulue and toek Adames kynde
> To wyte what he hath soffred in thre sundry places,
> ...
> To wyte what al wo is, þat woet of alle ioye.
> (C.20.231-234)

These radical images suggest that God seeks to be made complete, fulfilled, through the act of incarnation; that he *needs* to redeem humankind, as much as we need that redemption.

Most often, this figure of divine need is expressed through metaphors of hunger, thirst, and eating.[51] In his discussion of the Trinity in Passus 19, for example, the Samaritan describes the "sone þat sente was til erthe" (C.19.121) as one who "Touchede and tasted /...Seynte Marie, a mayden, and mankynde lauhte" (C.19.122–123); and as he harrows Hell, Christ proclaims to Lucifer:

> Y fauht so, me fursteth ȝut, for mannes soule sake.
> Sicio.
> May no pyement ne pomade ne preciouse drynkes
> Moiste me to þe fulle ne my furst slokke
> Til þe ventage valle in þe vale of Iosophat,
> And I drynke riht rype must, *resureccio mortuorum*.
> (C.20.408-412)

51 Jill Mann explores the significance of metaphors of ingestion in "Eating and Drinking in *Piers Plowman*," *Essays and Studies* 32 (1979): 26–43.

Christ's thirst for mankind's love cannot be quenched until the moment of re-union between God and man, the resurrection of the dead. Behind these daring images is a kind a mutual hunger on the part of both God and man to "eten al þat barn and his bloed dronken" (C.19.88). Such shared need ultimately redeems the rift between human and divine, not by privileging one destination over the other, but by reconfiguring that gap as the site of a discourse of mutuality, of recuperative faith.

Nede's speech provides a solution to the struggle between images of poverty and allegorical representation in *Piers Plowman*, a means for reaching at once through and beyond the rift within allegory. In the poem's earliest visions, the horrors of the actualities of indigence on the half-acre caused the breakdown of the allegorical discourse of need, exposing, if you will, the rupture in the sign by forcing our attention to an historically immediate material world—advertising only the disparity between real and ideal, signifier and signified. Images of the poor in *Piers*'s central visions repaired that rift by representing poverty not as a personal indignity or social evil, but rather as a means of moral strengthening and spiritual renewal. These images were overtly ideal, powerfully and successfully allegorical, underpinned by that Augustinian "faith" in the possibility of direct referentiality. Nede's speech, however, articulates a space within which both the literal and spiritual dimensions of poverty might *mean* with equal weight; a position that looks neither to the union of the sign, which requires the sublimation of the things of sense, nor to its failure, which denies even the possibility of representation, but rather within the tension between these two destinations. In both its recovery of the literal—the *experience* of need—and its emphasis on the mutuality of need between God and humankind, the de-stabilization of allegory precipitated by images of poverty in *Piers Plowman* has, at least momentarily, enriched and redeemed the mode, providing significance *within* the epistemological void constitutive of allegorical discourse: in the face of the world, where fish have their homes, but humans have need.[52]

---

[52] My thanks to Stephen Barney and Linda Georgianna for their thoughtful comments on an earlier version of this essay.

Notes on Contributors

JOAN BAKER is Associate Professor of English at Florida International University, Miami. She has published several essays on Robert of Sicily, and, most recently, on gender issues in Chaucer and Langland.

STEPHEN BARNEY is Professor of English at the University of California at Irvine. He has written several articles on *Piers Plowman* and is currently preparing part of a collaborative commentary on the poem. He has also written books on allegory (*Allegories of History, Allegories of Love* [1979]), Old English vocabulary (*Word Hoard* [1985]), and on Chaucer's *Troilus and Criseyde* (1980), as well as producing an edition of the latter for the *Riverside Chaucer* (1989).

C. DAVID BENSON teaches English and Medieval Studies at the University of Connecticut at Storrs. He has written or edited books on Chaucer, Lydgate, and the medieval Troy story, and written essays on a number of other Middle English writers, most recently Langland.

MARY CLEMENTE DAVLIN, O.P. is Professor of English at Dominican University. She is author of *A Game of Heuene: Word Play and the Meanings of Piers Plowman B* (1989) and *The Place of God in Piers Plowman and Medieval Art* (forthcoming).

ANDREW GALLOWAY is Associate Professor of English and Medieval Studies at Cornell University. Currently Editor of *The Yearbook of Langland Studies*, he has most recently written on medieval historical writing (in the *Cambridge History of Medieval English Literature* [1999]), textual scholarship of *Piers Plowman* (*Studies in Bibliography* [1999]), eleventh-century

Latin satire (*Medium Ævum* [1999]), Chaucer's negotiations with "authority" (in Peter Brown, ed., *A Companion to Chaucer Studies*, forthcoming),
and Gower's view of legal ethics and "the literature of 1388" (for a volume
edited by Emily Steiner and Candace Barrington). He is collaborating in an
annotation of *Piers Plowman*, and, with Russell Peck, an edition of Gower's
Confessio Amantis.

KATHLEEN M. HEWETT-SMITH is Associate Professor of English and
Medieval Studies at the University of Richmond. She has published several
articles on Langland and Chaucer, and is presently completing a book on
poverty and allegory in *Piers Plowman*. She has served as Associate Editor of
The Yearbook of Langland Studies.

SUSAN SIGNE MORRISON is Associate Professor of English at Southwest Texas
State University. She is author of *Women Pilgrims in Late Medieval England:
Private Piety as Public Performance* (2000) as well as articles on Chaucer,
Malory, medieval children's literature, and medieval German literature.

JAMES J. PAXSON is Associate Professor of English at the University of Florida.
He is author of *The Poetics of Personification* (1994), and has co-edited
Desiring Discourse: The Literature of Love, Ovid through Chaucer (1998)
and *The Performance of Middle English Culture: Essays on Chaucer and the
Drama in Honor of Martin Stevens* (1998). He also serves as Associate Editor
of *Exemplaria: A Journal of Theory in Medieval and Renaissance Studies*.

ELIZABETH ROBERTSON is Associate Professor of English and Director of the
Center for British Studies at the University of Colorado at Boulder. She has
written many articles on gender issues in medieval English literature and is
co-founder of the *Medieval Feminist Newsletter*. She has also published two
books, *Early English Devotional Prose and the Female Audience* (1990) and,
edited with C. David Benson, *Chaucer's Religious Tales* (1990); a third,
Representing Rape in Medieval and Early Modern Literature, edited with
Christine Rose, is forthcoming.

STEPHEN H. A. SHEPHERD is Associate Professor of English at Southern
Methodist University. He has edited Norton critical editions of *Middle
English Romances* (1995) and Malory's *Morte D'Arthur* (forthcoming).

JAMES SIMPSON is Professor of Medieval and Renaissance English at the
University of Cambridge. He has published one book, *Piers Plowman: An
Introduction to the B-Text* (1990), and many articles on *Piers Plowman*; his
more recent work focuses on traditions of medieval humanism (*Sciences and
the Self in Medieval Poetry*, 1995), and on the relations between medieval
and early modern writing.

Index

Abingdon,
  abbey of, 22-26
  abbot of, 22-23
Adam of Usk, 19-20
Aelred of Rievaulx, 56, 62
Aers, David, 125, 175, 178-179
Alford, John A., 70, 122, 123
allegory
  in *Piers Plowman*, 43-46, 195-253
alliterative line
  Chaucer's use of, 107-109
  Langland's use of, 103-117, 130
Ambrose, 247-248
Anima, 44-46, 156-158, 162-165, 218-222
anticlericalism, 13
Aquinas, Thomas, 9, 15, 120, 247-248
Arundel, Bishop, 160
Athlone project, 90-93
audience
  of *Piers Plowman*, 60-67
author(ship)
  in *Piers Plowman*, 83-88, 93-95, 145-148, 225-231

Ball, John, 19, 27
Barnes, Richard, 130
Bataille, Georges, 215-216
Bennett, J. A. W., 120, 127, 134, 140
Bennett, Judith, 171, 179-180
Benson, David, 126-127, 189-190
Beton the Brewster, 180-181
The Book of Vices and Virtues, 50-51, 201
Bloomfield, Morton, 122, 123, 217
Bowers, John, 28, 61, 92, 146
Brewer, Charlotte, 60, 146
Bright, Alan, 89
Brinton, Thomas, 79
Burrow, J. A., 94-95, 147
Butler, Judith, 173
The Canterbury Tales
  alliterative line in, 107-109
  fabliau in, 66, 107
  pathos in, 121-122, 125-133
  poverty in, 134-137
  prosody of, 103-117, 130
  religious verse in, 119-141
  romance convention in, 113-114
  satire in, 111-116